Backroad Mapbook

Welcome to the Third Edition of the Backroad Mapbook for Vancouver Island!

Thank you for making us a number 1 best seller since 1994. Over that time, we are proud to say we have sold over 50,000 of the two previous Vancouver Island editions of the Backroad Mapbook Series.

Despite this success, we have not remained stagnant. We have listened to our readers and have spent countless hours revising the book. Most notably, readers will find a completely different look to the maps. In addition to updating the maps, we also rescaled them and added more colour. The rescaling will especially help travellers exploring the north and the northwest coast of the Island.

We did not stop at improving the maps. We have been busy tracking down new recreational pursuits for you to enjoy. You will find some new information, some information removed (mostly closed trails) and even new sections.

The Islands have always been a favourite holiday destination for locals and for travellers from around the province and the globe. The fantastic scenery, the unparalleled Island hospitality and the endless recreational opportunities are just a few of the reasons why this is such a popular destination.

With the Backroad Mapbook as your guide, we are certain you will find all the infromation needed to plan the perfect outdoor retreat. From short day trips to week or month long adventures, the maps will show you how to get there and our reference section will let you plan what to do once you arrive.

If you enjoy the outdoors, we are sure you will have as much fun using the Backroad Mapbook as we did in developing it!

Foreword

The Backroad Mapbook is truly a unique product. No other source covers Vancouver Island with as much detail or information on outdoor recreation activities as this book.

The reference section found in the guide includes information on both saltwater and freshwater fishing, paddling routes, parks and wilderness camping (recreational sites), multi-use trails (hiking/biking, and off road trails) and winter recreation. Countless hours have been spent in researching this book, making it the most complete compilation of outdoor recreation information you will find on the region anywhere. This information can be enjoyed by anyone who spends time in the great outdoors.

The maps in this book highlight the rural and logging road networks, trail systems and recreation opportunities throughout the Islands. A unique feature of the maps is that all recreation activities are labelled, allowing for quick and easy referencing when researching a specific area. Further, no other source provides as much detail and accuracy on the road and trail networks of Vancouver Island.

Continuous referral to our maps and the reference sections, will help you become acquainted with the area you are interested in. If you know the activity you are planning, you simply turn to that reference section and find the option you are interested in. If you are planning a trip to a specific area, you should consult the index to find the appropriate map(s) and look for the various recreation opportunities highlighted.

By popular demand from GPS users, we have included UTM Grids (NAD 83) and longitude and latitude for reference points. We must emphasis that these are for reference only. We have created a recreation guide and our maps do not offer the accuracy needed for GPS users.

Generally, Vancouver Island has a well established secondary road system that provides easy access to the backcountry. With numerous 4wd roads and trails, a good portion of the region is accessible by vehicle. Unfortunately, not all of the roads and trails shown on the maps are accessible. Some logging and rural roads are restricted or closed to the public. Be sure to pay attention to road signs and always watch for logging trucks.

We emphasis that our mapbook should only be used as an access and planning guide. We have gone to great lengths to ensure the accuracy of this book. However, over time, the road and trail conditions change. Always be prepared!

Please respect all private property and close any gates behind you. Above all, have fun!

British Columbia

Vancouver Island

Victoria   Vancouver

Table of Contents

Outdoor Recreation Reference Section

Backroads of Vancouver Island .... Reference 5

Caving & Hot Springs .... Reference 6

Saltwater Fishing .... Reference 7-10

Freshwater Fishing .... Reference 11-26

    Lake Fishing .... Reference 11-23

    Stream Fishing .... Reference 24-26

Paddling Routes .... Reference 27-30

    Canoe Routes .... Reference 27

    Whitewater Paddling .... Reference 27-29

    Ocean Routes .... Reference 29-30

Parks .... Reference 31-38

    Gulf Island Parks .... Reference 31-33

    South Vancouver Island Parks .... Reference 33-35

    North/West Vancouver Island Parks .... Reference 35-38

Wilderness Camping .... Reference 39-45

    Campbell River Forest District .... Reference 39-41

    Port McNeill Forest District .... Reference 41-43

    South Island Forest District .... Reference 43-45

Multi-use Trails .... Reference 46-60

    Campbell River Area .... Reference 46-47

    Comox/Courtency Area .... Reference 47-48

    Cowichan Valley/Duncan Area .... Reference 48-49

    Gulf Island Trails .... Reference 49-50

    Nanaimo Area .... Reference 50-52

    North/Northwest Island Trails .... Reference 52-53

    Pacific Rim Park/West Coast Area .... Reference 53-55

    Parksville/Qualicum Area .... Reference 55

    Port Alberni Area Trails .... Reference 55-57

    Port Renfrew Area Trails .... Reference 57

    Strathcona Provincial Park Trails .... Reference 57-59

    Victoria and Area Trails .... Reference 59-60

Winter Recreation .... Reference 61-62

    Cross-country Skiing .... Reference 61

    Backcountry Skiing & Snowshoeing .... Reference 61

    Snowmobiling .... Reference 62

Index .... Reference 63-72

Map Section

Vancouver Island Maps 1-47

Adam & Eve Rivers 42

Bamfield 6

Brooks Peninsula 30

Cameron Lake 15

Campbell River 36

Carmanah Walbran Park 7

Clayoquot Sound 11

Coal Harbour 38

Courtney 29

Cumberland 22

Cymox Glacier 21

Duncan 9

Elk River 27

Forbidden Plateau 28

Georgie Lake 46

Gulf Islands 10

Gold River 26

Holberg 45

Hotsprings Cove 19

Jordan River 2

Kennedy River 13

Kyuquot 31

Lake Cowichain 8

Memekay River 35

Nanaimo 17

Nanaimo Lakes 16

Nootka Island 24

Nootka Sound 18

Port Alberni 14

Port Alice 39

Port Hardy 47

Port McNeill 40

Port Renfrew 1

Qualicum Beach 23

Robson Bight 41

Rock Bay 44

Sayward 43

Schoen Lake 34

Sooke 3

Tahsis 25

Tofino 12

Ucluelet 5

Victoria 4

Westmin Mine 20

Winter Harbour 37

Woss 33

Zeballos 32

www.backroadmapbooks.com

Backroad Mapbooks

DIRECTORS
Russell Mussio
Wesley Mussio
Penny Stainton-Mussio

EDITOR IN CHIEF
Russell Mussio

CONTRIBUTING WRITERS
Richard Blier
Trent Ernst

COVER DESIGN
Brandon Tam

PRODUCTION
Shawn Caswell
Trevor Daxon
Farnaz Faghihi
Brett Firth
Dale Tober
Jennifer White

SALES / MARKETING
Shawn Caswell
Jason Marleau
Russell Mussio

WRITERS
Russell Mussio
Wesley Mussio

Canadian Cataloguing in Publication Data

Mussio, Russell, 1969-
Backroad mapbook: an outdoor recreation guide
Includes index. Cover title.

Written by Russell and Wesley Mussio.
Contents: v. 1. Southwestern B.C. - v. 2.
Vancouver Island (including the Gulf Island) - v. 3.
Kamloops/Okanagan - v. 4. Kootenays - v. 5. The
Cariboo- v. 6. Central B.C.
ISBN 0-9697877-0-7 (v. 1) - ISBN 1-894556-10-0
(v. 2) - ISBN 0-9697877-2-3 (v. 3) - ISBN 0-
9697877-3-1 (v. 4) - ISBN 0-9697877-4-x (v. 5) -
ISBN 1-894556-06-2 (v.6)

1. Recreation areas – British Columbia – Maps.
2. British Columbia – Maps. I. Mussio, Wesley,
1964- II. Title.

G1170.B23 1997   912.711   C98-011809-3

Published by:

232 Anthony Court
New Westminster, B.C. V3L 5T5
P. (604) 438-3474   F. (604) 438-3470
E-mail: info@backroadmapbooks.com
www.backroadmapbooks.com

The Authors

Wesley Mussio (right) is a Registered Professional Forester and a Lawyer practicing as a trial lawyer with the law firm of Kane, Shannon and Weiler in Surrey, BC.

Russell Mussio (left) graduated from the University of British Columbia with a degree in Leisure and Sports Administration. He formed Mussio Ventures Ltd. in 1993 with his brother, Wesley, in order to publish, distribute and market the Backroad Mapbook Series.

Wesley and Russell are avid outdoorsmen. Whenever they are not working on the Backroad Mapbook or Fishing BC projects, they are enjoying the great outdoors.

Acknowledgement

This book could not have been created without the hard work and dedication of the Mussio Ventures Ltd. staff, Leslie Bryant, Shawn Caswell, Trevor Daxon, Farnaz Faghihi, Brett Firth, Sherma Juanico, Dale Tober and Jennifer White. Without their hard work and support, this comprehensive mapbook would never have been completed as accurately as it was. We would also like to thank the following for helping with the project: Richard K. Blier for his word on Island Backroads and Trent Ernst for his tireless contribution to the reference section.

In addition, we would like to thank all those people behind the scenes. These include helpful individuals such as the Ministry of Forests and Ministry of Environment staff, the Region District personnel as well as the informative Chamber of Commerce tourism personnel. Their knowledge and assistance with the research has been invaluable. In particular the logging companies have been more than helpful in providing incredible logging road and recreational information. These comapnies include Canfor, Interfor, TimberWest, Western Forest Products and Weyerhaeuser.

Most of all, we would like to thank Nancy Mussio and Penny Stainton-Mussio. Their patience and support helped us during the many hours spent working on, researching and writing the Backroad Mapbook Series.

The Backroads of Vancouver Island

By Richard K. Blier

Vancouver Island's gravel backroads lead to dozens of backroading, hiking, paddling, camping, fishing, boating and spectacular outdoor destinations. The routes run through public Crown Land and Tree Farm Licences (TFLs) as well as forestlands that are privately owned by logging companies. Most logging mainlines and BC Forest Service roads are regularly maintained, well travelled and seasonally passable for passenger vehicles. Some routes and secondary roads may not be suitable for RVs or larger trailered boats. Spur roads are rougher and could require a high-slung vehicle or 4 x 4. Conditions and access restrictions on Vancouver Island backroads constantly change. Call local BCFS or logging company offices for available information on road conditions and access policies.

Logging Roads:

There are several classifications of Vancouver Island logging roads: **restricted access**, **combined-use**, **inactive** and **deactivated** roads. Some routes are signposted as private industrial roads. Read and comply with all posted notices.

Restricted access roads (often marked with a red, octagonal stop sign) go to and through active logging areas and can include mainlines where heavy hauling is ongoing. The loggers maintain radio contact with each other at designated checkpoints and do not expect unannounced traffic in unauthorized areas. Public access is permitted only after working hours on weekdays or all day on weekends and holidays. Contract loggers may haul on weekends and holidays resulting in periodic road closures. Some active logging areas are closed to the public at all times for safety and security reasons. Private forestlands are usually gated and open gates could be locked at night.

Combined-use roads are open to the public twenty-four hours a day, but logging trucks and other industrial traffic may be frequent. Expect crummies (small buses that transport the loggers to and from work sites), heavy-duty company pickups, graders, fuel carriers and both loaded and unloaded logging trucks. The frequency, location and hours of hauling operations vary throughout the year. (A yellow, inverted triangle is sometimes used to identify these roads.)

Logging trucks and company vehicles have the right-of-way at all times. If you meet any, signal your intentions to the other driver and safely head to the nearest pulloff (no matter which side of the road it's on) and stop. Occasionally you may have to back up quickly to a pullout. Always stop on the inside of any curves to avoid potentially hazardous sweeper logs (some over 20 metres long) that may overhang the back of logging trucks. Don't be in a hurry to get going again; there could be a second truck following the first. You may be required to wait for, and then follow a company vehicle. Be particularly wary on narrow roads and when trucks are travelling downhill. Loaded trucks cool their brakes with water on downhill runs. In dry weather watch for telltale watermarks on the road. To avoid dodging logging trucks or company buses, time your travels to after weekday working hours (usually between 5:00 pm and 6:00 am) or on weekends and holidays.

Inactive roads are always open to the public. Though on these arteries logging traffic is rare, the roads may be overgrown, rough or impassable (even in a 4 x 4) due to lack of maintenance and washouts. (A welcoming green circle sometimes marks these backroads.) Along the older routes you could encounter confusing and unmarked side roads, steep washboard hills, switchbacks, loose gravel, sharp rocks, gravel ridges, potholes or deep puddles and water holes. Streams and runoff can undercut roads and bridges to create hidden sinkholes. Ribbons, branches or rocks sometimes mark these danger spots. Carry a shovel, winch or come-along. Avoid the temptation to continue downhill on really rough roads; it may not be as easy getting back up again. In places you may have to build up the roadway using rocks and logs. Some backroads may be impassable due to seasonal washouts, flooding, landslides, fallen trees or deep snows.

Deactivated roads are secondary routes on which the logging companies have dug ditches and water bars and/or removed bridges in compliance with Forestry and Fisheries guidelines. In many cases negotiating these roads requires a 4 x 4. Bridge closures or removal may preclude any vehicular travel.

Road Closures:

Many districts are subject to periodic fire closures, even when BC Forest Service restrictions are not in effect. Threats of poaching, vandalism and public safety or security concerns may also limit entry. Access roads that run through private property or into fragile regions where 4 x 4 use is destroying vegetation are often closed. Co-operation among government, industry, private property owners and outdoor enthusiasts will ensure continued public access. Carry out your litter, follow seasonal fire, hunting and fishing regulations and don't cut trees.

Travel Hints:

Be prepared. Don't forget to gas up before travelling into isolated regions. Vancouver Island backroads can tax your vehicle's brakes and the suspension, cooling and exhaust system. Your vehicle should be in good condition. Carry engine oil, antifreeze or summer coolant; brake fluid, a set of tools and a repair manual. Good tires will reduce the chance of a flat. Check your spare tire. In the off-season you could encounter slippery or frosty roads. Consider bringing chains, sand or even kitty litter for traction. In dry weather the backroads can be extremely dusty. Top off your vehicle's windshield washer fluid and always drive with your headlights on. Being sure you can see other travellers and they can see you is a good safety precaution. Most Automobile Association memberships do not cover logging road breakdowns.

Be ready for wilderness conditions and use common sense. Know your personal limitations and your vehicle's capabilities. Pack extra food, water and warm clothing in case of a mechanical breakdown, even on day runs when you may not have overnight gear. Always let someone reliable know your destination and leaving and returning dates. Take your time on Vancouver Island backroads. A slower pace is easier on your nerves and you won't miss any scenery. Be alert, drive defensively, and pull over and allow following traffic to pass. Leave no valuables in your vehicle and be sure to lock up.

Use the maps with area topographical charts. If possible, travel with someone familiar with the area you visit. Carry a notebook and jot down key junctions and cutoffs. You can gather valuable information by talking with locals.

Bio:

Outdoor writer, photographer and angler, Richard K. Blier, has explored Vancouver Island backroads, campsites, trails, lakes and coastlines for over 25 years. He is author of three guidebooks: **ISLAND BACKROADS: Hiking, Camping and Paddling on Vancouver Island** (Orca Book Publishers, 1998); **MORE ISLAND ADVENTURES Volume 2: An Outdoors Guide to Vancouver Island** (Orca Book Publishers, 1993); and **ISLAND ADVENTURES: An Outdoors Guide to Vancouver Island** (Orca Book Publishers, 1989). He also revised and edited **HIKING TRAILS II: South-Central Vancouver Island and the Gulf Islands** (8th edition, 2000), published by the Vancouver Island Trails Information Society. His outdoor stories and photos have appeared in magazines and newspapers. You are invited to visit his BACKROAD ADVENTURES ON VANCOUVER ISLAND website at http://members.nbci.com/rkblier.

Editors Note:

We have spent countless hours updating our road systems. Where possible we have destinguished the roads to allow you to choose whether to stick to the mainlines or venture a little off-road.

Generally speaking, the thick lines on the maps are good gravel or paved roads that can be driven by most vehicles, including RVs and cars. The very thin lines should be left to high clearance 4wd vehicles, ATV's or walkers. Where possible, we have also tried to distiguish deactivated roads with thin dashed lines.

If you are using our maps for the first time, you will need to refer to the legend found at the beginning of the map section. The legend will help you identify the symbols we have used but more importantly, it will help you understand our road classifications.

Caving & Hot Springs

Caving

A mixture of geology and rain has combined to create one of the richest caving areas in North America, with over 1,050 known caves, ranging from a few metres to 7.6 km long. Caving has become an extremely popular past-time on Vancouver Island, because of the sheer number and quality of the caves. Five of the top ten longest caves in Canada are located on Vancouver Island. There is also plenty of karst topography, especially on the northern section of the island. Karst is the name given to a group of geological formations that either accompany or presage cave formation, like sinkholes, disappearing rivers, streamless canyons, and deep, narrow crevices cut into the limestone rock.

Despite the number of caves, we are only including a handful in this guide. If you are serious about caving, you'll know how to find the rest; if you're not, one can get into trouble fast in a cave. And treading carelessly can destroy works of natural art that have taken millennia to grow. The caves listed here are a good introduction to the sport. If you want to get involved in caving, contact an area group, like the Vancouver Island Cave Exploration Group, or a cave tour guide. Vancouver Island cave resources can be found through the Canadian Caver website, www.cancaver.ca.

Devil's Bath (Map 39/D6)
The largest cenoté north of Mexico. What's a cenoté? Basically its a big hole in the ground filled with water. Geological interesting, but it doesn't make the most exciting viewing, especially without any interpretive signs. However, the entire area around the Benson River displays karst features (sinkholes, springs that flow out of the ground then go underground again, etc.), of which Devil's Bath is the most prominent.

Horne Lake Caves (Map 23/A7)
Located in its own provincial park, you can explore two of the Horne Lake caves either by yourself or with a tour guide. There are also caving clinics, which range from a 1.5 hour interpretive session to a seven hour epic underground adventure. This is one of the most popular caving sites on Vancouver Island. Because it is so popular, it has its own website: www.hornelake.com. If you are visiting the caves without a guide, we recommend bringing a hard helmet and headlamp.

Karst Creek Interpretive Trail (Map 28/A7)
This trail, located in Strathcona Provincial Park, is an easy 2 km (45 min.) walk, passing by sinkholes, disappearing streams and other karst features.

Little Hustan Cave (Map 32/D1)
Little Hustan is not what most people consider a classical cave. For one thing, it has entrances at both ends. And, at 250 metres long, it is more a tunnel or an archway than a cave. There area is part of a regional park and hosts other smaller arches, sinkholes and karst features.

Upana Caves (Map 26/B3)
There are at least 15 entrances and nearly 1,500 m (4,920 ft) of passages in the Upana Cave system, which were first mapped in 1975. The Upana River runs through these caves, disappearing, then reappearing 30 m further on. Other caves in this system include Tunnel Cave, Corner Cave, and the aptly named Insect Cave.

Vanishing/Reappearing River (Map 39/G7)
If you thought the Upana River (see Upana Caves, above) disappearing for 30 m then reappearing again was a cool trick. Well, the Vanishing River starts out above ground, then disappears for over a kilometre before the Reappearing River appears, just before it joins up with the Raging River. There are a pair of short (200 m) trails to viewing platforms, one to where the river vanishes, and one to where the river reappears. Stay well away from the edge of Vanishing River: if you get swept in, chances are you're not getting out again.

Hot Springs

There is no greater reward for a day's outing in the wilds of British Columbia than to relax in a hot spring. Unfortunately, Vancouver Island has not been blessed with an abundance of these therapeutic soaks. But what it lacks in quantity, it makes up in quality, namely Hot Springs Cove. None of these springs have been developed, but that speaks more to the difficulty in accessing the springs than the quality of the springs.

Ahousat (Flores Island) Warm Springs (Map 11/E1)
Located at the end of Matilda Inlet in Gibson Provincial Marine Park, Ahousat Warm Springs have been spurned in favour of the warmer and more picturesque Hot Springs Cove. The water is warm, at 25°C (77°F), but not warm enough for extended soaks, and the concrete pools are often filled with algae, making the soak a less than pleasant experience unless you take the time to clean it out. There is no road access to the hot springs, but you can charter a boat or plane from Tofino.

Hot Springs Cove (Map 19/A7)
Considered by many to be one of the finest hot springs in Canada, Hot Springs Cove is located in Maquinna Provincial Park, at the tip of Openit Peninsula on the West Coast of Vancouver Island. The beautiful area is found 37 km (as the crow flies) from Tofino and can be accessed by power boat, kayak or airplane. The very hot (51°C or 124°F) springs are located a 1.5km hike from the government dock along a picturesque boardwalk. The main pools are located at the very edge of the open ocean and the hot water flows in over a 3m (10 ft) waterfall.

Mate Islands Warm Spring (Map 19/A7)
Located across Hot Springs Cove from the springs, there is a warm (25°C or 77°F) seep located just above the low water tide. The seep is usually covered by ocean water, and even when it's not, the ground is too rocky for soaking. There is another vent of the southwest tip of Mate Islands, covered by about 15m (50 ft) of water.

Abbreviations Used Throughout the Book	
$	Canadian Dollar
+	plus
2wd	2 wheel drive
4wd	4 wheel drive
cm	centimetres
FSR	Forest Service Road
ft	feet
ha	hectares
hrs	hours
Hwy	Highway
kg	kilograms
km	kilometres
m	metres
Mt	Mount
Mtn	Mountain
Prov	Provincial
Rec	Recreation
RV	Recreational Vehicle
X-C	Cross-country

www.backroadmapbooks.com

Saltwater Fishing

Anglers come from around the world to fish the waters off Vancouver Island. This is the stuff of legends, and many a legendary fish has been caught here.

Unfortunately, perhaps a few too many legendary fish have been caught here. Add to that recent harsh environmental conditions and the Vancouver Island fishery has suffered some major setbacks over the last decade.

In 1998, the Department of Fisheries and Oceans began a long-term strategy to help rebuild stocks of the hardest hit fish, primarily coho. Currently, there are very few openings for coho as the DFO tries to regenerate stocks. Openings are often on hatchery stock, which can be identified by the lack of an adipose fin, which is clipped before the stocks are released. This conservation strategy is expected to be in place until 2004 or 2006 (and likely beyond), with the emphasis on preservation and rehabilitation. Regulations include barbless hooks on all salmon, and special conservation areas around sites that have been historically over-fished. Check the fishing regulations for closures and gear and size restrictions, which have become far more prevalent in the last few years.

Some bottomfish stocks, especially rockfish, are also under considerable environmental and angling pressure, partially because, unlike salmon, decompression effects on fish caught from depths as shallow as 10 metres (30 feet) can be fatal. Because of this catch mortality, all rockfish should be retained, regardless of size. Rockfish mature slowly—some species live to be 150 years old—and do not reproduce until they are quite mature—some may be as old as 15 to 20 years before they reproduce.

This is not to say that there are not still opportunities to catch a trophy fish here. The west coast of Vancouver Island is an angler's paradise, and there are also some opportunities along the east coast of the island as well. But the nature of sport fishing is changing, and you need to be aware of these changes.

What we are providing here is an overview of popular fishing areas as well as a few fishing tips. Fishing varies not just from month to month but from day to day, and if you really want to know where the hot spots are, talk to a local tackle shop or marina, or better yet, go with a guide who knows the area. Remember that with changes to the sport fishing regulations, areas can open and close to sport fishery on a moment's notice. This information, too, is available from tackle shops and marinas, or from the local DFO office.

Barkley Sound/Bamfield (Maps 5-6, 13-14)
Although there is some action in Barkley Sound in January, the year really gets rolling in February, when herring return to the Sound. The feed brings feeder chinook in the 5-6kg (10–12 lb) range for those willing to venture to Vernon Bay (13/G7, 14), Rainy Bay (6/B1, 14), Pill Point (6/A1), Swale Rock, Diplock Island (6/A1), Seapool Rocks (5/F4) the Bamfield Wall (5/G3) or Cape Beale (5/F4)). In poor weather, many anglers stick closer to the mouth of Bamfield Harbour (6/A3). Your best bet is to fish deep (25-40m/80–130 ft) early in the morning or on a slack tide using anchovies on a long leader or herring. It is best to use a fast troll in the area where the chinook are feeding. Make sure your bait has a fast roll by shortening the leader to (80-105cm/32–42 in). It is also best to have four lines staggered about 3m (10 feet) apart to attract the fish. Hoochies (white, glow, white and black, white and green) on a 105cm (42 inch) leader behind a Hot Spot flasher can also be effective. The glow Hoochie is best just before daybreak if you charge it with a flashlight. Lures that have proven to be effective in the past are the Tom Mac Spoon, Apex and Diamond King. Give your Hoochies a 48-70cm (19–28 in) leader.

Halibut season also starts in February. The best fishing being up to 20 miles offshore in the early season, and closer to shore (like in Tapaltos Bay 5/G4) in June–July. Trolling deep can work, but jigging a Lucky Jig, But Slammer or Norwegian Jig in 45-90m (150–300 feet) of water is better.

June kicks off the migratory chinook season, with the best fishing coming in late July and early August. These big fish can reach tyee sizes of over 13kg (30 lbs) and are found off Meares Bluffs (5/E3), Pill Point (6/A1), Rainy Bay (6/B1, 14), Diplock Island (6/A1), Swale Rock, Folger Island (5/F3), King Edward Island (5/F3) or in Leach Inlet. Mooching or jigging can work, but trolling works best, with a white or green Hoochie, anchovies or herring strips all with a green or orange flasher. In the past few years, salmon fishing has been restricted in-shore from August until October, though there is still some good fishing in the offshore banks.

In June, there is a chance to catch a sockeye as they make their way through the sound and into the Alberni Inlet. June also brings coho to Folger Island (5/F3), King Edward Island (5/F3) and Cape Beale (5/F4). By mid-September, they have moved a little farther out, with the best fishing being around Cree Island (5/D3) and Meares Bluffs (5/E3). For best results, troll a bucktail along the surface, 7-10m (25–35 feet) behind the boat. Radiant squirts and Apexes have also proven to be effective lures for coho.

Campbell River (Map 36)
The self-proclaimed Salmon Capital of the World, Campbell River is indeed a great place to hook a chinook, catch a coho or net yourself a sockeye, chum or pink.

Feeder chinook appear around Salmon and Willow Points (36/G7) in mid-September and stick around until March. You can also find them on the east side of Quadra, around Rebecca Spit and Drew Harbour (36/G4). The best way to catch feeders is troll deep (25-35m/80–110 ft) with green Hoochies, Tomic plugs or cut plug herring. Winter bucktailing for chinooks off Willow Point can also work.

The larger migratory chinooks (7-14kg/15–30+ lbs) start to trickle into the area in April, but the fishery really gets rolling in mid-May and peaks in the third week of June and then again in mid-August. The big tyees (30+ lbs) arrive in mid-July and stick around until mid-September. The most popular method of catching these beauties is cut-plugging off Cape Mudge (36/G7) near the drop-off. You can also troll anchovies, Apexes or Hoochies at Willow Point (36/G7), Copper Bluffs (36/F4), Menzies Bay (36/D4) or Quathiaski Cove (36/G6). Be aware that there is a Special Management Zone around the mouth of the Campbell River: artificial lures only and no downriggers.

The coho fishery is currently closed along the east coast of Vancouver Island, though there have been occasional opportunities on hatchery coho; as always, check the regulations and updates. If and when it does open, Wilby Shoal and Francisco Point are where you will have the best luck finding them. Try Bucktailing or trolling an Apex. Cut-plugging can also be effective.

Pink and Sockeye run from August to mid-September. You can try fly fishing at river mouths, but your best chance is trolling with a green or orange flasher and a pink Hoochie.

Comox/Courtenay (Maps 22-23, 29)
Migratory chinook begin to appear in April, but the season really gets going in mid-May, peaks in August, and ends in mid-September. The best areas to fish are off Denman and Hornby Islands (22/G2, 23). There is also an excellent winter spring (chinook) fishery from January to March. Try trolling deep using a Hoochie, herring or plug.

The coho fishery is currently closed along the east coast of Vancouver Island, though there have been occasional opportunities on hatchery coho; as always, check the regulations and updates. When the fishery is open, try laying your line down around Bates Beach and Little River (29/D5), or off the south tip of Denman and Hornby Islands (23/B4).

Pink and Sockeye run from August to mid-September. You can try fly fishing at river mouths, but your best chance is trolling with a green or orange flasher and a pink Hoochie. Pinks are present in greater numbers during odd-numbered years (2001, 2003, etc.). There is also a small chum salmon run in September and October.

Gulf Islands

Denman Island (Map 22-23)

Komas Bluff (22/G1), along the northeast side of Denman, is a popular place to troll for chinook from June–September. You will also find coho here, but chances are you won't be able to keep them unless there is a random, unpredictable opening announced. You will find coho from June–September around Chrome Island (23/B4) near the drop-off, and both coho and chinook can be found in the 12-18m (40–60 ft) range near Palliser Rock on Sandy Island (22/F1). Drift fishing or trolling works best.

Gabriola Island (Map 17/D4)

From May–July, there are tyee (30+ lb chinooks) in the water off the east coast of Gabriola (in the Flat Top Islands and Grande Cliffs area), and to a lesser extent off the west coast as well. As the summer progresses, the chinook tend to move to the reef structures like Thrasher Rock, Orlebar and Brant Reef. In the morning, you will find them around 26-43m (120–140 feet) below the surface, but as the day progresses they move down to between 67-73m (220–240 feet), especially on a hot, sunny day. Try trolling strip herring, a plug or an army truck, fluorescent or white Hoochie.

Winter Chinook arrive in December and stay until April. You will find them in 45-76m (150–250 feet) of water around Flat Top Islands, or in the 40-60m (130–200 foot) range off Thrasher Rock and Orlebar Point. Herring strips or fluorescent blue/green, army truck or white Hoochies are your best bet.

In July, the cohos also arrive, but chances are you will not be able to keep any. The coho fishery is currently closed along the east coast of Vancouver Island, though there have been occasional opportunities on hatchery coho; as always, check the regulations and updates.

Galiano & Mayne Islands (Map 10/A1-G4)

There are small feeder chinooks to be found around both Galiano and Mayne Islands in the winter. Try the south end of Galiano Island off the west coast beneath Mt Galiano (E3), or off the east coast around Gossip Island (F2), as well as the north end of Mayne Island at Georgiana Point (F3). Even though it is a high traffic area, Active Pass (F3) can also be productive; just watch out for that ferry. Halibut arrive in the area in February, in the 9-36kg (20–80 lb) range, while larger chinook show up in March and hang around for most of the summer.

Hornby Island (Map 23/B3)

In late June, there is good fishing for chinook and coho (though summer openings are rare for coho; check with DFO or a local shop for day-to-day updates) around the Shingle Spit (23/A1). There is a good chinook hole near Flora Island just off Downes Point. Drop anchor and drop your line down to about 30m (100 feet). You will also get good results trolling south from Whale Station Bay during the summer (June–September) or by mooching along the kelp beds off the island.

North & South Pender Islands (Map 10, 10 Inset)

The hotspots around Pender Island are Pender Bluffs and the mouth of Bedwell Harbour (G6 or Inset). Chances are, if there are fish in the area, they at one of these locations. You can also try Otter Bay on the North Island, though, as the locals say, "You'll never know what you'll catch in Otter Bay."

January kicks of with feeder chinook ranging from barely legal and below to mid-teens (~7kg). Halibut from (9-36kg) (20–80 lbs) move into the area in February (remember, the smaller the halibut, the better the eating) and stick around until September. They can usually be found in either Plumper Sound (G5) between Pender and Saturna or in Swanson Channel (F5) between Pender and Saltspring.

By March, larger feeder chinooks (in the 9kg or 20 lb range) can be found in most of the hotspots around Pender. Fish deep (up to 60m or 200 ft) and try trolling larger cuts of herring strip, anchovies and 4–5 inch Tomic Plugs

Sockeye show up around the Bluffs in late July, while Pinks start showing up in the same area in August.

Saltspring Island (Map 10)

Saltspring Island can be one of the most productive of all the Gulf Islands and there are lots of places that fish tend to congregate. The following is a list of hotspots to try: between the north tip of the island and Kuper Island (A1), along the western shore at Parminter Point (A2), Booth Bay (A3), Erskine Point (A3), Maxwell Point (A4), through the Sansum Narrows (A5), Bald Bluff Point (A5), Musgrave Point (A5) and through the Satellite Channel (A6) between Saltspring and the Saanich Peninsula, all the way to Elanor Point (D6). Beaver Point (D5) in Ruckle Provincial Park, in the southeast corner of Saltspring can also be productive.

Saturna Island (Map 10 Inset)

Winter is a time for smaller feeder chinook off the waters of Saturna Island, while larger chinook move into the area in March. Halibut also move into the area in spring (usually in late February). Popular areas include off the west coast of Saturna in Plumper Sound and in the Tumbo Channel, especially around the south end of Tumbo Island.

Kyoquot Sound (Maps 30-31)

This is one of the few areas that has allowed chinook to be caught inside the 1 mile limit during August and September migration. Occasional coho openings during this time allow for fast fishing for generally smaller chinook (in the 9kg/20 lb range) and nice size coho (over 5kg/10 lbs). Trolling or mooching with anchovies or herring in 6-12m (20–40 ft) of water near Spring Island works well. From early December to April, there is also a good fishery for mostly smaller feeder Chinooks. Weather (and regulations) permitting, Rugged Point is another good area. Fish deeper near the wall. There is also a good halibut spot 5 miles off shore (from Spring Island).

Nanaimo (Map 17)

Although the big northern tyees do not come down this far south (catching anything over 30 lbs is a rarity), there is good fishing in the waters around Nanaimo. In winter, smaller feeder chinooks appear in droves, and what they lack in size they make up for in numbers. Your best bet is to troll at 25-50m (80–160 feet) using an army truck or lime green Hoochie or herring strips around Entrance Island (17/D3) and Five Fingers (17/A3). In May and June, two runs of larger 7-11 kg (15–25 lb) chinook migrate through this area. This is one of the best times to be out on the water. The springs are generally taken on a deep troll—down to 67m (220 feet) or so. From July to September, your best bet for chinook is to try drift fishing in shallower waters.

Pinks and sockeye show up in July and August and are best taken on a red or pink Hoochie with a red or green flasher.

The coho fishery is currently closed along the east coast of Vancouver Island, though there have been occasional opportunities on hatchery coho; check the regulations and updates. There are two runs of coho; the first run lasts from June to August, and the second from September to October. This second run has larger fish, often in the 3-5kg (8–12 lb) range.

Chum run in October and November.

There are also bottom fishing opportunities. The reefs around Thrasher Rock and Entrance Island produce ling and rock cod and sometimes the odd halibut.

Nootka Sound/Tlupana Inlet (Maps 18, 24, 25)

You will find 4-7kg (10–15 lb) winter chinook in the waters of Nootka Sound from November to May. The best spots outside the sound are between Burdwood Point and Escalante Point (18/C2) or Between Maquinna Point and Yuquot Point (18/A1) on the eastern tip of Nootka Island. Be well aware of the marine reports, if the weather is nasty, you are not going to want to go out onto the open seas. Try near Saavedra Islands (18/B1) or off Verdia Island (25/C7) instead. The preferred method is to troll a Hoochie—either white or white and green—a medium sized herring strip, Tomic plug or spoon in 18-45m (60–150 feet) of water.

The big guys (chinook between 9-18kg/20–40 lbs) begin to appear in the inside passage in early July and peak in the first week of August. They like to go after large herring or white or fluorescent Hoochies with a Hot Spot flasher trolled at 9-18m (30–60 feet). If the in-shore area is open, expect crowded fishing conditions, especially at Camel Rock (25/D7). The shallow waters of Friendly Cove offers a fun option if the bay isn't too crowded with other boats.

In September, the coho start to appear, and last until mid-November. There are occasional openings, so keep an eye out. Bucktailing or using Apex spoons can be productive.

Nootka Sound has historically been a good place to find Halibut all year round (except during January), with the best time being spring and summer. The north end of the mouth of Esperanza Inlet (24/C2), off the Nootka Light (18/B1) or a little bit farther south at Maquinna Point (18/A1) are popular spots with the locals.

Parksville/Qualicum Beach (Maps 16, 23)
Like many places along the east coast of the island, the year begins with smaller 4-7kg (10–14 lb) feeder chinook chasing schools of herring through deeper water close to shore. Try looking for them around the Ballenas Islands, Mistaken Island or Cottam Reef (23 Inset).

Larger migratory chinook and coho (currently closed; check for openings) show up in the summer and the season lasts from June–September. If you are after chinook, troll shallow at dawn, and move deeper—into the 60m (200 foot) range—as the day warms up. The best lure is a Hoochie behind a red or green Hot Spot flasher with a 45-75cm (18–30 inch) leader. Other methods that can work are trolling plugs or jigging with a Zzinger, Perkins or Striker off the Eaglecrest Golf Course (23/G7) or across the strait around Lasqueti Island (from Sangster Island to Sisters Islets). If there is an opening for coho, try bucktailing around Lasqueti Island from Squitty Bay to Sangster Island and Sister Islets or west from Brant Point (23 Inset).

Sockeye and pinks appear in July and August. They are usually found between 15-30m (50–100 feet) and can be caught with a pink or orange Hoochies, pink squirts or red Krippled K on a 45-75cm (18–30 inch) leader behind a red or green Hot Spot flasher. Troll dead slow across tide lines and make sharp corners to entice the fish to bite.

Cod, red snapper, sole and halibut can be found in the many fishing holes around Lasqueti, Ballenas (23 Inset) and the Winchelsea Islands (16/F1) and are open year-round.

Port Alberni/Alberni Inlet (Map 14)
The Alberni Inlet is famous for its sockeye salmon run, which begins in mid-June and peters out by the end of August. Your best chance to snag a sockeye is between July 1 and August 10 when the run in at its peak. The sockeye, which number in the millions, range from 2-5kg (5–10 lbs) and are usually taken at 9-30m (30–100 feet) on a pink Hoochie with an 45-75cm (18–30 inch) leader and a red or green Hot Spot flasher. To attract the fish try stacking two lines on each downrigger, 6m (20 feet) apart. This will space your four lines 3m (10 feet) apart.

Large chinook (9-14kg/20-30+ lbs) move into the inlet in mid-August and congregate in the deeper water off of the river mouths—around Franklin River, Coleman Creek and the Nahmint River. You can catch these big chinooks on glow Hoochies on a 120cm (48 in) leader at daybreak or with a pink Hoochie on a 75-100cm (30–40 in) leader behind a red or green Hot Spot flasher later in the day. You can also try a red Hoochie, Tomic plug without a flasher, or whole anchovies with a 1.5m (5–6 foot) leader, a green Rhys Davis Anchovy Special and a red or green Hot Spot flasher. Troll at 6-15m (20–50 feet) at daybreak, and move down to 15-35m (50–120 feet) as the day progresses.

The coho run is in late August and September. Although coho fishing is usually closed, there have been some openings over the past few years. As always, check with the DFO before heading out.

Port Hardy/Port McNeill (Maps 39-41, 46-47)
The North Island is a big place with lots of places to find big fish. It also has enough islands and is tucked around the eastern side of the island to offer some relatively sheltered spots during the winter storms.

One of the best spots to find salmon is in Blackfish Sound, from Donegal Head on Malcolm Island to the mouth of the Baronet Passage (40/F1-41/B2). You will find smaller feeder chinooks throughout the year, while the larger migratory chinook pass through here in early June.

Migratory chinook appear around the end of March and the season peaks in August. These chinook are usually smaller than elsewhere on the island, but the rare 14kg (30 lb+) tyee can be landed. Troll slowly at 18-45m (60–150 feet) using whole, strip, or cut-plug herring on a

105-120cm (42–48 inch) leader with a pink, green or red trimmed flasher. Apex, Tomic plugs, Swimmertail spoons or green or green and white Hoochies behind a flasher can also be effective. Mooching and strip casting can also work at times. The best time to catch chinook is at dawn or dusk, especially on a flood tide.

In mid-June the sockeye season begins, and runs until early September. The peak of the run comes around the end of July. Try trolling dead slow at 9-15m (30–50 feet) with a small pink Hoochie with most of the strands removed on a 40-55cm (16–22 inch) leader behind a flasher.

Coho usually appear in mid-July, while the big 9-11kg (20–25 lb) northerns show up in September/October. Remember, there are very few openings for coho, so keep an eye on the updates. Trolling for coho is similar to chinook but remember coho like shallower water and a faster troll.

During even years (2002, 2004, etc.) there is a strong run of pinks in July and August. Troll slowly with a pink Hoochie behind a red or green Hot Spot flasher. Pinks tend to stay in the 9-15m (30–50 ft) depth range. The average catch is usually between 1 and 3kg (3-7 lbs).

Chum season is from August to October. Chum average 3-4kgs.

There is a strong halibut fishery during spring and fall, which sags during summer and disappears during winter.

Other than Blackfish Sound, there is good fishing around Port Hardy (Maps 46/G3-47/B5) at Dillon, Daphne and Duval Points, Gordon, Duncan, Masterman, Heard and Hurst Islands, Bate Passage, the Deserters Group Islands, Hardy Bay and Telegraph Cove. Areas around Port McNeill (Maps 39-41) include Cormorant Island, Cracroft Point, Cluxewe River mouth, Neil Ledge, Haddington, Pearce Passage, Bold Head to White Cliff Islets and Wells Passage.

Port Renfrew (Map 1)
The northwest coast of Vancouver Island is a maze of inlets, channels, sounds, islands, bays and passages. Not so the southwest coast. From Sooke to Bamfield, the only real shelter offered is the Port of San Juan, a small crack in the otherwise unsheltered coastline. All this is to say that during the winter months, fishing around Port Renfrew is often a non-event as the coast is hammered by winter storm after winter storm. When there are windows of opportunities, local fishers love to chase after the small (always under 9kg or 20 lb) chinook in the Juan de Fuca Strait. Pound for pound, they say, winter chinook fight better than any other fish on the coast.

If you go during this season, plan on waiting many days for the storms to pass. If you do get a chance to head out, winter chinook can usually be taken by trolling hoochies with a flasher or anchovies and small herring strips, fished at the 30-40m (100–140 ft) depth.

The main saltwater fishery usually gets underway in May. Halibut and other bottom fish can be found around Logan Creek (1/C2), Walbran Creek (1/B2), Bonilla Point (1/A1) and Carmanah Point (1 Inset) and offshore at the Swiftsure Banks (you'll find halibut here all year). Chinook fishing is spotty during May, but if you're going to catch salmon, it'll probably be at the Can Buoy, Owen Point (1/E2) or Camper Bay (1/D2). The first strong summer run of chinook shows up sometime in the first couple weeks of June, and fishing for chinook is usually good until the end of September. Camper Bay and Owen Point are the real hotspots. The fish usually like to hang out in 5-15m (15 to 50 ft) of water. Anchovies trolled behind rotating flashers on 1.5m (5–6 ft) leader work well, as does cut plug herring. In July, you will find chinook starting to school at Hammond Rocks, Rock Pile and the Sand Bank.

Cohos show up in late summer, with the peak season coming at the end of September. Remember, closures on coho are almost universal. Although the Port Renfrew area has had some of the best returns on the island recently, verify openings before you go.

Quatsino Sound (Maps 37-38)
You still can not catch chinook inside the Sound during August and September (a closure that has been in place for quite a few years now), but there is a good chinook fishery from early December to April. Though these are mostly smaller feeder chinooks, the occasional 11-14kg (25–30 lb) giant can be pulled in during the winter. Winter chinook are caught on a fast troll below 18m (60 feet) with cut plug herring. Orange or pink Hoochies, Apex, Tom Mack, Gibbs Stewart or McMahon lures also work.

Saanich Inlet (Maps 4, 10)

This sheltered inlet is a great place to fish during winter storms, but because of its proximity to Victoria, has been historically overfished. Finding fish that are biting can be difficult.

In early May, chinook (5-9kg/12–20 lbs) bound for the American River arrive in the Inlet. In June, the first of the larger (14kg/30+ lbs) summer stock hit the Inlet and stick around until September. Results vary, but trolling a strip teaser head without a flasher or an anchovy behind a #3 Pal Dodger has been known to produce. For something a little different, try jigging a green minnow or white Buzz Bomb off Wain Rock, McCurdy Point, Sawluctus and Sananus Isls or near the Coles Bay buoy.

Coho openings are rare (check for updates) and when the summer run does appear, they usually stay deep (up to 75m/250 feet). Try your luck by mid-channel trolling a green and white Hoochie or a green and blue Squirt behind a flasher. The October run bound for the Cowichan River stick closer to the surface and the traditional bucktailing method usually works well.

Halibut as big as 70kg (160 lbs) can been pulled from these waters but are more traditionally chickens (6-9kg/20–30 lb range).

Popular fishing spots include near the Bamberton Cement Plant, Sawluctus Island, Willis Point, Chesterfield Rock, Misery Bay, Coles Bay, Slugget Point, Indian Bay, Tanner Rock and Tozer Rock.

Tahsis Inlet (Map 25)

You will find 4-7kg (10–15 lb) winter chinook around Tahsis from November to May. The chinook follow the feed fish like herring into the deeper waters. Sometimes you have to go as deep as 70m (230 feet) to find them, though you are more likely to find them between 40-55m.

The big tyees (14kg/30+ lbs) begin to appear early July and peak in the first week of August. They like to go after large herring, or white or fluorescent Hoochies with a Hot Spot flasher. Mooching cut plug herring near the kelp beds works, too.

In September, the coho start to appear and last until mid-November. There are occasional openings, so keep an eye out. Bucktailing or using Apex spoons can be productive.

You will find halibut here all year round, with the best time being spring and summer. Six Mile Reef is a popular stomping ground for halibut, which can weigh up to and over 90 kg (200 lbs).

Tofino, Ucluelet and Clayoquot Sound (Map 5 Inset, 11-12)

Winter brings pounding storms to the Tofino area and when the gales start rocking the coast, you will need a big boat or a sheltered cove to ride out the storm. Fortunately, there is a lot of protected water in Clayoquot Sound. Winter Chinook in the 3-6kg (6–14 lb) range like to hang out in these areas, too. When the weather's not raging, try off Rapael Point (11/B1) on Flores Island.

By mid-March winter storms have given way to spring storms, and the halibut season begins. The historical hotspots have been about 5 miles offshore from Rapael Point and south to Portland Point (12/B5) and Ucluelet's South Bank (5 Inset) and La Perouse or Big Bank. Trolling, mooching a cut plug or drift fishing all yield good results. Fish the Tofino waters at 42-48m (140 to 160 feet) and the Ucluelet area waters at 55-90m (180 to 300 feet).

By mid-April, larger Chinooks (8-14kg/18–30 lbs) also start to show up in these areas. They stay until mid-July.

In mid-June, coho in the 2-3kg (4–7 lb) range begin to show up. If there are openings, try bucktailing in both the offshore areas and in the shallow, protected waters of Clayoquot Sound. A second appearance by coho—this time northern coho—begins in September and continues into mid-October.

In summer (July and August) the salmon fishery moves closer to shore, and around areas like Wilf Rock (11/G3), Blunden Island (11/E2), Ahous Point (11/E2), Kutcous Point (11/E1), Bartlett Island (11/D2), Wya Point (5 Inset) Florencia Bay (12/F7) and Little Beach. The most effective method of fishing is trolling anchovy, cut plug herring or a Hoochie (green and white, blue and white, white, black or silver) behind a flasher. Mooching cut plug herring or jigging can also yield favourable results. For added variety why not try fishing with live needlefish on a banana weight.

Victoria/Sooke (Maps 3-4)

Winter chinook season begins in late November and tails off into April. The Victoria Waterfront is an option for springs up to 7kg (15 lbs) but watch for closures. Other areas around Victoria include the Sooke Bluffs, Powder Wharf, Bedford Island, Beacher Bay and Sidney Channel. Around Sooke try Possession Point, Secretary Island, or Otter Point. Try trolling in the 45-61m (150–200 foot) range with a (army truck, white, green and white or black) Hoochie, whole herring strips or a medium anchovy in a glow head holder. The average size is 4kg (9 lbs), though chinook as large as 11kg (25 lbs) have been taken this early in the year.

Big chinook from the Columbia River stock run from mid-May until the last run goes through in late August. For most of these try trolling a medium or large anchovy on a 1.5-2m (5–8 foot) leader behind a dodger trolled at a depth of 7.5-10m (25–35 feet). For later runs you might have to go deeper—down to 25m (80 feet). Dawn, dusk, or the hour just before high tide are your best fishing times. Good areas to try include close to the shore around Otter Point, Secretary Island, the Trap Shack, Church Rock, Beechy Head, Aldridge Point, Cudlip Island, the William Head Prison, Race Passage, Christopher Point, Bedford Island, Sheringham Point, Whirl Bay or Possession Point.

Halibut, which can reach over 90kg (200 lbs) can be found from March–June. Nice size fish in the 9-14kg (20–30 lb) range are more likely. Try herring or octopus jigs, and leave the bait on the sandy bottom and let the tide do the work. The best place for halibut is the Sidney Channel (4/F1) or Cordova Channel at the D'Arcy Island buoy (4/G2) during slack tides.

Pinks arrive between June 1 and August 30 on odd years (2001, 2003, etc.). They range from 2-6kg (4–12 lbs) and are usually caught between 9-21m (30-70 feet) down.

Sockeye run from July 1 to August 15, and are caught with a red Hoochie and green or red flasher on a slow troll. The run is bigger during even (2002, 2004, etc.) years.

Coho run from May–October, with the larger northern run showing up in mid-August. Remember, the coho fishery is currently closed, with the occasional opening, usually on hatchery stock. If there is an opening, bucktailing near the surface is usually the most exciting way to catch a coho.

Freshwater Fishing

(Lake and Stream Fishing)

Lake Fishing

Vancouver Island offers many opportunities for fishermen to catch rainbow and cutthroat in the freshwater lakes. The odd brown trout, bull trout/dolly and smallmouth bass are also available. Given the popularity of the saltwater and stream fishery, the numerous freshwater lakes that dot the island often go unnoticed.

Unfortunately, the Vancouver Island lakes are usually acidic, nutrient deficient bodies of water compared to the lakes of the southern interior of B.C. Thus, it takes far longer to grow a large fish and so the average fish size is smaller than other parts of the province.

The most productive lakes are those lakes with the least rainfall and small outflow creeks. This is because the nutrients are not flushed away as rapidly. Also, the urban lakes nearby to farmland or residents are often more nutrient rich than lakes with forested slopes. This is because some of the nutrients from the farms and residents seep into the lake improving the nutrient level of the lake.

Beginning in March, the low lying lakes begin to produce rainbow and cutthroat. The first hatches of chironomids occur and so fly fishermen should focus on nymph and pupae imitations. In larger lakes, the cutthroat begin to congregate near the spawning streams so try trolling a stickleback minnow imitation, leech or large dragonfly nymph imitation past the mouth of the creeks.

April is considered the best month for fishing the low level Island lakes. Not only are there chironomid hatches but also, mayfly hatches begin to occur. The fish are now feeding vigorously after a long, cold winter.

By late May, the fishing at the low level lakes begins to tail off as the water warms. The fish begin to retreat to the depths of the lake. Where the lakes have smallmouth bass, that fishery begins to heat up.

By summertime, your best bet is to head north or to the hills. Higher elevation lakes do not warm up as much and offer a better chance to catch fish.

As the fall approaches, the water temperature in the low lying lakes begins to decline and fishing starts to pick up again. The subalpine tarns are still a good bet until the snow begins to fall. By late November, trolling a bucktail or a minnow pattern in the shallows of some of the bigger lakes produces some big cutthroat. In the smaller lakes, casting from shore or trolling along the drop-off is a good bet as the fish tend to move closer to shore as the winter approaches. Some say it is because of oxygen deprivation problems in the deeper holes.

The fishery grinds to a halt when the fall rain begins to pelt the coastline. Most of the Island lakes remain ice free throughout the year but fishing is quite slow during the cool, wet winters.

South Vancouver Island and Saltspring Lakes

If you are looking for more details on South Vancouver Island lakes, we recommend picking up a copy of **Fishing BC** the Vancouver Island South edition. This book focuses on 100 of the best lakes in the area and is loaded with helpful hints on lake fishing.

Anderson Lake (Map 7/C7)

Anderson Lake is a remote mountain lake located in the Carmanah Walbran Provincial Park on the West Walbran Trail. The 183.4 ha lake is at 165 m in elevation and offers good fishing for rainbow and cutthroat. Since the lake is 78.7 ft (24 m) deep and the lake is seldom fished, fishing is good throughout the ice free season. Please note that there are artificial fly only, bait ban and catch & release restrictions at the lake. Rustic camping is possible.

Antler Lake (Map 26/E3)

Just north of Gold River, Antler Lake offers fair fishing for small cutthroat (to 30 cm/12 in) by fly fishing or spincasting. The lake is 20 ha in size and is at 150 m in elevation. A car can access the lake which has a picnic site and cartop boat launch. No power boats allowed.

Arrowsmith Lake (Map 15/D2)

Off the Arrowsmith Lake Main, this 15ha lake has good numbers of small rainbow. Try trolling, fly fishing or spincasting in the spring.

Ash Lake (Map 22/A5)

Ash Lake is found north of Great Central Lake off a spur road from Branch 102. The 64.8 ha lake is 108 ft (32.9 m) deep and has good fishing for small rainbow and cutthroat (ave. 20-30 cm). The odd bull trout to 1.5 kg (4 lbs) is also caught. Since the lake averages 14.1 m (46.3 ft) deep, the waters stay cool enough in the summer to allow for some good fishing. It is possible to launch a cartopper at the lake.

Bainbridge Lake (Map 15/A2)

This lake has fair numbers of small rainbow, cutthroat and bull trout (dolly varden). Fishing is best in the spring or fall with a spinner or fly. Fishing is from shore only and there is an age restriction. The lake is on the Cameron River Road.

Battleship Lake (Map 28/E6)

Battleship Lake is found on Forbidden Plateau within Strathcona Provincial Park. The lake is reached by walking 1.5 km (1 hr) from the Paradise Meadows Trailhead nearby to the Mt Washington Ski Area. The lake has good fishing for small rainbow (<35 cm/14 in). The fishing season starts later in the year (early July) because the lake is at 1170 m in elevation and is in a high snowfall area. However, this means that fishing remains good throughout the summer months, particularly in August.

Bear Lake (Map 8/E4)

This small (10ha) lake next to Cowichan Lake has fair numbers of small rainbow, cutthroat and bull trout. Fishing is best in the spring or fall with a spinner or fly.

Bear Creek Reservoir (Map 3/B3)

Bear Creek Reservoir is found northwest of Sooke. A truck is highly recommended to access the 44 ha lake. There is a 20 m high earth dam at the west end of the lake so the reservoir is subject to draw down throughout the year. At 330 m in elevation, Bear Creek Reservoir offers fair fishing for small cutthroat and rainbow (to 35 cm) in the spring and fall. The lake is best fished by trolling.

Beaver Lake (Map 4/D3)

Beaver Lake is found nearby to the town of Lake Cowichan. The lake has fair numbers of small rainbow, cutthroat and bull trout. Since Beaver Lake is at 181 m in elevation, fishing begins as early as April. As the lake is only 24.6 ft (7.5 m) deep, it is best to use light tackle or a fly rod in the spring or fall.

Black Lake (Map 6/A5)

This remote lake offers good fishing for small cutthroat taken on a fly or by spincasting throughout the spring to fall. The lake requires a 3 km (one-way hike) along an old logging road. The lake is 60 ha in size and at 160 m in elevation.

Blackjack Lake (Map 16/D4)

Blackjack Lake is located north of the Nanaimo River Valley and the Nanaimo Lakes. You will definitely require a truck to reach the lake. The lake is 3.9 ha in size and contains stocked cutthroat, which average 20-25 cm (8-10 in) in size. The lake is very shallow (6 m/19.7 ft) and at an elevation of 290 m so fishing is best in the early spring (April-May) or later in the fall.

Blind Lake (Map 17/A6)

Blind Lake is located nearby to the Nanaimo River Road. It has good numbers of small rainbow and cutthroat, which are stocked annually. Fishing is best in the spring or fall although you can have some success during the summer months. The lake is 4.2 ha in size and is at 396 m in elevation. It is fairly shallow (8.5 m/27.9 ft). There are no developed facilities at the lake.

Blue Grouse Lake (Map 6/D6)

Blue Grouse Lake is located in the Oyster River Valley and accessed by a 4wd road. The lake is very good for small rainbow (to 35 cm/14 in) especially in the spring or fall. It is at 450 m in elevation and is 49.2 ft (15 m) deep. The water is deep enough to allow a summer fishery. Trolling is possible if you stick to the middle of the lake. At the south end of the lake, you will find a boat launch together with a rustic camping site.

Boneyard Lake (Map 3/E5)

Boneyard Lake is located on the Boonyard Main north of Sooke. The lake is only 2.4 ha in size and is very shallow with a maximum depth of only 5 m (16.4 ft). It has good numbers of small rainbow, which are stocked every second year. The lake is ideal for a float tube with fly fishing being the preferred method of catching fish. Launching a small boat is possible.

Boomerang Lake (Map 16/D3)

Boomerang Lake is located southwest of Lantzville off of Branch 160. A truck is necessary to reach the lake. The 10.9 ha lake is stocked annually with cutthroat and is found at 365.8 m in elevation. The cutthroat tend to remain small with a 30 cm fish being a good sized fish. Most fishermen cast flies or a small lure tipped with a worm. Trolling is possible as the lake is 12.5 m (41 ft) deep so long as you stay out from shore. Boomerang Lake has a cartop boat launch and a picnic area at the south end of the lake.

Botley Lake (Map 7/D7)

Botley Lake is a hike-in lake in the remote Carmanah Walbran Provincial Park nearby to Anderson Lake. The lake holds good numbers of rainbow and cutthroat.

Boulder Lake (Map 3/C4)

Boulder Lake is located northwest of Sooke nearby to the Bear Creek Reservoir. The 3.4 ha lake is stocked with rainbow that average 20-25 cm (8-10 in). Most of the lake is very shallow except at the northwest corner of the lake where the water drops off to 36.1 ft (11 m). There are no facilities at the lake.

Brannen Lake (Map 16/G2)

Brannen Lake is a popular urban lake next to the Nanaimo Parkway (Hwy 19). The lake is a productive lake and is known for its large cutthroat and rainbow, which can grow to 2.5 kg (5 lbs). There is an annual stocking program for both cutthroat and rainbow and there are some kokanee in the lake. Trolling is your best bet particularly during late March to mid June and again in the fall. A campsite and boat launches are available.

Buttle Lake (Map 20/G1, 27/G5, 28/A7)

This large, long man-made lake is over 4,200 ha in size and easily accessed off the Westmin Mine Road within Strathcona Provincial Park. The fishing is good from spring to fall for small cutthroat, rainbow and bull trout (to 40 cm/16 in) primarily by trolling. Many campsites and boat launches are offered. The lake is at 220 m in elevation and is prone to strong winds.

Cameron Lake (Map 15/C1)

Cameron Lake is a pretty lake found next to Highway 4. The deep lake is unique as it contains some brown trout. These fish are notoriously hard to catch but do reach enormous sizes (6 kg/14 lbs). There are also rainbow, cutthroat and kokanee. Fishing with a small boat or a float tube is tough because the lake is known for sudden strong winds that may blow in the wrong direction. A resort, a picnic area and a boat launch are all found at the east end of Cameron Lake.

Chemainus Lake (Map 9/E2)

Chemainus Lake is south of the town of Chemainus and is easily accessed off the Trans-Canada Hwy. The lake is 4.25 ha in size and offers a good smallmouth bass fishery. There are also small rainbow and cutthroat in the lake. Indeed, a 35 cm fish is considered a trophy. Fly fishing or spincasting from March-June and in the fall (September-October) produces the best. The lake is at 91 m in elevation and is only 26 ft (7.9 m) deep. Other than a rough cartop boat launch and wharf, there are no facilities at the lake.

Circlet Lake (Map 28/C6)

Circlet Lake is a gorgeous lake found in the Forbidden Plateau area of Strathcona Provincial Park. The deep lake has surprising large rainbow that average 30-35 cm (12-14 in) in size. The stocked trout are usually eager to take your fly or small lure during the summer months. There is a designated camping site for backpackers situated at the northeast corner of the lake.

Comox Lake (Map 21/G1, 29/A7)

Comox is found 10 km southwest of Courtenay. The large 2,100 ha lake is very deep (109 m/358 ft) and offers year round fishing for cutthroat, rainbow and bull trout to 2 kg (5 lbs). There are also kokanee in the lake. Trolling is the proven method to catch fish. At the Cumberland Lake Park you will find a boat launch, campground and a picnic area. A boat launch is also located at the northeast end of the lake off Comox Lake Main. Watch for fishing restrictions.

Cowichan Lake (Map 7/G1, 8/C3)

Cowichan Lake is one of the largest and most popular lakes on the Island. The 40 km long lake is 6,201 ha in size. and contains rainbow, cutthroat, kokanee, dollies and a few brown trout. The trout are said to grow to 3 kg (7 lbs) but you are more likely to catch one in the 1-1.5 kg (3 lb) range. The kokanee tend to be very small and are usually not targeted by fishermen. The lake is 499 ft (152 m) deep and is at 158 m in elevation. Given the fishing pressure, the lake is now heavily regulated. Cowichan Lake offers numerous campgrounds, resorts and two parks.

Crabapple Lake (Map 3/G4)

Crabapple Lake is found north of the Sooke Mountain Provincial Park and a high clearance vehicle is recommended to access the area. The lake is very shallow at its south end but the northern part of the lake drops off to 10 m (33 ft). Given the size of the lake and its contours, it makes an ideal float tube lake, especially in the spring and fall. Expect small rainbow and cutthroat.

Croteau Lake (Map 28/E6)

Croteau Lake is found on the Forbidden Plateau of Strathcona Provincial Park. The lake can be accessed by trail from the Mount Washington Ski Area. The tiny 3.4 ha lake has many rainbow in the 30-35 cm (10-12 in) range easily caught using a fly or small lure. There are rustic campsites located on the eastern shoreline of the lake.

Crown Lake (Map 6/G3)

Crown Lake is located a few kilometers west of Flora Lake on the Flora Lake Main. The lake offers fair fishing for small trout. Spincasting and fly fishing are the preferred methods of fishing the lake.

Crystal Lake (Map 17/A6)

Crystal Lake is a dark water lake located nearby to Timberland Lake. Crystal Lake has good cutthroat fishing in the spring with the average fish being 30-40 cm (12-15 in). In particular, the chironomid hatch in April and May can be a great time to fish if you use a brown coloured pupae imitation. There is a cartop boat launch next to a decaying dock and camping nearby. The cutthroat are stocked regularly.

Cusheon Lake (Map 10/B4)

On Saltspring Island, this 30 ha lake is at 90m in elevation and offers full facilities (boat launch and resort). Expect fair fishing for cutthroat to 1.5 kg (3 lbs) taken by trolling, fly fishing and spincasting. Smallmouth bass are also present at the lake in good numbers. There is an electric motor restriction.

Darlington Lake (Map 7/A1)

Darlington Lake is one of two lakes nearby to Franklin Camp on the way to Bamfield. This 13 ha lake has good fishing for small rainbow and dollies. The lake is deep so you can either troll, fly fish or spincast from a float tube or small boat. Since the lake is at 240 m in elevation, fishing is best in the spring (April-June) and fall (September-October).

Delphi Lake (Map 16/A7)
A tiny (4ha) lake with stocked rainbow. Fishing is generally good in the spring or fall.

Dickson Lake (Map 22/A6)
Dickson Lake is accessed by both the Ash River Road (car is sufficient) and Branch 102. It is a perfect fly fishing lake given its many bays and shallows. The lake has good numbers of small cutthroat and rainbow. On the rare occasion, some of the summer run steelhead are able to navigate over Dickson Falls and enter the lake. Please note the fishing restrictions.

Diver Lake (Map 16/G3)
Diver Lake is easily located off the Old Island Highway northwest of Nanaimo City. Although fishing is generally slow for rainbow, cutthroat and smallmouth bass, the trout can reach 2 kg (4.5 lbs). The trout are stocked and average 30 cm (12 in) in size. There is an electric motor only restriction on the marshy lake, which offers a cartop boat launch.

Dixie Lake (Maps 8/A1, 16/A7)
Off the East Shaw Main, this 6 ha lake is stocked with small rainbow. Try fly fishing or spincasting.

Diversion Reservoir (Maps 2/G3,3/A3)
Off the East Main, the reservoir has both stocked rainbow and cutthroat. Fish tend to be small in this 42ha lake and are best caught by trolling.

Donner Lake (Map 27/A5)
Found in Strathcona Park southeast of Gold River, Donner Lake offers many small cutthroat. This 565 m high lake has good fishing from June through the summer. Branch 140 is a rough deactivated 4wd road that doesn't quite reach the lake. A new campsite has been proposed at the north end of the lake. No power boats are allowed.

Doran Lake (Map 21/E7)
Doran is a small mountain lake located at the end of Branch 500, a 4wd road north of Sproat Lake. The lake offers good fishing for steelhead and rainbow that can grow to good sizes (1 kg/2+ lbs). The best time to fish the lake is in August-October as the lake is quite high in elevation at 670 m. A small boat can be launched at the lake.

Dougan Lake (Map 9/G7)
Dougan Lake is located next to the Trans Canada Highway just north of the traffic light at the Cobble Hill Road junction. The lake has fair numbers of rainbow and cutthroat to 4 lbs (1.5 kg) but most of the trout are around 25 cm in size. Fly fishing and bait fishing in March-May and in September-October is your best bet as there is an algae bloom in the summer months that puts a halt to the fishing. Dougan Lake is known as a good chironomid lake with the hatch beginning in April. Electric motor only boats can be launched at the end of the access road found on the east side of the lake.

Douglas Lake (Map 28/F7)
Douglas Lake is found on the Forbidden Plateau and can be reached by trail from either the Mount Washington Ski Area or the old Forbidden Plateau Ski Hill. The 7.2 ha lake has some good sized rainbow but the average fish is 30-35 cm (10-12 in). The stocked trout are easily caught in the summer using a fly or small lure. There is a primitive camping area at the lake.

Drum Lakes (Map 27/A2)
On Highway 28, these 20 ha lakes hold fair numbers of small rainbow, cutthroat and bull trout (dollies). Fly fishing and spincasting during the spring or fall is your best bet. A picnic site and cartop boat launch are found at the lake, which is at 305 m in elevation.

Durrance Lake (Map 4/C2)
Durrance Lake is located within the Gowlland Tod Provincial Park and can be accessed by the Durrance Road. It contains smallmouth bass and stocked rainbow and cutthroat. The lake receives heavy fishing pressure given its easy access and close proximity to Victoria. Since the lake is at 129 m in elevation and only 16 m (52.5 ft) deep, it suffers from the summer doldrums due to warming water. Therefore, it is best to fish the lake in April-June and then in September-October. Facilities include an electric motor only cartop boat launch and a dock.

Elk & Beaver Lakes (Map 9/A6)
Elks and Beaver Lakes are located next to the Pat Bay Highway (Hwy 17) north of Victoria. The lakes are joined by a wide channel with Beaver Lake being the southern most lake. The popular lakes are unique because they have smallmouth bass and reports of perch and largemouth bass. There are also rainbow and cutthroat, which are stocked annually. The low elevation lakes offer an early season fishery beginning in late March and are known as good chironomid lakes. The lakes are home to the Elk Beaver Lake Regional Park, a popular daytime retreat for the residents of Greater Victoria.

Elsie Lake (Map 21/G4,22/A4)
Elsie Lake, which is accessed by the Ash River Road, is very popular especially on weekends. The 1,107 ha lake has been known to disappear during summer drawdown. April-June and September-October are the best times to fish with trolling being the preferred method. Cutthroat, rainbow and stocked steelhead can reach 1.5 kg (3 lbs) but average 25-35 cm. A couple rustic boat ramps and camping areas are found near the east end of the lake.

Esary Lake (Map 22/G7)
Esary Lake is a catch & release fishery located east of Horne Lake. The 13 ha lake is rather shallow and has fair numbers of cutthroat. It is recommended to fish in the early spring or in the fall. There are no facilities at the lake.

Fairy Lake (Map 2/A1)
Fairy Lake is located nearby to Port Renfrew off the paved Harris Creek Main. The lake offers good early season fishing for cutthroat and bull trout, which average 30 cm (12 in). The cutthroat are both resident and sea run. There is a popular rec site, with a dock, sandy beach and a cartop boat launch as well as a nature trail in the area. Restrictions include an engine power restriction (10hp).

Father & Son Lake (Map 15/C5)
Father & Son Lake is a high elevation lake reached by a 1 km (one-way) hike. The lake offers good fishing for rainbow to 2.5 kg (5 lbs) although the average fish is 25-30 cm. Try fly fishing or spincasting in the early summer and into the fall. A rustic campsite is found at the lake.

Fetus Lake (Map 7/C7)
Tiny Fetus Lake is found south of Anderson Lake on the West Walbran Trail within the Carmanah Walbran Provincial Park. It holds some trout.

Fishtail Lake (Map 15/D2)
From Arrowsmith Lake, a 2 km hike will bring you to a sub-alpine lake with good fishing for small stocked rainbow. Fly fishing or spincasting in the summer or fall produce best results. Rustic camping is possible.

Flora Lake (Map 7/A3)
Flora Lake is a remote lake best accessed off the Flora Lake Main by way of a high clearance vehicle. The lake holds many small stocked rainbow and wild cutthroat, which can be caught throughout the year. The rainbow are stocked every second year. The rec site at the north end of the lake offers rustic lakeshore camping as well as a dock and cartop boat launch.

Florence Lake (Map 4/B4)
Florence Lake is found east of Victoria off the Trans-Canada Highway. It is a very shallow lake that is best fished in the early spring (March-May) and later in fall (October). The lake holds a few rainbow and cutthroat, which tend to be small (20-25 cm/8-10 in in size). It is possible to launch a small boat at the lake.

Forbush Lake (Map 21/F3)
Forbush Lake is a canoe access lake located west of Willemar Lake. Forbush Lake receives less fishing pressure than other lakes and has good numbers of small trout.

Francis Lake (Map 7/A1)
Francis Lake is one of two lakes nearby to Franklin Camp on the way to Bamfield. At Franklin Camp on the Bamfield Road, head southeast on South Main for about 2km and you will pass by Darlington Lake then Francis Lake. This 42 ha lake has numerous small rainbow and bull trout caught by trolling, fly fishing or spincasting. There is a campground with a dock at the northwestern end of the lake.

Frederick Lake (Map 6/B3)
Frederick Lake is located just east of Bamfield on the West Coast. At 73.2 m in elevation, the lake offers an early season fishery for fair numbers of small trout (rainbow, cutthroat and bull trout). September is the best time to fish. There is a boat launch and picnic site located at the north end of the lake.

Fuller Lake (Map 9/F2)
Fuller Lake is an urban lake surrounded by private residences, a golf course and a park (with picnic tables and a boat launch) south of Chemainus. The lake offers a good early season fishery beginning in late March and remaining steady until June. Some large rainbow and cutthroat (up to 3 kg/6 lbs) are pulled out annually. Catchable size trout are continually stocked to help maintain the fishery. An electric motor only restriction applies.

Glen Lake (Map 4/B5)
Glen Lake is located southwest of Langford off Glen Road. The low elevation lake receives heavy fishing pressure but the fishing is still fair for smallmouth bass and stocked rainbow. An irrigation system was installed in recent years to help water quality and the fishery. Glen Cove Park, off Glenview Drive, has a boat launch for small (electric motor only) boats. A number of private residences line the lake.

Gracie Lake (Map 14/A2)
Gracie Lake is located along the Stirling Arm Road near the west end of Sproat Lake. The lake is considered one of the better rainbow fisheries in the southern part of Vancouver Island. A wilderness campground and a natural boat launch are found on the northwestern side of the deep lake. There is also an electric motor only restriction at the lake.

Grass Lake (Map 3/G5)
Grass Lake is found north of the Sooke Mountain Provincial Park on a rough road. The lake has good numbers of small rainbow and cutthroat that can grow to 35 cm (14 in). Spincasting and fly fishing in the spring or fall are the preferred methods of fishing as the lake is too shallow to troll effectively.

Great Central Lake (Map 21/E6, 22/B7)
At 80m in elevation, this 5,000 ha lake is a popular recreation lake. The lake has fair numbers of cutthroat averaging 1 kg (2 lbs) as well as bull trout (to 3 kg/6 lbs) and stocked steelhead. Trolling in the spring or fall is best especially near the creeks that run into the lake. Try using a gang troll or kwikfish (with or without) a worm. A Tonic plug and small Apex also work. There are good boat launching facilities, a resort and campsites found along the long lake. Some fishing restrictions apply.

Green Lake (Map 16/G2)
Green Lake is an urban lake found 13 km northwest of the Nanaimo city centre. It is easily accessed off Highway 19 via Jenkins Road. It is a shallow lake and has rainbow and cutthroat last stocked in the 1980's as well as some bass. The fish tend to be small with a 35 cm (14 in) fish being considered big. There is an electric motor only restriction at the lake.

Harewood Lake (Map 17/A5)
Harewood Lake is situated off White Rapid Road south of Nanaimo. It is the largest of a series of lakes at 10 ha. It has small stocked cutthroat, which are best fished in the spring or fall by trolling, spincasting or fly fishing. Nearby lakes include Stark Lakes, Blind Lake, Myles Lake and Overton Lake.

Hawthorn Lake (Map 14/G6)
On the Lizard Pond Road, this small lake has many small cutthroat caught by spincasting or fly fishing. A rough boat launch and picnic site is available.

Healy (Panther) Lake (Map 16/A4)
Healy Lake is located north of the Nanaimo Lakes off Branch C-26. The higher elevation lake is (at 527 m) is very shallow. Since the lake is artificial fly only, bait ban, barbless hooks and catch & release, it has good numbers of small rainbow (to 35 cm) best caught throughout May-June and September-October. At the northeast end of the lake you will find the Healy Lake Rec Site. It offers rustic camping as well as a cartop boat launch.

Heart Lake (Map 16/A6)
The gated access to this lake limits anglers in the area. The mountain lake offers summer fishing for average sized trout.

Heather Lake (Map 7/F1)
Heather Lake is a mountain lake that is accessed by foot off the blocked roads north of Cowichan Lake. Given the poor access, the lake is seldom fished and has good numbers of trout caught by spincasting or fly fishing.

Henry Lake (Map 15/C3)
Henry Lake is a sub-alpine tarn (at 1006 m in elevation) accessed by truck via a spur road off Cop Creek Main. The 8 ha lake is only 4 m (13 ft) deep and is subject to winterkill. However, the lake was stocked with steelhead trout and the last reports say that the fish are still doing well in the lake. The trout tend to be small with a 35 cm (14 in) fish being a large one. Given the depth of lake, shore fishing and trolling are limited. Most fishermen fly fish, bait fish or spincast from a small boat. When you reach Henry Lake, you will find a rustic campground as well as a dock at the north end of the lake.

Hidden Lake (Map 15/D2)
From Arrowsmith Lake, a 2 km hike will bring you to a subalpine lake with good fishing for small stocked rainbow. Fly fishing or spincasting in the summer or fall produces best. Rustic camping is available.

Holden Lake (Map 17/C5)
Holden Lake is located off Cedar Road and offers a nice park and cartop boat launch. Despite the elevation (15 m) and close proximity to Nanaimo, it offers a fairly descent year round fishery for small rainbow, cutthroat and smallmouth bass. The cutthroat are stocked annually at the 40 ha lake.

Holland Lake (Map 9/C1)
Found near Ladysmith, this is another South Island lake that has a gated access road. Fishing is best in the spring and fall for average sized trout.

Horne Lake (Map 23/B7)
Horne Lake is lined with private residents and is easily accessed by an all season road (Horne Lake Road). The lake has fair numbers of small stocked cutthroat and steelhead as well as a a few kokanee in the lake. The lake is deep and large enough to offer consistent trolling throughout the year. Boat launches campsites are found at both the west and east ends of the lake.

Indian Lake (Map 15/F5)
A 10 ha lake requiring a 1 km hike (one way). The lake has small rainbow and cutthroat best caught in the spring or fall by fly fishing or spincasting.

Jarvis Lake (Map 3/D2)
Jarvis Lake is nearby to the Greater Victoria Watershed and is reached by driving north on the Cragg Main. The lake is at 647 meters in el-

evation and is quite shallow. Your best bet is to work the fringe area using a lure with a worm or try fly fishing. The 15 ha lake has good numbers of small stocked rainbow to catch. Launching a cartop boat or camping are certainly possible at the lake.

Johnson Lake (Map 28/E7)
Johnson Lake is a long walk from either the Mount Washington Ski Area or the old Forbidden Plateau Ski Hill. This high elevation Forbidden Plateau lake offers some good fishing for surprisingly large rainbow, which average 30-40 cm (12-14 in). There are two areas to camp near the south end of the lake.

June Lake (Map 21/F4)
June Lake is found northeast of Oshinow Lake on Branch 110. The lake forms part of the Ramsay Creek drainage in Strathcona Provincial Park and offers fair fishing for small trout.

Junior Lake (Map 21/E4)
Junior Lake is north of Toy Lake on Branch 110. It is 5 ha in size and is at 480 m in elevation. The lake offers many small rainbow and cutthroat easily caught by fly fishing or spincasting in the spring or fall. The lake is extremely shallow at only 1.5 m (4.9 ft) deep so it is subject to winterkill. A rustic campsite and boat launch are found at the lake.

Kammat Lake (Map 15/C3)
Kammat Lake is a scenic lake found in a sub-alpine area southeast of Port Alberni. The lake is located off Cop Creek Main and you will need a truck to reach the lake. The lake holds good numbers of small steelhead, which are stocked regularly. The small lake is an ideal lake for fly fishing from a float tube. There is a rustic campsite and a place to launch small boats at the lake.

Kemp Lake (Map 3/D6)
Kemp Lake is easily accessed by the Kemp Lake Road off Highway 14. At 38 m in elevation, Kemp Lake offers an early season fishery beginning in late March and continuing to June. It is preferable to fish the lake from a (non-motorized) boat as the shallow lake is lined with weed beds making shore casting hard. The lake holds fair numbers of cutthroat and rainbow to 40 cm (16 in). There are a number of private residences but there is a cartop boat on the western shores of the lake.

Kennedy Lake (Map 12/G6,13/A5)
Kennedy Lake is a large West Coast lake at 6,500 ha in size. The lake is considered one of the island's best cutthroat lakes. Try fly fishing or spincasting a stickleback imitation. That baitfish represents the cutthroat's main diet in this lake. With easy access off Highway 4, there are developed campsites and boat launches on the lake. Watch for strong winds.

Kunlin Lake (Map 26/G5)
Located southeast of Gold River off the Ucano Road (truck recommended), Kunlin Lake has great fishing for small cutthroat. The 260 m high lake offers fishing throughout the summer. An undeveloped campsite and boat launch are found at this Strathcona Park Lake.

Labour Day Lake (Map 15/F4)
Labour Day Lake is at 890 m in elevation and offers good fishing for small rainbow throughout the summer and fall using a fly, bait or a lure. It is a hike-in lake found off the Lake Road. A truck is needed to reach the trailhead.

Lacy Lake (Map 23/A7)
Found south of Esary Lake, Lacy Lake has fair numbers of cutthroat and rainbow. Spincasting and fly fishing in the spring and summer is your best bet. The lake does not have any developed facilities but it is possible to launch a small boat at the lake.

Lady Lake (Map 28/E6)
Lady Lake is best accessed by trail from the Paradise Meadows Trailhead near the Mount Washington Ski Area. It is another one of the high elevation Forbidden Plateau lakes that offers a good summertime alternative. The small rainbow can be found near the expansive shallows at the southwest end of the lake near the river estuary. There are two rustic camping sites located near the south end of the lake.

Lake Beautiful (Map 28/D7)
Lake Beautiful is one of the many lakes found in the Forbidden Plateau area of Strathcona Provincial Park. It contains aggressive rainbow that average 30-35 cm (12-14 in) in size and are waiting to take your fly or small lure.

Lake Helen McKenzie (Map 28/E6)
Lake Helen McKenzie is located to the west of Battleship Lake in Forbidden Plateau. It is reached by a 6.8 km (3 hr) return hike from the Mount Washington Ski Area. The 55 ha lake offers very good fishing for small rainbow (up to 35 cm/14 in) on a fly or by spincasting. Fishing is best from July until early October due to its 1,145 m elevation and the fact that the lake is iced over most years until June. Since the lake is one of the closer ones to the parking lot, it is possible to pack in a float tube.

Lake Weston (Map 10/D5)
This 18 ha lake on Saltspring Island has remarkably good fly fishing for rainbow to 2.5 kg (5 lbs) in the spring and fall. The access to the lake, which is at 80 m in elevation, is off the paved Beaver Point Road.

Landslide Lake (Map 27/B4)
A beautiful but remote hike-in lake found in Strathcona Provincial Park. The long hike discourages anglers despite the plentiful rainbow. The small, stocked trout are best caught by fly fishing or spincasting in this 14ha lake.

Langford Lake (Map 4/B5)
Langford Lake is an urban lake located west of Victoria. The 61 ha lake has good sized rainbow and smallmouth bass (to 3 kg/7 lbs). There are also some cutthroat in the lake. The lake is ideal for fly fishing from a float tube and is known as a good chironomid lake. A wooden walkway provides access for shore anglers wishing to fish from a pier. An aeration system was installed in order to improve the quality of the water for the fish. There is also a boat launch for non-motorized boats at the southwest end of the lake.

Larry Lake (Map 13/B4)
Larry Lake or Hydor Hill Lake is located next to the Pacific Rim Hwy (Hwy 4). The fishery for small rainbow is best in the early spring and in late fall. Since the lake is quite small, it is well suited for a belly boat and can be effectively fly fished. Spincasting a lure with a worm or other bait is also a good idea.

Lizard Lake (Map 2/C1)
Lizard Lake is a popular destination about 18 km northeast of Port Renfrew. It is easily accessed off the Harris Creek Main. The 8.7 ha lake has good numbers of stocked rainbow that can reach 35 cm (14 in) in size. Since this is a low elevation lake (91.4 m), fishing is good during April-June and again in October. The Lizard Lake Rec Site offers a gravel boat launch, nice dock and five camping spots. There is an electric motors only restriction at the lake.

Lizard Pond (Map 14/G6)
Off the Lizard Pond Road (car is adequate), this 10 ha lake holds fair numbers of small cutthroat taken with an artificial fly only. The best fishing is in June or in the fall. There are no developed facilities.

Lois Lake (Map 9/D7)
Lois Lake is accessed by truck southwest of Duncan. The lake is at 669 meters in elevation and offers a late spring or early summer rainbow trout fishery. The lake is unique because it also has brown trout that grow to 3 kg (7 lbs) but are notoriously hard to catch. Please note that this lake is an artificial fly fishing only lake and there is a one fish limit per day. There is a rough boat launch and camping is possible at the north end of the lake.

Long Lake (Map 16/G,29/B6)
Long Lake is located about 7 km northwest of the city of Nanaimo right next to the North Island Hwy. The 33.6 ha lake has good sized smallmouth bass (4-5 lbs) as well as some rainbow and cutthroat. It is found at 122 m in elevation and is 46 ft (14 m) deep. The lake has a cartop boat launch as well as a Bed & Breakfast.

Loon Lake (Map 15/A1)

Loon Lake is also known as Summit Lake due to its location along the Highway 4 pass. The 7 ha lake holds surprisingly large rainbow and cutthroat, which average 40 cm (16 in) in size. The lake is best fished during the spring (April-June) and the fall (September-October). Fly fishing or spincasting are your best bets as the lake is difficult to troll. It is possible to launch non-motorized boats and a trail circles the lake.

Lost Lake (Map 28/F3)

Without a good map and some local knowledge, you may indeed find out why they call this water body Lost Lake. The small lake offers good fishing for small stocked cutthroat. April-June and September-October are the best times to fish. The lake is deep enough to troll but given its size, it is well suited for a belly boat and fly rod. It is easy enough to camp at roadside and launch a small cartop boat.

Lowry Lake (Map 22/A6)

Lowry Lake is found off the Thunder Mountain (Branch 83) Road, which is a fairly good road. The lake is considered a good fly fishing lake because the shoreline is lined with weed beds, which make good cover for the trout. The lake has stocked cutthroat and wild rainbow that grow to 35 cm (14 in). The best times to fish the lake are in April or May and also in the fall. There is a rec site at the southeastern end of the lake that offers lakeshore camping and a cartop boat launch.

Lucid Lake (Map 16/F4)

Lucid Lake is accessed by a 4wd road found south of Mount Benson. This tiny lake has good fishing for small stocked cutthroat and rainbow. Since the lake is at 610 m in elevation, fishing does not get started until June but the shallow lake warms significantly in the summer months. By September-October, the fishing begins to get good again. During severe winters, there is the prospect of winterkill.

MacDonald Lake (Map 3/F3)

MacDonald Lake is a tiny lake found to the southwest of Sooke Lake off Cragg Main. It has small cutthroat and rainbow, which are best fished beginning in April until June and again in September-October. The summer months are very slow as the water warms significantly at that time of the year. There are no developed facilities at the lake.

Maggie Lake (Map 16/B7)

This medium sized, 250 ha West Coast lake is only 50 m above sea level. Fishing is fair fishing for cutthroat, rainbow and bull trout to 1 kg (2 lbs). Trolling in the spring or fall is best. The lake has a cartop boat launch and rustic camping.

Maple Lake (Map 29/C7)

Maple Lake is found north of Cumberland next to the last phase of the Inland Island Hwy. The 28 ha lake is best fished in the spring (April-June) or fall (September-October). It is possible to troll, fly fish or spincast for the stocked cutthroat and rainbow to 1.5 kg (3 lbs). There is a rough cartop boat launch available for non-motorized boats.

Mariwood Lake (Map 28/D6)

Mariwood Lake is one of several small hike-in fishing lakes found in the Forbidden Plateau area of Strathcona Provincial Park. The lake is a fly angler's dream lake with numerous islands and bays offering great casting terrain. It offers good fishing for rainbow averaging 30-35 cm (12-14 in) that are easily caught on a fly or by spincasting. The lake, which is at 1,170 m in elevation, has no developed facilities.

Marshy Lake (Map 23/A7)

A tiny (2 ha) lake requiring a short hike to reach the good fishing for small rainbow. Try a fly or lure in the spring or fall.

Matheson Lake (Map 4/A7)

Matheson Lake is a popular fishing lake found within the Matheson Lake Regional Park to the southwest of Victoria. The lake is accessed by car and offers an early season fishery (April-May) for small cutthroat and rainbow trout. There are also a few larger bull trout (to 1.5 kg/3 lbs) and bass. There is an electric motors only restriction at the lake and the bass must be released. A picnic area and beach area are situated at the east end of the lake.

Mayo Lake (Map 9/A4)

Mayo Lake is located nearby to Highway 18 (Cowichan Valley Highway) and is accessed via the paved Mayo Road. The lake holds small rainbow trout primarily because 1,000 catchable size rainbow are stocked in the lake each year. The lake is very shallow at 2.5 m (8.2 ft) and is best suited for a float tube and light tackle. The 8.4 ha lake is at 180 meters in elevation and is best fished in March-May and in October-November. Please note that you must be 16 years or younger to fish in the lake.

McBride Lake (Map 21/A6)

In Strathcona Park, this 18 ha lake is accessed by boat then bushwacking from Great Central Lake. You can expect great fishing for small rainbow and cutthroat. Try a fly or spinner.

McClure Lake (Map 7/E5)

Regardless of which mainline you take, it is a long bumpy road in. The 16 ha lake does offer a campsite and boat launch. Fishing is fair for stocked brook trout and rainbow caught primarily by trolling in the spring or fall.

McKay Lake (Map 17/A6)

McKay Lake is found east of the Nanaimo Airport on Branch 100 from the McKay Lake Forest Service Road. A truck is recommended to access the 5.5 ha lake, which offers very good fly fishing for small stocked cutthroat. Fishing is most productive in the spring (March-June) and fall (September-October) since the lake is at 155 m in elevation and is 8 m (26 ft) deep. It is stocked annually with yearling cutthroat and is considered a good chironomid lake. A large parking area is located on the west side of the lake and is idea for camping and picnicking.

McKenzie Lake (Map 28/F7)

McKenzie Lake is one of 10 good hike-in fishing lakes found in the Forbidden Plateau area of Strathcona Provincial Park. The lake is best accessed by trail from the old Forbidden Plateau Ski Hill. At 935 m in elevation, this 10 ha lake is one of the lowest elevation lakes in the area. As a result, fishing begins a week or two earlier than the other lakes (late June to early July) and extends into late October. It offers good fishing for small rainbow and cutthroat up to 35 cm (14 in) in size. A stocking program maintains the fish population.

McKenzie Lake (Map 3/C4)
McKenzie Lake is located at the north end of the Thetis Lake Regional Park nearby to Victoria. This small, 2.9 ha lake is only 5 m (16.4 ft) deep. It does holds small rainbow which are best caught using a float tube and casting a fly or lure towards the weeds. No power boats are allowed on the lake.

McLaughlin Lake (Map 22/A5)
McLaughlin Lake is accessed off the Ash River Road and offers good fishing for small rainbow and cutthroat throughout the spring (April-June) and fall (September-October). The 40.9 ha lake is stocked with cutthroat every second year and there are also a few dollies in the lake. There is a cartop boat launch and picnic site at the west end.

Mesachie Lake (Map 8/E4)
Mesachie Lake is found nearby to the town of Lake Cowichan off the South Shore Road. The 58.3 ha lake has cutthroat, rainbow, bull trout and kokanee that tend to be small although some of the fish reach 40 cm (15 in) in length. All the fish species are in low numbers compared to other south Island lakes making fishing somewhat sporadic.

Michael Lake (Map 17/D6)
Off Doole Road, this 10 ha lake has fair fishing for small cutthroat and rainbow. Trolling is the preferred method of fishing. No power boats allowed.

Mitchell Lake (Map 4/B3)
Mitchell Lake is located north of the tiny community of Millstream off the Millstream Road. The lake is best fished beginning in March until May and again in September-October for small trout.

Moat Lake (Map 28/C7)
Moat Lake is another one of the many lakes found in the Forbidden Plateau area of Strathcona Provincial Park. The lake is best fished in July to September because of the high elevation (1163 m). The best month is August as the insect hatches are in full swing at that time and the fish are actively feeding. The 94.6 ha lake has good numbers of rainbow, which are stocked frequently. Pitching a tent along the eastern shoreline at three locations is certainly possible.

Moriarty Lake (Map 15/G4)
This 7 ha lake is accessed by trail off a rough branch road (a truck is needed). You can expect good fishing for small rainbows, especially in the spring or fall with a fly or lure.

Muriel Lake (Map 12/F4)
Muriel Lake is accessed off the deactivated West Clayoquot Main, which will require a high clearance vehicle to negotiate. The 145 ha lake offers good fishing for small cutthroat from May to October primarily by trolling. Rustic camping is possible.

Nahmint Lake (Map 14/B3)
Nahmint Lake is located off the Nahmint Mainline south of Sproat Lake. This lake holds large rainbow and steelhead as well as some small cutthroat. Try fly fishing or spincasting where the river enters and leaves the lake. Watch for fishing restrictions such as releasing the larger fish.

Nanaimo Lakes (Map 15/G6, 16/D5)
Nanaimo Lakes are a series of four popular recreation lakes located southwest of Nanaimo on the Nanaimo River Road. The road is paved to the east end of First Lake. The Nanaimo Lakes offer a fishery for small rainbow and cutthroat trout along with a few bull trout and kokanee. Some of the cutthroat and rainbow do reach 2 kg (4 lbs) but that is a rare fish. Fishing is best in April-June and September-October because of the low elevation of the lakes. Camping is available at the first and fourth lakes and boat launches are found on all lakes.

Nimnim (Long) Lake (Map 22/A3)
Nimnim Lake is also known as Long Lake and is found north of Elsie Lake off Branch 121 (a car is adequate). The lake is located at 671 m in elevation and has both stocked rainbow and wild cutthroat. The trout grow to 2 kg (4.5 lbs) but the average size is only 25-30 cm. Rustic camping and a cartop boat launch are offered at the lake.

Oshinow Lake (Map 21/D4)
Oshinow Lake is found within the Strathcona Provincial Park and forms part of the Ash River drainage. It is a narrow deep lake, which gives up fish very rarely. The 263 ha lake is accessed off Branch 110 via truck and is at 420 m in elevation. Rainbow and cutthroat reach 2 kg (4.5 lbs) but average 25-35 cm in size. The lake is well suited for trolling. There are two camping areas along the southern end of the lake.

Pachena Lake (Map 6/B3)
Pachena Lake is located next to the Bamfield Road about 11 km from Bamfield but does not receive a lot of fishing pressure. It has fair numbers of small rainbow and cutthroat with the odd bull trout (dolly). The lake is nutrient poor so the fish are slow growing and are generally small. The low elevation lake is best fished in April and May and in September-October. It is possible to launch a small boat.

Panther Lake (Map 28/E7)
Panther Lake is situated on the Forbidden Plateau of Strathcona Provincial Park. The lake can be accessed by trail from either the Mount Washington Ski Area or the old Forbidden Plateau Ski Hill. The lake has rainbow that average 30-35 cm (12-14 in) and are caught by fly fishing only. The high elevation lake is best fished from early July to late October-early November.

Patterson Lake (Map 22/C7)
Patterson Lake is a 12 ha lake on the Ash River Road (a car is adequate) and has fair numbers of small cutthroat caught during the spring and fall. Fly fishing and spincasting are the proven methods. A primitive boat launch is offered.

Peak (Henry) Lake (Map 15/D4)
At 1000 m in elevation, this 8 ha lake offers good fishing for small rainbow and stocked steelhead from July to September. Fly fishing or spincasting is best. A rustic campsite is at the lake, which is located on a rough spur road off Cameron River Main.

Pear Lake (Map 22/A3)
Pear Lake is located to the southeast of Comox Lake and is easily accessed off the Valley Link Hwy (Toma Main) at the 43 km mark. The 14 ha lake is at 420 meters in elevation and is only 4.5 m (14.8 ft) deep. Fly fishing and spincasting produces small trout in April-May and September-October. There is a cartop boat launch at the lake.

Pearl Lake (Map 28/A6)
At the end of Oyster River Main a short 1 km trail leads to this high elevation, remote lake. Good numbers of stock rainbow (to 35 cm/14 in) can be caught in this 22 ha lake.

Pixie Lake (Map 2/D1)
Pixie Lake is located east of Port Renfrew on Lens Main. This small 5.8 ha lake is very shallow (4.3 m/14 ft) and is at 91 m in elevation. It has a few rainbow, which tend to be small (less than 30 cm). Fly fishing or spincasting are the preferred methods of fishing. It is possible to launch a small boat at the lake.

Priest Lake (Map 17/D6)
Priest Lake offers an early season fishery (April-May) as well as later in the fall (October-November). The lake is perfect for a belly boat given its small size. The lake is easily accessed by taking the Cedar Road southeast of Nanaimo.

Prior Lake (Map 4/C4)
Prior Lake is located within the Thetis Lake Regional Park off Highland Road or via McKenzie Creek Trail. The lake has surprisingly good fishing for small cutthroat (to 30 cm) in the spring or fall despite the fishing pressure. It is best suited for fly fishing and spincasting. No power boats are allowed at the lake.

Prospect Lake (Map 4/C3)
Prospect Lake is a popular south island lake located north of Victoria. The lake has a good size population of cutthroat, rainbow (both stocked) and bass. In the spring (April-May) and fall (September-October), the 148 ha lake has good fishing near the surface in the early morning and late into the evening. There is a boat launch available.

Quamichan Lake (Map 9/G4)

Another popular fishery that is easily accessed east of Duncan. The lake has stocked rainbow and wild cutthroat that can reach 2.5 kg (5 lbs) but are generally small. The fishing is generally slow although can be productive in the early spring (March-May) or later in the fall. It is better to fly fish or spincast the shallow lake. The Art Mann Kinsman Park, at the end of Indian Road, has a picnic area and boat launch.

Quennell Lake (Map 17/D6)

This 121.4 ha lake is one of the most productive lakes on the island due to its slow nutrient run-off. The stocked rainbow and wild cutthroat are known to grow to 2 kg (4-5 lbs) whereas the smallmouth bass reach 3 kg (6-7 lbs). Due to the elevation and shallow depth, fishing is best in the early spring or late fall using light tackle or a fly.

Ranger Lake (Map 3/C4)

Ranger Lake is located southeast of the Bear Creek Reservoir on the TW 40 branch road (4wd access). The last reports indicate that Ranger Lake has good numbers of cutthroat and rainbow, which are generally small (ave. 20-25 cm/8-10 in). The lake is ideal for a float tube and spincasting or fly fishing. There are no developed facilities at the lake.

Reagan Lake (Map 28/E3)

Found off Rossiter Main, Reagan Lake is 20 ha in size and has fair numbers of cutthroat and rainbow averaging 35 cm (14 in). Fishing is best in the spring and fall primarily by fly fishing or spincasting. Rustic camping is available at the lake, which 530 m in elevation.

Rheinhart Lake (Map 8/F1)

Rheinhart Lake is found on the Rheinhart Road off the Copper Canyon Main and is considered a good fly fishing Lake. The lake has small rainbow and cutthroat to 30 cm (12 in) in size caught throughout the spring and fall. The lake tends to warm during the summer given its shallow depths.

Rhododendron Lake (Map 16/B3)

Rhododendron Lake makes up part of the South Englishmann River drainage off Branch 155B (a truck is necessary). The 5.7 ha lake has fair numbers of small cutthroat (stocked), rainbow and steelhead. Fly fishermen and spincasters can do well at the lake during late April-early June and in late September-early October. Cartop boat launching is possible on the southern shores of the lake.

Rosseau Lake (Map 6/C3)

Rosseau Lake is located off the Central South Main (good 2wd access) nearby to Frederick and Pachena Lakes. The lake has good fishing for small rainbow and cutthroat that average 20-25 cm (8-10 in) in size. There are also some small kokanee and smallmouth bass. You can launch a small boat off the northeastern shore of the lake.

Rossiter Lake (Map 28/D5)

Off the Rossiter Mainline, this 4 ha lake requires a short hike on a deteriorating road. Small stocked steelhead are available in good numbers. Try a fly or spinner.

Round Lake (Map 16/E3,22/C7)

Round Lake is located north of the Nanaimo River Valley off Dumont Road or Bonnell Main (a truck is necessary). The lake is at 310 m in elevation and offers an early season fishery for small rainbow and cutthroat. The lake is only 10.0 m (32.8 ft) and is best fished in April to early June and in September to October using light tackle or a fly rod.

Rowbotham Lake (Map 15/E2)

This 13 ha lake has good numbers of small stocked rainbow due to its hike-in access. Try in the spring or fall using a fly or lure.

Sarita Lake (Map 6/E1)

Sarita Lake is located northeast of Bamfield next to the Bamfield Road. The 135 ha lake offers good fishing for small cutthroat, rainbow, bull trout and kokanee from April to October including the summer months. The lake is well suited for trolling and offers a rec site with a boat launch, campground and picnic area.

Shawnigan Lake (Map 3/G1, 9/G7)

Shawnigan Lake is one of the more beautiful recreational lakes found on the East Coast of Vancouver Island. Paved road circles the popular lake providing good access to the many cabins and facilities on the lake. The 537 ha lake has fair numbers of rainbow and cutthroat averaging 40 cm (16 in) in size along with a few small kokanee and smallmouth bass. The lake is stocked annually with up to 30,000 rainbow and cutthroat to maintain the fishery. Trolling during March-June and September-October is most productive for the trout and kokanee.

Shelton (Echo) Lake (Map 16/A4)

Shelton Lake is located in the Nanaimo River Valley off a rough branch road. The 36 ha lake offers good fishing for small stocked rainbow. Fishing is best during the spring (May-June) or fall (September-October) using a lure or fly. There is a rec site at the south end of the lake offering rustic camping as well as a small boat launch.

Sherk Lake (Map 9/C1)

Sherk Lake is accessed via truck on Branch F from the Chemainus River Road. The lake is at 853 m in elevation and is only 6 m (19 ft) deep. It has good numbers of rainbow, which average 20-25 cm (8-10 in) if there is no winterkill. The lake is well suited for a float tube and spincasting or fly fishing. There are no facilities at the lake.

Shields Lake (Map 3/G5)

Shields Lake is found north of the Sooke Mountain Provincial Park on a rough road that requires a high clearance vehicle. The lake is at 393 m in elevation and has descent fishing for small rainbow and cutthroat in May and June and in October. Fly fishing and spincasting are the more popular alternatives.

Silver Lake (Map 9/C2)

Silver Lake is a good fly fishing lake for small cutthroat (to 35 cm/14 in). The lake is 10 ha in size and is found along a 4wd spur road at 860m in elevation. The shallow lake warms in the summer meaning the spring and fall are the best times to fish.

Somenos Lake (Map 9/F4)

Somenos is a popular South Island lake. It is found just east of Duncan on the Drinkwater Road and is easily accessed by car. This 95 ha lake has stocked rainbow and cutthroat (ave. 25-30 cm) as well as some brown trout. The lake is best suited for spincasting or fly fishing in March-early May before the algae bloom begins in May. A good boat launch is on the western shores of the lake.

Spectacle Lake (Map 4/A2)

Surrounded by a nice park, Spectacle Lake is found north of Victoria near the Malahat Summit on the Trans Canada Highway. This 4 ha lake offers the only eastern brook trout fishing on the Island. The fish can grow to 40+ cm (16 in) but most of the fish tend to be small. There are also some cutthroat in the lake. If you plan to launch a boat, it is a 100 m carry from the parking area.

Spider Lake (Map 23/C7)

Spider Lake is a popular fishery accessed by car on either the Lakeview Road to the south or Turnbull Road to the north. The Spider Lake Provincial Park provides a popular picnic area and beach. This 41.4 ha lake has good fishing for stocked rainbow and steelhead as well as some cutthroat. The trout can grow to 1 kg (2 lbs) but are generally small. There is also a very good smallmouth bass fishery throughout the year. No power boats are allowed at the lake.

Sproat Lake (Map 13/G1, 14/A-D1)

Found next to Highway 4, this large 3,800 ha recreational lake has private resorts, several campsites and good boat launching facilities. The lake has fair numbers of rainbow, kokanee and cutthroat to 2 kg (4.5 lbs). Fishing begins in late February and lasts until October. Trolling is your best bet using a gang troll or Kwikfish (with or without worm). A Tomic plug or small Apex also works. Try fishing near the creeks that enter the lake. In March and April, trolling the shallows of Taylor Arm with a minnow imitation can produce some cutthroat in the 4-5 kg (10 lb) category. Watch for fishing restrictions.

St Mary Lake (Map 15/C1)
This 2 ha high elevation (1,070 m) lake offers good fishing for small cutthroat and rainbow. Try a fly or lure from June-September. There is a rustic campsite and cartop boat launch on the lake which is located near the Mt. Arrowsmith Park on a 4wd branch road off Pass Main.

St Mary Lake (Map 10/A2)
On Saltspring Island, St Mary Lake has a good fishery for small cutthroat and steelhead throughout the year but the summer is generally slow. The lake also has perch as well as a very good smallmouth bass fishery with the odd bass reaching 3.5 kg (7 lbs) in size. Trolling, fly fishing and spincasting all work. There are non-motorized boat launching facilities, a resort and camping at this 195 ha lake.

Stocking Lake (Map 9/C1)
Stocking Lake is accessed by truck on Davis Road south of Ladysmith. The 17 ha lake is at 366 m in elevation and has fair numbers of rainbows averaging 20-25 cm (8-10 in) in size. The lake is well suited for trolling in April-June and September-October but no power boats are allowed on the lake.

Stowell Lake (Map 10/C5)
Stowell Lake is found on the paved Beaver Point Road on Saltspring Island. The lake is 6 ha in size and is at 90m in elevation. It has a fair number of cutthroat reaching 1.5 kg (3 lbs). Fly fishing and spincasting in the early spring and fall is your best bet. Electric motors only.

Thetis Lakes (Map 4/C5)
Upper and Lower Thetis Lakes are very popular urban lakes located in the Thetis Lake Park nearby to Victoria. The lakes offer an early season fishery beginning in March and extending to June. The lakes have some inviting bays and islands around which to fly fish or spincast. Anglers will find smallmouth bass, rainbow and cutthroat that can grow to 35 cm (14 in).

Timberland Lake (Map 17/A7)
Timberland is found east of the Nanaimo Airport on a gravel logging road. Despite its good fishing and close proximity to Nanaimo, it does not receive a lot of fishing pressure. The 5.5 ha lake offers stocked cutthroat (to 30 cm) caught by fly fishing or spincasting in the spring (March-June) and fall (September-October). Timberland Lake has a few lakeshore camping sites as well as a cartop boat launch.

Toy Lake (Map 21/E4)
Toy Lake is found within the Strathcona Provincial Park next to the Branch 110 (a truck is recommended). The 10.2 ha lake offers good fly fishing for small cutthroat and rainbow. Given that the lake is only 5 m (16 ft) deep, the lake is best fished during the early spring and late fall using light tackle or a fly rod. The lake is susceptible to winterkill given its shallow depth. However, cutthroat are stocked every second year to maintain the fish stock. There are no developed facilities at the lake.

Trail Pond (Map 22/D7)
Trail Pond is located less than a kilometer from the Turtle Lake Trailhead on Branch 73. The lake has good numbers of small trout. Fly fishing and spincasting are the preferred methods of fishing.

Tuck Lake (Map 7/D1)
Tuck Lake is a remote lake accessed by a long walk (or ATV) along a series of abandoned roads (Z Branch) from the Nitinat River Road. The 44.5 ha lake has good numbers of cutthroat and rainbow to 1 kg (2 lbs). Fly fishing and spincasting in spring or fall is your best bet.

Turnbull Lake (Map 22/A5)
Turnbull Lake is right next to the Ash River Road. The 22.7 ha lake has good numbers of small rainbow and cutthroat plus a few bull trout to 2 kg (4.5 lbs). Fishing is best in the early spring and late fall with spincasting light tackle and fly fishing being the best methods of fishing. A cartop boat launch is at the lake.

Turtle Lake (Map 22/D7)
Turtle Lake is reached by driving past the powerline on Branch 73, parking and then hiking 1.3 km hike to the south end of the lake. The 16.2 lake is best fished in the early spring or late fall using a float tube and light tackle or a fly rod.

View Lake (Map 21/D6)
Accessed by boat on Great Central Lake then a 2.5 km hike along an old road, View Lake has good numbers of small rainbow and cutthroat.

Weeks Lake (Map 3/C1)
Weeks Lake is found on the gated Leech Main west of Sooke Lake. The lake is at 518 m in elevation and is best accessed by a truck. The 23.6 ha lake offers very good fishing lake for stocked rainbow. The fish are usually 20-25cm in size but the odd fish grows to 35 cm. There are also reports of some cutthroat in the lake.

Westwood Lake (Map 16/G4)
Westwood Lake is a popular recreation lake for Nanaimo residents. The shallow lake offers generally slow fishing for stocked rainbow and cutthroat that can reach 1.5 kg (3 lbs) in size but are usually 20-30 cm. Trolling or fly fishing in the early spring or later in the fall is most productive. The Westwood Lake Park is situated on the northern shores of the lake and has a nice picnic site and good boat launch.

Wild Deer Lake (Map 9/D7)
Found north of the Koksilah River on the blocked West Main, Wild Deer Lake offers a rustic campsite, rough boat launch and wharf at the south end of the lake. The 7.6 ha lake has decent fishing for stocked rainbow that can reach 2 kg (4 lbs) but average 30 cm. There are also some cutthroat in the lake. Both fly fishing and spincasting in the spring and fall are productive methods of fishing the lake.

Willemar Lake (Map 21/G3)
Willemar Lake is found to the south of Comox Lake and is part of the Puntledge River drainage. It is a productive lake, which provides good fishing for cutthroat, dollies and kokanee throughout the spring and fall. The fish are generally small but plentiful and are caught by trolling, spincasting or fly fishing. The odd cutthroat is known to grow to 2.5 kg (5 lbs). The deep lake has many deadheads and wind is a problem for light boats. Restrictions include a bait ban and the use of single barbless hooks restriction at the lake.

Wolf Lake (Map 28/G5, 29/A5)
Wolf Lake is found about 16 km northwest of Courtenay on the Duncan Bay Main. The 156 ha lake offers fair fishing for small rainbow and cutthroat (to 35 cm/14 in). The lake is easily trolled with a gang troll and best fished in the spring and fall.

Young Lake (Map 3/D6)
Young Lake is situated on the Young Lake Road northwest of Sooke. The lake is at 80 m in elevation and offers an early season fishery for small trout. The shallow lake is best fished by casting a lure or fly.

North Vancouver Island Lakes

Alice Lake (Map 39/B24)
One of a series of good fishing lakes near the Port Alice Highway, Alice Lake offers some large rainbow, cutthroat and bull trout. Fishing is best left to the spring and fall although the summer can be productive at times. Trolling is your best bet using a minnow imitation. Campsites and boat launches line the 1,200 ha lake, which is 71 m (234 ft) deep. Check the gear and fishing restrictions.

Amor Lake (Map 36/A3)
At 198 m in elevation, this 362 ha lake forms part of the Sayward Canoe Route. The lake offers good fishing for cutthroat and rainbow to 2 kg (4.5 lbs) that average 35 cm (14 in) in the spring and fall. A few bull trout and many small kokanee are also present. The lake is well suited for trolling as it is 49 m (160 ft) deep. There are several recreation site s and a boat launch on the lake.

Antler Lake (Map 26/E3)
Antler Lake is situated 4 km north of Gold River on the E-7 branch road. The 20 ha lake offers descent fishing for small rainbow in early April to June and in late September to October. The lake is at 152 m in elevation and is fairly shallow (10.4 m/34 ft) meaning that the lake is better suited for spincasting or fly fishing. There is a boat launch and picnic site at the west end of the lake. Power boats are prohibited.

Anutz Lake (Map 40/C7)
Anutz Lake is situated to the south of Nimpkish Lake off River Main (a truck is recommended). The lake contains stocked cutthroat as well as rainbow and bull trout. There is a rec site with a boat launches at the 98 ha lake, which is deep enough to troll. Fly fishing and spincasting are also productive, primarily in the spring and fall.

Atluck Lake (Map 32/C2)
Atluck Lake is a pretty 308 ha lake found next to Atluck Road at 137 m in elevation. It contains fair numbers of small, stocked rainbow and dollies caught by trolling, fly fishing or spincasting in the spring (May-June) or fall (September-October). A nice recreation site and a boat launch are found on the 77 m (254 ft) deep lake. As the lake is situated in a narrow valley, it is subject to strong winds.

Beaver Lake (Map 39/D1)
Next to Highway 19 south of Port Hardy, Beaver Lake is a small (7 ha) shallow lake with a lovely picnic site and a cartop boat launch. The lake offers fair numbers of small rainbow and stocked cutthroat as well as a few bull trout and smallmouth bass to 1.5 kg (3 lbs). Found at 99 m in elevation, your best bet is to fly fish or spincast the lake in the spring or fall and avoid the summer.

Beavertail Lake (Map 36/A7)
Elk River Mainline and Beavertail Road provide access to this 103 ha lake at 270 m in elevation. The lake offers fair fishing for small stocked rainbow. Kokanee, cutthroat and bull trout also inhabit the lake. Rustic camping areas and good boat launches skirt the lake. Trolling, spincasting and fly fishing all work in this 28 m (92 ft) deep lake.

Benson Lake (Map 39/E5)
This 72 ha lake has large rainbow, cutthroat and bull trout by Island standards. Trolling during the spring and fall is your best bet as the lake is 55 m (180 ft) deep. A private boat launch gives access to the lake which is found at 76 m in elevation.

Bonanza Lake (Map 40/G6)
On the 2wd Main Road South, this 901 ha lake contains fair numbers of rainbow, bull trout and cutthroat. A rainbow stocking program is in effect. There are two popular recreation sites and boat launches on the lake, which is at 267 m in elevation and 161 m (528 ft) deep.

Boot Lake (Map 36/A5)
Off the Merrill Lake Road, this 86ha lake has fair numbers of stocked rainbow, wild cutthroat and bull trout (dollies). Trolling during the spring or fall is your best bet. A recreation site with a cartop boat launch is at the south end of the 56 m (105 ft) lake.

Brewster Lake (Map 35/G4)
One the larger lakes on the Sayward Canoe Route, this 773 ha lake is easily accessed. The lake, which is 56 m (185 ft) deep, holds good numbers of stocked cutthroat and rainbow trout and the odd bull trout. Since the lake is at 213 m in elevation, the lake warms in the summer; reducing fishing success. There are two recreation sites on the lake with cartop boat launching available for trollers.

Cedar Lake (Map 36/A2)
On the gated Mud Lake Road, this 33 ha low elevation (230 m) lake has good fishing for small cutthroat to 35 cm (14 in). A recreation site and a cartop boat launch is situated at the 21 m (68 ft) deep lake.

Claude Elliot Lake (Map 41/D7)
Set below Mt. Ashwood, this remote lake requires bushwhacking to reach it. The lake is an artificial fly only lake that holds both rainbow and cutthroat. It receives little fishing pressure so the fishing is good although the fish are quite small (to 25 cm/10 in).

Cross Lake (Map 31/G1)
This remote, mountain lake is best accessed from the south. The artificial fly only lake has a one fish limit. Subsequently, the 7 ha lake offers good fishing for small stocked rainbow.

Darkis Lake (Map 27/F3)
Starting from the Buttle Narrows Campground, this 11 ha lake is accessed by a short walk 300 m along the Partius Lake Trail. The lake has many small cutthroat and stocked rainbow (to 30 cm/12 in). Try fly fishing or spincasting with a float tube or small boat as the lake is shallow and lined with log jams.

Diane Lake (Map 32/D1)
A small 21 ha lake with small rainbow and cutthroat. The lake is found on a spur road off the Atluck Relocation Road and is best fished in the spring or fall with a lure, bait or fly.

Echo Lake (Map 36/C7)

On Highway 28, this 24.4 ha lake has fair numbers of stocked rainbow and cutthroat as well as wild bull trout. A good boat launch for non-motorized boats is available. The lake is best fished in the spring or fall by trolling, fly fishing or spincasting.

Farewell Lakes (Map 35/G2)

Off the overgrown Blackwater Lake Road, Farewell Lake offers good fishing for small cutthroat and rainbow. The artificial fly only lake offers a small cartop boat launch and a few rustic campsites. Try fly fishing the weedy shoals in the spring or fall.

Georgie Lake (Map 46/E5)

West of Port Hardy this is an acidic nutrient poor lake with good numbers of slow growing small cutthroat, rainbow and bull trout. The lake receives sporadic fishing pressure and 1.5 kg (3 lb) cutthroat is not uncommon. A recreation site and cartop boat launch are found at the east end of the 42 m (139 ft) deep lake. Fishing is good in the spring through fall (except August) by trolling.

Gosling Lake (Map 36/B5)

On the Sayward Canoe Route and accessed off Gosling Lake Road, this 65 ha Lake is found at 225 m in elevation. The lake has fair fishing for stocked cutthroat, wild rainbow and the odd bull trout in the spring and fall. There is a recreation site and cartop boat launch at the south end of the lake.

Grace Lake (Map 35/G3)

Located on the 146 Main, this lake has good numbers of cutthroat and rainbow trout. Spring (April-June) and fall (September-October) are the best time to fish this 20 ha lake which is at 335 m in elevation. Thre is a small cartop boat launch at the lake.

Hoomak Lake (Map 33/D2)

10 km east of Woss along Highway 19, this 94 ha lake offers good fishing for small cutthroat and bull trout throughout the spring (May-June) and fall (Sept-Oct). Fly fishing and spincasting from a float tube are the best methods of fishing this 37 m (121 ft) deep lake. A rest area with a cartop boat launch and forestry trail are found next to the lake.

Hustan Lake (Map 32/C1)

This small 186 ha lake has fair numbers of small cutthroat and rainbow. Fishing is best in the spring and fall as the elevation of the lake is only 76 m. The lake is found on a spur road off Atluck Road south of Nimpkish Lake.

Kains Lake (Map 46/D6)

On the Holberg Road 14 km west of Port Hardy, this 218 ha lake holds good numbers of slow growing small cutthroat. It receives little fishing pressure and has a cartop boat launch. It does not have a developed campground. Best fishing is in the spring (April-June)and fall (September-October) with bait or a lure. The lake is 23.5 m (77 ft) deep.

Kathleen Lake (Map 39/D5)

Kathleen Lake has fair numbers of small cutthroat and rainbow (to 35 cm/14 in) with a few bull trout (to 1.5 kg/3 lbs). Fishing is best during the spring (April-June) or fall (Sept-Oct) by spincasting or fly fishing. There is a recreation site and cartop boat launch on the lake.

Keogh Lake (Map 39/G3)

On the Keogh Main, this 80 ha lake offers good fishing for small cutthroat and rainbow to 40 cm (16 in). Fly fishing and spincasting in the spring (May-June) and fall (September-October) are your best bet. There is a cartop boat launch at the 43 m (142 ft) deep lake, which is at 245 m in elevation and can be accessed by a car.

Klaklakama Lakes (Map 33/E3)

Some call these shimmering lakes the highlight of the Nimpkish Valley. They are a combined 352ha in size and located at 295 m in elevation. A car can be used to access the lakes where two recreation sites and good boat launches are found. Fair fishing for small cutthroat (to 30 cm/12 in) and bull trout (to 2 kg/4.5 lbs) is available. Trolling, spincasting or fly fishing in the spring or fall are the most effective methods of fishing lakes.

Lower Campbell Lake (Map 36/B6)

This large man-made waterbody (2,250 ha) has several different access points and camping areas. The lake contains fair numbers of rainbow, cutthroat and bull trout reaching 2 kg (4.5 lbs). Steelhead trout were recently stocked. Despite the elevation, fishing remains consistent throughout the year for patient trollers. Fish production is fair due to water fluctuation hampering insect and plant growth.

Martha Lake (Map 35/G6)

Found on a deactivated 4wd, this 10ha lake offers good fishing for small stocked rainbow (to 30 cm/12 in) in April-June and again in September-October. The lake is at 274 m in elevation and is best suited for fly fishing and spincasting.

Mary Lake (Map 36/C4)

On the rough Mary Lake Road, this 10 ha lake has small stocked cutthroat. The lake is at 275 m in elevation and is best fished by fly fishing or spincasting.

Maynard Lake (Map 39/F5)

This 85ha lake has good numbers of small cutthroat (+30 cm) and is 38 m (125 ft) deep. Trolling, fly fishing or spin casting all work, particularly in the spring (April-June) and fall (September-October). Access is by way of the Keogh Main (a car is adequate). The lake has a cartop boat launch and recreation site.

McCreight Lake (Map 43/G7)

On the well travelled Rock Bay FSR, this 272 ha lake has fair fishing for stocked cutthroat and wild rainbow and bull trout to 1 kg (2 lbs). The best fishing is by trolling in the spring (April-June) and fall (September-October). Three recreation sites are found on the lake along with several cartop boat launches.

McIvor Lake (Map 36/D7)

On Highway 28, this 123 ha lake offers fair trolling for small stocked steelhead. The lake, which is at 133 m in elevation, is best fished in the spring and fall and has a campsite and picnic site.

Mirror Lake (Map 36/D7)

On the Elk River Main (a car is adequate), Mirror Lake has small stocked cutthroat. The lake is 6 ha in size and is best fished in the spring or fall by spincasting or fly fishing.

Mohun Lake (Map 36/B4)

This 620 ha lake is part of the Sayward Canoe Route and is accessed by good logging roads on both sides of the lake. Expect some fair fishing for rainbow, cutthroat and bull trout (to 45 cm/18 in). Fishing is best in the spring (April-June) or fall (September-October) by trolling or spincasting. There is a recreation site with a good boat launch at the south end of the lake and the northern campsite is located in Morton Lake Provincial Park. The lake is at 190 m in elevation.

Morton Lake (Map 36/B4)

A small (22.6 ha) lake with a recreation site and cartop boat launch. The 15 m (49 ft) deep lake contains fair numbers of stocked cutthroat best caught in the spring or fall on a fly or with a lure.

Muchalat Lake (Map 26/B2)
This 650 ha lake at 210 m in elevation has an abundance of small rainbow and cutthroat but some of these trout can reach 1.5 kg (3 lbs). The lake also has a few kokanee and bull trout. Trolling or spincasting seem to work better than fly fishing. A car or RV can easily access the large recreation site and cartop boat launch next to the lake.

Mud Lake (Map 36/A2)
This 18 ha lake is found off Highway 19 via the Lakeview Correctional Camp Road. It has small stocked cutthroat.

Mukwilla Lake (Map 32/E2)
Off Atluck Road (a car is adequate), this 42 ha lake has many small wild rainbow and stocked cutthroat (ave. 25 cm/10 in) as well as a few kokanee. Fly fishing, spincasting or trolling during the spring or fall is your best bet. The lake offers a cartop boat launch.

Nahwitti Lake (Map 46/A6)
On the paved road to Holberg, this lake, which is located at 221 m in elevation, offers excellent fishing for slow growing small cutthroat, dollies and kokanee. The 262 ha lake does not receive a lot of fishing pressure and is very good from June to October (except August). It has a recreation site and cartop boat launch.

Nimpkish Lake (Map 40/C7)
Located along the Island Highway, the long, narrow lake has some large rainbow and cutthroat. As long as the windy is not too strong, trolling is the best method from the spring to fall. There are recreation sites and boat launches on the lake.

Nita Lake (Map 42/E7)
On the rough UA 103 branch road, this small 3 ha lake offers some fairly good fly fishing and spincasting for small stocked rainbow.

O'Connor Lake (Map 39/E2)
Off West Main, this 40 ha lake has good fishing for cutthroat and rainbow to 40 cm (16 in) the average 25 cm. The lake is at 180 m in elevation and is best fished with a fly or by spincasting in the spring or fall. The lake is popular for water sports in the summer and offers a recreation site and cartop boat launch at the lake.

Perry (Malaspina) Lake (Map 25/C2)
This 13 ha lake offers good fishing for small stocked rainbow (25-30 cm). Fishing is best in the spring and fall using an artificial fly only. There are no facilities at the lake, which is at 235 m in elevation.

Pye Lake (Map 35/G1, 43/G7, 44/A7)
This 370 ha lake is accessed off the Pye East and West FSRs. The lake is at 150 m in elevation and offers fair fishing for small cutthroat, rainbow and bull trout (to 45 cm/18 in). Three recreation sites with boat launches line the deep lake, which is best trolled in the spring or fall.

Quatse Lake (Map 38/G1, 46/G7)
Near Coal Harbour, this 16 ha lake has fair numbers of small cutthroat, rainbow and kokanee. Try trolling, spincasting or fly fishing in the spring or fall.

Quinsam Lakes (Map 27/G2, 28/A-D1)
These three lakes are found on the Quinsam River southwest of Campbell River. All three lakes have fair numbers of larger rainbow, cutthroat and a few smaller bull trout throughout the spring and fall by trolling, fly fishing or spincasting. The lakes were recently stocked with steelhead trout. **Quinsam Lake** is the best for summer fishing. It is accessed off the Gilson Main and has a cartop boat launch. **Middle Quinsam Lake** is reached by truck off Argonaut Main and offers good fly fishing using nymph patterns near the weed beds. It has two recreation sites and a cartop boat launch. **Upper Quinsam Lake** is found along Argonaut Main (truck only) and has two recreation sites plus a good boat ramp.

Reginald Lake (Map 36/A7)
Off the rough Beavertail Road, Reginald Lake is 18 ha in size and is stocked with small steelhead. Try trolling in the spring or fall.

Roberts Lake (Map 36/A1)
Beside the North Island Highway (Hwy 19), this 161 ha lake has stocked rainbow and cutthroat trout and some bull trout (dollies). The fish are generally small but can reach 35 cm (14 in) in length. They are taken by trolling primarily in the spring and fall. The deep lake does offer fishing through the summer despite being only 167 m in elevation. There are cabins, camping facilities and good boat launches on the lake. Watch for fishing restrictions.

Rooney Lake (Map 42/C6)
On Highway #19, this 15 ha lake has fair numbers of small cutthroat taken on a fly or by spincasting in the spring and fall. There are also a few bull trout to 1.5 kg (3 lbs) in the lake, which is at 230 m in elevation. A campsite and boat launch is located on the north side of the 21 m (69) deep lake.

Roselle Lake (Map 40/B3)
This 16 ha lake has excellent fishing for small cutthroat and rainbow by fly fishing in the spring or fall. The cutthroat have been stocked in recent years to ensure that the population remains steady. A cartop boat launch is found on the shallow, low elevation lake.

Santa Maria Lake (Map 43/A7)
On the A20 branch road, this 6 ha lake has fair numbers of small stocked cutthroat. Try fly fishing or spincasting in the spring or fall.

Schoen Lake (Map 34/A3)
This lake, at 440 m in elevation, has a mixed population of cutthroat and rainbow and offers good fishing even in the summer. The pretty lake is best fished by fly at the mouth of the creeks entering the lake or by trolling. Camping and boat launching facilities are provided.

Second Lake (Map 35/D5)
On the Memekey Salmon Hookup (Branch SR5), Second Lake is a 6.5 ha lake with small stocked cutthroat. Try a fly or lure in the spring or fall. At 152 m in elevation, the shallow lake warms in the summer.

Snakehead Lake (Map 36/A7)
Located at the picnic area on Highway 28, this 20 ha, weedy lake holds many small stocked cutthroat and rainbow (to 35 cm/14 in). Fly fishing (try a March Brown or wooly worm fly) or spincasting during the spring (March-June) or fall (September-October) are your best bets on this shallow lake. It is possible to launch a small boat.

Spirit Lake (Map 35/F2)
A truck is needed to access this 31 ha lake with good numbers of rainbow and cutthroat. Fishing is best left to the spring or fall as the lake is at 270 m in elevation. A small cartop boat launch is available at the 21 m (69 ft) deep lake.

Stella Lakes (Map 36/A1, 44/A7)
Off the Rock Bay FSR, these two lakes have fair numbers of rainbow, stocked cutthroat and bull trout to 40 cm (16 in). The larger Stella Lake is 423 ha in size and is at 150 m in elevation. It has a recreation site and a cartop boat launch. Fishing at both lakes is best in the spring and fall. Trolling, fly fishing and spincasting all work.

Stewart Lake (Map 34/F5)
At 465 m in elevation, this 46 ha lake provides a good fishery for small stocked cutthroat as well as kokanee and bull trout. The 27 m (89 ft) lake is best accessed by truck and offers a rustic camping area and boat launch. Watch for fishing restrictions such as electric motors.

Tahsis Lake (Map 33/C7)
Rumour has it that this mountain lake is now accessible by road. There are good numbers of small trout best caught in the summer.

Three Isle Lake (Map 39/F4)
This scenic lake can be accessed by car and offers a rec site and cartop boat launch. The 38 ha, 11 m (36 ft) lake has small cutthroat best caught using a fly or by spincasting during the spring or fall.

Tlowils Lake (Map 34/F1)
On the Tlowils Lake Branch (truck only), this 26 ha lake has many small rainbow and cutthroat. Fly fishing and spincasting are productive primarily in the spring and fall. There is a rustic campsite and a (non-motorized) boat launch at the lake.

Tsiko (Loon) Lake (Map 32/E1)
Tsiko Lake is a 32 ha lake at 200 m in elevation. A truck is needed to reach the lake which has no developed campground but does have a cartop boat launch. The lake has good numbers of stocked cutthroat to 40 cm (16 in) that are caught primarily in the spring or fall.

Twin Lake (Map 36/A2)
Forming part of the Sayward Canoe Route, this lake is accessible by a 2wd road from the North Island Highway. Cutthroat and rainbow (up to 1 kg/2 lbs) inhabit the 15 m (49 ft) deep lake.

Upana Lakes (Map 26/B3)
Off the Head Bay FSR, this 45 ha lake has small rainbow trout (to 30 cm/12 in) easily taken on a fly or by spincasting. The lake is at 520 m in elevation and is near the popular Upana Caves.

Upper Campbell Lake (Maps 27/F1, 35/G7)
This large man-made lake skirts Highway 28 on the way to Gold River. Fishing is fairly good for small cutthroat, rainbows and bull trout (dollies) from spring to fall primarily by trolling. There are many campsites and boat launches as well as accommodations along the lake. Up to 40 m (130 ft) deep, the lake can be quite windy.

Vernon Lake (Map 33/F6)
Anglers can expect fairly good fishing for small rainbow and cutthroat by trolling during the spring and fall. The lake is 780 ha in size and quite deep. A large recreation site with beach and a cartop boat launch are found at the north end of the lake.

Victoria Lake (Map 39/B6)
5 km east of Port Alice, this large 1,576 ha lake is productive by Island standards. It holds some good size rainbow, bull trout and cutthroat. Trolling is the preferred method of fishing using a plug such as a Tomic Plug or Rapalas. There are two recreation sites and boat launches on the 110 m (360 ft) deep lake.

Wolfe Lake (Map 32/E2)
Off Pinder Main, Wolfe Lake has good numbers of larger cutthroat, rainbows and bull trout particularly in the spring (May-June) and fall (September-October). The good option on the 20 ha lake is to fly fish the outflow creek. The lake is at 240 m in elevation and 14 m deep.

Woss Lake (Map 33/B3)
Woss Lake is a large 1,395 ha lake easily accessed by car. Trolling produces fair numbers of small (stocked) cutthroat, rainbow and bull trout (ave. 45 cm/18 in) from spring (April-June) through the fall (September-October). Watch for strong winds on this deep lake. A large recreation site and boat launch are found at the north end.

Stu Grundison & Wesley Mussio at Kyuquot

www.backroadmapbooks.com

Stream Fishing

An impressive number of salmon and steelhead bearing rivers attract thousands of anglers annually. Outside of the south and east coast rivers, many of the Island streams do not get heavy fishing pressure. Combine the remote fishing with steelhead, salmon and resident trout and you see why Island rivers make such an excellent year-round fishery.

Unfortunately, over the last decade, the pressure on Vancouver Island rivers has skyrocketed. A combination of natural factors and over-fishing has lead to the closure of almost all the rivers that drain the east coast of Vancouver Island during winter steelhead season for the last three seasons (1997–2000). Sources at the BC Fish and Wildlife office say that it will probably be a few more years yet until these rivers are open again.

The situation is similar for east coast coho. Fortunately, most of the west coast rivers remain open to winter steelhead and coho, but before you set out for any of these rivers, check for closures and for gear and other restrictions put in place.

Wild steelhead are catch and release only! There is some catch and keep hatchery fish (look for the adipose clip) but, as always, check current restrictions before you set out. For information, contact the BC Fish and Wildlife Regional Office, 2080A Labieux Road, Nanaimo, (250) 751-3100. Current quotas on hatchery steelhead are two per day and ten per year. Steelhead anglers must purchase a steelhead conservation stamp to attach to their license, even if fishing catch and release.

Steelhead remains the fish of choice for Vancouver Island river anglers, but most rivers also support a resident population of trout, be it cutthroat, rainbow, bull or, less often, brown. The other species of fish you'll encounter here is salmon, primarily coho and chinook.

Below we have grouped the larger streams into two sections, the more remote North Island and the more popular South Island. A short blurb will help you estimate when the fish are running. We did not mention a lot of smaller streams due to space constraints. As a general rule of thumb, most smaller streams hold resident trout. Be sure to visit the local retailer to ask for the latest information and to ensure you have the latest gear. Please ensure you check current restrictions before you set out.

South Island

Ash River (Map 21/C3, 22/B6)
Originating in Strathcona Park and flowing all the way to the Stamp River, north of Port Alberni, the Ash is a good summer steelhead river from July to September. From February to March is the smaller winter steelhead run. You will also find good runs of chinook in September and October, and coho in October. Parts of the river are closed to fishing.

Bedwell River (Map 20/E4)
A remote, boat access only river, the Bedwell is rarely fished. There is a good natural run of winter steelhead in February and March, while bull and sea-run cutthroat inhabit the estuary as well.

Big Qualicum River (Map 22/G6, 23/B7)
When the Big Q opens, there's always a crowd. Unfortunately, it will not be open to winter steelhead for a few more years. Returns have been terrible despite a steelhead hatchery and habitat enhancement. Year round cutthroat (best in the fall), and fall runs of chinook and coho should keep Qualicum Beach residents happy. Please note, fishing at the mouth is trespassing and closed to non-native anglers.

Campbell River (Map 36/E6)
At a mere 5 km, the Campbell does not rank up there among the longest rivers on the island. However, along its short banks, you'll find some great fishing spots, though you'll probably have to contend with dozens, even hundreds of other anglers fighting for the best location during the August-September chinook run and the September-November coho runs. There are also summer (June-October) and winter (mid-November to mid-April) runs of Steelhead. The nearby steelhead hatchery on the adjoining Quinsam River helps maintain the numbers. Note: this river has been closed during steelhead and coho runs the past few years.

Caycuse River (Map 7/D4)
The Caycuse flows into the tidal Nitinat Lake and offers small summer (June) and winter (February-March) steelhead runs.

Chemainus River (Map 9/D3)
Draining the restricted Nanaimo Watershed, this river is known to offer a small spring (April–June) steelhead run and a tiny summer run. Resident trout are also available.

Cous Creek (Map 14/E3)
This creek is worth noting because of its summer and winter steelhead runs. As with most streams, resident cutthroat and rainbow are also present.

Cowichan River (Map 8/G4, 9/A5)
The famous Cowichan is one of those rivers which fishing magazines love to highlight. The fabulous scenery, and excellent fishing bring anglers from around the world. For trout enthusiasts, there is excellent rainbow trout and even brown trout fishing all year. The runs include a winter run of steelhead (December–April), coho (October–November) and chinook (September–November). There is a steelhead hatchery on the Cowichan, though production has been cut back in the past few years due to a low brood stock. This is a highly regulated river. It is also one of a very few rivers (as of this writing) where hatchery steelhead are catch and keep.

Cypre River (Map 20/A7)
A remote, west coast river with good winter and summer steelhead runs, a coho run in the fall and resident rainbow throughout the year.

Englishman River (Map 15/F2, 16/A1)
This pretty stream receives more than its share of anglers and is now facing closures. Winter steelhead (February to April), fall coho and chinook (September–December) and some sea-run cutthroat, especially in the estuary, make this a dynamic river. Note: this river has been closed during steelhead and coho runs the past few years.

Franklin River (Map 14/G5, 15/A5)
Found west of Alberni Inlet, this river has a good resident population of cutthroat, as well as a winter steelhead and fall coho run.

Gordon River (Map 1/F1, 7/G7, 8/A4)
The Gordon has a small winter steelhead run, and fall runs of coho and chinook. The Gordon Main provides good access most of the stretch from Gordon River Camp to Port Renfrew. Note: this river has been closed during coho and chinook runs the past few years.

Harris Creek (Map 2/C1, 8/C7)
This small scenic yet fast flowing creek is known for its many canyons, waterfalls and pools. A small summer steelhead run in July, and slightly larger winter run in February and March add to the resident trout fishing opportunities. Fishing is closed upstream from Hemmington Creek.

Jordan River (Map 2/G5, 3/B2)
The mouth of the Jordan is now a popular surfing location. For anglers, a winter steelhead run enhances the year round resident cutthroat fishery.

Klanawa River (Map 6/F4)
The remote Klanawa, which flows through Pacific Rim National Park, supports winter and summer steelhead runs and resident cutthroat.

Little Qualicum River (Map 15/D1, 23/E7)
There are a ton of restrictions, regulations and closures on this extremely popular yet beautiful river. Chinooks return in August, as do sea-run cutthroat. Hatchery enhanced winter steelhead run is February to April, but they have been closed the past few years. Check with BC Fish and Wildlife for up-to-date information.

Megin River (Map 19/F3)
A secluded river in Strathcona Park, the Megin is foot or air access only, with most anglers opting for the latter. There is a small winter steelhead run in March and April. To help flyfishing enthusiasts, there is a bait ban and single barbless hook restrictions.

Millstone River (Map 16/G2, 17/A3)

The Millstone is a short river that flows from Brannen Lake, through downtown Nanaimo and into the sea. Closed to anyone between the ages of 16 and 65, the Millstone is home of an ambitious enhancement program called Salmon in the City. Coho, chum, steelhead and cutthroat are the prime catches in the Millstone.

Moyeha River (Map 20/C3)

A remote, boat access only Strathcona Park river, the lower Moyeha is slow moving, and it is possible to canoe upstream for a distance. There is a small summer steelhead run in June and a winter run in March and April. Coho also run in the fall.

Nahmint River (Map 13/F2, 14/A2)

This short, fast flowing river flows out of Nahmint Lake, through a series of drops and pools and into Alberni Inlet. Its once-famous steelhead run has been almost decimated, and the river is closed in the winter. There is still good coho fishing in October.

Nanaimo River (Map 16/F6, 17/B6)

This popular fishery is currently closed during the winter steelhead run and the fall coho run. Chinook and catch and release sea-run or resident cutthroat provide action during the remaining months, though it is best to check for current closure information.

Nitinat River (Map 7/D2)

A small summer (June–July) and slightly larger winter (February–March) steelhead run draw anglers to the Nitinat, but the real catch here is cutthroat. There is a chinook hatchery on the lower Nitinat, and this is one of the few rivers where it is possible to retain chinook. The Nitinat is currently closed above Parker Creek. Check with BC Fish and Wildlife for current information.

Pachena River (Map 6/B4)

Found east of Bamfield on the west coast, the Pachena has a few winter steelhead. There is also fair cutthroat fishing in the spring and fall.

Puntledge River (Map 29/B7)

Another great steelhead river, another decimated stock, another seemingly permanent closure even with hatchery enhanced stock. Now, your best bet for this rural river is coho and chinook in the fall, and cutthroat and rainbow trout year round.

San Juan River (Map 1-3/A1, 9/G7)

Flowing into Port Renfrew, this South Island stream offers a larger river angling experience. The runs include a summer steelhead run in late May to early July, and winter returns from January through to April. There is also a fair chinook run in September and a good coho run in November.

Somass River System (Map 14/F1, 22/E7)

The Sproat and the Stamp join forces to create the Somass, which flows into the Alberni Inlet. They all have coinciding salmon and steelhead runs. The chinook run is late August, early September, the coho run is September to October, while the hatchery enhanced winter steelhead run on the Stamp begins in mid-December. This is a highly regulated river system but you might be able to keep some of the hatchery steelhead. Check for closures and current restrictions.

Sooke River (Map 3/F5)

A popular steelhead fishery when it opens, which isn't often. The Sooke is currently closed during the winter steelhead run and the fall salmon runs. There are resident rainbow trout. Check current closures before you go.

Taylor River (Map 13/F1, 21/C7)

A medium-size river with a very short, catch and release fly fishing only season for the large cutthroat that spawn in spring. Rainbow trout are also available.

Toquart River (Map 13/C5)

Found to the east of Long Beach, this small river can be quite secluded. A small summer steelhead run in June and July and a larger wither run in February and March attract anglers. There is also a good coho run in October, as well as resident cutthroat throughout the year.

Trent River (Map 22/C1, 29/E7)

This small river with a small winter steelhead run, is located south of Courtenay.

Tsable River (Map 22/D3)

Found further to the south than the Trent, the Tsable is another small river with a small winter steelhead run. Resident rainbow are also found in the lower reaches of the river.

Walbran Creek (Map 1/B1, 7/D7)

A small, fast flowing creek that cuts through virgin Sitka spruce (at least in the lower regions; the upper Walbran has been logged). Access to the Walbran is limited, in the upper regions due to active logging, and in the lower regions because there is no road and a very sketchy trail. There is a good-sized summer steelhead run in July and August, while the West Walbran has catch and release trout, char and even konanee.

North Island

Adam River (Map 42/C6)

Don't confuse this with the famous Adams River, located in the interior of BC. Here, you will find steelhead, salmon, resident trout and rainbow trout below the falls, while above the falls you'll find rainbow, brown and cutthroat trout. The river is currently closed to fishing. Check with BC Fish and Wildlife for future openings.

Artlish River (Map 32/B4)

The Artlish has good steelhead fishing March to April, while in the fall sea-run cutthroat and coho are the catch of the season. This is a remote river that is accessible at points by the Artlish Road.

Benson River (Map 39/F6)

This small river leads into Benson Lake. The river boasts a fair rainbow trout population.

Burman River (Map 19/G1, 20)

A remote, boat access only river, the Burman sees good runs of summer steelhead (June-July), winter steelhead (February-March), coho (October) and chinook (September-October).

Cluxewe River (Map 39/G1)

Found west of Port McNeill, this river offers a good year round fishery. Every second year (even numbered), the mouth of this river has a good fishery for pinks in mid-August. It also has a winter steelhead run (February–April), sea-run cutthroat (fall), bull trout (spring) and coho (fall). This is one of the few rivers (currently) with an allowable catch of hatchery steelhead.

Davie River (Map 33/D2, 34/A3)

The Davie River links Schoen Lake with the larger Nimpkish River. The Davie offers winter and summer steelhead runs (February to March and June to July respectively), as well as rainbow trout in summer.

Elk River (Map 27/C2)

A good catch and release river for rainbow trout. Currently fly fishing only, the Elk River is located in Strathcona Provincial Park and can be accessed by highway or trail.

Eve River (Map 33/G1, 42/B6)

A major tributary of the Adam River, you'll find steelhead in the winter, coho in the fall and cutthroat all year round. Most of the river has good road access.

Fisherman River (Map 37 Inset, 45/A5)

A hike-in access only river in Cape Scott Park, this remote river has winter steelhead, fall coho and resident cutthroat.

Gold River (Map 26/E2)

Considered one of the ten best steelhead rivers in Canada, Gold River has one of the largest winter steelhead runs in BC from January to March. There is a smaller summer steelhead run in June and July. Chinook and coho also run in August and September respectively. Currently, fishing is closed above the Machalat confluence.

Heber River (Map 26/F3, 27/A1)

The Heber flows into the Gold River at the small town of Gold River. This smaller river has remote sections and offers a small summer (June–July) steelhead run. There is a year round bait ban and the river is closed below the top of the lower canyon.

Jacklah River (Map 19/D1, 26/D7)

They do not get much more remote than this. This small river flows into Muchalat Inlet south of Gold River and requires a boat to access. Expect a small summer steelhead run (June–July).

Keogh River (Map 39/F2, 47/D7)

There is a pink fishery every even-numbered August on the Keogh. The Keogh also supports spring and fall sea-run bull trout, fall coho and sea-run cutthroat, and a hatchery-enhanced winter run of steelhead.

Kokish River (Map 40/F4, 41/A5)

Summer (June–July) and winter (February–March) steelhead are the big draws to this North Island river, which is found south of Beaver Cove. There are also resident cutthroat.

Leiner River (Map 25/C1)

Small summer runs (June–July) and winter runs (February–March) of steelhead, and a good fall coho run if the river is running high. Getting to the Leiner requires a bit of a bushwhack off the Head Bay FSR.

Mahatta River (Map 38/B5)

A small but productive river for summer steelhead in June and July. The fish tend to congregate in a few larger pools because the river is low in summer. Fishing is currently closed from November 1 to April 30.

Marble River (Map 39/A2)

A beautiful little river with a nice fisherman's trail providing access. The roaring Marble River is one of the Islands better steelhead rivers, with a good summer run in July, and a small winter run in February and March.

Nahwitti River (Map 45/G4)

There are a few resident cutthroat, an excellent sea-run bull trout fishery near the mouth and also a winter steelhead run from February to April. The lower reaches of this small northern river are accessible by boat or a long, tough bushwhack.

Nimpkish River (Map 32-34, 40)

The largest river system on Vancouver island, the Nimpkish boasts summer steelhead from June to September, winter steelhead from January to April, sea-run bull trout in the spring, and resident cutthroat all year round.

Oyster River (Map 28, 29/A2)

Once home to one of the best winter steelhead runs on Vancouver Island, this river, like so many before it, has been nearly decimated. Now the Oyster's best run is pinks during August on even-numbered years. There's also cutthroat trout, both wild and hatchery-enhanced, with your best chance of finding them is in the estuary. The open banks make this a fine flyfishing river.

Perry River (Map 25/C2)

This small river is found at the head of Tahsis Inlet and has relatively good road access. There is a small summer run (June–July) and winter run (February–March) of steelhead, and good fall coho if the river is running high.

Quatsie River (Map 46/G7, 47/A7)

A fair winter steelhead run from February to April and fair sea-run cutthroat and resident bull trout. Found south of Port Hardy, this is one of the few rivers with an allowable catch of hatchery steelhead.

Quinsam River (Map 28/D1, 36/E7)

This small, fertile river can be quite busy since it flows into Campbell River, near the city. There are hatchery enhanced runs of steelhead, coho and chinook, as well as cutthroat, though returns have been terrible in recent years. As of this publication, there is a winter steelhead closure in effect, but you can check the current status of returns by calling BC Fish and Wildlife.

Salmon River (Map 27/A1, 35, 43/B7)

This big river produces the biggest steelhead (up to 11.5kg/25 lbs) on the island, but the winter steelhead run is now partially closed due to over-harvesting, clearcut logging around the river's headwater and poor returns over the last few years. Check the current status of closures and restrictions by calling BC Fish and Wildlife. Resident and sea-run cutthroat (in May to October) and bull trout offer good fly angling, especially in the lower reaches of the river.

Stranby River (Map 45/C5)

There are a few resident cutthroat and excellent sea-run bull trout fishing near the mouth of the river and also a winter steelhead run from February to April. This small, remote northern river, is accessible by boat or a long, tough bushwhack.

Tahsis River (Map 25/B1, 33/B7)

Forming the headwaters of the long, narrow Tahsis Inlet, expect small summer runs (June–July) and winter runs (February–March) of steelhead. If the river is running high, fall coho numbers can be good.

Tahsish River (Map 31/G3, 32/A1, 40/A7)

Running through old growth Sitka spruce, this is a gorgeous river to lay down a line. The lower reaches are water-access only, preferably by canoe. The summer steelhead run is between June and July, while the winter run is between March and April. Cutthroat trout are found throughout the river at all times of the year but beware of the year round bait ban.

White River (Map 34, 35/A1, 43/A7)

A narrow, deep river with many pools, the White has a fair run of summer steelhead in June and July and a smaller winter run in February and March. There are bull trout throughout the year, cutthroat in spring and fall and a coho run in October. Watch for the year round bait ban and other restrictions.

Zeballos River (Map 32/F6)

This beautiful north island river is known for its clear, swift running water. Expect a small steelhead run in June and July, a winter run in February through April, chinook in September, and coho in October and November. There are also resident cutthroat. Watch for the year round bait ban and other restrictions.

An Island Fly Fisherman

Paddling Routes

(Canoe Routes, Whitewater & Ocean Paddling)

Canoe Routes

Although whitewater and ocean kayaking take the lion's share of the attention given to Vancouver Island paddling, there are three noteworthy canoe routes on the island, as well as many lakes for the avid canoeist to explore. If you are interested in exploring one of the seemingly endless lakes, you can simply look for any number of lakes on the maps. Our freshwater fishing and wilderness camping sections also provides more insight into the lakes.

Main Lake Chain (Map 36/G2)
On the north end of Quadra Island, the route includes Village Bay, Main and Little Main Lakes. Only about 12 km from Village Bay Lake to the end of Little Main Lake, this route is neither difficult nor extensive. It is, however, just remote enough for a peaceful, lazy paddle and wilderness camping on beaches or islands. The passage between Village Bay and Main Lakes is shallow, choked with reeds, and hard to navigate.

Nitinat Triangle (Map 6/F6, 7)
A difficult, remote paddle through the Pacific Rim National Park Reserve best accessed from Knob Point Rec Site. It is the portages that define this 3-4 day trek: rough, muddy, rooty, and difficult enough to hike, let along carry a canoe along. For your effort, you'll visit an area few others have the courage to travel, along unspoiled lakes and through virgin coastal rainforest. Hobiton and Tsusiat Lakes and Tsusiat River make up one side of this triangle of Nitinat Lake, the second. The third side is either a risky open ocean paddle off the headlands of Vancouver Island's wild west coast, or a 7 km carry from Tsusiat Falls to the Nitinat Narrows along the West Coast Trail. Do not attempt to canoe through the Narrows. Also be prepared for tides and wind on the larger Nitinat Lake.

Sayward Canoe Route (Map 35/G5, 36/A5)
The most popular canoe route on the islands, the 47 km long trek is best traveled in a counterclockwise direction from Gosling Bay on Campbell Lake, although there are many other starting points. There are 7.5 km of portages, and many Forest Service campsites along the route, which covers 14 different lakes. Because most of these sites are road-accessible, this route is not as remote as the Nitinat Triangle is, nor is the scenery quite so pristine. Still, this is an enjoyable, popular 3–4 day route, and a good introduction to canoe touring.

Whitewater Paddling

Vancouver Island rivers offer a bit of everything for river enthusiasts. From easy floats to hair-raising descents, the variety is fantastic. If you are a serious whitewater paddler, the Island rivers are at their best in the winter. The high rainfall and mountain snowmelt combine to swell the rivers. The summer sees lower water levels and is a good time to fine-tune those skills. For a completely different twist, surfing is a popular alternative at such locations as the mouth of the Jordan River or Long Beach.

In this section, we have including the majority of river routes found on Vancouver Island. For each, we have included the put-in and take-outs, the length of each run, as well as the grade of the run, based on the International River Classification System. Remember that the difficulty of a river can change daily. A river in full spring flood will be a different beast than the same river at the end of a dry, hot summer. Trees fall in, creating sweepers. Advance scouting is essential!

Grade I: Flatwater or slow moving water with small waves with virtually no obstruction. Suitable for novices in canoes and kayaks.

Grade II: Moderate rapids requiring moving around obstacles, though channels are easy to spot, even without scouting. Suitable for intermediate paddlers.

Grade III: Numerous rapids, boulders and eddies. Scouting is required. Experts in open canoes, or advanced whitewater kayakers.

Grade IV: Long, challenging rapids with powerful, irregular waves. Scouting is required, as is navigating through a complex series of obstacles. Suitable for experts in closed canoes or whitewater kayaks. Eskimo roll ability is recommended.

Grade V: Severe, extended rapids with narrow, dangerous routes and obstructions. Errors can be fatal! Professional paddlers in closed boats only.

Please remember that river conditions are always subject to change and advanced scouting is essential. The information in this book is only intended to give you general information on the particular river you are interested in. You should always obtain more details from your local merchant or expert before heading out on your adventure.

Adam River (Map 42/C6)
Highway 19 to Rooney Lake Junction
Put in: Highway 19 bridge

Take out: Bridge at Rooney Lake Junction.

This 4.3 km (1 hour) section of the Adam is rated grade II, with a few play waves, some sweepers and a tendency to flood at the first sign of rain. The best time to kayak is from October to June.

Adam River Canyon
Put in: Rooney Lake Junction

Take out: Forest Service site just past confluence with Eve River.

This 10.9 km (3.5 hour) section is rated grade II, III+, with a class IV drop and a class VI (60 metre) waterfall, which is portagable. Through the canyon, the Adam is fast and dangerous, narrowing down to as little as 2-metres. At high water levels, this section is unrunnable. Watch for sweepers and be alert for flash floods.

Campbell River (Map 36/E6)
Put in: Elk Falls Provincial Park below power plant.

Take out: Logging bridge, 1.9 km down river off Highway 28.

This 1.9 km (1 hour) grade II section of Campbell River is fast flowing with very few pools to rest at but not technically difficult. There are few rocks and fewer sweepers but don't let that lull you into thinking there are no obstacles. Whale Rock, near the confluence with the Quinsam, is just one exception. The river is dam controlled and offers a constant flow year round.

Chemainus River (Map 9/D3)
Put in: First bridge past Sally Creek on Copper Canyon Main

Take out: Near truck water tower between the 8 km and 9 km signs on Copper Canyon Main

This 12.9 km (2.5 hour) alternates between hairy technical sections (rated as high as Grade IV) with easy downstream floats. The last drop—the most difficult section—sees the 30 metre river narrow to 3 metres. Watch for sweepers and flooding.

Cowichan River (Map 9/A5)
Put in: Below Skutz Falls

Take out: Campsite at Marie Canyon

This 3.9 km (3 hour) section of the Cowichan is mostly Grades II and III, but at lower water levels some of those turn into Grade IV. At high water, this is a pretty mundane river as the high water washes out all the drops and waves.

Davie River (Map 33/D2, 34)
Put in: 10.5 km from Highway 19 on road to Schoen Lake Park.

Take out: Just southeast of Woss, at bridge over Nimpkish River.

This 14 km (4 hour) section of the Davie and Nimpkish Rivers is an extended boulder garden, rated mostly grade II+/III+, with two grade IV drops and one class V waterfall. The waterfall is portagable and in low water, some of the drops are unrunable.

Eve River (Map 42/B6)

Put in: At bridge where Main and East Main Roads meet, a few kilometres off Highway 19

Take out: At bridge over Eve River on East Main logging road

This 10.9 km (3.5 hour) trip is along a beautiful but dangerous section of the Eve River. The low volume of the river offers mostly grade II and III+ water but there is one grade IV drop and one grade V or VII waterfall (portagable). The safest time to run this river is during spring runoff. Watch for sweepers/logjams.

Gold River (Map 26/E2-6)
Upper Canyon

Put in: Second bridge from Gold River traveling north on Port Hardy Road (marked as Muchulat Pools and put-in on our maps.

Take out: First bridge from Gold River traveling north on Port Hardy Road

A 6.1 km (4 hour) bash through grade III and IV sections. At high water levels, expect some grade V rapids. This seemingly remote voyage takes you through a virgin canyon, yet it is easy to access. This is a popular place for playboating. Watch for sweepers.

Shawn Caswell paddling along the coast

Middle Section

Put in: First bridge traveling north from Gold River on Port Hardy Road.

Take out: Gold River Campsite, south of Gold River on Highway 28

This 9.7 km (4 hour), mostly easy (grade II+/III+) is usually free of sweepers, this section is a good training ground for novices looking for something a little bit harder than just grade II.

Lower Canyon

Put in: Gold River Campsite, south of Gold River on Highway 28

Take out: The large parking area near pulp mill, 9.2 km past Gold River Bridge.

This 5.8 km (1 hour) section of Gold River offers a mixed bag for the experienced kayaker. The popular Big Drop, a 350 metre section of river, has been called the biggest-water boating experience on Vancouver Island. The Lower Canyon of Gold River is Graded II+, but there are a lot of III+ and IV drops.

Kennedy River (Map 12/E4)

This would be an easy 20 km (5 hour) river and ocean paddle from Kennedy Lake to Grice Bay on Tofino Inlet. Unfortunately, there is a rough section of rapids that require a nasty 5 km portage to avoid.

Koksilah River (Map 3/D1, 9/G7)
To Burnt Bridge

Put in: 5 km from Burnt Bridge, at a large parking lot.

Take out: Burnt Bridge on Koksilah Main, just after it turns off Port Renfrew Road.

A 6.0 km (1.5 hour) section of the Koksilah, that is perfect for novices with a bit of experience and looking for a few grade III sections. It is best run at just right water levels (not too high; not too low).

Canyon Section

Put in: Burnt Bridge

Take out: Bridge on Koksilah Road, 2 km west of junction with Highway 1.

A difficult 14.8 km (6 hour) grade III section with grade IV and even V drops that are almost impossible to portage around. Once you're on this section, it's difficult to bail out, other than the infamous Kinsol Trestle partway into the route. There is one easy, mandatory portage.

Marble River (Map 39/A2)

Put in: A bridge just below where the Marble flows out of Alice Lake on Port Alice Highway. The actual put in is below the falls north of the bridge.

Take out: The Government Dock in Coal Harbour is as good a place as any, but many other options exist. Look for road access to Rupert Inlet/ Holberg Inlet/ Quatsino Inlet or Neroutsos Inlet.

A series of waterfalls, which are portagable, and still clear pools, are linked by a 7.6 km (4 hour) mostly grade II route. From the mouth of the river it is 9 km (1.5 hours) to Coal Harbour. The scenic ocean paddle can be extended if you choose another take-out point.

Nanaimo River (Map 16/F6, 17/A6)
Nanaimo Lakes to Weyerhaeuser Bridge

Put in: Where the Nanaimo river runs out of First Lake along the Nanaimo River Road.

Take out: Weyerhaeuser Bridge. Left off Nanaimo River Road at about Kilometre 23 (Mile 17).

An easy 4 km (1 hour) grade II float.

Weyerhaeuser Bridge to White Rapids Mine

Put in: Weyerhaeuser Bridge.

Take out: White Rapids Mine on Nanaimo River Road, 2.6 km from where the White Rapids Road junction.

An 11.9 km (4 hour) run along a grade II/III medium volume river. At high water levels, some drops are grade IV. This is a popular section for playboaters.

Pumphouse to Cranberry Bridge

Put in: Where Highway 1 crosses the Nanaimo River

Take Out: Cranberry Bridge, on Cedar Road

An easy 5 km (1 hour) paddle along the slow moving lower section of the Nanaimo River.

Nimpkish River (Maps 32/F1, 33, 34/A7)

Duncan Road Bridge to Woss

Put in: Duncan Road Bridge, just off Rona Road (Map 33/B2).

Take out: Just southeast of Woss, at bridge over Nimpkish River.

This 8.2 km (3 hour) run builds in intensity from an easy grade II to a stiff grade III. You can end off with a class IV waterfall (or you can pull out right before). There's even an optional grade V fish ladder to test your skills (please do not attempt this when the salmon are running).

Kaipit Creek to Nimpkish Camp

Put in: Bridge over Kaipit Creek on Nimpkish Road (Map 32/F1)

Take out: Nimpkish Camp (40/D7)

This grade II (one short class II+ rapid) is an easy place for novices to take their first solo trip, or for more experienced kayakers to go for a sightseeing tour. Limestone caverns, deep black pools and a final destination on Nimpkish Lake, with its broad sandy beaches, make this a very scenic route indeed.

Puntledge River (Map 29/A7)

Put in: Below the dam where the Puntledge flows out of Comox Lake

Take out: Puntledge Park.

An easy 5 km (1 hour) paddle along a dam-controlled grade II river. The water level is pretty constant over the year, but watch for sudden releases from the dam.

San Juan River (Map 1, 2/D1)

Put in: San Juan Bridge Rec Site

Take out: Port Renfrew

An easy year round, 19 km paddle down the San Juan River. The toughest water you'll face is Grade II but lookout for log jams.

Sooke River (Map 3/F5)

Put in: Sooke Potholes

Take out: South Fairgrounds

An easy 5 km paddle down a grade I/II river. The river is best paddled after a rainfall but it is subject to flash floods

Tsitika River (Map 41)

Put in: Follow Tsitika Main to junction with Tsitika West Elliot. Bridge is just off Tsitika Main.

Take out: Follow Tsitika Main about 10 km past junction with Tsitika West Elliot to bridge over Tsitika River.

This 10 km (3 hour) can be a bit of a pinball run at low water levels as there is very little water and lots of rocks. At moderate water levels, it is generally a grade III run.

White River (Maps 34, 35, 43/A7)

Put in: A difficult approach down a rough, bramble-lined trail 700 metres past where the 303 Main Road veers off of White River Road. Look for a sign to waterfall.

Take out: Bridge over White River on Salmon River Main (43/A7).

A 16 km (4 hour) paddle along a grade II/III+ section of the White River (at high water levels, it can be rated grade IV). Watch for sweepers, especially at low water levels when every obstacle on the low volume river is revealed.

Woss River (Map 33/B2)

Put in: Woss Lake Campground

Take out: Where the powerlines cross Nimpkish River

The Woss river flows from Woss Lake into the Nimpkish River. The Woss is an excellent river for beginners with mostly grade II water. There are some major obstacles (including a log jam that blocks the entire river) that don't make it the easiest to navigate.

Ocean Paddling

We are limited in what we can say about ocean paddling around Vancouver Island because there are just so many places to go. Hundreds upon hundreds of destinations from pocket beaches in hidden coves to rocky islands to narrow fjords, the variety is amazing. Ocean paddlers can make short day jaunts from coastal towns or string together islands for a weeklong venture. Even month-long excursions along the wild outer coast or the slightly more sheltered inner coast of Vancouver Island are possible.

Below we offer just a few general suggestions. For more ideas, check out the Provincial Parks section or look on the maps for the   symbol.

It is important to know where you are and where you are going. Although large swaths of the north island coastline remain undeveloped Crown Land, areas along the southern island, and especially the gulf islands, might be under private ownership. Thankfully, most beaches are public property up to the highest tide line.

Although sea kayaking is by far the most common form of open ocean paddling, there are still a number of brave souls who head out in canoe, though in rough water, a closed deck—either canoe or kayak—is a must.

Note that distances are given in nautical miles, not kilometres. Also note that most of the open ocean routes, especially on the West Coast of Vancouver Island are best left to experienced paddlers, due to tides, currents, fog, wind, and other adverse weather conditions. Before any outing it is essential that you review the Tides and Current Tables, as well as the Marine Weather Broadcasts.

Alert Bay/Malcolm Island (Map 40/C1)

Whale watching, historic Native and Finnish sites or quaint fishing villages are the appeal of this North Island adventure. Common launching points include Telegraph Cove or any of the ferry landings (Port McNeill, Alert Bay or Sointula). Strong currents, ferry and boating traffic and fog and wind can make this a real challenge.

Bligh Island Marine Park (Map 25/D7)

This marine park is found in a sheltered inlet of Nootka Sound. Most paddlers start from the busy Cougar Creek Rec Site and allow at least 3 days to explore this beautiful west coast location. Wilderness camping, a few historical sites and plenty of marine life make this a paddling delight.

Broken Island Group (Map 5/D2)

Part of Pacific Rim National Park Reserve, this group of about 100 islands in Barkley Sound between Ucluelet and Bamfield is an international destination for sea kayakers. A combination of protected inner waters, a riot of marine life, sea birds beyond number and a rugged, untamed beauty makes this area a paradise. Experienced kayakers can make the long, dangerous open water crossing from Toquart Bay near Ucluelet. The rest catch the Lady Rose passenger ferry (call 250-723-8313 for info). In March and April there is a chance to paddle with the gray whales as they make their annual migration. You will need a minimum of three days, preferably a week or more, to explore the 50 nautical miles of paddling. Camp only in designated areas. Hazards include unpredictable weather, fog, strong tides and exposed outer islands.

Brooks Peninsula/Bunsby Islands (Map 30/G5, 31, 32/A6)

Located just south of Brooks Peninsula, accessing the rugged Bunsby Islands involves a mostly sheltered, 50 km (3 day) paddle from Fair Harbour. Be sure to visit the quaint Village of Kyoquot and allow time to explore the endless coves and small islands along route. Venturing past the Mission Group Islands (to the Bunsby Islands or Brooks Peninsula) is for the experienced west coast paddler only. The weather can get extremely rough. Bring drinking water and emergency supplies.

Chatham and the Discovery Islands (Map 4/G5)

From the Oak Bay Marina, it is a 5 nautical mile loop around Chatham and Discovery Island Marine Provincial Park. There are many small islets in the area, as well as the larger Chatham and Discovery Islands to explore. Wilderness camping is possible on Discovery Island.

D'Arcy, James and Sidney Islands (Map 4/G2)

These three islands are a popular destination for kayakers planning on spending the night at D'Arcy Island Marine Park. There are numerous shoals and reefs in the area, most of which won't cause kayakers any problems, but keep an eye out anyway. This is a 5 mile route from Island View Beach.

DeCourcy Group Islands (Map 17/E5)

Off the southern shore of Gabriola Island, the DeCourcy Group is an 11 mile paddle from Vancouver island, or 3 miles from Gabriola. Cliffs with caves and sandstone beaches highlight the area. There is wilderness camping available at Pirates Cove Marine Provincial Park.

Deer Group Islands (Map 5/G3, 6)

This spectacular paddle does not receive the press or popularity of the nearby Broken Island Group. The Deer Group Islands are also geographically and climatically similar to the more popular group across the channel. These islands are more exposed to the open ocean and are recommended for experienced paddlers only. Other hazards include unpredictable weather and fog. Starting from Port Desire or Haggard Cove, allow 3-4 days to explore the islands.

Denman Islands (Maps 22/G3, 23/A4)

The smooth coastline of Denman offers good paddling opportunities and a fairly sheltered coastline on the west side of the island. It is 10 miles from the ferry landing to the sandy beaches of Sandy Island Marine Provincial Park of the north tip of Denman. Another popular destination is Boyle Point Park and the tiny Chrome Island at the South end of the island, though there is no camping in Boyle Point Park.

Gabriola Island (Map 17/D4)

Gabriola is a quiet, friendly island with numerous bays and beaches to explore. Popular destinations include the Flat Top Islands, off the northeast corner of the island, Sandwell Park and Whalebone Beach. Be aware that the currents move pretty fast around Gabriola.

Galiano (Map 10/D2)

This long, narrow island forms the eastern edge of the gulf islands. The exposed east coast, the swift currents at the north end and the busy Active Pass at the south end limit paddling opportunities. One of the most popular paddles is a 9 mile paddle through Montague Harbour to Ballingall Islets.

Hornby Island (Map 23/B2)

Hornby is a popular recreational island, with some great paddling. Some popular trips include the 4 mile trip from Whaling Station Bay to Helliwell Bluffs, a 3 mile trip from Ford Cove to Shingle Spit or south from Ford Cove to Norman Point.

Mayne Island (Map 10/G4)

Active Pass, between Mayne and Galiano, is one of the most dangerous places for kayaking and canoeing to be in the Gulf Islands. The high volume of boating traffic, including a BC Ferries main route from Tsawwassen to Swartz Bay, and dangerous tides make this a hazardous area for small boats. There are a number of small islands about Mayne, perfect for short circumnavigations, as well as many bays (Village, Horton, Bennett, Gallagher, Piggot) to sample.

Pender Islands (Map 10/G5, 10 Inset)

There are hundreds of bays and beaches between the 61 kilometres of coastline shared by the two Pender Islands. Although very few of these beaches are private property, they are also accessible by car. Don't assume that a cozy little beach is as private and secluded as it appears from the water. Some popular routes include a 17 mile paddle from Port Washington to Bedwell Harbour, and an 8 mile route through Browning Harbour and Bedwell Harbour.

Port Alice/Quatsino Sound (Maps 37/G4, 38/D1, 39/B2)

Port Alice offers an excellent starting point for endless sea-kayaking adventures. The area is known for its blue waters surrounded by the forested slopes around the sheltered Neroutsos, Holberg and Rupert Inlets. Venturing on Quatsino Sound requires experience with rougher conditions. If you are brave enough, the rewards of a west coast paddle to sandy beaches of Harvey Cove, Gooding Cove and Side Bay. These areas are popular camping locations.

Portland and Moresby Islands (Map 10/E7)

From Swartz Bay, it is a 12 mile paddle around these two islands. There is wilderness camping on Portland Island and plenty of marine life (river otters and harbour seals). Watch for ferries and stiff south winds through the Moresby Channel.

Quadra Island (Map 36/F3)

Quadra Island is not a great paddling island because the currents around the island have a tendency to carry kayakers well away from their destination. There are a couple sheltered routes to try. The 12 mile paddle from Granite Bay to Small Inlet takes you past recent logging, old mines and a fish farm to the secluded inlet. The small beaches and interesting rock formations highlight a 10 mile paddle from Heriot Bay to Open Bay. The later offers a possible side-trip to Brenton Island.

Saltspring Island (Map 10/B4)

Saltspring is the largest and most populated of the Gulf Islands. It's also one of the most popular paddling destinations. Some of the more popular paddles include an 18 mile paddle from Drummond Park on Fulford Harbour to Musgrave Landing, a 10 mile paddle from Southey Point to the Secretary Islands (wilderness camping available), and an 8 mile jaunt from Arbutus Beach to Vesuvius Bay.

Saturna Island (Map 10 Inset)

Saturna Island is largely undeveloped island with virgin shores and sandstone cliffs. Tides through Boat Passage between Saturna and Samuel Islands are very fast. Other hazards include winds and tides off East Point and Taylor Point. There is camping at Cabbage Island and Fiddler's Cove.

Thetis, Kuper and Tent Island (Maps 9/G1, 17/F7)

A 9 mile route around three large islands located off the inner coast near Chemainus. The draw to these islands includes sheer cliffs that rise straight out of the ocean and pocket beaches. There is camping on tiny Tent Island to the south.

Parks

(National, Provincial & Regional Parks)

In this section you will find a wide variety of parks. From the world famous Pacific Rim National Park to the ever popular provincial and regional parks, outdoor enthusiasts can pursue pretty well every imaginable activity. We have added recreational symbols beside each park name to show you some of the more popular activities pursued in the area.

To make things easier when you are planning a trip, we have grouped the parks into separate regions. Below you will find parks grouped under the Gulf Islands, South Vancouver Island and North/West Vancouver Island. If you are unsure where a park lies on the island, you can consult the index at the back of the book. This index will tell you the map number and reference page number.

BC Provincial Park Campgrounds generally operate from early spring through to fall. Some stay open all year. Most charge a fee for overnight stays. BC Parks has six fee levels, which vary according to the facilities and services provided and are based on a per party per vehicle per night rate. Parks with the least developed campgrounds have the lowest fees, while those with showers and flush toilets have the highest. There is usually a reduced fee for off-season camping. We have noted the parks that currently offer a call-in reservation system through Discover Camping, but more are being added each year. Call 689-9025 (add 1-800 outside Greater Vancouver) to reserve, or check out their website at www.discovercamping.ca.

Gulf Island Parks

The Gulf Islands are a popular destination for city dwellers. The quiet, rural setting, dry climate, spectacular scenery, marine life and unique flora and fauna make them an ideal destination. Although camping is limited on those islands that are accessible by ferry and car, there are many boat/kayak accessible islands with beautiful beaches and camping areas. Day-users can enjoy the many picnic areas, beaches and trails the islands host.

Ballingall Islets (Map 10/C2)
A string of islets found off the west coast of Galiano Island. These islets make an ideal paddling or boating retreat.

Beaumont Prov Marine Park (Map 10/G6)
Beaumont Provincial Marine Park is located in Bedwell Harbour on South Pender Island and is accessible by boat or land. Fees are applied for mooring buoy and walk-in camping at 15 campsites charged from May to Sept. 30. There are no fees and no services in the off-season.

Bellhouse Provincial Park (Map 10/F3)
This picturesque picnic site is located an easy walking distance from the Sturdies Bay Ferry on Galiano Island. Busy Active Pass and Mayne Island make for a nice backdrop.

Bennett Bay Protected Area (Map 10/G3)
Located on the northeast shore of Mayne Island, this 10.93 ha protected area was established as part of the Pacific Marine Heritage Legacy (PMHL) program. BC Parks will be responsible for the overall management of this area for the next few years when a decision will be made on what to designate the area: national park, provincial park or ecological reserve. Camping and fires are not permitted in this area.

Boyle Point Park (Map 23/A4)
A scenic park on the southern tip of Denman Island. The park offers a nice hike to the lighthouse.

Brooks Point Regional Park (Map 10/F1)
A new 3.9 ha park reserve at the southeast tip of South Pender Island features a rocky beach and a sheltered beach.

Cabbage Island Prov Marine Park (Map 10 Inset)
Located off the northeast tip of Saturna Island, this small (4 ha) park features a sandy beach for sunbathing or swimming. There is also good scuba diving in the area. On a clear day, you can enjoy watching passing ships in the Strait of Georgia against the backdrop of the mainland mountains. Fees are collected from May to September 30th, there are no fees or services in the off-season.

D'Arcy Island Prov Marine Park (Map 4/G2)
This 81 ha island in Haro Straight West of Sidney Island is densely forested and has no sheltered anchorage. It was once the site of BC's first leper colony, from 1891 to 1926. These days, it is a provincial marine park, with 10 walk-in campsites and various water-based opportunities (like diving and swimming) being the big draw. Open year round, fees are collected and from June 1 to September 30. From October 1, the park is open with no services or fees.

Dionisio Point Prov Park (Map 17 Inset)
Private property and an Indian Reserve restrict land access to this spectacular park. The rustic 142 ha provincial park overlooks Porlier Pass at the northern tip of Galiano Island. Sandy beaches, rocky headlands, abundant marine life and amazing sunsets attract visitors. There are 30 walk-in campsites, as well as day-use facilities. Several nice hiking trails are found in the area.

Discovery Isl Prov Marine Park (Map 4/G5)
Located 2 nautical miles east of Victoria, this 61 ha undeveloped marine park was donated to the province by Captain E.G. Beaumont, who once lived here. It has no sheltered anchorage but offers four walk-in campsites for sea kayakers. The northern portion of this island is Indian Reserve land. Please respect these areas. Fees are collected from June 1 - August 31. From September 1st on the park is open but offers with no services and has no fees.

Drumbeg Provincial Park (Map 17/F4)
Located at the south end of Gabriola Island overlooking Gabriola Passage, this park features shelving sandstone rocks and a small sandy beach for sunbathing. Scuba diving and fishing are also popular in the area.

Fillongley Provincial Park (Map 23/A2)
The 10 oceanfront campsites in this 23 ha park fill up very quickly, especially on weekends. Short trails lead through an old growth cedar forest and by a salmon spawning stream. There is good road access and the park accepts reservations.

Gabriola Sands Provincial Park (Map 17/B3)
Located at the north end of Gabriola Island fronting Taylor Bay and Pilot Bay, this parkland was donated by the Gabriola Sands Company. The sandy swimming area is ideal for children. It is recommended that you boil the water from the hand pump.

Helliwell Provincial Park (Map 23/C3)
The cliffs overlooking the Strait of Georgia provide excellent vantage points to watch marine traffic and wildlife. A good trail system and picnic facilities attract day-users to this beautiful 2,872 ha park on Hornby Island.

Isle-de-Lis Prov Marine Park (Map 10/G7)
Rum Island is a tiny island in the Haro Strait, with pleasant walking trail and beaches. Open year round, fees are collected and full services are provided June 1 to September 30 for the three wilderness/walk-in campsites. Sea kayakers will find this an ideal retreat.

Main Lake Chain Provincial Park (Map 36/G2)
Located on east-central Quadra Island, this 2,454 ha park protects an area of both biological and historical significance. Over 72 bird species, 234 plant species, as well as ochre pictographs are found on Main Lake. Be sure to take your time and explore the area while enjoying the Main Lake Chain Canoe Route.

Montague Harbour Prov Park (Map 10/D2)
This popular 97 ha park on the southwest side of Galiano Island starts five metres below sea level and climbs 180 metres to a steep rocky precipice. White sand and shell beaches, open meadows, a tidal lagoon, towering forest and craggy headlands are yours to explore. The park is accessible by land or water and has 25 drive-in and 15 walk-in campsites, which can be reserved. A nice trail circumnavigates the peninsula and leads to isolated beaches and good vantage points.

Mouat Park (Map 10/B3)
A small regional park is found south of historic Ganges on Saltspring Island. The day-use site is accessed of Drake Road.

Mount Maxwell Provincial Park (Map 10/B5)
At 594 metres (1,948 ft), Baynes Peak is the highest point on Saltspring Island. Visitors to the park are rewarded with superb views of Vancouver Island and the other Gulf Islands. Recent logging in the area makes road access from the north difficult. For this reason, it is best to hike up from the trailhead to the south.

Newcastle Isl Prov Marine Park (Map 17/A3)
Newcastle Island is the large island that greets BC Ferries passengers as they pull into Departure Bay in Nanaimo. People wanting to visit this 336 ha park can take a 10-minute ride on a foot passenger only ferry across the water. The island is the site of Saysetsen Village, a former native settlement on the island that was deserted well before Vancouver Island's first coal mine was built here in 1849. These days, visitors can spend their days exploring the islands trails, swim in Kanaka Bay or set up camp at one of the 18 wilderness campsites. The park is open all year.

Octopus Islands Prov Marine Park (Map 36/G1)
This 360 ha boat access park is located at the southern tip of Sonora Island at the junction with Quadra and Maurelle Islands. The series of small islands are a popular site for boaters and kayakers.

Pirates Cove Prov Marine Park (Map 17/E5)
Best known as home to BC's infamous Brother XII in the 1920's and 30's, DeCourcy Island lies south of Gabriola Island. This 31 ha park is located on the south end of DeCourcy, well away from the Brother XII settlement. The park offers 12 walk-in campsites, nice beaches and a sheltered anchorage. Trails lead to middens (historical areas used by transient natives when harvesting fish or seashells), past unique plant life and to a pebble beach.

Prevost Island Protected Area (Map 10/D4)
Prevost Island is recognized as one of the last remaining, relatively intact landscapes within the Gulf Islands biotic region. The island is largely unchanged and contains much the same environment that would have existed 100 years ago. The area contains large cedar and arbutus groves. Although not developed, there is a small campsite at James Bay. This protected area was established as part of the Pacific Marine Heritage Legacy (PMHL) program. BC Parks will be responsible for the overall management of this area for the next few years when a decision will be made on what to designate the area: national park, provincial park or ecological reserve.

Princess Margaret Marine Park (Map 10/E6)
A gift from the province to Princess Margaret, then from Princess Margaret to the province, the beaches of this 575 ha park encompasses all of Portland Island. The island makes a popular destination for South Island boaters and during summer months the five walk-in campsites are hotly contested.

Prior Centennial Provincial Park (Map 10/F5)
While many of the parks in the Gulf Islands are marine access only, Prior Centennial is vehicle accessible. At 16 ha, setting up camp is about all you're able to do. Reservations are possible. Fortunately, it is close to Mt Norman Regional Park and Beaumont Provincial Marine Park, which both offer excellent hiking and picnicking opportunities. Camping reservations are accepted.

Rebecca Spit Marine Park (Map 36/G4)
This 177 ha hook of land juts out into the Strait of Georgia to create Drew Harbour. It is a popular park for picnicking and beachcombing along the beaches that line both sides of the spit. The park is accessible by both water and land.

Ruckle Provincial Park (Map 10/D5)
Ruckle Park is the largest provincial campsite on the Gulf Islands. It has 70 walk-in sites and 10km of easy hiking trails. The park is also popular with scuba divers, fishermen and kayakers interested in exploring the southeastern shore of Saltspring Island. Campers can expect drinking water, pit toilets and wheelchair accessible sites. The facilities are closed from October to April.

Russell Island Protected Area (Map 10/D6)
This 16.2 ha island between Portland and Saltspring Islands is currently undeveloped, though plans are underway to develop basic amenities. A part of the Pacific Marine Heritage Legacy program. Russell Island was purchased by one of the original Kanaka (Hawaiian) families in 1886 and remained a farming homestead until 1960. Russell Island may be the only remaining intact example of Kanaka settlement in BC. The original homestead with a heritage orchard site dates from 1902-1906.

Sandwell Provincial Park (Map 17/C3)
This small day-use provincial park is located at the north end of Gabriola Island. The oceanfront park offers a nice sandy beach for picnics and swimming.

Sandy Island Prov Marine Park (Map 22/F1)
This boat access park includes Sandy (Tree) Island the Seal Islets off the northwest tip of Denman. During low tide, it is possible to walk to Sandy Island from Longbeck Point on Denman Island. As the name indicates, there are nice beaches as well as wilderness camping and anchorages.

Sidney Spit Prov Marine Park (Map 4/F1)
This popular 400 ha park is made up of mostly white sandy beaches backed by towering bluffs. Beachcombing is also fun in the sweeping tidal flats and salt marshes teeming with birds, mammals and marine life. For small crafts, there are sheltered anchorage on west side of spit as well as a wharf and landing floats. 30 walk-in campsites, swimming, sunbathing and trails add to the fun.

Small Inlet Provincial Park (Map 36/G1)
This 487 ha water access only park protects the area around Small Inlet, as well as a chain of tiny lakes. It is found at the northeast side of Quadra Island and can be accessed by foot or boat.

South Otter Bay Protected Area (Map 10/F5)
The site of a former resort, Roe Lake is the only natural lake left on both North and South Pender Islands. The area provides wetland habitat for Virginia rails and American dippers, and was the reason this area was protected as part of the Pacific Marine Heritage Legacy program. Currently undeveloped, BC Parks will be installing facilities over the next few years. There are a number of small cabins in the protected area that are closed to public access.

Tribune Bay Provincial Park (Map 23/C3)
At over a kilometre long, Tribune Bay boasts the largest beach in the Gulf Islands. This 95 ha park also boasts the warmest salt water swimming in the islands, or indeed, in all of BC.

Tumbo Island Protected Area (Map 10/G1 & Inset) 🏊
The 121.41 ha Tumbo Island Protected Area lies off the northeast end of Saturna Island. Currently undeveloped, the island is a popular sea kayaking destination.

Wallace Island Marine Park (Map 10/A1) ⚓ 🛶 🏊 🧍 🐟 🏕
A 72 ha park on a long, narrow, low-lying island in Trincomali Channel between Galiano Island and the northern tip of Saltspring Island. A trail runs from tip to tail and there are 12 walk-in campsites a sheltered anchorage and docks for boaters.

Whaleboat Island Prov Marine Park (Map 17/F6) 🛶 🏊 🐟
A small, undeveloped, rocky island is found south of Ruxton Island and west of Valdes Island. The area is popular with sea kayakers.

Winter Cove Provincial Park (Map 10/F1) 🛶 ⚓ 🛶 🏊 🧍
Winter Cove is a 91 ha park with broad sand and mud beaches on the northeast side of Saturna Island. The area offers a small boat launch and an exposed anchorage. The strong tidal currents that rush through Boat Passage, provide whitewater excitement for kayakers.

South Vancouver Island Parks

There is an amazing range of scenery, landscape and wildlife on South Vancouver Island, and for each new area, there's usually a regional or provincial park to preserve a part for future generations. Some of these parks are islands of refuge for endangered flora and fauna, some are wilderness experiences for the truly self-sufficient, while others are just great places to take the family for a day of fun in the sun or a couple days camping at the lake.

Albert Head Lagoon Regional Park (Map 4/C6) 🧍
A small lagoon with cobble beaches is the focus of this 7 ha park, popular with bird watchers.

Ayum Creek Regional Park (Map 3/G6) 🧍 🏕
A new 6.7 ha park reserve east of Sooke.

Bamberton Provincial Park (Map 4/B1) 🏊 ♿ 🛶 🧍 🏕
There are 47 vehicle/tent campsites in this beachfront park on the west side of Saanich Inlet. There is also a popular day-use area for families coming to picnic and to swim in the inlet, which is shallow and often warmed by the sun.

Bear Hill Regional Park (Map 4/D3) 🧍 🧍 🐎
Bear Hill is a hilltop park in a mixed woodland area found at the north end of Elk Lake. This 49 ha park contains the oldest rock on Vancouver Island and offers outstanding views of the Saanich Peninsula and Haro Strait from the top of the 220 metre (720 ft) Bear Hill.

Bright Angel Provincial Park (Map 9/F6) 🏊 🛶 🧍 🐟 🏕
There's 11 km of hiking trails in this 11 ha park found south of Duncan. The are is popular for picnicking and swimming while campers can call ahead to find out about the campsite (250)746-4762.

Carmanah Walbran Provincial Park (Map 1,B1, 7/B7) 🏊 🧍 🏕
The fame of this 16,450 ha wilderness park is founded mostly on the many old growth giants in the park. Although the most famous of them all, the Carmanah Giant, currently has no trail access, there are still many other giant trees. 95 metre (310 ft) tall spruce trees estimated to be 800 years old and 1000 year old cedars are found throughout the park. The large Sitka spruce ecosystem represents two per cent of BC's remaining old-growth forest. A day-use area offers 40 picnic tables, while there are to rugged trails and designated wilderness camping locations for the hardy backpacker.

Chemainus River Provincial Park (Map 9/C3) 🐟 🏕 🛶
This 86 ha day use park on the Chemainus River is a popular picnicking site/swimming hole in the summer. It also offers angler's access to the Chemainus River.

Coles Bay Regional Park (Map 4/C1) 🏕
This tiny 4 ha park on muddy Coles Bay is known to be rich in tidal lagoon life. The picnic area also offers nice views of Saanich Inlet.

Cowichan River Provincial Park (Map 8, 9/B5) 🏊 🛶 🧍 🐟 🏕
This spectacular 873 ha park on the Cowichan River protects significant stretches of this Provincial Heritage River. The river is world-renowned for its wild salmon and steelhead fishery. Established in 1995, it was the first new provincial campground on Vancouver Island in over a decade. There are 39 drive-in and 4 walk-in sites at Stoltz Pool and the Horseshoe Bend Group campsites, which are only open in the summer. Full services (such as water, firewood) are available for a fee. The Cowichan River Trail and the newly established Trans Canada Trail route are found in the area. Camping reservations are accepted.

French Beach Provincial Park (Map 3/A6) 🏊 🧍 🐟 🛶
This 59 ha park on the Strait of Juan de Fuca near Jordan River was named after pioneering naturalist James French. This remarkable man took two years to cross Canada by land, losing half his toes to frostbite along the way. The park is a great place to experience the West Coast as you wander up and down the 1.6 km sand and gravel beach and watch for whales offshore. There are 69 drive-in campsites and the park is open all year. Fees for full services collected from March 15 to October 31, while winter fees apply the rest of the year. Camping reservations are accepted.

Galloping Goose Regional Park (Map 3/F5, 4/A6) 🧍 🐎 🚲
A 57 km long rails-to-trails park corridor weaves through most of the municipalities in the Capital Regional District. The popular route links many of the area's parks as it winds its way through urban, rural, and semi-wilderness landscapes. The section from Johnson Street Bridge to the Luxton Fairgrounds (south of Langford) forms portion of the Trans Canada Trail.

Goldstream Provincial Park (Map 4/A4) 🏊 🧍 🐟 🏕 🛶
One of the highlights of this 388 ha park, is Niagara Falls, which is actually higher than the famous falls in Eastern Canada. Other highlights include the salmon spawning in fall and a trail to Mount Finlayson, which hikes past 600 year old Douglas fir and western red cedar. You will also find remains of gold mining, for which the park was named. The 173 campsites here are open all year. Fees for full services are collected from March 15 to October 31, while winter fees apply the rest of the year. Camping reservations are accepted.

Gordon Bay Provincial Park (Map 8/C4) 🏊 🛶 🧍 🐟 🏕 ♿ 🛶
Cowichan Valley boasts the highest average annual temperature in Canada. At the eastern end of the valley, the large, warm Cowichan Lake attracts beach lovers to the sandy beaches of Gordon Bay. The 126 campsites in this 51 ha park are usually packed during summer. The full service campground is open from March 15 to September 30th. In the off season, the lake makes an excellent fishing destination. Camping reservations are accepted.

Gowlland Tod Provincial Park (Map 4/B2) 🧍 🏕 🚴
This 1,219 ha park is the jewel in the crown of the Commonwealth Nature Legacy and protects a significant portion of the Gowlland Range and the shores of Tod Inlet. The park's focus is to preserve a heritage of green space in the area for future generations, so recreation opportunities are limited. Many rare or endangered plant and animal species can be found in the park. In order to protect their extremely fragile habitat, portions of Gowlland Range Trails have been closed or seasonally relocated.

Hemer Provincial Park (Map 17/C5) 🧍 🐟 🏕
A pocket park on Holden Lake southeast of Nanaimo offers a popular picnic spot. There are a few walking trails and good fishing in the lake.

Hitchie Creek Provincial Park (Map 7/A4) 🏊 🐟
A 226 ha wilderness park adjacent to Pacific Rim National Park on the southwest coast of Vancouver Island. The park was established to protect the area old growth and a salmonid stream. There is no trail or road access into the area.

Horth Hill Regional Park (Map 10/C7) [symbols]

A 31 ha hilltop park found near the northern tip of the Saanich Peninsula. The area offers panoramic views of the peninsula and the Gulf Islands.

Island View Beach Regional Park (Map 4/E2) [symbols]

It is the beach that draws most people to this 40 ha park nestled on the eastern shore of the Saanich Peninsula. Bird watchers, fishermen and sea kayakers also frequent the park.

John Dean Provincial Park (Map 4/C1) [symbols]

In 1921, John Dean donated 32.4 ha of land to the province to form a park. It was the first time anyone had donated land for a park, and it forms the core of the now 155 ha park. The park is located on the Saanich Peninsula, north of Victoria, overlooking the pastoral peninsula, the Gulf Islands and the Cascade Mountains. Area activities include hiking and picnicking and just observing and enjoying nature.

Juan de Fuca Prov Park (Map 1/G3, 2/D5) [symbols]

Home to the Juan de Fuca Marine Trail, this 1,277 ha park stretches along the southwestern coast of Vancouver Island. From the Botanical Beach tidal pools to the popular China Beach, this stretch of the west coast is being compared to the more famous trail and park further up the coast. China Beach offers a full service 78 site campground that is wheelchair accessible. There are designated wilderness sites for trail walkers located along the 47 km long trail. Camping reservations are accepted.

Kapoor Regional Park (Map 3/F4) [symbols]

A new 16.6 ha park forms the western terminus of the Galloping Goose Regional Trail in Sooke.

Koksilah River Prov Park (Map 3/E1, 9/F7) [symbols]

Found on the Old Port Renfrew Road, there is one main site, which offers 10 drive-in campsites as well as a smaller, more isolated camping location further along the river. The undeveloped 210 ha park is popular with all sorts of recreationists, including trail riders, whitewater paddlers and fishermen.

Lone Tree Hill Regional Park (Map 4/B3) [symbols]

The lone tree is now dead, but still standing at the top of this 388 metre (1,273 ft) hill. Hiking to the top is a favourite past-time here, as is watching the raptors that like to soar in the currents above the hill.

Manley Creek Regional Park (Map 10/A7) [symbols]

Found north of Mill Bay, this shaded picnic site overlooks the ocean. There is a series of short but steep trails leading down to the shore.

McDonald Provincial Park (Map 10/C7) [symbols]

There is little to do but camp in this small (12 ha) park located near the Swartz Bay Ferry Terminal on the Saanich Peninsula. There's 49 sites for campers/RVs looking for little more than a place to set up shop while exploring the area or waiting for the ferry.

Matheson Lake Reg Park (Map 3/G7, 4) [symbols]

A former provincial park, this 162 ha park is now a stop along the former railway recreation corridor, the Galloping Goose Trail. The lakes makes a fine picnic and/or fishing destination east of Sooke Basin.

Symbols Used for Parks

[symbol]	Campsite / Trailer Park
[symbol]	Road Access Recreation Site
[symbol]	Trail or Boat Access Recreation Site
[symbol]	Day-use, Picnic Site
[symbol]	Beach
[symbol]	Boat Launch
[symbol]	Hiking Trail
[symbol]	Mountain Biking Trail
[symbol]	Horseback Riding
[symbol]	Cross Country Skiing
[symbol]	Snowmobiling
[symbol]	Mountaineering / Rock Climbing
[symbol]	Paddling (Canoe / Kayak)
[symbol]	Motorbiking / ATV
[symbol]	Swimming
[symbol]	Cabin / Lodge / Resort
[symbol]	Interpretive Brochure
[symbol]	Anchorage
[symbol]	Fishing
[symbol]	Diving
[symbol]	Viewpoint
[symbol]	Wheel Chair Accessible

Matthews Point Regional Park (Map 10/E3) [symbols]

Overlooking Active Pass, this new 14 ha park reserve features good views from the top of the bluffs.

Memory Island Provincial Park (Map 3/G1) [symbols]

A small island at the south end of popular Shawnigan Lake offers a great picnic location. Fishing and swimming are enjoyed in the area.

Mill Hill Regional Park (Map 4/C5) [symbols]

Home to the Capital Regional District Park headquarters, this 50 ha park is a mix of cool woodland along Millstream Creek and a 200 metre hilltop with open views and wildflowers.

Morden Colliery Provincial Park (Map 17/B5) [symbols]

This 4 ha park stands as a reminder of the coal mining industry on Vancouver island. This was the former site of the Morden Mine, from which 76,000 tonnes of coal were removed. Little remains other than an old coal tipple.

Mount Work Reg Park (Map 4/C2) [symbols]

A 536 ha wilderness park has three freshwater lakes for swimming or fishing in, 11 km of trails and the Hartland Surplus Mountain Bike Area. Hiking to the summit of Mount Work is a popular activity.

Nitinat River Prov Park (Map 7/D2) [symbols]

This 160 ha park is made up of two locations along the Nitinat River. The area was established to protect Summer Steelhead habitat, as well as winter range for Roosevelt elk. Fishing is not allowed at the Falls site, though it is allowed at the Bridge Pool site.

Petroglyph Prov Park (Map 17/A4) [symbols]

Established to protect hundreds, perhaps even thousand of year old rock carvings, this park contains both the original petroglyphs and castings from which rubbings can be taken. It makes for a nice break when travelling the Trans Canada Highway.

Quarry Regional Wilderness Park (Map 9/G7) [symbols]

The big draw to this park is a 3 km return hike to the top of Cobble Hill. Why not pack in a lunch and enjoy the panoramic views of the ocean.

Roberts Memorial Prov Park (Map 17/D6) [symbols]

A 15 minute walk from Yellow Point Road brings you to a nice picnic spot along a sandstone beach.

Roche Cove Regional Park (Map 3/G7) [symbols]

Linking up with both Sooke Basin and Matheson Lake Park, this 159 ha wilderness park features 7 km of trails and a picnic area. The popular Galloping Goose Trail dissects the park.

Sooke Hills Wilderness Reg Park (Maps 3/G5, 4/A5)

This 4,000 ha former non-catchment area of the Greater Victoria Water District is now a wilderness park reserve. It is not open to the public at this time.

Sooke Mountain Provincial Park (Map 3/G5) [symbols]

Made up of 450 ha of undeveloped wilderness north of Sooke, there is a gated road (no vehicle access) that leads to the park. The three lakes in the area attract fishermen, while the old road system is popular with hikers and bikers.

Sooke Potholes Provincial Park (Map 3/F5)
A popular picnic and swimming area found north of Sooke. Whitewater paddlers also use the park as a put-in location.

Spectacle Lake Prov Park (Map 4/A2)
An excellent trail system and a small lake form the hub of this park. It is possible to swim, canoe, fish or picnic at the lake.

Thetis Lake Regional Park (Map 4/C4)
Thetis Lake Park is one of the more popular recreational retreats in the Victoria area. The 635 ha area covers a diverse landscape, from swamps and lakes to forest and hilltops. There is supervised beach area (during the summer) along with a fabulous trail system. Anglers will be pleased with the fishing in the lakes in the area.

West Shawnigan Lake Park
(Map 3/G1, 9/G7)

A small lakeside picnic area with a boat launch is found on the western shores of Shawnigan Lake. The warm lake makes this an ideal place for all manner of watersports.

Witty's Lagoon Regional Park (Map 4/B6)

A 56 ha nature reserve featuring a sheltered lagoon with sandy beaches and rocky headlands. There is excellent bird watching and 5 km of trails in the area.

North/West Vancouver Island

The further north or west you are willing to venture, the further from civilization you will find yourself. For many this is the ideal wilderness experience that they are looking for. The scenery is spectacular, the parks are isolated and weather is unpredicable. One thing for sure, the raw beauty of this region will not disappoint.

Arbutus Grove Provincial Park (Map 16/E2)
A small nature site is found along the island highway north of Lantzville. There are no facilities.

Artlish Caves Provincial Park (Map 32/E4)
There is no official development at this 234 ha park northwest of Zeballos. Local area residents, who lobbied for many years to have this last remaining undisturbed karst unit made a park, have created hiking trails. This is a sensitive ecosystem, so do not disturb anything while you are here.

Big Bunsby Provincial Marine Park (Map 30/G5)
The 639 ha boat-accessed park is situated on the west coast of Vancouver Island between Brooks Peninsula and Kyuquot. The park was created to pull kayakers away from the adjacent Checleset Bay Ecological Reserve. The area hosts the rare sea otter as well as many other marine animals and birds. A number of known archaeological sites are also in the area.

Bligh Island Provincial Park (Map 18/C1, 25/C7)
A popular boating and fishing destination, this 4,456 ha park encompasses the southern portion of Bligh Island and the Spanish Pilot Group of Islands (Villaverde, Pantoja, Verdia, Vernaci, Navarez, Clotchman, and Spouter Islands). It offers sheltered anchorages and deep bays. This park is part of the Mowachaht First Nations traditional territory,

and was a major fur trade centre during the early years of European contact and settlement.

Brooks Peninsula Provincial Park (Map 30, 31/A2)
Brooks Peninsula is becoming a popular recluse for west coast paddlers. The remote, rugged wilderness area is found northwest of Kyuquot. This 51,631 ha park includes an extensive wild ocean coastline, long sheltered fjords, rugged mountain ranges, pristine estuaries and old-growth forests. Sea kayakers should be prepared for extreme weather conditions and should bring their own drinking water.

Cape Scott Prov Park (Maps 37 Inset, 45/A5)
The 21,849 ha Cape Scott is accessible only by foot or boat, and is a magnificent area of rugged coastal wilderness at the northwest tip of Vancouver Island. Established in 1973 and named after the site of a lighthouse that has guided mariners since 1960, Cape Scott has 64 km of ocean frontage stretching from Nissen Bight in the north to San Josef Bay in the south. Over 23 kilometres of this stretch is beach. The area is popular with backpackers but there is a large camping area (San Josef Campsite) near the entrance that allows day-users to access a few of the shorter trails and beaches. In addition to the infamous lighthouse and beaches, there are historic Dutch settlements to explore.

The Nahwitti-Shushartie coastal corridor has recently been added to Cape Scott Provincial Park. This 6,750-hectare strip is undeveloped. Some historic heritage trails exist with

Trying to set up the tent on a windy day

this new park area but they are not well defined.

Catala Island Provincial Marine Park (Map 24/A3)
This 850 ha park in Esperanza Inlet on the west coast of Vancouver Island protects reefs, islands, islets and marine ecosystems. Catala Island itself is forested with mature trees, twisted and stunted from the wind, a lake and bog area.

Claude Elliot Lake Provincial Park (Map 41/C7)
A popular sport fishing destination, this 289 ha park plays a key role in protecting elk and deer habitat.

Clayoquot Arm Provincial Park (Maps 12/G3, 13/A2)
This 3,491 ha park was created as a result of one of the largest environmental campaigns in history, and encompasses the lower Clayoquot River, Clayoquot Lake and the forested slopes northwest of the Clayoquot Arm of Kennedy Lake. The park contains rare old-growth forests of Sitka spruce in the Clayoquot Lake and lower Clayoquot River areas, and excellent salmon spawning conditions in Clayoquot River. An unusual phenomena occurs in Clayoquot Arm, where sockeye salmon spawn 20 m (65 ft) below the surface.

Clayoquot Plateau Provincial Park (Map 13/B2)
This 3,155 ha high elevation plateau is a mix of old growth forests, karst topography and subalpine meadows. There is no development, save for a few challenging hiking routes.

Cormorant Channel Provincial Park (Map 40/E1)
A series of undeveloped islands, popular amongst the sea kayaking group. The park is 744 ha in size and found north of Telegraph Cove.

Dawley Passage Provincial Park (Map 12/C3)
The fast current through Fortune Channel creates a riot of marine life off the coast of this 154 ha boat-access only park. The park is situated at the south end of Fortune Channel northeast of Tofino.

Dixie Cove Provincial Marine Park (Map 31/F6)
This 156 ha park on Hahoae Island in Kyuquot Sound, features a sheltered anchorage for boaters. This beautiful area makes a fine fishing or sea kayaking destination.

Elk Falls Provincial Park (Map 36/E6)
This 1,087 ha park takes its name from where the Campbell River plunges over a 25 metre (80 ft) precipice into a rock walled canyon. Other attractions include 8 km of magnificent forest trails, 122 campsites, a nearby salmon hatchery and in autumn, salmon spawning in the Quinsam and Campbell Rivers. Camping reservations are accepted.

Englishman R. Falls Prov Park (Map 16/A1)
Englishman River Falls Park is named after not one but two beautiful waterfalls which cascade along the river bed. There is a spectacular canyon in between the two falls and 3 km of viewing trails. At the lower falls, there is a swimming hole with a small rocky beach area to sunbathe. This 97 ha park also contains 103 drive-in campsites and a large day use area. Camping reservations are accepted.

Epper Passage Provincial Park (Map 11/G1)
The waters surrounding the two small islands, Dunlap and Morfee, make up this 306 ha park. The area is rich in marine life, including rare massive purple ascidians (sea squirts).

Flores Island Provincial Park (Map 11/D1, 19/B7)
Flores Island is home to a population of wolves, which are becoming habituated due to people feeding them. This is bad news, as wolves have had to be destroyed due to man's ignorance. The 7,113 ha of remote west coast wilderness also protects old growth Sitka spruce and undisturbed watersheds. Migrating Gray whales and Nuu-chan-nult heritage sites are popular attractions for sea kayakers.

Fossli Provincial Park (Map 14/D1)
A grassy picnic site on the south shores of Sproat Lake makes a nice base to explore the lake or to relax the day away.

Gibson Provincial Marine Park (Map 11/E1)
The little brother of Flores Island Park, Gibson Marine is home to Whitesand Cove, with its broad, sandy beaches, and Ahousat Warm Springs. This area does not get the attention the more popular Hotspring Cove does.

God's Pocket Provincial Marine Park (Map 46/G3)
A 2,025 ha park comprised of a group of small islands including Hurst, Bell, Boyle and Crane Islands is found northwest of Port Hardy. The park protects a seabird breeding colony and bald eagle habitat as well as the area's marine and terrestrial landscapes.

Gold Muchalat Provincial Park (Map 26/D2)
This pristine 653 ha park, a popular spot for sport fishers, also protects important habitat for the Marbled Murrelet, deer and Roosevelt elk. The area is only reached on foot.

Hesquiat Lake Provincial Park (Map 18/F3)
A 62 ha boat-access nature appreciation park north of Boat Basin is found on the east side of Hesquiat Lake. Enjoy the rare plant life or look for spawning salmon at nearby Satchie Creek in the fall.

Hesquiat Peninsula Provincial Park (Map 18/C5)
The bulk of this prominent, low-lying peninsula is now a provincial park, protecting heritage sites, old-growth stands of Sitka spruce, lodgepole pine, white pine and yellow-cedar. The 7,891 ha park also

encompasses a variety of coastal ecosystems including extensive off-shore reefs (which create a navigational hazard), boulder, cobble and sand beaches, sea caves, sheltered bays, kelp beds, and mudflats.

Horne Lake Caves Prov Park (Map 23/A7)
The caves are the center piece for this 123 ha park, ranging from a simple self-guided tour of two of the smaller caves, to guided seven hour underground epics. The park also serves as a base for the many different activities possible, including camping, canoeing or fishing on Horne Lake.

Kennedy Lake Prov Park (Map 12/G6, 13/A6)
The 379 ha Kennedy Lake Park is comprised of two day-use sites along the south shore of Kennedy Lake, adjacent to the Pacific Rim National Park. The lake makes a popular picnic and boating area.

Kennedy River Bog Provincial Park (Map 12/F5)
A unique, low-acid bog along the Kennedy River is protected within this 11 ha park.

Kwakiutl Lawn Point Provincial Park (Map 37/G7)
A 560 ha park south of Quatsino Sound offers a nice area to relax and get away from the constant west coast swell. The beaches and wild west coast make this a fabulous sea kayaking area for experienced paddlers.

Little Qualicum Falls Park (Map 15/C1, 23)
It is the river, not the falls, that has the designation as little in this 440 ha provincial park. The park actually has two different locations along Highway 4 west of Parksville. The first location offers 91 drive-in campsites and the popular hike to the falls. The larger area skirts the south end of Cameron Lake and has a beautiful picnic location. Swimming and fishing are popular pastimes on the lake.

Loveland Bay Provincial Park (Map 36/B5)
A former forest service rec site cum provincial park, this 30 ha site has 50 drive-in campsites, some of which are wheelchair accessible. The wooded area is found on a lovely bay of the man-made Lower Campbell Lake. When the water level is right, there is a beach area.

Lower Nimpkish Provincial Park (Map 40/B2)
The Nimpkish River meanders through a steep-sided previously logged valley that has still some old growth. The 265 ha park is important black bear and salmon habitat, but is also popular among recreational fishers. A trail skirts the east bank of the river.

MacMillan (Cathedral Grove) Prov Park (Map 15/B1)
This extremely popular 136 ha park is one of the most accessible stands of giant Douglas-fir trees in British Columbia. As you round the bend of Highway 4 at the west end of Cameron Lake you will find a jammed pack parking area. Regardless of the crowds, the 800-year-old trees are truly amazing and the short trails on both sides of the highway make for a perfect break for travelers heading west to Long Beach and the Pacific Rim National Park.

Maquinna Prov Marine Park (Map 18/F5, 19/A6)
Hot Springs Cove is the big draw to this 2,667 ha park found west of Flores Island in the infamous Clayoquot Sound. Outside of the boardwalk trail and popular hot springs, there is not much development in the park. The extensive coastal area offers sea kayakers a variety of coastal ecosystems including extensive offshore reefs, boulder, cobble and sand beaches, sea caves, sheltered bays, kelp beds, and mudflats.

Marble River Provincial Park (Map 38/G2, 39/A2)
Marble River flows through a shallow canyon bordered by forest covered bench lands. At the east end of the park next to the highway, a developed 33 unit campground provides a good base to explore the area. A hiking/fisherman trail starts from the campground and follows the south bank of the river past a hatchery to an old fort at the river mouth.

Miracle Beach Prov Park (Map 29/B3)
The broad oceanside sandy beach is the big draw to this 137 ha park. This is a popular family getaway and offers a 193 campsites and a separate picnic area. The park is open all year, with winter fees charged in the off-season. Camping reservations are accepted.

Morton Lake Provincial Park (Map 36/B4)
Morton Lake Provincial Park includes all of Morton Lake and a section of shoreline on Mohun Lake. The trout fishing is exceptional and the nearby Sayward Canoe Route can be accessed from the park. A fine sandy beach and picnic area attracts swimmers and sunbathers, while 24 drive-in campsites and a boat launch on Mohun Lake are also available.

Nimpkish Lake Provincial Park (Map 40/B7)
A 3,950 ha wilderness area has been set aside to protect the old growth western hemlock forest of the Tlakwa Creek Watershed. This remote area is only accessible by boat.

Nuchatlitz Provincial Park (Map 24/C3)
A 2,135 ha wilderness park protects a diverse range of west coast environments, both on land and in the sea. This is another remote area that only has boat access.

Nymph Falls Regional Park (Map 29/B7)
Located along the Puntledge River, this 55.5 ha park offers access to Nymph Falls. Trails in this park hook up with a larger trail system along the Puntledge River.

Quatsino Provincial Park (Map 38/B3)
An undeveloped 654 ha wilderness park is found on the east side of Koprino Harbour. The area is popular among sea kayakers.

Pacific Rim National Park (Maps 1, 5-7, 12)
Certainly one of the most beautiful places to visit both on and off Vancouver Island, Pacific Rim National Park is actually broken into three separate units.

Long Beach Unit (Map 12/D5) is the most accessible and popular of all three units. This section is dissected by Highway 4 between Tofino and Ucluelet and offers easy access to sandy beaches and inland rain forests. Long Beach may be the focal point of the region but visitors will find plenty of short trails, an old radar site, good surfing, as well as plenty of offshore treats (including salmon fishing, ocean kayaking and whale watching). Green Point Campground is the only vehicle access campground in the park reserve and offers 94 drive-to sites as well as walk-in sites. It is a good idea to reserve a spot well in advance of your trip. Call 1-800-689-9025. The campgroud offers well-spaced sites with flush toilets, running water and two access points to the beautiful beach. The over conscious park staff, the possibilities of bear encounters and the fee for wood can deter from the camping experience. Outside of the park visitors will find a few private campgrounds, plenty of tour operators and full amenities in both Tofino and Ucluelet.

Broken Group Islands Unit (Map 5/D2) is a world class kayaking and canoeing destination. Encompassing over 100 small islands and rocky islets in the open waters of Barkley Sound, there are endless nooks and cranies to explore. Many paddlers elect to take the passenger ferry (1-800-663-7192) to and from the islands but experienced paddlers can brave the open crossing between Toquart Bay and the Broken Island.

West Coast Trail Unit (Maps 1, 5, 6 & 7) surrounds the world famous West Coast Trail. Stretching from Port Renfrew in the south to Bamfield in the north this area is known as the Graveyard of the Pacific. Hikers interested in the trail should be prepared for a gruelling trek. Call 1-800-663-6000 for reservations. There are also a few shorter trails and the infamous Nitinat Triangle Canoe Route to explore in the area.

Raft Cove Provincial Park (Map 37/B1)
This gorgeous sandy bay is certainly a wilderness treat. The rugged west coast environment and the lack of development make this a fine paddling or hiking destination. The 670 ha park is found at the outlet of the Macjack River south of Cape Palmerston.

Rathtrevor Beach Prov Park (Map 23 Inset)
The 175 drive-in and 50 walk-in campsites, nestled in a towering old growth forest, are some of the most coveted on all Vancouver Island during the summer months. Book ahead and book early. The huge tidal flats warm the water and makes swimming or beachcombing at this 347 ha park extremely pleasant. Camping reservations are accepted.

Robson Bight (Michael Bigg) Ecol Reserve (41/C4)
Three highly sensitive marine ecological reserves have been combined to make this 5,460 ha park. The area is internationally known as a haven for killer (orca) whales, which often use the pebble beaches to rub their bellies. The closest access is Telegraph Cove; alternatively there are a many different tour operators to choose from. Please note that land access to the area is not permitted.

Rock Bay Provincial Marine Park (Map 44/C7)
A spectacular area at the junction of Discovery Passage and Johnstone Strait, this 525 ha park is comprised of two bays and a rocky headland with a lighthouse. A private campground and boat launch (which can be used for a fee) provide access to the area. Strong currents limit sea kayaking in the area but fishing and watching the massive cruise ships pass on by are popular alternatives.

Rosewall Creek Provincial Park (Map 22/G4, 23/A4) 🚶🐟♿
This 54 ha nature park protects an important area for wintering waterfowl northwest of Qualicum Beach. The park is found next to the highway and has an easy 2 km hiking trail.

Rugged Point Prov Marine Park (Map 24 Inset)
🚣🚶🐟⛺🖼
As the name indicates, this is an exposed area on the beautiful west coast of Vancouver Island. The remote, water access only park is found on the westernmost tip of land south of Kyuquot Channel. Isolated pocket beaches, which are linked by an interesting trail, and sheltered coves are the big draw for boaters and kayakers. The main beach area offers an outhouse.

Santa Gertrudis-Boca Del Infierno Park (18 Inset) 🚣🐟⛺
Located near Friendly Cove on south Nootka Island, this 435 ha water-access only provincial park protects the coastal marine environment and an old-growth forest. The sheltered anchorages are popular with boaters and sea kayakers. The tongue-twisting name is certainly one of the most unique in the province.

Schoen Lake Prov Park (Maps 33/G3, 34) ⛷🚣🚶🐟⛺🖼
This large 8,430 ha park is soon to have another 259 ha added in the Davie River Area. The beautiful area is a popular recreational retreat with 9 drive-in campsites and a boat launch on Schoen Lake. Backpackers and paddlers will also find wilderness camping options and some fantastic trail systems. Nisnak Meadows, glaciers, small lakes and plenty of wildlife are just some of the attractions in the area.

Seal Bay Regional Nature Park (Map 29/D5) 🚶🚴🐎
A maze of hiking and multi-use trails link the 563 ha Seal Bay Forest and the 152 ha Seal Bay Nature Park. Mountain bikes are restricted to the west side of the park. On the east side, trails lead to an escarpment overlooking a rocky beach, often populated by seals.

Spider Lake Prov Park (Map 23/C7) ⛷🚣🚣🐟⛺♿🖼
A picnic site on the uniquely shaped lake is a great place for a swim. The water warms nicely in the summer and makes for an interesting canoeing area. The lake is also known to provide good fishing in the spring and fall.

Sproat Lake Prov Park (Map 14/D1) ⛷🚣🚣🐟⛺♿🖼
Located on the north shore of Sproat Lake, 13 km northwest of Port Alberni, the 39 ha Sproat Lake Park is a watersports haven. Swimming, fishing, water skiing and when the wind is blowing, wind surfing are all popular activities. The east end of the park contains one of the finest panels of petroglyphs in British Columbia. There are also 58 drive-in campsites that are available by reservation.

Stamp River Provincial Park (Map 22/E7) ⛷🚶⛺🚴
A combination of two former parks (Stamp Falls and Stamp River Money's Pool), this 327 ha park has 22 drive-in campsites. In addition to trails to the two areas listed above, watching salmon spawn in the fall is a popular past time. Camping reservations are accepted.

Strathcona Provincial Park (Maps 19-21, 26-28, 34, 35)
⛷🚣🚣🚶🐟⛺▲🖼🎿➕♿
Designated in 1911, Strathcona is the oldest provincial park in BC. At 253,772 ha it is the largest park on Vancouver Island, comprising almost 8% of the island's total landmass. Most of the park is high alpine and sub-alpine and provides some of the best ridge (hiking) routes in BC. There are 160 drive-in campsites between the Buttle Lake and Ralph River campgrounds, with the Buttle Lake campground accepting reservations. There is also wilderness camping throughout the park, along the many kilometres of trails and backcountry hiking routes. The park also offers winter activities such as backcountry skiing and snowshoeing routes. Pretty well every outdoor pursuit can be sampled in this fabulous area. Spend a day or a month, the park is yours to explore.

Strathcona Westmin Provincial Park (Map 20/G1) 🖼🚶▲
A class B 3,328 ha park that is hidden in the heart of the massive Strathcona Park on the southwestern shores of Buttle Lake. The B designation gives Boliden Westmin resources the right to operate a mine in the area. For recreationists, this means good road access to the middle of the park. Camping reservations are accepted.

Sulphur Passage Provincial Park (Map 19/E5) 🚣🚶🐟
Known as the Upper Shelter area, Sulphur Passage Park is situated in the northeast portion of Clayoquot Sound, between Flores Island and the Megin River watershed. The 2,299 ha park, comprised of Obstruction Island, and the surrounding shores of Vancouver island in Sulphur Passage, is a popular area for sea kayakers

Sydney Inlet Provincial Park (Maps 18/G3, 19/A3) 🚣▲
The 2,774 ha park is situated in the northern Clayoquot Sound area between Hesquiat Lake and Pretty Girl Lake. It is one of the best examples of a fjord on Vancouver Island, and a popular destination for boaters and sea kayakers.

Tahsish-Kwois Provincial Park (Maps 31/G2, 32/A3) 🚣🚶▲
A popular sea kayaking destination, the 10,829 ha Tahsish-Kwois Park is also accessible by logging roads. Located at the head of Kyuquot Sound on the west coast of Vancouver Island, the park is rich in wildlife values, including habitat for Roosevelt elk and waterfowl. The park features low elevation old-growth forests, steep forested slopes, rugged mountains and spectacular karst features.

Taylor Arm Provincial Park (Map 14/B1) 🚣🚶🐟⛺▲🖼
Found on the north shore of Sproat Lake, this pleasantly wooded park is not as busy as other parks in the Port Alberni area. Along with an undeveloped beach, there are three campsites and a separate day-use area. The campsites are intended primarily for group camping (by reservation only).

Thurston Bay Prov Marine Park (Map 44/E6) 🚣🚶🐟⛺♿🖼
This undeveloped wilderness park on the northwest side of Sonora Island contains several small but attractive beaches. Visitors can also hike into nearby Florence Lake.

Tranquil Creek Provincial Park (Map 20/F7) 🐟🚶▲
Bushwhacking from the end of the Tranquil Creek logging road can access this remote hike in only park. The 299 ha area encompasses the headwaters of Tranquil Creek, Paradise Lake. There is no development.

Vargas Island Provincial Park (Map 11/F3) 🚣🚶🐟▲
The 5,970 ha park protects the rugged, outer coast of Vargas Island, Blunden Island, and the Cheland Island Ecological Reserve in Clayoquot Sound. Found just west of Tofino, this section of the west coast is also a prime area to watch gray whales migrate off shore. Other than the Cheland Island Ecological Reserve, which has no public access, you can also explore the islands on foot.

Weymer Creek Provincial Park (Map 25/B2)
A 307 ha area south of Tahsis has been established to protect undisturbed karst topography. There is no development in the park.

White Ridge Provincial Park (Map 26/G4)
This 1,343 ha undeveloped park takes its name from the easily identifiable karst landscape. There are no facilities, road access or developed trails into this park.

White River Provincial Park (Map 34) 🐟
This small 70 ha park's prime recreational activity is fishing in the White River. The area also protects prime woodland habitat for Roosevelt Elk and black bear. The area is not marked on the maps.

Woss Lake Provincial Park (Map 33/B5) 🚶🐟▲🎿
Most people access this steep, seldom visited 6,634 ha wilderness area by boating across Woss Lake, as there is no road access. The aptly named Rugged Mountain and the glaciers of its north-facing slopes dominate the remote, beautiful park.

Wilderness Camping
(Forest Recreation Sites)

Forestry recreation sites (rec sites) are scattered throughout Vancouver Island. These sites have been developed by the BC Forest Service and various forestry companies as a base from which to explore our wilderness areas. The sites are usually small, rustic campsites, offering little more than a clearing, a fire ring, a pit toilet and a picnic table. Accessing some of these sites can be quite the challenge; long, 4wd access only roads that are sometimes unmarked are par for the course. The rewards are often remote and beautiful locations—lakes, rivers and coastal areas—that are often less crowded and more rustic than provincial park campsites.

Rec sites are user maintained; if you pack it in, you pack it out. There is an $8/night or $27/year fee for most rec sites, and a slightly higher enhanced camping fee at some of the busier sites.

We have organized these sites according to Forest Service District boundaries, of which there are three on Vancouver Island: Campbell River, South Island and Port McNeill.

In our descriptions, we have used to following the terms:

small: less than 10 vehicles.

medium: 11 to 20 vehicles.

large: more than 20 vehicles.

open: a large, open area with few or no trees. Very little privacy between camping parties. Ideal for group camping, RVs and trailers

semi-open: some trees, as well as a large open area. Some privacy is possible, and the open area is usually big enough for RVs and trailers.

treed: heavily forested. Campsites are usually well separated. A tenter's dream, these sort of sites can be difficult, if not impossible for an RV to access.

Campbell River District

This vast 1.5 million hectare area covers roughly the middle of the Island as well as a few of the Northern Gulf Islands. From the populated east coast to the remote and rugged West Coast one can expect all extremes of a wilderness experience. The area also hosts a wide variety of wildlife; from Roosevelt Elk to world-renowned salmon and steelhead rivers, from bald eagles to killer whales. The mild climate allows for recreation year round. The popular Sayward Canoe Route, endless fishing in lakes, streams and on the ocean, fantastic trail systems as well as old logging roads to explore are just a few activities to sample in this beautiful area.

Aldergrove Rec Site (Map 43/G7)
Located near an old railgrade that intrepid explorers can follow, this small (2 unit) treed site is found near the south end of picturesque McCreight Lake. Most visitors here are after the cutthroat, bull and rainbow trout that inhabit the lake. Good road access is found along the Rock Bay FSR.

Amor Lake Rec Site (Map 35/G3)
This small (10 unit) semi-open site has a rough boat launch. Although Amor Lake is located along the Sayward Canoe Route, most canoeists forgo this road-accessed site in favour of Mr. Canoehead located a short portage to the south. The Amor Lake Rec Site is popular with anglers and drive-in campers who can endure the rough access along Blackwater Lake Road from the south.

Apple Point Rec Site (Map 35/G5)
A small (8 unit) open site with a gravel boat launch on Brewster Lake, this site is shared by canoeists paddling the Sayward Canoe Route and drive-in campers alike. It is also popular with anglers chasing after the lake's ample supply of cutthroat and rainbow trout. The site has good 2wd road access just off Salmon River Main.

Bear Creek Rec Site (Map 43/G7)
There used to be a fish hatchery just above where Bear Creek Flows into Amor De Cosmos Creek. The site has been converted into a small (7 unit) site that can be accessed by the 2wd Bear Bight Road.

Big Bay Rec Site (Map 36/C6)
This medium (11 unit) site on Lower Campbell Lake offers a gravel boat launch and a small wharf for boaters. The fairly remote spot is popular with cartop campers and fishermen. If you are boating, watch for hazards in the lake.

Boot Lake Rec Site (Map 36/A6)
Although this site is located within the circumference of the Sayward Canoe Route, Boot Lake is not a part of the chain. Instead, this small (3 unit) semi-open site has a rough boat launch designed to give anglers access to the lake. 4wd vehicles can access the quiet site along Boot East Road.

Brewster Camp (Map 35/G5)
Located just off the southern tip of Brewster Lake, this small (6 unit) open site is designed for destination campers. The site is large enough for RVs and has good 2wd access. There is a short trail down to the water's edge.

Brewster Lake Rec Site (Map 35/G4)
Although this medium (12 unit) semi-open site is accessible to drive-in campers via a long, narrow access road, it is a prime camping spot for canoeists along the Sayward Route. Water enthusiasts will enjoy the sandy beach.

Brittany Bay Rec Site (Map 35/G5)
A small (3 unit) site on Gray Lake with a narrow access road and restricted turn around room for RVs or trailers. Because there is no boat launch, most anglers will head for the Gray Lake Rec Site to the south. This quiet site is ideal for tenters or canoeists on the Sayward Route.

Camp 5 (Map 35/G4)
This small (8 unit) semi-open site with a car top boat launch for anglers or canoeists is the site of the historic camp 5 logging camp on Brewster Lake. Salmon River Main provides good 2wd access.

Campbell Lake Rec Site (Map 36/A6)
The views from here are big, wide and open—on a clear day you can see the Coast Mountains. The medium (20 unit) semi-open site has a gravel beach and lots of space for trailers and RVs. Campbell Lake Road provides good road access.

Cedar Lake Rec Site (Map 36/A2)
An old logging railgrade runs along the shores of Cedar Lake, a small lake with an even smaller (4 unit) semi-open site. Hikers and bikers can follow the old railgrade north or south. Cedar Lake is also popular with fishermen. Accessed off the gated Lakeview Centre Road.

Conuma River Rec Site (Map 25/G4)
A small site on the banks of Conuma River is found just upstream from the Conuma Fish Hatchery along the good gravel Head Bay FSR. The site is owned and maintained by Western Forest Products and provides a good place to watch black bears feeding on salmon in the fall. Please keep a safe distance.

Cougar Creek Rec Site (Map 25/E6)
A large, popular (49 unit) semi-open site is found on the Tlupana Inlet at the mouth of Cougar Creek. The long bumpy logging road does not discourage the hoards of saltwater anglers looking for tyee (30 lb+ chinook salmon) in august. The gravel boat launch and wharf are also popular with West Coast paddlers.

Dogwood Bay (Map 36/A6)
This small (5 unit) semi-open site is found on Lower Campbell Lake. The site is a popular starting point for the Sayward Canoe Route and offers a rough boat launch as well as a sand/gravel beach. Good access can be found along the Lower Campbell Lake Road.

Elk Bay (Maps 36/C1, 44/C7)
Two small rec sites (7 units total) have been added to the shores of Elk Bay in Discovery Passage. They share a boat launch between them and offer good ocean views.

Elk Creek (Map 43/A7
A small (7 unit) treed site is found just off the North Island Highway on the White River Road. This site has good access but is quite close to the highway, and if you're a light sleeper, the hum of traffic will probably keep you awake all night.

Fair Harbour (Map 31/G6)
The long access road does not deter visitors from accessing this medium (15 unit) rec site near government dock and boat launch of Fair Harbour. This is a popular place for anglers with small boats and kayakers to access beautiful Kyoquot Sound (larger boats usually use the boat launch at the end of the Artlish Main).

Fir Grove (Map 36/A6)
Fir Grove is one of many small sites on Lower Campbell Lake. This (3 unit) semi-open site boasts a gravel beach and is a great launching point for canoeists on Sayward Forest Canoe Route. Although the road access is good the small site in not suitable for RV or trailer.

Fry Gravel Pit (Map 36/A6)
The Lower Campbell Lake Road provides good gravel road access to many small recreation sites. This (7 unit) RV friendly site offers a rough boat launch that can be used by anglers or canoeists.

Fry Trestle (Map 36/A6)
Another new site found in the popular Sayward Forest west of Campbell River. This small (6 unit) site has a short, rough access road and limited turn-around space if the site is full. Look for it off the Lower Campbell Lake Road.

Garden Point (Map 24/D3)
The West Coast offers a beautiful yet rugged experience for those willing to brave the elements. This small boat access only site is found on Esperanza Inlet and offers a pebble beach and some places to pitch a tent in an old growth forest.

Gosling Bay (Map 36/B6)
This is one starting point for canoeists doing the Sayward Forest Canoe Route but canoeists should be prepared for a 1.1 km portage to Gosling Lake. The small (6 unit) rec offers a small boulder beach and a rough boat launch.

Gosling Lake (Map 36/A6)
Gosling Lake is another popular starting point for canoeists doing the Sayward Forest Canoe Route. The small (5 unit), semi-open site offers a wharf and is a popular spot for anglers. Gosling Lake Road limits access to smaller camper units and trucks.

Gray Lake (Map 35/G5)
Canoeists, anglers or cartop campers will enjoy this small (6 unit) semi-open site along the Sayward Forest Canoe Route. Gray Lake Road provides 2wd access to the site, which also offers a boat launch and wharf.

Junction Pool (Map 42/B5)
A medium (10 unit) semi-open site is found at the confluence of Adam and Eve Rivers via a 2wd access road. The site is popular with both kayakers and anglers.

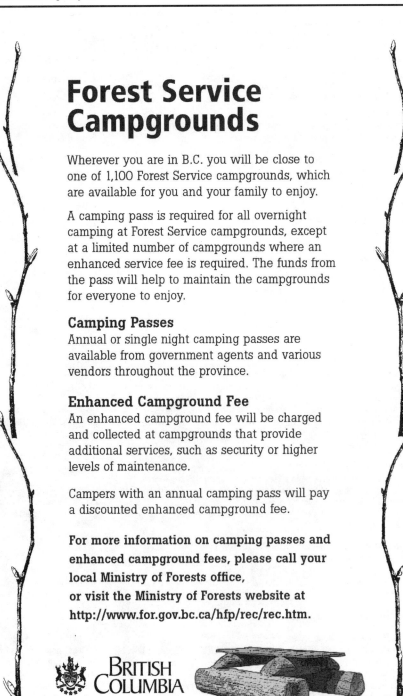

Forest Service Campgrounds

Wherever you are in B.C. you will be close to one of 1,100 Forest Service campgrounds, which are available for you and your family to enjoy.

A camping pass is required for all overnight camping at Forest Service campgrounds, except at a limited number of campgrounds where an enhanced service fee is required. The funds from the pass will help to maintain the campgrounds for everyone to enjoy.

Camping Passes
Annual or single night camping passes are available from government agents and various vendors throughout the province.

Enhanced Campground Fee
An enhanced campground fee will be charged and collected at campgrounds that provide additional services, such as security or higher levels of maintenance.

Campers with an annual camping pass will pay a discounted enhanced campground fee.

For more information on camping passes and enhanced campground fees, please call your local Ministry of Forests office, or visit the Ministry of Forests website at http://www.for.gov.bc.ca/hfp/rec/rec.htm.

BRITISH COLUMBIA
Ministry of Forests

Leiner River (Map 25/B1)

Leiner River Rec Site is a small (9 unit) treed site found a few kilometres east from where the river flows into Tahsis Inlet. This site is popular with anglers. Head Bay Road provides good gravel road access.

Little Bear Bay (Map 44/A6)

Found in a tiny bay Johnstone Strait, this medium (15 unit) open site offers a rough boat launch (if the tide is right). This is a popular site with anglers as there is good fishing just outside the bay. This beautiful ocean side site also makes a great destination resort for campers and small trailers. There is a short trail to a waterfall and a couple amazing fir trees that have survived the logging that has desimated the area. The steep access road off Little Bear Main can be trouble when it is wet.

Little Espinosa Picnic Site (Map 32/E7)

This small day use site is found 6km southwest of Zeballos on Fair Harbour Main. The rec site has a rough boat launch and is a popular place for kayakers to explore the small inlet from. There are tidal rapids to be wary of at the west end of the inlet.

Long Point (Map 36/A6)

On the southern shore of Campbell Lake, this small (8 unit) site offers a sandy beach and is often used by canoeists and water sport enthusiasts. It is possible to access the site of the Strathcona Dam Road.

Loon Bay (Map 36/A6)

The sandy beach, which grows larger later in summer as the water levels drop, and the fact there is space for larger trailers make this a popular choice. The medium (10 unit) site is found in a semi-open area and offers a good launching area. Anglers and canoeists doing the Sayward Forest Canoe Route frequent the area. The site is found along Lower Campbell Lake next to the good gravel road.

Malaspina Lake (Map 25/C3)

This small lake is found next to the busy Head Bay Road. A new day use site offers a picnic area and a short trail to sandy point on the south side of lake.

McCreight Lake (Map 43/G7)

Found next to the busy Rock Bay Road the pretty lake offers 4 semi-open sites spaced widely apart in the forest above the lake (but below the road). There is a small, rocky beach and a steep gravel boat launch that is frequented by anglers.

Merrill Lake (Map 36/A5)

A small (3 unit) treed site is tuck away on Merrill Lake. The gravel boat launch is well used by anglers with cartop boats. Merrill Lake Road provides 2wd access.

Miller Creek (Map 36/C7)

A new medium (11 unit) sized, treed site is found in a sheltered bay along the south shore of Campbell Lake. There is a short trail out to the point that runs beneath the hydro lines, as well as a maze of old logging roads that can be explored by the intrepid hiker or mountain biker. Elk River Main provides access for 2wd vehicles.

Mr Canoehead (Map 36/A3)

This boat access only site provides the ideal setting for explorers of the Sayward Forest Canoe Route. There is room for about 5 tents at the north end of Surprise Lake, which is a short portage south of the bigger Amor Lake.

Mohun Lake (Map 36/A4)

Menzies Main provides good access to this small (3 unit) open site. There is a rough boat launch and a wharf for anglers and canoeists to enjoy.

Muchalat Lake (Map 36/C2)

This large (20 unit) site is suitable for RVs and offers a boat launch, a float and gravel beach. Anglers can try their luck for lake trout. The area is accessed off Nimpkish Road, a good gravel road.

Naka Creek (Map 41/F3)

This is certainly pretty coastal area with the added bonus of being close to the infamous killer whales viewing in Robson Bight area (remember landing in the Bight is restricted). The small (7 unit) site offers a boat launch and is found beside the Naka Creek logging camp off the good gravel Naka Creek Road. This is a popular launching point for kayakers and anglers onto Johnstone Strait.

Orchard Meadow (Map 35/G6)

Found at the end of the Lower Campbell Lake Road, this medium (11 unit) site is big enough for RVs. There are two spots set away from the main site that are used by canoeists or tenters willing to walk a bit. The gravel boat launch is used by anglers and canoeists.

Pye Bay (Map 43/G7)

Pye Lake is a popular fishing lake and this rec site sees a lot of traffic from anglers despite the rough 2wd access along Pye East Road. The small (7 unit) semi-open site also has a small beach area.

Pye Beach (Map 44/A7)

Found a bit further to the south than Pye Bay, Pye Beach is another small (6 unit) site with a sandy beach.

Pye Lake (Map 43/G7)

Found off the rough Pye West FSR, this is another small rec site on the pretty lake found sandwiched between the highway and Johnstone Strait. The small (5 unit) semi-open site has a small beach and a boat launch is found just south of this site.

Resolution Park (Map 24/F1)

A small (7 unit) semi-open site is nestled on the sheltered shores of Zeballos Inlet. The cobble beach, wharf and boat launch can be accessed by either a 4wd vehicle (off Zeballos Main) or by boat from Zeballos or points farther afield.

Santiago Creek (Map 25/B4)

Popular with kayakers exploring the Tahsis Inlet, this is a small (5 unit) boat access only beach site. The area is found where where Santiago Creek flows into Tahsis Inlet.

Sitka Spruce Beach (Map 43/F7)

A small, walk-in or boat access site with a sandy beach is found on the southern end of McCreight Lake. The picturesque lake is a popular fishing lake. The site is found a couple hundred metres off the Rock Bay FSR.

Star Lake (Map 26/F5)

Found southeast of Gold River off the good Ucona Road, this is a small day-use only site. There is a rough boat launch, wharf and the Star Lake Trail to explore.

Stella Beach (Map 44/B7)

A medium (12 unit) semi-open site is found on the western arm of Stella Lake. 2wd vehicles can access the site of the Rock Bay FSR. There is a boat launch in the area for anglers or pleasure boaters to use.

Sterling Beach (Map 36/A3)

In the last few years, a couple new boat access only sites have been developed for users of the Sayward Forest Canoe Route. Sterling Beach is one of them and offers a small (2 unit) tent site on Amor Lake.

Sterling Island (Map 36/A3)

Another new 2 unit boat access only tent site is found on Amor Lake. The island site is one of the better canoe access sites on the Sayward Forest Canoe Route.

Strathcona Dam (Map 35/G7)

Located in the shadow of the Strathcona Dam, this medium (11 unit) open site is maintained by BC Hydro. The campsites are located along the water's edge, and there are wheelchair accessible outhouses. The Campbell Lakes—both Lower and Upper—offer fine fishing, and there is a small beach for suntanning or swimming. If camping in the shadow of a few million tonnes of water is disconcerting, BC Hydro assures us that the dam probably won't break, even if there is an earthquake.

Tsitika Crossing (Map 41/C4)

A small (4 unit) site is found next to the Tsitika River where the Tsitika Main (2wd access) crosses the river. This is a popular take-out spot for kayakers on the Tsitika River.

Port McNeill Forest District

A good bet for a little more peace and solitude, the Port McNeill Forest District covers the North Island and several islands including the beautiful Broughton Archipelago Islands. Endless logging roads and isolated stretches of ocean waters provide access to some of the most remote and beautiful recreation sites in the province. While in the area be sure to allow time to sample one of the many inland lakes or explore one of the fantastic geological features tucked away in the mountains.

Alice Lake (Map 39/B4)
A medium (10 unit) site with a boat launch has been designed primarily to offer anglers access to Alice Lake, which boast some of the biggest trout on the island. Non-fishers can enjoy swimming or sunbathing on the beach or just soaking in the ambiance of this wild North Island Lake. The site is access ed off Branch 25 off the Port Alice Highway.

Anutz Lake (Map 40/D7)
A large, open picnic or camping area and beach are found on Anutz Lake. The beautiful site is frequented by anglers and is easily accessed by larger units off River Main from the south.

Atluck Lake (Map 32/C2)
A semi-open site offers a nice gravel beach and boat launch. Like most rec sites on the shores of North Island lakes, this site sees a lot of action from anglers, chasing after the numerous rainbow trout that inhabit the lake. Cartop campers will also enjoy this relatively remote rec site, which has 5 campsites and picnic tables. Atluck Road provides good road access.

Beaver Lake (Map 39/D1)
Located just off Highway 19, this is a large, open day-use only site. The wharf is helpful for boaters or anglers heading out on this tiny lake.

Blinkhorn Peninsula (Map 40/G2)
Located just west of Robson Bight and east of Telegraph Cove, this is a small water access only day-use only site. The area makes a scenic and popular place for kayakers and boaters to pause for lunch before continuing on their search for orcas. People can also stretch their legs along the Old Telegraph Line or a couple old logging roads that can be followed for a kilometre or so inland.

Bonanza Lake North (Map 40/F5)
This small (3 unit) semi-open site is found on a former log sorting area. Bonanza Lake has some fair trout fishing and the lack of a boat launch at the north site means there is a little less angler traffic than the south site. Both sites are easily accessed of a good gravel road.

Bonanza Lake South (Map 40/F7)
A medium (14 unit) site with a boat launch, a sandy beach and enough wind to make this a good spot for sailboarding.

Camp Henderson (Map 39/B1)
A medium sized day use area that is located accross from the closed Island Copper Mine. The site was formerly called Rupert Inlet and offers a covered picnic area, grass field and a beach. Fishing and crabbing are popular activities. There is also a group camping area.

Canyon Lake (Map 32/E1)
The sandy beach at this small day use site offers a good swimming area. For anglers and paddlers, there is a cartop boat launch for people who want to tool about the tiny Canyon Lake for a few hours. Atlcuk Road provides good gravel road access to the site.

Cape Palmerston (Map 37/A1)
Found on the ruggedly beautiful Cape Palmerston, this small (5 unit) area is set in a semi-open area. Although the walk is only about 50 metres to the actual camping area, it still discourages drive-to campers. The cobble beach and the the wild West Coast are the main attractions to the area. The site is found off Coast Main, a 2wd road.

Clint Beek (Map 39/G3)
This is a new site found on Keogh Lake that is still in good shape. The medium (10 unit) treed site offers a man-made sandy beach and is RV friendly.

Georgie Lake (Map 46/F5)
Despite the remote location, this is a small (5 unit), unimpressive site. There is a sandy beach and a boat launch for water enthusiasts. There is 2wd access to this lake.

Gooding Cove (Map 37/G6)
Although a 2wd vehicle can access this small day use site, it is more popular with kayakers and boaters. There is a nice sandy beach, which was created by the pounding surf of the wild West Coast.

Helper Creek (Map 46/A6
A small (5 unit) treed site is located a short walk from Nahwitti Lake. The site has good road access, as it is found at the end of Highway 19.

Ida Lake (Map 40/F4)
Next to Ida Lake, this small day-use site offers a boat launch for anglers and paddlers.

Iron Lake (Map 39/F6)
A small day use site that provides little more than a boat launch to access Iron Lake.

Kaikash Creek (Map 41/A3)
With small boat access only, this small site is almost exclusively the domain of sea kayakers. There is a small, informal tenting site found in a treed area as well as a gravel/cobble beach and a funky solar powered outhouse. The site is frequented by kayakers hoping to view killer whales near Robson Bight.

Kathleen Lake (Map 39/D6)
A small (4 unit) semi-open rec site with a boat launch. This is a popular spot for anglers as well as those exploring the rare geological formations in the area. Good road access is found on Alice Main.

Kinman Creek (Map 40/D7)
A large site near the south end of Nimpkish Lake, this is a popular windsurfing destination. The site is located just off Highway 19, and traffic noise can be an issue for some.

Klaklakama Lake, Lower (Map 33/F3)
There is a reason these are called Forest Service Sites. From this small (5 unit) site, you will see a lot of clearcuts on the surrounding hills. The lake itself is nice, with a rocky beach and good swimming. Both rec sites are accessed off the Nimpkish Main South, a good gravel road.

Klaklakama Lake, Upper (Map 33/F4)
A small (4 unit) open site with a sandy beach and a boat launch. Unlike the well-logged lower lake site, there are still a few ancient trees standing here.

Mahatta River (Map 38/B5)
This medium (10 unit) site is often used as a stopping point on the way to Gooding Cove. The site is a long haul along a good gravel road but the remote location and river access will help you enjoy the visit.

Marble River (Map 39/A2)
A large (33 unit), well maintained semi-open site that has good road access along the Port Alice Highway. A handful of the sites back onto the Marble River, while the rest are well-sheltered in the trees. The park in the area protects some old growth while anglers frequent the trail.

Maynard Lake (Map 39/F6)
Set within a valley of good fishing lakes, Maynard Lake is easily accessible on Keogh Main. The medium-sized, open, day use only rec site has a boat launch and picnic area.

Nimpkish Lake (Map 40/D7)
A large open site at the south end of this beautiful fjord-like lake is found just off Highway 19. There is a boat launch for anglers and pleasure boaters, and strong, consistent winds from the north make this a popular destination for sailboarders.

O'Connell Lake (Map 38/D6)
A small (2 unit) site is found on the southwest end of the fair fishing lake. There is a boat launch on the lake for anglers and paddlers.

O'Conner Lake (Map 39/E2)
Found off West Main, a good gravel road, this is a small, semi-open day use site. There is a boat launch and beach for water enthusiasts to use. Waterskiing and fishing are the main attractions to the lake.

Pinch Creek (Map 39/C5)
A small (3 unit) site is found near the south end of Alice Lake, where Pinch Creek flows into the lake. Alice Lake Main provides good road access.

Rupert Arm (Map 39/ B1)
A small (4 unit) undeveloped rec site is found on Rupert Inlet. Managed by Weyerhaueser, the site offers a gravel boat launch and cobble beach.

San Josef River (Map 45/C7)
The popular, medium sized (11 unit) rec site is located in an old growth spruce forest just outside Cape Scott Provincial Park. From here, the San Josef is a slow moving river and a boat launch provides access to the river and then down to the ocean. Managed by Western Forest Products, the site even offers free firewood. Most vehicles can access the area.

Spencer Cove (Map 38/A3)
A beautiful, medium sized (11 unit) site in hidden in a sheltered cove on Quatsino Sound. There is a boat launch nearby for anglers and pleasure boaters looking to explore the Sound or the North Island. The site is accessible by a 2wd vehicle.

Spruce Bay (Map 39/C7)
Located on Victoria Lake, this small (5 unit) open site offers a boat launch and a sandy beach. Victoria Lake Main provides good 2wd access.

Swan Lake Picnic Area (Map 45/D7)
This small picnic area is located on the sight of an old homestead on tiny Swan Lake. There is a canoe launch for people wanting to paddle around this quiet, small lake.

Three Isle Lake (Map39/F4)
A tiny day use site on a good 2wd road gives access to this pretty lake. There are picnic tables and a canoe launch. Since Three Isle Lake warms up in the summer and is a good place for a swim.

Vernon Lake (Map 33/E6)
A large (24 unit) open site is found at the north end of the lake. There is a boat launch, which is frequented by anglers in search of the elusive trout. Vernon Lake Road offers 2wd access.

Victoria Lake (Map 39/B5)
One of the larger day use areas is located on the western shores of Victoria Lake. A boat launch and a sandy beach give access to the lake, which is a popular and warm swimming hole.

Woss Lake (Map 33/B3)
A large (24 unit) treed site is located in a sandy cove on Woss Lake. The wharf and boat launch are used by anglers, while Woss Lake is a popular swimming hole for locals.

Zeballos (Map 32/F7)
This small logging and fishing community offers a riverside campsite. There is a good public boat launch onto the inlet.

South Island Forest District

The South Island Forest District is a large area that covers all of the South and Central Island as well as the the many offshore islands in the area. Easily the most populated region, private property can and does limit access to many areas. There is good highway, rural road and logging road access throughout the area but visitors should be prepared to encounter gates in the most annoying of places. Regardless, the South Island offers fantastic fishing, a variety of trails, unrivaled paddling and some of the most impressive scenery in the world.

Arden Creek Rec Site & China Creek Park (Map 14/G4)
This small treed site is located on the shores of the Alberni Inlet, across the water from the more popular China Creek Regional Park. Both sites offer similar activities. Water enthusiasts can enjoy fishing, boating or even windsurfing and there are hiking trails, although the Arden Creek Trail is shorter than the China Creek Trail. If you prefer slightly less crowded camping conditions, Arden Creek is your better bet.

Bald Mountain (Map 8/D3)
A small, secluded tenting site is found on Cowichan Lake across from the popular Gordon Bay Park. The site is only accessible by canoe (or small boat) or trail (a 1.5 hour hike). From the rec site, a series of trails lead to the top of Bald Mountain or out to Marble Bay Road. Please respect private property in the area.

Blackies Beach (Map 14/B4)
This small tenting site is found on the southwest shore of Nahmint Lake. It is only accessible by walking from Riverside Main or by boat.

Caycuse (Map 8/B2)
The South Shore Road is a good gravel road that cars and RVs will have no trouble negotiating. This large (27 unit) beach front site is set in the forest on the shores of Cowichan Lake and even offers a pump with water. As with most sites on the lake, it is a popular location.

Clayoquot Arm Beach (Map 12/G5)
A medium (12 unit), primitive site that is strung out along a sandy beach. There is a boat launch, popular with the kayakers and boaters, while nearby trails are worth exploring. In particular, look for the J.N. Godfrey Nature Trail, a short trail leading down to a sandy cove. West Main is a good gravel road.

Cobble Hill (Map 9/G7)
A small day use area is located on top of 335 metre (1,100 ft) Cobble Hill. From here, there are excellent views of the Cowichan Valley and wildflowers in season. It is a hike-in only site.

Fairy Lake (Map 2/A1)
Found east of Port Renfrew, this RV friendly site is accessed from the paved Harris Creek Main. The large (30 unit), open site offers a sandy beach, a dock and cartop boat launch to help anglers. A nature trail leads from the shoreline east along the creek. This popular campsite has a tendency to flood in heavy rains but should be high and dry during the busy summer months. It is gated and closed in winter.

Father and Son Lake (Map 15/C5)
This small, primitive tent site nestled in an old growth cedar, fir and hemlock forest is as picture perfect as they come. It is hike-in access only, along a 3 km trail that offers some stellar vistas and the lake offers some great fishing for rainbow trout. Hikers can use this site as base camp while exploring the meadows and ridges in the surrounding area.

Flora Lake (Map 7/A3)
Despite its small and primitive nature, the Flora Lake Rec Site is very popular with the angling crowd. The site is also used as a base to explore fishing in other small lakes in the area (Crown, Francis, Darington, Dorothy, Arthur, etc.). Flora Lake Main provides 2wd access.

Heather Campsite (Map 7/F1)
A large (40 unit) beautiful site is found at the west end of Cowichan Lake. The beach is enjoyed by water lovers, the lake offers fabulous fishing and there are many sites to enjoy in the area. Hikers may want to venture to scenic Heather Mountain but be prepared for a long, stiff climb up. Timber West owned and operated, the site has good gravel road access.

Jordan River Recreation Area (Map 2/G5)

An extremely popular RV friendly, large (40 unit) open site that is famous for it's beach access and views. In winter, this is a popular surfing destination, while many summer recreationists enjoy the good salmon fishing in the area. It's not the prettiest site, as you camp in a large, open gravel area, but the views of the Juan De Fuca Straight and the Olympic Mountains across the way are terrific. It's popularity might stem from the fact that it is located just off the main highway from Victoria to Port Renfrew.

Kissenger (Map 7/F1)

This medium (20 unit) site is found on a small lake just west of Cowichan Lake.

Knob Point (Map 7/A4)

Possibly the best sailboarding in the entire province is found on Nitinat Lake and Knob Point is one of the best places to catch the breeze that blows down this long, narrow lake. Knob Point is also a popular staging area for people canoeing the Nitinat Triangle. The site itself is a small, semi-open site with a gravel boat launch.

gravel road.

Labour Day Lake (Map 15/F4)

It's a short walk in to this small, rustic tenting site. You can carry a canoe with you and paddle about the small lake, or you can take a short hike on the trail that circumnavigates the lake. A longer trail heads up towards Tangle Mountain from the east end of the lake. This is a popular destination for anglers. In the winter, this area is high enough to receive snow, and is a popular destination for snowmobilers and cross country skiers in winter.

Lizard Lake (Map 2/C1)

This site has been upgraded to a large campsite complete with wharf and trail around the lake. The new site is now gated and charges a higher fee. The lake offers good fishing and a nice place to take a dip in the deep, clear water.

Lowry Lake (Map 22/A6)

A small, primitive site is found north of Great Central Lake on the much smaller Lowry Lake. During spring and fall this is a popular destination for anglers and there is a cartop boat launch. The rough 2wd access may discourge some visitors.

Mactush/Bill Motyka (Map 14/F5)

A huge (100 unit) well developed rec site offers 45 open and 55 treed campsites. Managed by Scouts Canada on behalf of Weyerhaeuser, the site is only open in the summer. Visitors will find two boat launches, one concrete, one natural, access to the beach and a number of eagle aeries in the area. The site is accessed by a good

Maple Grove (Map 8/B2)

Yet another nice place to camp on the popular Cowichan Lake. This large treed site has a gravel beach and a boat launch ramp that is not recommended for boats over 14 feet. The close proximity to the North Shore Road can make this site a little noisier than others on the lake.

Nahmint Lake (Map 14/B3)

A small site is located in an old growth forest next to this pretty lake. There is a cartop boat launch for anglers and paddlers. Although the Nahmint Main is accessible by most vehicles, this site is not recommended for RVs.

Nitinat Lake (Map 7/B4)

A medium sized site that is usually overrun with sailboarders. Anglers and paddlers will find a cartop boat launch. The small access road is found off South Main.

Nixon Creek (Map 7/G2)

Boaters and tenters looking for a bit more privacy may like this site since it is not a drive-to camping area. Instead a short trail leads to a large treed site with a fine gravel beach on the shores of Cowichan Lake. There is a nearby nature trail to explore.

Old Mill (Map 16/D5)

This area has long been a favourite destination of Nanaimo residents. Timberwest has been kind enough to formalize this site into a large (35

unit) wooded campsite. Found along the shores of First Lake, there is a boat launch, a beach and a 30 minute hiking trail to Windy Point.

Pine Point (Map 8/B2)

As the number of recreation sites and provincial parks indicate, Cowichan Lake is a fabulous South Island destination. Good fishing, paddling, swimming, nearby trails or just plain lounging around keep visitors coming back year after year. The Pine Point Rec Site is a large, open lakeside site located just west of Youbou. There is a small boat (less than 14 feet) launch.

San Juan Bridge (Map 2/D1)

A small (6 unit) site is found near a fine gravel beach on the San Juan River. The San Juan is a sluggish, shallow river and is great for wading about in on hot summer days. Shade is provided by a giant Sitka spruce.

Sarita Lake (Map 6/E2)

A small (2 unit) site provides a cartop boat launch for anglers and paddlers. Do not pitch your tent too close to the lake, especially in rainy weather, as the water level on the lake rises quickly. The Bamfield Road is a good (but bumpy) gravel road.

Scout Beach (Map 22/A6)

This medium sized site is set on the shores of Great Central Lake. The site is often used as a launching point for people looking to canoe to the end of Great Central, then hike up to Della Falls. The wind can blow up fast on the lake, and there are very few places to get off, so be careful. Branch 83 provides 2wd access.

Snow Creek (Map 13/G1)

A small (7 unit), rustic site is tucked away on the southwest end of Taylor Arm of Sproat Lake. There is a rocky (some would say cartop only) boat launch and a rocky beach. This site is popular with the windsurfing crowd and anglers. South Taylor Main provides good gravel road access.

Spring Beach (Map 8/E4)

This small walk-in tenting site on Cowichan Lake offers some peace and solitude as it is hidden from Meade Creek Road by the deep, dark thickets of hemlock and cedar. Unfortunately, one can still hear the distant rumble of logging trucks rolling by. The tenting spots are located on the edge of a large gravel beach, where you can enjoy a swim in the warm lake.

Toquart Bay (Map 13/C7)

A popular site on the north side of the picturesque Barkley Sound. The site sees a lot of traffic from kayakers heading out into the sound or to the Broken Islands. It is also a popular launching point for anglers heading out onto the Pacific, as there is a concrete boat launch. The campsite itself is a large, open, flat area with space for about 15 tents down by the ocean and a lot of room for any number of tents, RVs, cars and other campers behind. Great for accessibility, terrible for privacy.

Windy Point (Map 16/E5)

This popular camping area has finally formalize by the folks Timberwest. The large (30 unit) site is found where the Nanaimo River flows into First Lake. There is a boat launch onto the slow meandering river, a beach and a covered picnic shelter. A short 30 minute trail connects with the Old Mill Campsite.

Multi-use Trails

(Hiking, Mountain Biking, Horseback Riding and More)

Vancouver Island is home to one of Canada's—and possibly the world's—best known trails. But while the West Coast Trail gets all the press, and a fair bit of the traffic, there are other trails for everyone from day hikers to hardcore backpackers to enjoy.

This section contains brief descriptions of over 250 trails, including information about length, location and difficulty. Time and distance given is for a return trip, unless otherwise noted. Also included in each description is a symbol to indicate what the trail is used for—mountain biking, hiking, horseback riding, etc. Multi-use trail descriptions are written from a hiker's point of view, and mountaineering and climbing opportunities are also noted.

Finding the trailhead can often be the most difficult part of the journey. Always refer to the appropriate map to determine where the trail begins. Remember that trails that are accessed off of logging roads often have restricted access on weekdays.

Despite the wealth of trails listed below, it is still only presents a fraction of the outdoor opportunities on the islands. Game trails, old logging roads and half-forgotten trails lead the intrepid explorer ever onward. Our maps will help motor bikers and ATV users find endless road systems to enjoy.

Keeping track of mountain biking trails is especially difficult. New trails are often built illegally, enjoy a brief moment of popularity, then abandoned. Some trails have been logged over, while others are only known to a few secretive riders. For the most part, this guidebook will direct you to established trails or into popular mountain biking areas. Remember, it's always best to check with local riders or local bike shops to find the state of a particular trail, or to discover a hidden rat's nest of trails that has just been developed.

Hiking Trails are usually tagged with one of the following descriptors:

An **easy trail** has gentle grades, and is suitable for family excursions. A **moderate trail** can involve a long, steep hill, some scrambling and is probably enough to tax most users. Just because they're not considered difficult, doesn't mean that they aren't challenging. Don't overestimate your ability or underestimate the difficulty of the trail. Only experienced trail users should consider **difficult routes**. These trails are often rough and/or unmarked.

Also note that we use the word trail to describe marked, often well-travelled paths. The word route is used for unmarked and often rarely travelled, hard to follow routes. These are best left to experienced hikers with strong route-finding skills. These maps provide a general reference, but when travelling on long trails or unmarked routes, you should also carry a topographic map.

The same words are used to describe mountain bike specific trails, too, though they mean different things. An easy trail has gentle grades and is suitable for even the greenest of riders. A moderate trail will have more taxing climbs, faster downhills, tighter corners, and some technical sections (roots, boulders, etc.). A difficult trail is the sort of riding you'll see on the Outdoor Life Network: highly technical, with steep dropoffs and many more chances for you to land on your helmet. If you're not sure you're up to it, you probably aren't.

We have grouped our trails into the following sections:

- Campbell River Area
- Comox/Courtney Area
- Cowichan Valley/Duncan Area
- Gulf Islands
- Nanaimo Area
- North/Northwest Island Trails
- Pacific Rim Park/West Coast Area
- Parksville/Qualicum Area
- Port Renfrew Area
- Strathcona Provincial Park
- Victoria and Area

Campbell River Area

Beaver Lodge Forest Lands (Map 36/F7) 🚶 🐎 🚴
Close to 10 km of easy, interconnected trails crisscross this 415 ha parcel of forested land on the west side of Campbell River.

Canyon View Trail (Map 36/E6) 🚶 👣
A 6km (1.5hour) easy loop trail circumnavigates a portion of the Campbell River. The trail leads through a mix of natural beauty and man-made attractions, including salmon spawning channels, the John Hart Generating Station, and over a 24 metre (78 ft) high bridge that offers the canyon views the trail is named for.

Elk Falls Trail (Map 36/E6) 🚶 👣
There are 6 km of mostly easy trails in Elk Falls Park, which derives its name from the 25m (82 ft) waterfall on the Campbell River. The Elk Falls trail itself is 4 km (45 minute), return, although you can continue on along a more difficult trail to Moose and Deer Falls. The falls are best viewed in the winter when there's a higher volume of water flowing.

Goose Lake Trail (Map 36/B4) 🚶 🐟 🚴
An easy 2.7 km loop from pretty Morton Lake to the smaller and more remote Goose Lake.

McNair Lake Trail (Map 36/A1) 🚶 🐟 🚴
This easy 3.6 km trip takes you to McNair Lake, along an old railbed.

Menzies Mountain Lookout Trai (Map 36/B2) 🚶 👣 🚴
Although it's an easy trail to the former forestry lookout on Menzies Mountain (you can still get a 4wd up the old road), the climb does get a little stiff in some places. The open views from the top are well worth the effort.

Old Rail Grades (Map 35/G5) 🚶 🚴
An easy loop trail runs between Brewster Lake Road and Menzies Mainland along an old, partially overgrown logging railbed.

Oyster River Park Trails (Map 29/A2) 🚶 🚴
From Salmon Point Lodge, south of Campbell River this gentle ocean side walk can take up to 2 hours return. As with most ocean walks, there is plenty of marine life to watch for.

The Pumphouse (Map 36/F6) 🚴
This series of trails, mostly moderate to difficult, is found near Elk Falls Provincial Park. Park near the bridge, where Duncan Bay Main leaves Highway 28 and crosses Campbell River, then bike up to the Blue Water Trail, where the trails start. There are about 15 km of trails, and a lot of little tricks, whoop-dee-doos, drops, jumps, etc. There is a trail that connects to the Snowden Lake area.

Quinsam Nature Trails (Map 36/E6) 🚶 👣 📖
From Elk Falls Provincial Park, the Quinsam River Trail follows the Quinsam River for 4 km to the Quinsam Salmon Hatchery (2 hrs return). This is an easy hike.

Ripple Rock Trail (Map 36/D4) 🚶 👣
One of the more popular trails in the area, this is a fairly easy 8 km (2 hr return) hike. From the signed highway parking area the trail takes you through patches of old growth past Menzies Bay to Wilfred Point overlooking former Ripple Rock in Seymour Narrows. Ripple Rock was one of the most notorious marine hazards along the entire West Coast until the largest man-made, non-nuclear explosion in history blew it up in 1958. There are nice viewpoints and resting spots along the way, with the most notably being the beach at Nymphe Cove.

Salmon Lookout Trail (Map 35/D1) 🥾 🚴

From Highway 19, this short 6 km return hike leads to an old forestry lookout. The stiff climb is rewarded with excellent views of the Salmon River Valley.

Skidmarks (Map 36/D6) 🚴 🚵

You'll find the trailhead for this difficult 2.5 km trail near the top of Radar Hill (Johnson's Lookout). Lots of two and three foot drops, with connections to a couple other trails in the area, including Bohemian Drop Zone and The Needle.

Snowden Demonstration Forest Trails (Map 36/C5) 🥾 🚴 🚵

There are 30+ km of easy to moderate trails located in the Snowden Demonstration forest, mostly along old railbeds and logging roads. The longest single trail is 8.2 km (2 hrs), but you can easily string together any number of trails for a full day's hiking or a half day biking. The trails are divided into two sections, The Frog Lake Trail System, and the Lost Lake Trail System. There are also three very short (from 0.3 km to 1.1 km) interpretive trails along Snowden Road that are not connected to the main trail system.

To add to the mix, there are nearly 70 km of unmarked mountain biking trails, some developed illegally, some developed with mixed blessings from the Forest Service found in the area.

🥾 🚴 🚵

Enchanted Forest: A 4.3 km loop along a rough logging road. Cyclists will find it easiest to do clockwise.
Lookout Loop: A 3.2 km trail around Elmer Lake, with some moderate climbs to an open viewpoint over Lily Pond.
Old Rail Trail: A 4.2 km easy loop along a historical rail grade.
Riley Lake Connector: A 2 km trail that connects the Frog Lake Trails to the Lost Lake Trails.

🥾 🚴 🚵

Frog Lake Road: A 5.7 km link between Frog Lake Trails and Lost Lake Trails. Easy, except for Cardiac Hill, a long, stiff climb that'll tax the lungs of hikers and mountain bikers alike.
The Lost Frog: An easy 8.2 km loop along an old railbed that shares about 1.5 km of the path with the Lost Lake Trail.
Lost Lake Trail: A moderate 5.5 km loop around lost lake with a short side trail to a rocky viewpoint.
Mudhoney Pass: A 3 km trail through rock, salal and Douglas-fir forests.

Willow Creek Trail (Map 36/G7) 🥾 🚴

A 3.4 km (1.5 hour) easy hike with various access points along a salmon enhancement creek south of Campbell River. Erickson, Martin and Dahl Roads all access the trail.

Comox/Courtenay Area

Alone Mt Trail (Map 21/G1) 🥾 🚴

A good spring hike leads into the wildflower-filled meadows. The views from 847m (2,779 ft) summit make the challenging hike worthwhile.

B21/Boston Main (Maps 28/G7, 29/A7) 🚵

A moderate logging road that connects Forbidden Plateau to the Comox Lake mountain biking area. The roadbed has been washed out in many sections, and is very rocky throughout.

Cape Lazo (Map 29/F6) 🥾 🚴

More of a beach walk. This scenic area is enjoyed by beachcombers.

Comox Lake Mountain Bike Area (Map 29/A7) 🚴 🚵

There's a lot more trails in this area than just the named trails. Tucked into the corner formed by the Puntledge River flowing out of Comox Lake is a series of mountain bike trails—B21, Bics, Arbutus, Salamander, etc.—ranging from moderate (the ex-logging road B21, see above) to difficult (the highly technical Nymph Falls Trail, see below) .

Century Sam Trail (Map 21/D2) 🥾 ⛺ 🚴 🎣 🚵

This unmaintained, often rough 4.6 km moderate trail leads along the south side of Comox Creek to a small lake with good fishing and a nice campsite. The remote trail is difficult to access (a 4wd vehicle is necessary).

Comox Glacier Trail/Route (Map 21/D2) 🏔 🥾 ⛺

Give yourself three days to hike this difficult route, with the first and third days hiking to and from base camp at Frog Pond Wilderness Site. The trail to Frog Pond is fairly easy to follow, but beyond that, the route is rough and difficult to follow, over Lone Tree Pass and down onto Comox Glacier. This is also the beginning (or end) of a number of longer routes into Strathcona Provincial Park.

The Dump (Map 29/B7) 🥾 🚴 🚵

Not an area where you will find many hikers or casual bikers. The odour takes care of that. Serious mountain bikers dig the area around the Pigeon Lake Landfill as it is a good area for moderate singletrack, with some funky technical sections.

Forbidden Plateau (Map 28/D-G7) 🥾 🎣 ⛺ 🚴 🚵

For more information on hiking in this area, check out the Strathcona Park listings. For mountain bikers, grunt up the long access road, then pick your route down. Some of these trails (most notably B21) hook up with the Comox Lake area.

Idiens-Capes Lake Route (Map 21/E1) 🥾 🎣 🚴

A steep climb up a blazed route leads to a pair of picture perfect lakes on the Lee Plateau. A moderate 6.5 km trail also accesses a memorial cairn.

Kookjai Mtn to Comox Glacier Route (Map 21/E2) 🏔 🥾 ⛺ 🚴

The first two hours of whacking through bush isn't a very promising start to this alternative route to Comox Glacier. At the edge of Strathcona Park, you will hit old growth trees, which makes the going to Frog Pond a lot easier.

Mount Washington X-C Ski Trails (Map 28/E5) 🥾 🚴

A 35 km network of easy hiking trails on the fringe of Strathcona Park offers many rewarding views of the Strathcona mountain peaks (see also Cross Country Skiing).

Nymph Falls Trail (Map 29/B7) 🚶‍♂️🎣🚲

A moderate hike along the north shore of the Puntledge River. Mountain bikers will find this trail surprisingly difficult for such a level trail, with lots of obstacles.

Puntledge River Trail (Map 29/B7) 🚶‍♂️🎣🚲

A series of trails are found along the south banks of the Puntledge River. The eastern trailhead is found about 1.5km from the Duncan Bay Mainline that juts off the Comox Lake Trail/Road.

Seal Bay Park (Map 29/C5) 🚶‍♂️🎣🚲

There are over 24 km of easy trails through a park that encompasses both heavily wooded forest, marshy lowlands and oceanfront access. Mountain biking is restricted to the east side of the park.

Upper Puntledge River Trail (Map 21/F3) 🚶‍♂️🎣

You will have to canoe across Willemar and Forbush Lakes (there's a 300 metre portage between the two) to find the trailhead for this 8 km hike. Although the terrain is gentle, the overgrown nature of the old road may impede progress. The trail accesses an old growth forest and a pretty waterfall.

Cowichan Valley/Duncan Area

Bald Mountain Trails (Map 8/D3) 🚶‍♂️🎣

The Bald Mountain Trails consists of a trio of moderate interlocking loops. The longest trail, The Denninger Trail, is about 8 km long and climbs to an old forestry lookout on Bald Mountain over Cowichan Lake. The summit is located at the 629 metre (2, 064 ft) mark.

Bright Angel Park (Map 9/F6) 🚶‍♂️🎣🚲

There is about 5 km of easy, well kept trails on both sides of the Koksilah River in this small, provincial park found south of Duncan. The trails provide easy access to the river for fishing and swimming.

Burnt Bridge Area (Map 9/E7) 🚶‍♂️🚲

Oh, how the mighty have fallen. A few years ago, this was the hot spot for mountain biking in the Duncan area, maybe even all Vancouver Island. But the Burnt Bridge Race is no more, and active logging has not only decimated parts of some trails, but logging trucks add an unwelcome, unnatural hazard. As logging is ongoing at this time, there's no final word as to the state of the trails. They were in mostly good condition at press time.

Cobble Hill Trails (Map 9/G7) 🚶‍♂️🐎🎣

Over a dozen short, easy/moderate trails, ranging from a few hundred metres to about a kilometre are found north of Shawnigan Lake. There are four viewpoints from the top of Cobble Hill overlooking the Cowichan Valley and beyond. The northern side of the park offers the better viewing areas.

Cowichan River Footpath (Map 9/B5) 🚶‍♂️🎣🎣

This classic hike follows the Cowichan River for 20 km (40 km return), from Glenora (at the end of Robertson Road) to Skutz Falls. The trail is mostly easy, though its length may deter some. West of Skutz Falls, the newly established Trans Canada Trail route follows the abandoned CN Rail all the way to the Lake Cowichan town site. Some of the highlights of the area include the beautiful river views, sections of old growth trees and the revamped Marie Canyon Trestle. Be sure to bring your fishing rod.

Diddon Price Trail (Map 8/F3) 🚶‍♂️🎣

This trail is no longer maintained but a route does still access the old lookout and ridge beyond. A short (1.5 km), steep trail leads from the Satellite Station Road to a lookout over Cowichan Lake.

Heart Lake Trail (Map 9/C1) 🚶‍♂️🎣

This 6 km (3 hour) moderate hike starts up a steep trail before flattening out and circumnavigating the tiny Heart Lake. The total elevation gain from Davis-Battie Road in Ladysmith is 240 metres (787 ft).

Heather Mountain Trail (Map 7/F1) 🚶‍♂️🎣

From the northwest corner of Cowichan Lake, this hike is 14 km (6 hour) long if you can get past the gate and your vehicle can handle the rough access road. If not, add an extra 2 km (1 hour) both ways hiking up to where the logging road washes out. It's steep, but the alpine meadows flush with wildflowers (including heather) and panoramic views from the top are worth it.

Hill 60 Route (Map 9/B4) 🚶‍♂️🎣

Pick your way up to a 450 metre (1,476 ft) high ridge between the Cowichan and Chemainus valleys. It's a short, stiff hike up to the ridge from the Branch 8 logging road to the top of the ridge, which you can follow for 7 km (14 km return). A number of logging road crossings can confuse the issue. You can also access the route from any of the aforementioned logging roads.

Legion Trail (Map 3/G1) 🚶‍♂️🎣

East of Shawnigan Lake, this is an easy 3 km loop.

Lomas Lake/El Capitan Mountain (Map 8/C1) 🚶‍♂️🎣

There are two trails up to Lomas Lake, one from the west and one from the south. Both are about 7 km return of moderate hiking if you can get past the gate. If not, add a 6 km hike both ways along the logging road. Your best access is from the west, up a rough logging road and then an old miner's trail to this picture perfect lake nestled in the shadow of El Capitan Mountain. A difficult route beyond the lake (approx. 2 km return) takes you past an old mine and climbs 350 metres (1,150 ft) up El Capitan. You can also access Mount Landale and Mount Service along difficult, faintly marked or unmarked routes.

Maple Mountain Trails (Map 9/G3, 10/A3) 🚶‍♂️🎣

Four trails, ranging from a one hour jaunt along the easy Green Trail (2.6 km), to the two hour, slightly more taxing Blue Trail (5.1 km) take you up the mountain or down to the beach. Hikers will enjoy forested walks with great views over Sansum Narrows and the Gulf Islands.

Mesachie Mountain Trail (Map 8/E4) 🚶‍♂️🎣

It is about an hour from the trailhead to the 420 metre (1,377 ft) Mesachie Mountain summit, a mossy outcropping overlooking the Cowichan Valley.

Mount Prevost Area (Map 9/E4) 🚶‍♂️🐎🎣🚲

This is a rat's nest of trails, built by various interest groups, including the Boy Scouts, horse riders and mountain bikers. Near the 794 metre (2,605 ft) summit is a war memorial, with a great viewpoint looking east.

Mount Richards (Map 9/F3) 🚶‍♂️🎣

A steep, moderate scramble climbs 314m (1,030 ft) up a game trail to the summit of Mount Richards. Allow 45 minutes; longer if you enjoy the views.

Mount Sutton Trail (Map 8/A4) 🚶‍♂️🎣🎣

A moderate 5 hour climb to the scenic 1,170 metre (3,839 ft) summit of Mount Sutton. Currently the cable crossing over the Gordon River is out. The Sierra Club of Vancouver Island hopes to have this fixed by the summer of 2001.

Mount Tzouhalem (Map 9/G5) 🚶‍♂️🎣🚲

With Burnt Bridge losing popularity, Mt Tzouhalem is now the place to go for mountain bikers. The area east of Duncan is rife with trails, but is currently under scrutiny as various interest groups vie for access to the area. Good vantage points, rare plants, native flowers and Garry Oak make this an interesting place to visit. Check with a local cycle shop as to the current political climate before loading up your bike.

Nixon Creek Trails (Map 7/G2) 🚶‍♂️🏕️

From the South Shore Road, an easy 2km hike follows the beach to the Nixon Creek Rec Site, a walk-in campsite on the shores of Cowichan Lake. There is also a 1km long nature trail through the forest in the area.

Old Baldy Mountain Trail (Map 3/G1) 🚶‍♂️🎣

This unmarked and often hard to follow trail leaves the Easter Seal Camp property, crosses the railroad tracks, then heads up to a viewpoint at the summit of Mt Baldy. Expect a one hour hike.

Shaw Valley Routes (Map 15/E7) 🚶‍♂️🎣

An old game trail continues on from the end of West Shaw Mainline and up to Balmer Lake. From here, you can head west to the 1,491m (4,892 ft) high Mt Hooper, east to the 1,384m (4,540 ft) high Marmot

Mountain, or north to Sadie Creek or Nitinat River (both of which hook up with logging roads to either Port Alberni or Nanaimo). These are difficult day hikes that offer fine views and wildflowers in season.

Spectacle Lake Park (Map 4/A2)
A mix of secondary logging roads and 4X4 roads make up the 18 km moderate loop past the tiny Spectacle Lake, out of the park itself, and past the larger Oliphant Lake 1.5 km north before looping back to the beginning. You can also take a 6 km side loop around the 616 metre (2,020 ft) Mt Wood.

Gulf Island Trails

Trails in this section are listed alphabetically by island. Because the Gulf Islands have such a low profile, hiking is usually neither lengthy nor extremely challenging. Few trails are more than a few kilometres. This is not to say that all the trails are easy. Many 300+ metre (1,000 ft) mountains are climbed in little more than a kilometre, which can be too stiff a climb for some. The rewards include fantastic ocean and/or island scenery, arbutus trees, marine life and endless beaches. Mountain bikers should note that outside of a few notable exceptions, they are restricted to the more traditional on-road bike touring.

Denman Island
Boyle Point Park (Map 23/B4) is an easy 7 km hike through a second growth forest to the scenic Chrome Island Lighthouse.

Fillongley Park Trail (Map 23/A2) is an easy 2 km walk through an old growth forest and down to the sea. You can extend your hike along the beach

Gabriola Island
Seymour Road Area (Map 17/D4) offers several trails/old roads to explore in and around the area. Knit them together to make an hour or two of easy hiking.

Galiano Island
Bluffs Park (Map 10/E3) offers a couple of different options to explore. Off Bluffs Road, a trail leads north through the lush forest along a broad, well developed trail. This pleasant walk will take you to a down to Sturdies Bay Ferry Terminal. In all you will descend 400 ft (120 m) over 5km. It is a little more challenging to hike it from the ferry terminal (partly due to the difficulty in finding the trailhead). At the place called The Bluffs, a rough road leads to a spectacular lookout over Active Pass. From the lookout, broad trails head in both directions and offer several other vantage points. These easy trails also lead through the impressive forest. Between the two areas, one can easily spend a few hours exploring.

Bodega Ridge (Map 10/B1) is an easy, 3km ridge walk with great views, occasional wildlife sightings, and plenty of Arbutus trees. Considered by some to be the finest ridge walk in BC, the trail elevation gain is 282 metres (925 ft). If you start from the south end (off either Vineyard or Cottage Way), you can also stretch this hike into a challenging 14 km moderate trek to Dionisio Park. The route mostly follows old overgrown roads and crosses private property.

Mountain biking The Bluffs on Galiano Island

Coon Bay Trail (Map 17 Inset G1) starts at the end of Porlier Pass Road (park near the postal boxes). Be sure to ask for permission before crossing the Indian Reserve and continue through the gated road toward the lighthouse. Look for the faint trail through the old orchard that leads around the tiny inlet. This trail soon turns into a good trail, which picks it's way along the rugged northern coast of the island. There are several chances to explore the wave-swept shoreline or you can continue along the trail. It leads past a midden, an ancient Indian Village, to Coon Bay in Dionisio Point. From Porlier Pass to Coon Bay, the trail is about 1.5 km long. Do not be fooled by the distance, the pure beauty of the area and the many other trails to explore will make this a good day trip.

Dionisio Park (Map 17 Inset G1) is a marine (boat) access park that offers a short network (about 3km total) of trails. The trails lead through old growth forest, along the shoreline, or out to Dionisio Point. Set up a tent and stay awhile, fishing, swimming, or just watching life go by, Gulf Islands-style.

Montague Harbour Park (Map 10/D2) offers a lovely 3km (1 hour) trail that circles the forested Gray Peninsula, next to the lagoon. There are many beaches and viewpoints along the way, including a rare (and protected) white-shell beach to explore. Families should allow a little longer as the kids will surely want to explore every nook and cranny along the many beaches. The trail does have one set of stairs to negotiate.

Mount Galiano (Map 10/E3) is the highest point on Galiano Island, at a mere 311m (1,020 ft). From Georgeson Bay Road, follow the signs to Mount Galiano Trail. Here a trail climbs, initially through the forest and heavy canopy, to a fantastic lookout. The 6km (2 hour) return hike makes a fine destination on clear days when you can see many of the surrounding Gulf Islands.

Hornby Island

Coltsfoot (Map 23/B2) is a 6km trail (or old road) leading to the firehall on Central Road.

Helliwell Park (Map 23/C2) offers a 5 km (1.5 hour) easy loop. The trail starts in an old growth Douglas-fir forest before skirting along a sandstone cliff with lovely ocean views.

High Salal Trail (Map 23/C3) connects Helliwell Provincial Park with Tribune Provincial Park. This trail follows an old road 3.5km one-way along a bluff overlooking Tribune Bay.

Mount Geoffrey Regional Nature Park (Map 23/B3) is an area especially popular with mountain bikers. This 303 ha nature park on Hornby Island offers a mess of multi-use trails.

Summit Trail (Map 23/B3) offers a nest of trails that hook up with either Strachan Road or Central Road. The trail takes explorers up to the 330 metre (985 ft) summit of Mt Geoffrey. Depending on what route you take up, the length and time required will change. Expect to hike a minimum of 8 km in about 2.5 hours. Unfortunately, due to public abuse, both the Bench and

Spit Trails (which skirt the bluffs below) are no longer open to public access.

Mayne Island

Helen Point Trails (Map 10/F3) 🚶 🚴 begin on an easy 9 km (3 hour) trail along a Hydro road. There are fine views of Active Pass and access to beaches and coves in the area as well as side routes branching off the road to extend your adventure. The trail crosses the Indian Reserve on the western point of the island, so get permission from the band before you strike out.

Mt Parke (Map 10/F4) 🚶 🚴 offers several steep, unkept trails that climb the 255 metre (836 ft) peak of Mt Parke, Mayne's highest point. Watch for bald eagles and turkey vultures playing in the thermals and updrafts around the peak.

Pender Islands (North/South)

Mt Norman Regional Park (Map 10/G & Inset E1) 🚶 🚴 🚵 is highlighted by an easy, though steep, trail beginning from Ainslie Point Road. The 2 km (1 hour) hike climbs up to the 244 metre (800 ft) high Mt Norman. The trail also intersects with a 2 km trail through Beaumont Provincial Marine Park to a viewpoint over the tiny Skull Islet and Starvation Bay. The trail to Mt Norman continues over the top of the mountain and down to the beach below Canal Road. This will add an extra 4 km onto your round trip.

Quadra Island

Cape Mudge (Map 36/G7) 🚶 🚴 is the popular fishing area seen from the old Island Highway in southern Campbell River. Island dwellers can enjoy about 6 km of trails around Cape Mudge. From the village, the Oceanside walk leads past the lighthouse and lodge to secluded beaches.

China Mountain Trails (Map 36/F3) 🚶 🚴

are sometimes refered to as Chinese Mountain. By whatever name you call it, the trail is a moderate 5km (2 hour) hike up a steep trail and over the mossy knolls that form the twin peaks of this mountain. The south peak is your highest point at 327 metres (1,072 ft), 12 metres (39 ft) higher than the north peak. From either peak there are good views of the Mainland and Northern Gulf Islands.

Community Hall Trail (Map 36/G6) 🚶 is an easy 1.5 km hike leading from the Community Hall in Blenkin Park to Heriot Bay Road. It provides a leisurely stroll at the southern end of the island.

Morte Lake Trail (Map 36/F3) 🚶 🚴 is a moderate 6 km (3 hour) circuit leading to the shores of Morte Lake through the second growth forest and along the ridge at the foot of China Mountain. A second loop around the lake will add 3km (1 hour) to your trip. The trailhead is found of Morte Lake Road.

Newton Lake Trial (Map 36/F1) 🚶 🚴 🚵 starts from Granite Bay Main. This is a pleasant 6.5 km (2 hour) one-way hike leads along an old road and past a handful of (five) small lakes. Newton Lake is the largest of the bunch. Past Newton Lake, the trail continues on for another 3.5 km one-way past Small Inlet and through a canyon before ending at Waiatt Bay

Nugedzi Lake Trail (Map 36/F3) 🚶 🚴 is a 10 km (4 hour) moderate hike. The trail starts along a steep, rocky road through stands of old growth and continues on to a pair of mountain lakes. From the lakes you have the option to explore other routes, including the difficult, unmarked route to Mt Seymour.

Rebecca Spit Trail (Map 36/G4) 🚶 🚴 🏖 is the long, narrow spit rimmed by beaches that thrusts into Heriot Bay and forms Drew Harbour. The area is popular with beachcombers and birdwatchers. Allow about 1.5 hours to walk the easy 4 km route.

Saltspring Island

Channel Ridge (Map 10/A2) 🚶 🚴 offers a series of unmarked but easy trails. The main route travels about 4.5 km from the trailhead on Sunset Drive to Canvasback Road.

Hope Hill Trails (Map 10/C6) 🚶 🚴 can be stitched together any way you like, but you're probably going to cover about 7 km (4 hour) of ground. The moderate hike starts in a second growth forest and leads to the top of Hope Hill.

Mount Bruce Trails (Map 10/B5) 🚶 🚴 were once a popular retreat for hikers but logging and private property have decimated the northern flank of this area. Regardless the 6 km (3 hour) moderate hike up to the top of this 711 metre (2,333 ft) peak is rewarded with fine views, wildflowers (in season) and close encounters with the rare Arbutus Tree. The trailhead is found off Musgrave Road.

Mount Tuam Area (Map 10/C6) 🚶 🚴 is another area affected by logging. The trailhead is located off Mountain Road (to the south) but you can pick any variety of routes up the open slopes of Tuam, most of them carved by the sheep that graze here. From the trailhead it is about a 6 km (2 hour) easy hike to the 602m (1,975 ft) summit.

Mount Erskine (Map 10/A3) 🚶 🚴 is a difficult 2.8 km (2 hour) trail up a steep slippery slope to a lookout just below the 411 metre (1,348 ft) summit of Mt Erskine. The trail is on private property so don't go wandering off the beaten path.

Mount Maxwell Provincial Park (Map 10/B5) 🚶 🚴 offers 5 km of trails but most people strike out for the 594m (1,949 ft) Baynes Peak. The moderately stiff hike climbs about 175m in elevation to a series of viewpoints. The other park trails take you through a second growth forest and through the thick understory of salal.

Reginald Hill Trail (Map 10/D5) 🚶 🚴 begins from the gate off Morningside Drive. The trail is a stiff, difficult 3 km hike up to the top of Reginald Hill. The views over Fulford Harbour and the San Juan Islands are breathtaking. Please respect the private property in the area and do not wander off the beaten path.

Ruckle Park Trails (Map 10/D5) 🚶 🚴 offers 10 km of easy hiking trails, through second growth forest, on bluffs overlooking the ocean, and down to the beaches that line the shore of this popular provincial park. Ruckle Park is the largest provincial campsite on the Gulf Islands.

Wallace Island (Map 10/A1) 🚶 ⛺ 🚴

All but a tiny pocket on this narrow, 3.5 km long island in Trincomali Channel between Saltspring and Galiano Islands is dedicated as a provincial park. An easy trail runs the length of both the island and the park from Chivers Point to Panther Point.

Nanaimo Area

Hikers visiting the Nanaimo/Ladysmith areas may be interested in picking up the detailed brochures describing a few of the trails in the area. They are available for $2 each at the travel info centre on Bowen Road in Nanaimo.

Baldy Mountain/Copley Mountain (Map 16/F2) 🚶 🚴

On a clear day, you can see Mount Baker, as well as closer points west. On a cloudy day, this trail offers little more than exercise. It is a moderately strenuous hike that takes about 2.5 hours to Baldy Mountain or 4.5 hours to Copley. Most of the trail follows an old roadbed.

Benson Creek Falls (Map 16/F3) 🚶 🚴

Benson Creek is currently an undeveloped area, though trail development is ongoing. The 24 metre (79 ft) high Ammonite Falls is easily the most popular destination and can be accessed from Jameson Road, from the first yellow gate you pass off Kilpatrick. Be warned, the hike through Benson ravine has claimed a number of careless hikers; don't be one of them.

Blackjack Ridge (Map 16/E3) 🚶 🚴 🚵

There is a 12 km moderate mix of roads and trails in the Round Lake area, usually accessed from Dumont Road. Much of the riding is accomplished on logging roads, but there is also some singletrack in the area. Ardent riders will find a good mix of other trails in the area, including the Malaspina Trail, a moderate, technical 5 km loop. Fishing is popular in the small lakes in the area.

Buttertubs Marsh Sanctuary (Map 17/A3) 🚶🧗

This 20 ha nature sanctuary at the end of Buttertubs Drive is a popular bird watching destination. There are 4.5 km of trails in the area that allow for easy stroll around the slough. These trails form part of the Trans-Canada Trail.

Cable Bay (Dodd Narrows) Nature Trail (Map 17/C4) 🚶🧗

An easy 6 km (2 hour) hike north and then east from the Harmac Mill Landfill on Nicola Road to Joan Point in Dodd Narrows. The shoreline is rugged and awe inspiring, and you might just catch a glimpse of a killer whale (Orca) from Joan Point. This is also a great place to watch the tidal surge as the ocean tries to squeeze between Vancouver Island and Mudge Island. If you turn west instead of east when you hit the shoreline (about 2 km into the hike, but you'll know it when you see it), you travel along Cable Bay to a logging boom, which doesn't sound exciting, but the boom is a known hangout for sea lions from fall through spring.

Colliery Dam Park (Map 17/A4) 🚶🛶🧗🚴

Another piece in the Trans Canada Trail puzzle, there are 2.5 km of easy trails around two small, dammed lakes that are popular swimming and fishing holes for locals. There are two access points to the trails, one at the parking lot on Nanaimo Lakes Road, the other from the corner of Wakesiah Avenue and Sixth Street.

Christie Falls Trail (Map 17/B7) 🚶🧗

A moderately difficult hike leads to Christie Falls on Bush Creek. Although the trail starts on a private access road, the Ladysmith Fish and Game Club Road, hikers are allowed. At the end of the road you will find a fish hatchery. Just before the hatchery, a narrow trail leads left from the road, skirting the parking lot and up to Christie Falls.

Extension Mine Trails (Map 17/A5) 🚶🧗🚴

Known to mountain bikers as the Abyss, a reference to a deep, narrow crack that the trail passes, the Extension Mine Trails are now a part of the Trans Canada Trail. This is a haven for both hikers and mountain bikers, who love following any of the dozens of trails that spiral off of the main trail. The Abyss/Extension Mine Trail itself is about an 8 km loop, and is considered a moderate ride or hike. Other biking trails in the area range from moderate to difficult. Watch out for old mine shafts. The trails can be accessed from either end, but is usually hiked from North to South to North, parking under the high voltage lines on Harewood Mines Road.

Green Mountain Area (Map 16/A6) 🚶🧗🚴

Written up as a popular hiking destination in many sources (including the previous edition of this guidebook), this former ski hill is home to 13 of the last 41 Vancouver Island Marmots. Although access to the area isn't closed to hikers, Green Mountain above 800m (2,600 ft) is designated a critical wildlife management area, and hikers are asked to avoid this area. Contact the Marmot Recovery Foundation (1-877-462-7668, www.marmots.org) for more information on the Vancouver Island Marmot, Canada's most endangered species.

Gemini Mountain Route (Map 16/A6) 🚶🧗

After an hour's hike up spur K30 on the road up to Green Mountain (see above), the road forks. Keep right. Keep right again when the main road up to Green Mountain switches back. The difficult 7 hour trail is marked with orange blazes. You will gain about 1,000m (3,280 ft) elevation by the time you reach the 1,508m (4,947 ft) summit. Be aware that parts of the trail up Green Mountain lie within the critical wildlife management area.

Hemer Provincial Park Trails (Map 17/C5) 🧗🚶🛶🐎🚴

There are a surprising amount of easy trails (about 10 km in total) lacing through this small provincial park on the shores of Holden Lake, about 7 km south of Nanaimo. The Morden Colliery Trail (see below) hooks up to Cedar Road, 2.4 km away. The plan is to eventually link Hemer Provincial Park with Morden Colliery Historic Park.

Mikola Downhill Delight (Map 17/A6) 🚴

A short (3km), steep, technical downhill ride is found near McKay Lake. Expect to take an hour to clear the technical singletrack section, then grunt back up Branch 1000 logging road to the start. The gate on Spruston Road is usually locked and is as good a starting point as any.

Morden Colliery Trail (Map 17/C5) 🧗🚶🚴

Following an old rail grade that used to link South Wellington with Boat Harbour, this easy 8 km route will someday link Hemer Provincial Park with Morden Colliery Historic Park. Currently, the middle section of the route is missing.

Morrell Lake Nature Sanctuary (Map 17/A4) 🚶🛶♿

Tucked in between the Island Parkway and Westwood Lake Park, there are 11.5 km of easy hiking through second growth Douglas fir and along the shores of Morrell Lake. Trails in this area also hook up with Westwood Lake Trails. One of the trails—Yew Loop—is wheelchair accessible.

Mount Benson (Map 16/F4) 🧗🚶🚴

There are several ways up to this 1,019m (3,343 ft) peak. The longest and most difficult route (some would also argue the most rewarding) heads out from Westwood Lake. It is a steep 7 hour climb to the summit. For easier access, try approaching from the southeast off of Nanaimo Lakes Road. There is a rocky 4wd road that will take you 3.5 km (1 hour) to the top. The last approach is from the northwest, where you can hike up the ridge to the top.

Nanaimo Parkway Trail (Map 16/G3) 🧗🚶🚴

A paved, 20 km trail that parallels the Nanaimo Parkway is a popular trail for carless commuters. If you are looking for an urban trail to stretch your legs a bit, maybe break out the in-line skates, well, this for you. If

you want to spend the day exploring Nanaimo green spaces, the Parkway also has links to many Nanaimo area parks and lakes. A part of the parkway, from Harewood Mines Road to Jingle Pot Road, is the designated route for the Trans Canada Trail.

Newcastle Park (Map 17/A3)

A short ferry ride from Nanaimo to the 306 ha Newcastle Provincial Park opens up 21 km of easy hiking trails that circle, intersect and dissect this wooded island. Bikes are allowed only on the Kanaka Bay and Mallard Lake trails. Popular destinations include Nares Point, Giovando Lookout, Kanaka Bay and Mallard Lake and you can swim in Kanaka Bay or off the wharf. If you want to circumnavigate the island, expect to take over 2 hours as there are many secluded coves to explore. The ferry for Newcastle is a short walk from Departure Bay and is a popular destination for mainlanders who walk on at Horseshoe Bay.

Westwood Lake Area (Map 16/G4)

The Westwood Lake area off Westwood Road is one of the best places to go to experience what hiking in the Nanaimo area is like. A mix of easy to moderate trails (almost all of which connect back to the Lake Trail) loop higher and higher up Westwood Ridge on the southwest side of the lake. The terrain ranges from the 5.5 km (1.5 hour) easy Lake Trail, to 7 hour grunt up to the top of Mount Benson (see above).

North/Northwest Island Trails

Adam Ridge Route (Map 34/C4)

A difficult 6 km (2 hour) route accessed off UA Main, just past the southern boarder of Schoen Lake Provincial Park and about 4 km from the Schoen Lake parking lot. This trail follows the long ridge that extends east from Mount Adam.

Antler Lake Trail (Map 26/E3)

This easy 4 km (2 hour) hike leads to a scenic picnic spot on Antler Lake. The trail is just a short way off the main highway (turn onto spur road C1, then again onto Head Bay Forest Service Road).

Beautiful Bay Trail (Map 47/B1)

On the north side of Malcolm Island, this scenic trail winds along a ridge and through the coastal rainforest. The trail is accessed from the Bere Point Park.

Calvin Creek Trail (Map 24/F7)

A 2.5 km trail off of Crawfish Main leads down to a rugged, remote West Coast beach.

Cape Scott Park Trails (Map 37 Inset, 45/A)

Cape Scott Provincial Park offers a series of trails along old settler's roads and a telegraph line, through dense rainforest to the remotest point of Vancouver Island. Although the trails offer an unparralleled wilderness experience, one should expect unpredictable weather with wind, rain and lots of mud.

Cape Scott Trail is the signature trail within the park, a difficult, 23.6 km (8 hour) one-way hike through the heart of Cape Scott Provincial Park. The trail can be muddy, rocky and rooty but leads past historic Danish settlements, to the very tip of Vancouver Island and the infamous Cape Scott lighthouse. There are few places on the island as remote—or as wet—as this.

Eric Lake is an easy 3 km (1 hour) one-way hike along the Nissen Bight/Cape Scott trail to a camping spot on this warm, picturesque lake. Take a few minutes to check out a 7.2 metre (23.6 ft) diameter Sitka spruce located another 20 minutes past the turnoff to the Erick Lake camping area.

Nissen Bight is one of the most picturesque spots you can imagine but you're going to have to work to get here. It is a difficult 15 km (5 hour) one-way hike to the bight, which boasts a 2km long white sand beach in a slightly sheltered nook along the north coast of Vancouver Island.

San Josef Bay, An easy 2.5 km (1 hour) one-way hike takes you to the beaches at San Josef Bay.

Mount St. Patrick, Sea Otter Cove and Lowrie Bay, At 422m (1,385 ft), Mount St. Patrick is the highest point in the park. A difficult, rugged 5 km one-way trail leads to the summit, then continues on for another 5 km down to the beach in Sea Otter Cove. Continue overland to reach a campsite at Lowrie Bay. This

trail is poorly marked and rarely travelled; a sirens song to avid explorers, and a warning to everyone else. Expect to take about 5 hours one-way.

Sushartle River Trail, A difficult overgrown, almost non-existent trail leads 35 km (3 days) one-way east from Nissen Bight to the remote Sushartle River. The trail starts out well for a road that hasn't seen any work put into it for 70 years, but as you travel on, it often disappears into the salal and bush. There are also no remaining bridges, making crossing the Stranby and the Nahwitti Rivers difficult at the best of times and impossible during high water.

Deserted Lake Trail (Map 25/D5)

An easy 1.2 km hike leads from Hisnet Inlet to Deserted Lake.

Gold Lake Trail (Map 34/G7, 35/A7)

Give yourself about 2 hours to hike an easy 5 km one-way along an old road/trail from Salmon River Main logging road to the tip of Gold Lake. Starting in the northernmost reaches of Strathcona Park, the trail continues on, in much poorer condition, for another 3 km, hooking up with East Main Logging road. This is a high mountain trail, so expect snow well into June.

Grant Bay Trail (Map 37/D4)

A typical North Island trail (remote, rocky, rooty and muddy), travelling first through some clear cut, then through an old growth forest down to isolated sandy beaches in Grant Bay. Budget 1.5-2 hours each way to the mud flat on Browning Inlet, and 2.5 hours to the beach at Grant Bay. The total distance is about 10 km return to Grant Bay.

Hesquiat Peninsula Trail (Map 18/C4)

This is a spectacular but difficult journey that exposes backpackers to many remote west coast beaches. The 32 km, weeklong trek requires some bushwhacking around headlands, as it takes you from Escalante Point to Boat Basin. Designed for people with strong backpacking skills, the trail also passes by a number of First Nation Reserves, especially as it makes its way along the inner coast of Hesquiat Harbour. Camping is not permitted at these sites. From Boat Basin, there is an extremely rough route to Hotsprings Cove along an old telegraph trail (not shown on our maps).

Hoomak Lake Trail (Map 33/D2)

An easy 3km interpretive trail begins at the rest area off of Highway 19 and meanders to the shores of Hoomak Lake. This trail is also used as a footpath for anglers heading to Hoomak Lake.

Kaipit Lake Trail (Map 32/G3)

More of a route than a trail, this unmaintained, difficult 6 km trail follows an old fire access road from the end of Kaipit Road to the lake. This is a beautiful hike through some rugged north island terrain. The adventurous angler will find good fishing.

Lac Truite Port McNeill (Map 39/F7)

Once an informal fisherman's footpath to the tiny Lac Truite, this trail had been improved and is now managed by the Forest Service, in co-operation with MacMillian Blodel. This easy trail is 1 km long one-way.

Louie Bay Area (Map 24/C5)

There is about 3 km of trails in this remote, boat/floatplane access only knob of land along the northwest coast of the island. One trail (about 1 km long) leads south to sandy beaches, while another trail leads west to land's end and the ruins of a World War II radar station. For the more adventurous, the Nootka Island Trail is described below.

Malcolm Island (Map 47 inset)

Malcolm Island offers a relatively flat 12 km mountain bike route that offers beach access, spectacular views and camping. From Sointula (where the ferry lands) follow the main road, past Rough Bay to the north side of the island.

Marble River Trail (Map 39/A2)

An old fisherman's trail that is now the central trail in Marble River Provincial Park. This easy 7.4 km trail follows the southern bank of the Marble River on the bench above a shallow canyon, through a mature hemlock/balsam forest to several popular steelhead fishing spots. You can access the trail from Port Alice Road.

Matchlee Mountain (Map 26/G7) 🛶🚶

A rough, undeveloped route starts from the end of an equally rough logging road. The route travels over rugged alpine terrain and is mostly used by climbers heading up Matchlee. It is about 2 km one way from the logging road to Matchlee Peak.

Mount Cain Park (Map 33/G1) 🚶🏂⛷🛶

Trails cut for skiing in winter provide hikers and bikers summer access to alpine on this 1,804 metre (5,919 ft) peak. From the lodge at the base of the ski area, it's a 458m (1,503 ft) climb to the top of the lifts, and another 128m (420 ft) to the top of Cain. Your best bet is to follow the ridge (it heads left from the lodge if you're looking up the mountain) to the top of the lift.

Nootka Trail (Maps 18 & 24) 🚶🛶⛺

Though people have been hiking this coastal trail for twenty years, it is only in the last few years that it has started to develop interest outside a handful of backpackers. Skirting the west coast of Nootka Island, this difficult trail/route runs 30 km from the Louie Bay Lagoon to the Village of Yuquot at Friendly Cove, and takes most hikers about 6 days. One of a series of trails that is claimed to be a worthy successor to the West Coast Trail, the Nootka Trail is one of a very few that can actually live up to the claim. At 30 km, the trail is less than half the length of the West Coast Trail but makes up for it by its sheer remoteness. While the West Coast Trail has 56 walk-ons a day, the Nootka Trail is lucky to see that many a month. Because of it's remoteness, it costs more to get to (either by float plane or boat) but with trail fees on the West Coast Trail skyrocketing, it might not be that expensive an alternative. The trail is a lot of beach walking punctuated by difficult bushwhacks around headland along sometime cleared trails.

Owossitsa Lake Trail (Map 24/D3) 🚶🐟

A moderate 1 km bushwhack skirts past some old growth spruce on the way to this remote West Coast Lake.

Raft Cove Park (Map 37/A1) 🛶🚶⛺

At 1.2 km (45 minutes), this surprisingly difficult trail wasn't built for people looking for extended hikes. Rather, it provides access to a mile long beach on the surf-pounded coastline.

Schoen Lake Park Trails (Maps 33/G3, 34/A3) 🛶🚶🐟⛺

This park is accessed from either side, from Davie Road in the west or the Upper Adam Road in the east. This park is wild, rugged, and partially dissected by a logging road to the south that improves access.

Compton Creek is a difficult 5 km route following an old trap line that starts at the end of Compton Creek Main. The route follows the south bank of Compton Creek to beautiful Schoen Lake.

Mount Adam Route is a difficult route that heads south from Nisnak Lake. You can start from the Compton Creek trailhead (see above) or hike about 2.5 km from Upper Adam Main (see below). You can also access the curved ridge southeast of Mt Schoen up a steep gully or follow the route to the top of Mt Adam, just outside the southern border of the park.

Nisnak Lake starts from Schoen Lake on the south side of Nisnak Creek and leads up to Nisnak Lake and a lakeside campsite. Just east of the lake the trail splits, one trail crossing the meadows of the Adams River headwaters and hooking up with the Upper Adam Main Logging Road (about 45 minutes hiking) and the other heads up to a lovely waterfall on the flanks of Mt Schoen. It is about 3 km one-way from Schoen Lake to Nisnak Lake.

Vancouver Island Recreational Corridor

An ambitious plan to link Sooke in the South to Port Hardy in the North, the dream of a Vancouver Island Recreational Corridor (VIRC) took its first step toward reality in 1994 with the establishment of the Vancouver Island Recreational Corridor Works Society.

The plan is to have a flexible corridor, with trails for four main recreational users groups: hikers, mountain bikers, horseback riders and motorcyclists. Rather than establish a park corridor, the VIRC is planned to run through the working forest of Vancouver Island. As a result, the "trail"—rather, a route along currently inactive logging roads for the most part—would change, depending on which areas were seeing active logging.

Although this route is currently non-existent, the VIRC works society hopes to have an active route in place in the next few years, perhaps as early as 2002. For more information on this ambitious project, or if you're interested in hiking/biking/riding from one end of Vancouver Island to the other, contact the VIRC Society at (250) 701-0705, or email vircbrig@telus.net.

Schoen Creek Route

is a 5km (2 hour) difficult route following the steep southern lakeshore of Schoen Lake. The trail is overgrown and hard to follow in many places. Beyond Schoen Creek, experienced route finders can continue for eight more arduous hours to the saddle of Mt Schoen.

Skidder Lakes Trail (Map 39/G3, 40/A4) 🚶🐟

This rugged, hard to follow trail climbs 3 km one-way to three small mountain lakes.

Songhees Trail (Map 46/E5) 🚶🐟

An easy 5 km trail takes you from the Forest Service Campground on Georgie Lake to Songhees Lake. The trail is popular with anglers looking for cutthroat trout.

Spring Island (Map 31/B7) 🚶🛶⛺

You will find this unmarked trail in the quiet, picturesque bay on the east side of the isolated Spring Island. The short trail follows an old road, complete with a rusting cannon ball, to a former World War II lookout offering spectacular coastal views.

Tahsish River Trail (Map 32/A1, 40/A7) 🚶🐟

A moderately difficult hike with some tricky log crossings skirts the beautiful Tahsis River. The remote trail can be found off the J. Main Spur and continues north towards Tahsis Lake.

Tex Lyon Trail (Map 47/D2) 🚶🛶

This is a difficult, challenging coastal trail that hugs the coast of Beaver Harbour, east of Port Hardy. From the trailhead in Beaver Harbour Park, the trail cuts 7 km through the forest and along the rocky shoreline to Dillon Point.

Pacific Rim Park/West Coast Area

For further information about trails in the Tofino-Ucluelet area please consult, "A Hiking Guide to Pacific Rim Trails." This guide is available at the Rainforest Interpretive Centre in Tofino.

Bedwell River (Oinimitis) Trail (Map 20/E4) 🚶⛺🛶

Although this trail hooks up with the Bedwell Lake Route in Strathcona Park, (a two or three day trek, see Strathcona Park section), most people access this trail by boat via Bedwell Sound. It is a moderate 17 km (9 hour) hike along the untouched Bedwell River to You Creek.

Big Cedar (Mosquito Harbour) Route (Map 12/B2) 🚶⛺🛶

Do this one at your own risk! A difficult 20 km (2–3 day) backpacking route follows part of the old Big Cedar Circle Trail north from the Great Cedar Trail (see below) to Mosquito Harbour. Whatever trail used to be here has since disappeared into the rainforest. From Mosquito Harbour, experienced backpackers can follow an even sparser route south to Fundy Creek, southeast to C'is-a-qis Bay, then overland to Meares Creek.

Botley Lake Trail (Map 7/C7) 🚶🐟🛶

This remote trail is a moderate 5 km route that is found about 4 km from the Glad Lake West Main along the rugged West Walbran Trail (see below). Do not forget your fishing rod as the trail is leads past Botley Lake to Auger Lake in the Carmanah Walbran Provincial Park.

Carmanah Valley Trail (Map 7/B6) 🚶⛺🛶

The Carmanah Walbran Provincial Park was created to preserve a section of old growth forest on the West Coast. The 20 km (8 hours +) Carmanah Valley Trail is a difficult one-way trek from tip to tail that dissects this fabulous area. As you trek through the Carmanah River Valley, you will pass by some giant spruce trees. If you are not into a rugged backpacking experience, shorter hikes include the 7.4 km (2

Penny Staunton-Mussio and a giant Red Cedar

hours) return route to the three sisters, 17.4 km (8 hours) to August Creek campsite or 7.8 km (2.5 hours) downstream to Heaven's Grove. The trail to the Carmanah Giant—the single tree around which environmentalists rallied to have this park formed—is closed for "safety" reasons.

Clayoquot Plateau Route (Map 13/B2) ⊞ ⚠ ℹ

Though there was talk at one time of developing this into a full-blown trail, there has been little to no work done in the last number of years. This is still an unmarked, unfettered, extremely difficult route in the headwaters of the Clayoquot River. Part of this route follows the Clayoquot Witness Trail (see below), which hooks up with a number of climbing/cave access routes on Clayoquot Plateau. The distance and time depends on how long and how far you want to go. A topographic map and compass skills are a must.

Clayoquot Witness Trail (Map 13/A1) ⊞ ⚠ ℹ

Another difficult route, this time a 28 km (2–3 day) trek, cuts through the Clayoquot River watershed. During the Clayoquot Sound controversy that peaked in 1993, environmentalists put an awful lot of work into this trail but since the area has been protected, there has been few hikers and even less trail maintenance on this remote trail. Though the north end (to Norgar Lake) is still in good condition, only a few brave souls do the entire route every year and the south end is being reclaimed by the forest.

Great Cedar Trail (Map 12/A3) ⊞ ℹ

Some of the oldest living cedars in Canada thrive on Meares Island, which was home to an environmentalists versus logging controversy in the 1970's. At that time a spectacular but rugged circle route was established. Only pieces of this route can be found. The Great Cedar Trail is found on the southeast part of the island and is an easy 2.5km loop trail. Allow yourself plenty of time to gawk as you walk through an old growth cedar forest. At low tide, you can also hike along the southern shore of Meares Island to a 49 metre (160 ft) tall Sitka spruce on Meares Creek.

Lone Cone Trail (Map 12/A2) ⊞ ℹ

A stiff 5 km hike from sea level at the Kakawis Indian Village climbs to the 721m (2,365 ft) peak of Lone Cone on Meares Island. Enjoy the view before the knee jarring decent back down again.

Pacific Rim National Park

⊞ ℹ 🗎 ♿ 🚌 🚡

The world famous Long Beach Unit encompasses a large swath of the oceanfront property between Tofino and Ucluelet. There are a number of short trails (less than 5 km) that will take you from the highway down to the beach, through old growth forests or coastal rainforests. Interpretive signs are located throughout the well developed trail systems to help you learn more about the geology and history of the area.

Schooner Cove Trail (C5) is a short, easy 0.8 km (one-way) boardwalk leading to the north end of Long Beach. From here it is another 500 metre beach walk (one-way) to Schooner Cove at low tide. At high tide, there is a moderately difficult, rough bypass trail through the underbrush just off the beach.

Gold Mine Trail (F7) is an easy 3 km trip along Lost Shoe Creek, past the remnants of an old gold mine, to Florencia Bay

Rain Forest Trail (E6) is actually two boardwalks, each about 1 km in length. The trails cut through an undisturbed (well, unlogged) rain forest and are found on either side of the highway.

Shorepine Bog Trail (E7) is an easy 0.8km boardwalk through a bog known for the unique looking stunted pine trees called shorepine.

South Beach Trail (E7) is a 1.5 km round trip found on the road to Wickaninnish Beach.

Spruce Fringe Trail (D6) is an easy 1.5 km trail through a windswept pine forest north of Wickaninnish Beach.

Wickaninnish Trail (E7) is an easy 5 km trail connecting Long Beach and Florencia Bay.

Willowbrae Trail (F7) is a steep, but fairly easy 2.8 km trail leading to Halfmoon Bay or Florencia Beach.

Pacific Rim National Park

⊞ ⚠ ℹ 🚌

The West Coast Trail (Maps 1 & 6) gets all the glory when it comes to BC Trails. Known internationally, the trail is becoming almost too popular for its own good, and as a result has become heavily regulated. The trail is only open from May 1 to September 30 and only 52 people are allowed to head out onto the trail each day. A reservation system has been put into place, which usually fills in a matter of minutes. Reservation fees (non-refundable) are currently $25, plus additional trail fees of $75/person. These fees have been climbing steadily for the last few years, so call ahead to confirm: 1-800-663-6000 or (250) 387-1642 (Internationally). There are indeed other trails to enjoy in the area.

Cape Beale Trail (Map 5/G4) is a moderate 4.5 km one-way spur found off the Keeha Bay Trail. The trail takes you to Cape Beale overlooking the dramatic Pacific Ocean.

Cheewhat Lake Trail (Map 7/A7) is a short but difficult 2 km hike along a rough, poorly marked trail found off Rosander Main southwest of Nitinat Lake. The trail leads to a series of giant cedars, including one that stands over 59 metres (195 ft) tall, near Cheewhat Lake.

Keeha Beach Trail (Map 5/G4) is a moderate 8 km hike leading past Keeha Lake to a remote beach just across from Pachena Bay and the West Coast Trailhead.

West Coast Trail is a difficult, demanding 75 km one-way trek from Bamfield to Port Renfrew along the rugged west coast of Vancouver Island. The trail is now noticeably tamer than it was even a decade ago, when boardwalks were a luxury and cable crossings and ladders were unheard of. Still, the scenery is much the same as it was a century ago, when the lifesaving trail was first built for the benefit of shipwrecked sailors along the treacherous coast. You can still see many of the wrecks, along with other man-made and natural points of interest.

West Walbran Trail (Map 7/C7) ⊞ 🛶 ⚠ ℹ

A difficult, rugged 14.5 km wilderness trek hides in an old growth forest along the West Walbran Creek valley bottom. The Botley Lake Route (see above) connects up with this trail about 1 km past Anderson Lake, while the West Walbran Trail continues past Walbran Falls and over

Walbran Creek in a cable car. BC Parks discourages hikers from this area, but a rough route does exist.

Wild Pacific Trail (Map 5 Inset) 🚶 🚻 🚻 ♿

Perhaps the most dynamic of all the trails in the Long Beach area is the newly established Wild Pacific Trail. This trail is found off Peninsula Road south of the town of Ucluelet but will eventually sprawl 16 km along the oceanfront. Currently, the trail joins up with the unique He-tin-kis Park Boardwalk you can make a 5 km (1.5 hour) walk through the dense coastal rainforest, which is dominated by coastal views over wave smashing headlands. The overabundant viewpoints and benches allow you to view the dramatic coastline from every conceivable angle. Another highlight of the trail is a close view of the historical Amphitrite Point Lighthouse.

Wild Side Trail (Map 11/E1, 19/C7) 🚶 ⛺ 🚻 🖺

This 16 km trail links the village of Ahousat with the 902m (2,960 ft) high Mount Flores. The spectacular route skirts several remote beaches along the west side of Flores Island. Currently the user fee is $20, which is payable at the Walk the Wild Side office in Ahousat.

Parksville/Qualicum Area

Big Qualicum Corridor (Map 23/B6) 🚶 🐟

There is a network of trails along the west side of the Qualicum River between the river and Fish Hatchery Road. Although the route is used mostly as access trails for anglers, hikers can string these trails together into an easy hike up to 12 km long, return.

Clay Bank (Map 16/B1) 🚶 🐟 🚊

We have not marked this one on the maps since it is on private land and access is not guaranteed. The moderate 5 km (1.5 hour) forested hike has also nearly disappeared into the undergrowth and is difficult to locate. Regardless, the route leads along the southeast side of the Englishman River to a viewpoint overlooking the river. It is also possible to make your way down to the water's edge and a nice swimming/fishing hole. Look for tiny wild strawberries in the summer season.

Cochrane Road/Nile Creek Main (Map 23/B6) 🚶 🐟 🚴

An easy 14 km trip follows (for the most part) a mainline logging road to the bridge over Nile Creek. From here, you can scramble down to the creek and follow an unmarked but well-used angler trail through a scenic gorge.

Englishman River Trails (Map 16/B1) 🚶 🚻 🚴

There are a number of trails to explore along the northwest shores of the Englishman River, between Allsbrook Road to the north, Little Mountain to the east, and the river itself. Most of this is on private land, and access is not guaranteed.

Englishman River Falls Park Trails (Map 16/A2) 🚶 🚻

There are 3 km of hiking trails within this popular park, located 13 km southwest of Parksville. The main trail loops through the forest, crosses a pair of bridges built over top two waterfalls on the Englishman River and then returns to the parking lot.

Fisher Road Trail (Map 15/G1) 🚶 🚻 🚴

An intermediate 2 hour hike starts near the Dudley Marsh on the gated Fisher Road. The route follows an old road up to a viewpoint over the Strait of Georgia.

Hammerfest Race Area (Maps 15/G2, 16/A2) 🚴

Though there is a Hammerfest Race every year, the course itself keeps changing as logging infringes upon (and destroys) parts of the trail. For current info on the course, or on other biking opportunities in the area, contact a local bike shop or Tranquility Woods Resort.

Kidney Lake Trail (Map 16/D3) 🚶 🐟 🚴

An easy 3 hour trail runs along the gated mainline next to Bonnell Creek. You will eventually come to Kidney Lake where it is possible to meet up with the Blackjack Ridge Trails described in the Nanaimo section. Fishing is certainly possible in the small lakes in the area.

Lighthouse Country Trail (Map 23/B6) 🚶 🏇 🚻 🚴

An easy 10 km trail network is currently separated into two, unconnected loops on either side of Nile Creek. The Regional District of Nanaimo hopes to have the creek bridged in the next few years. The north loop is the shorter of the two, at 2.5 km long. The longer southern

loop is 7 km long (but not open as of the fall of 2000). Eventually, this trail should connect Rosewall Creek Provincial Park to Nanaimo as part of an ambitious regional trail project to hook up with the Trans Canada Trail.

Little Mountain View Trail (Map 16/A1) 🚶 🚻

There is a road leading to the top of Little Mountain off of Bellvue Road. At the top, a series of short trails circle the mountain and offer panoramic views of the area. The trail skirts some steep cliffs, so be careful.

Morrison Creek Trails (Map 16/A1) 🚶 🚴

A patch of undeveloped forest, which is currently in the process of becoming a regional park, is riddled with unofficial trails and bridges developed by local area mountain bikers. The area offers some fine riding but it is best to check with a local shop for current information on the area. Your best access is currently from the end of Leffler Road.

Northwest Bay Trails (Map 16/C1) 🚶 🏇 🚴

A network of roads, both old and new, leads through a culturally modified (logged) forest. Please respect the area as it is on private land.

Top Bridge Mountain Bike Park (Map 16/B1) 🚴

A series of singletrack trails are carved through the salal and Douglas-fir along the east bank of the Englishman River near the site of the former bridge. The old road leads to the riverbank and stops, then picks up on the other side. A non-vehicular, multi-use bridge is currently in the works and will link an easy 5km route from the gravel pit to Rathtrevor Beach Provincial Park. The more serious biker should look for trails like Ridge Rocket, a fast, difficult stretch of singletrack along the edge of the Englishman River.

Port Alberni Area Trails

Alberni Mountain Bike Trails (Map 15/A1) 🚻 🚴

There is a rat's nest of biking trails, over 20 km worth, accessed off the Log Train Trail (see below). Most of the trails are found to the east and above the old railway bed around the Old Alberni Lookout (see below). The trails range from the easy Hare Scrambler to the extremely difficult Talent.

Brigade Lake Trail (Map 13/E1) 🚶 🐟

Angler's have beaten a well used, moderately difficult, 5.5 km path along South Sutton Creek to Brigade Lake. From Brigade Lake, it is possible to follow footpaths tramped by fishermen to other lakes in the area, which locals have named Weismuller, Richards, Middle and Vincent Lake.

Cathedral Grove (MacMillan Park) (Map 15/B1) 🚶 🐟 🚻

If you can find space to park your vehicle, you can wander about and gaze up in awe at the giant old growth found in this popular roadside stop. The actual trails are found on both sides of the highway and are only short loop trails.

China Creek Trail (Map 14/G4) 🚶 🚴 🏕

A moderate 5 km (2 hour) interpretive trail parallels Bamfield Road along the heavily wooded China Creek. Also in the area are more than a dozen named trails that are enjoyed by mountain bikers. The trails range from moderate to difficult.

Climbers Trail (Map 13/C3) 🚻 🚊 🚶

As the name implies, this rough, 10 hour-plus route is best left to experienced backcountry types. The trail climbs up to the bluff west of the McKenzie Range peaks. From here, there are various hiking and mountaineering opportunities to explore.

Della Falls Trail (Map 21/A4) 🚻 🚶 ⛺

At 440 metres (1,444 ft) Della Falls might be the highest waterfall in Canada, but the difficult access makes it quite the adventure to get to. The trail starts at the head of Great Central Lake and requires a powerboat, canoe, or water taxi to access it. You will then need to climb 825m (2,710 ft) over the course of a difficult 16 km (7 hour) hike one-way. The falls are found in the heart of Strathcona Park, and there are a few backcountry routes (see Della or Love Lake below) in the area to explore. There are also few wilderness camping areas to base camp from. For more information on the water taxi, contact Ark Resort.

Della Lake Route (Maps 20/G4, 21/A4)

The route to Della Lake is so difficult it borders on climbing. Indeed, the cables that were strung to help mere hikers up have been removed by park staff, as it encouraged people who shouldn't be attempting this route to attempt this route. Just over one kilometre long, this route leaves the Della Falls Trail (see above) just below the falls and climbs to the pristine Della Lake, from where the falls cascade.

Father and Son Lake Trail (Map 15/C5)

A steep 3 km trail leads from Thistle Mine Road to a primitive forest service site nestled in an old growth cedar, fir and hemlock forest. The trail offers some stellar vistas, while the lake is known for its rainbow trout fishing. Their is a trail that circumnavigates the lake, while the more avid adventurers can use the rec site as a base camp while exploring the meadows and ridges in the surrounding area, including Mt McQuillan, which looms over the lake's eastern shore.

Fossli Lake Provincial Park (Map 14/D1)

A pair of trails, one 4.5 km and one 2.5 km, bring you from Stirling Arm Road to Fossli Provincial Park. The East Access trail is the longer of the two as it skirts along the shores of Stirling Arm on Sproat Lake.

Gibson-Klitsa Route (Map 13/F1)

A difficult, 14 km (8 hour) one-way trail (depending on how far you can negotiate the washed out, old logging roads) follows a blazed but unmaintained trail to a sub-alpine paradise. The area is set on the Gibson-Klitsa Plateau below Mounts Gibson and Klitsa. Once you have made it up, you can ramble through the meadows, fish or camp at the sub-alpine lakes or follow the ridges up to the summit of Klitsa. You will have climbed about 1,600m (5,250 ft) by the time you reach the top of the 1,642m (5,387 ft) Mt Klitsa.

Horne Lake Trail (Map 15/A1, 23/A7)

Following part of a historic native trail to Barkley Sound, this is an easy 10.5 km (2.5 hour) trail. The route follows the old roads through second growth forests from Lacy Lake Road to the popular park on the west side of Horne Lake. In all, expect to gain about 300m (985 ft) of elevation gain.

Labour Day Lake Trail (Map 15/F4)

An easy 6 km (2 hour) trail leads to and around a secluded mountain lake. There is a rec site to enjoy while at the lake, which is frequented by anglers. It is also possible to bushwhack to Indian Lake from the south end of the Labour Day Lake.

Limestone Mountain (Map 15/B5)

How far you need to hike to reach the 1,470m (4,820 ft) summit of Limestone Mountain, depends, as is so often the case, on how far you can make it up the logging roads. Once you access the ridge, it's a moderate, unmarked ridge route to the top.

The Log Train Trail (Maps 14, 15/A1, 22)

Built on the bed of an old rail grade, this historic 20 km (5 hour) one-way trail is broad, level and very enjoyable to travel. A slightly more challenging 3 km extension continues through the Rogers Creek Ravine at the south end. The Rogers Creek Nature Trail (see below) intersects the Log Train Trail near the footbridge over the creek.

Love Lake Trail (Map 21/A4)

Leaving the Della Falls trail after about 15 km (see above), the Lovely Lake Trail switchbacks up the steep valley side to the 1,231m (4,039 ft) high Love Lake. From here, you can hook up with many Strathcona Park routes (see Strathcona Section below).

Mount Apps Trail (Map 22/D5)

You will gain most of the 1,525m (5,000 ft) to the summit of Mt Apps on logging roads, which you can drive most of the way up, depending on your vehicle. From the end of the last logging road, it is only a moderate 1 km pitch up a ridge to the top.

Mount Arrowsmith Area (Map 15/D2)

Rarely is high, sub-alpine country as easily accessible as this. That accessibility has come at a cost, and this area is no longer pristine. It is still pretty and is an easy sub-alpine area for the whole family to enjoy, with some stiffer hikes for the more adventurous.

The Cokely Saddle Route, A moderate 3 hour route leads to the Cokely Saddle, between Mt Cokely and Mt Arrowsmith, where it hooks up with the Judge's Route. Rather than return the way you came, you can come out along the Rousseau Trail (see below) for a slightly different perspective on this area.

The Judge's Route, A difficult route takes you up to the top of Mount Arrowsmith (at 1,819m or 5,968 ft), then over to Mount Cokely (at 1,631m or 5,350 ft). This 8 km route starts from a spur off the main access road and includes some moderately precipitous rock scrambling. The lower part of the trail has recently been reflagged.

Lookout Trail, This easy 3 km trail used to be part of the Old Arrowsmith Trail (see below). To access the lookout, follow the Old Arrowsmith Trail for about 2.5 km from the parking lot or from Branch P40 (about 3 km from Pass Main).

Old Arrowsmith (CPR) Trail, For those who do not like the thought of easily accessed sub-alpine, you can take the hard way up. The Old Arrowsmith Trail is a steep, switchbacky 7 km (5 hour) one-way trail that climbs 1,486m (4,875 ft) from Cameron Lake to the top of Mount Cokely. The majority of the pitch is covered near the start of the trail. For those looking to add distance and elevation, you can continue on to Mt Arrowsmith along The Judge's Route (see above). This addition will cover just over 2 km but requires 2 hours of difficult scrambling.

Rousseau Trail, A moderate 3 hour route follows the ridge to Mt Cokely, where it hooks up with the Judge's Route. Rather than return the way you came, you can head out along the Cokely Saddle Route (see above).

Mount Hankin (Map 14/G3)

From the Coulson Sawmill on the shores of Alberni Inlet, this trail is a difficult grunt up the steep but scenic mountainside. The route gains 580m (1,900 ft) over 3 km (2 hours) one-way.

Mount Horne Trail (Map 15/B1, 23/B7)

A scenic 6 km (4 hour) hike heads up trails and old logging roads from Cameron Lake to the 900m (2,950 ft) summit of Mt Horne. The trailhead is located about 1.5 km along north shore of Cameron Lake.

Mount McQuillan Trail (Map 15/C5)

A 6 km trek leads to the top of Mt McQuillan from the end of Thistle Mine Road, about 1 km south of the Father and Son Lake Trailhead (see above). The two trails can be strung together into a sort of loop, though the route to Father and Son Lake is not well marked. If you do this loop, plan on spending the night at the forest service site on this picturesque lake.

Mount Moriarty (Map 15/F4)

Following the Labour Day Lake Trail for just over a kilometre, the Mount Moriarty Trail is a steep, difficult 4 km hike. You will climb almost 700m (2,295 ft) to the top of the 1,596m (5,236 ft) Mt Moriarty. Almost all of the climb is over the last two kilometres (that's almost one vertical metre for every two metres traversed, or a 45% angle).

Old Alberni Lookout Trail (Map 15/A1)

An easy 7 km hike follows a rough logging road up to the Old Alberni Lookout.

Passive Reflector (Map 14/F2)

From the trailhead on Cous Main, this is an easy 2 km hike that follows a 4wd road almost all the way to a microwave tower (the so-called passive reflector). Once at the top, a series of bluffs overlooking the Alberni Inlet provide open views up and down the Inlet.

Robertson Creek Hatchery (Map 22/C7)

Two easy trails, one 2 km and one 1 km long, head in opposite directions along the Stamp River from the parking lot at Robertson Creek Fish Hatchery. The upper trail to Great Central Lake passes a small waterfall, and ends at a weir just before the lake. From here, you can walk back along the road or retrace your steps. The Lower Trail follows the river north past some good steelhead fishing holes and to a picnic area. This is a great place to watch spawning salmon in the fall, just keep an eye out for bears.

Rogers Creek Nature Trail (Map 14/G1, 15/A1) [icons]

An easy 6 km (3 hour) nature trail is found in the Rogers Creek ravine area. The trail follows the east side of Rogers Creek for about 2.5 km but there are a number of shorter trails that intersect with the main footpath. This trail also connects with the Log Train Trail to the north.

Ward Lake Trail (Map 14/D1, 22/C7) [icons]

An easy, obvious trail cuts through a second growth forest to this small lake. Ward Lake is found at the about the 2 km mark but the trail continues on for another 2.5 km.

Wesley Ridge Trail (Map 15/C1, 23/D7) [icons]

From the upper falls bridge in Little Qualicum Falls Park, it is a moderate 16 km (5 hour) hike along a ridge towards Mt Wesley. The trail terminates at a nice viewpoint overlooking Cameron Lake but you can also continue on to the top of the 908m (2,980 ft) Mt Wesley. The mountain requires and additional 8 km (3 hours) of moderate hiking.

Port Renfrew Area Trails

Botanical Beach Trails (Map 1/F3) [icons]

There are a number of short trails that lead down to Botany Bay and one, the Shoreline Trail, that leads to cliffs overlooking the beach. They are all short, easy (about 1 km long) hikes down to the bay, where you can wander up and down along the beach in an area that has been described as a "natural outdoor laboratory." 230 plant species, 101 invertebrates, plus gray whales, killer whales, otters...a veritable explosion of marine life.

Deacon/Beauchene Trail (Map 1/G1) [icons]

This trail is an easy 1.9 km (30 minute) hike alongside the Gordon River, occasionally detouring out onto some sandbars. The trail gets its name from the fact that it passes through the site of the old Deacon Homestead, the first settlers in the valley, circa 1889, who were joined in 1899 by Art Beauchene. This trail can be muddy in moist weather and flooded in really wet weather.

Fairy Lake Nature Trail (Map 2/A1) [icons]

An easy 2 km (40 minute) nature trail dissects the second growth forest around Fairy Lake. The trail runs from the Harris Creek Mainline, through a second growth forest, to the Fairy Lake Rec Site.

First and Second Creek Trail (Map 2/A2) [icons]

This easy 3.2 km (2 hour) trip takes you through the wetlands in the First and Second Creek area south of the San Juan River. Wet is the operative word here. Bring good footgear, especially during the rainy season. Spring is the best time to visit this river delta since the fawn lilies are in bloom.

Harris Creek Camp II Trail (Map 2/B1) [icons]

An easy 6km (3 hour) hike east from Granite Creek Main, follows an old rail grade to a historic logging camp on Harris Creek.

Harrison's Plankboard Trail (Map 1/G2) [icons]

An easy 3.5 km stroll follows an interesting old road made out of planks (also called a corduroy road). This trail is named for Stan Harrison, an early logger in the area.

John Quinn Trail (Map 1/G2) [icons]

Found west of the Plankboard Trail, this old timber road is now an easy 4 km trail. In the 1930s shingle bolts were cut from the trees in the hills above Port Renfrew. The logs were sent down log chutes to waiting trucks, which would drive out along what is now the John Quinn Trail to the shingle mill.

Juan de Fuca Marine Trail (Map 1/G3 & 2) [icons]

The jury is still out on the Juan de Fuca Trail. Some love it, others consider it a far inferior route to the West Coast Trail just up the coast. It doesn't help that much of this area has been logged; ancient cedars replaced with spry alders. And it runs parallel to Highway 14, often close enough that you can hear traffic. Still, there are remnants of old growth, plenty of wildlife and marine life and the beaches, especially Botanical Beach, are phenomenal. Most of the old beach trails in the area have been closed, leaving only four access points along this 49 km trail. The day-use sections range from easy to difficult, depending on which section you are hiking. If you want to run the whole route, you

expect to take 3–4 days to hike from China Beach to Botanical Beach. There are six designated campsites, which can be used for a fee.

Lens Creek Trail (Map 2/B1) [icons]

An easy 3 km (1 hour) round trip takes you through Chester's Grove, a stand of old growth on the banks of the San Juan River. There are other pockets of big trees and Ben's Beach, a nice swimming hole on the San Juan, make this a nice hike to explore.

Lizard Lake Nature Trail (Map 2/C1) [icons]

Starting at the Forest Service Recreation Site, an easy 1.5 km (35 minute) hike circles Lizard Lake. In spring, the trail is lined with wildflowers. While in the area, be sure to look for the 82 metre (269 ft) tall Harris Creek Spruce Tree. It is found just off the road about 8 km beyond the rec site (you'll probably want to drive along the uninspiring logging road) towards Cowichan Lake. This giant spruce is wheelchair accessible.

Red Creek Fir (Map 2/D2) [icons]

A narrow gravel trail leads to a giant Douglas fir. The trail is short (1 km) and easy.

San Juan Ridge/Kludahk Trail (Map 2/C-G3) [icons]

There is talk of having this trail ultimately link the Galloping Goose Trail to Port Renfrew and the trailhead of both the West Coast and Juan de Fuca Trails. Currently the moderate route stretches 36.5 km along the San Juan Ridge from Diversion Reservoir to just south of Port Renfrew. Spectacular vistas and remote cabins make this a fantastic destination type trail.

Sombrio Beach Trails (Map 2/B4) [icons]

It is the beaches that make the Juan de Fuca Marine Trail and one of the prettiest is Sombrio Beach. It is also one of only two place along the trail (other than the trailheads) accessible from the road. Several short trails, most of them quite rough and steep, provide access to the beach.

Strathcona Provincial Park Trails

BC's oldest provincial park is a backpacking paradise. Endless miles of developed trails and unmarked ridge routes offer a little something for everyone, from the family daytripper to the hardcore backpacker looking to get away for a month. Unlike many of the other high places in BC, Strathcona Park has interconnecting alpine ridges, which means you don't have to hike down 1,500 metres, then back up to access the next peak. Because much of this park is designated for wilderness conservation, there is no development—no pit toilets, no bridges...not even any signposts telling you where you are. Even area hiking groups have latched on to this no-trace ethic, not flagging routes or building cairns. If you plan to hike one of the many routes in Strathcona, be prepared. Because there are so many options for creating your own route, we are only going to mention some of the more popular routes, trails and destinations. For daytrippers, we recommend you stick to marked trails.

Gem Lake Trail (Map 28/C6) [icons]

This a moderate 3.5 km hike leads to a wilderness camping area on the shores of the aptly named lake. The access road, Oyster River Main, is a restricted road that is closed weekdays until 5pm but it does provide access to a few fabulous trails. Also in the area is the challenging Alexandra Peak route and the Sunrise Lake Route (see below).

Sunrise Lake Route (Map 28/C6) [icons]

Also found off Oyster River Main is the difficult 5 km route to the spectacular Sunrise Lake. En route, you travel past a number of smaller lakes. In addition to the scenery, Sunrise Lake is a fine fishing destination in the late summer.

Trails from Forbidden Plateau Ski Area (Map 28/G7) [icons]

Boston Ridge Trail is a 13 km (8 hour) easy hike starting along an old rail grade to Boston Ridge before turning into a fairly arduous ridge climb to the top of the 1,385m (4,544 ft) Mt Becher. You can return the way you came or via the Mount Becher Summit Trail (see below).

Forbidden Plateau Trail is a moderate hike that dissects the heart of the plateau that was given its ominous name by natives. There are many worthy destinations along the way but the 19 km (day) route to the campsite at Kwai Lake is one of the most popular. Other side routes include accessing the 1,363m (4,472 ft) peak of Mount Drabble or the campsite at McKenzie Lake, a good fishing destination.

Mount Becher Summit Trail has been a popular destination. In fact, the area was the site of the first known alpine skiing area on Vancouver Island. Enthusiasts used to slog through the snow all the way from Comox Lake up to a cabin that was built in 1928. Today, this moderate 5 km (2 hour) trail is a lot shorter and easier. The route follows blazes from the Forbidden Plateau ski lodge to Mt Becher, gaining 660m (2,165 ft) in elevation.

Trails from Paradise Meadows Trailhead (Forbidden Plateau Area) (Map 28/E6)

Castlecrag Mountain is found south of Moat Lake. Backpackers should be prepared for a moderate route, which gains (2,035 ft) and includes some scrambling up loose rock on the way to the summit of the 1,740m (5,708 ft) mountain.

Comox Glacier via Albert Edward Route is one of the most challenging and rewarding trips in the park. The route takes about ten days or so should only be attempted by experience mountaineers. From Mount Albert Edward (Map 21/C2), the Comox Glacier Route heads over Mount Frink, Mount George V, over the Aureole Snowfield, Mount Harmston and on to the Comox Glacier.

Helen McKenzie-Battleship Lake Loop is an easy 8 km (3 hour) hike looping past Battleship Lake, through sub-alpine meadows and around beautiful Lake Helen McKenzie. The elevation gain is a mere 70m (230 ft).

Helen McKenzie/Circlet Lake/Mount Albert Edward Route is a popular route leading past several sub-alpine lakes to the scenic Mount Albert Edward. Allow 4 hours to cover 9.5km of moderate terrain (the elevation gain is 270m or 885 ft) on the way to spectacular Circlet Lake, where a designated campsite is available. From Circlet Lake, you can continue on another moderate 6.5 km (5 hour) trail to Mount Albert Edward, gaining 935m (3,067 ft). A short ways past Moat Lake (2.5 km along), the trail becomes a route. From Circlet Lake there is also a 1.6 km (1 hour) trail north to Amphitheatre Lake.

Helen McKenzie-Kwai Lake-Croteau Lake Loop is an easy 14 km (6 hour) trail leading past a handful of beautiful sub-alpine lakes. The elevation gain on route is 185m (605 ft) and camping is available at Kwai Lake. From Kwai Lake, there is a 1.5 km (1 hour) trail that continues past Mariwood Lake and Lake Beautiful to a viewpoint overlooking the Cruickshank Canyon.

McKenzie and Douglas Lakes along the Forbidden Plateau Trail is a moderate to difficult 17 km (7 hour) trek climbing 770m (2,525 ft) to Douglas and McKenzie Lakes along the Forbidden Plateau Trail. The lakes are known for their good rainbow trout fishing and camping is permitted in the area above the lakes. A memorial cairn is also found at the north end of McKenzie Lake.

Paradise Meadows Loop Trail is an easy, 2.2 km (45 minute) walk loops through the sub-alpine meadows on a well-developed trail.

Trails from Buttle Lake/Westmin Mine Areas (Maps 20, 21, 27, 28)

Augerpoint Trail/Route (Map 28/A7) is a difficult 1,400m (4,595 ft) climb that accesses a sub-alpine plateau. Most of the climb is found in the first few switchbacking kilometres up from the trailhead at the Augerpoint Picnic Site. The original trail was burned out in a forest fire a few years ago but there is an unofficial rerouting of the trail (called Jack's Augerpoint Trail, after the trail's builder Jack Shark) north of the burn. It is about two hours to the top and the end of the trail. A rough route continues to Mount Albert Edward, about seven hours from the trailhead.

Bedwell Lake Trail (Map 20/G3) starts from Jim Mitchell Lake Road and is a moderate 12 km (7 hour) hike. The trail heads south to Bedwell Lake, climbing 600m (1,970 ft) along the way. There are a couple designated campsites at the lake from which to base camp. From here, routes lead southeast to Della Falls (see Port Alberni Trails), southwest to Bedwell Bay (see Pacific Rim National Park/West Coast Trails), west on the Burman Lake Route and east to Cream Lake and the Flower Ridge Routes (see below).

Flower Ridge Trail (Map 21/A1) is a difficult 6 km (5 hour) one-way hike. The trail starts out on a steep grade before opening up on a much easier alpine ridge walk. The pretty ridge is famous for its colourful display in season. Expect an elevation gain of 1,250m (4,100 ft).

Karst Creek Trail (Map 28/A7) is an easy interpretive loop trail leads past some karst landscape features, including a creek that disappears.

Lower Myra Falls Trail (Map 20/G1) is an easy 1 km (30 minute) trail is found on the southwest end of Buttle Lake. The trail takes you through an old growth forest to the falls.

Marble Meadows Trail (Map 27/G7) requires a boat to access the trailhead at the Phillip Creek Campsite. The moderate 6.6 km (6 hour) trail climbs 1,250m (4,100 ft) from the lake to Wheaton Hut in Marble Meadows. The route continues west to hook up with the Phillips Watershed Route (south) or a route to Mount McBride (north). Another access option is to trek 12 km one-way along the Phillips Ridge Route (see below)

Phillips Ridge Trail/Route (Maps 20/F1, 27/G7) is a moderate 6 km (4 hour) hike to Arnica Lake along a well graded, but steep, trail (you'll gain about 800m or 2,625 ft in elevation). The trail, which is more like a route, continues on to the 1,728m (5,670 ft) Mount Phillips, then down to the Phillips Creek Marine Campsite on Buttle Lake.

Phillips Watershed Route (Maps 20/F1, 27/E7) starts from the Phillips Creek Campsite on Buttle Lake. This difficult, weeklong route climbs up to Marble Meadows on a marked trail, then over Morrison Spire, down to Schjelderup Lake, then back to Arnica Lake to hook up with the Phillips Ridge Route (see above).

Price Creek/Cream Lake Route (Maps 20/G2, 21/A3) is a moderate 8.5 km (7 hour) trail following Price Creek. Overall you gain 1,200m (3,935 ft) to a campsite in the valley below Cream Lake. From here, it is just over a kilometre up a difficult route to Cream Lake. Beyond the lake are routes to Mount Septimus, Love Lake and Della Falls, Bedwell Lake and the Flower Ridge Trail.

Shepherd Creek Loop (Maps 21/A1, 28/A7) is an easy 2 km hike found just south of Ralph River. The trail is fairly flat (gaining 50m or 165 ft) as it showcases a pristine watershed.

Shepherd Creek Route (Maps 21/A1, 28/A7) is a route that was developed to assist hikers get down to the highway past the south end of Buttle Lake in an emergency. Some hikers trying to get up to the ridge east of Buttle Ridge now use this steep, difficult route.

Tennent Lake/Mount Myra Trail (Map 20/F2) is a steep 7 km (5 hour) one-way climb to Tennent Lake. An even steeper trail continues to the 1,814m (5,950 ft) summit of Mount Myra. The total elevation gain is 1,500m (4,920 ft) but from Tennent Lake it is a grueling 807m (2,648 ft) climb over 3.5 km.

Upper Myra Falls Trail (Map 20/F1) is an easy 3 km (2 hour) trail leading to the cascading Upper Myra Falls. The elevation gain is a mere 100m (328 ft). The route beyond, is a rough, bushwhack along a flagged route that eventually connects up with routes in the Mount Thelwood and Burman Lake areas.

Drum Lakes Area (Map 27/B3)

Crest Mountain is a difficult 5 km (4 hour) grunt up to the top of Crest Mountain. About 1 km into the hike, you will have to negotiate a rather hairy single log crossing over a fast moving creek. The trail starts at Highway 28 and climbs 1,250m (4,100 ft) to the top. After the first couple kilometres, you hit the alpine, with excellent views of the Elk River Valley.

Elkhorn Route starts 2.5 km along the Elk River Trail (see below). This well-travelled, though not marked route heads southeast to a sub-alpine campsite. The route is about a 3 km (6 hour) difficult hike from the trail junction. Beyond the campsite, the route degenerates into a serious scramble to the summit. Do not attempt this without a rope and a good leader.

Elk River Trail/Route follows an old elk trail, which is now well travelled and marked. The moderate 11 km (5 hour) one-way hike gains 600m (1,970 ft) to the impressive Landslide Lake. The lake is actually found a kilometre off the main trail but is the most popular destination in the area. The Elk River Trail continues on, petering off into a route to Burman Lake and the Golden Hinde Area. There are several locations to camp along this difficult 3–4 day route.

Kings Peak Route is a steep 5-7 km route depending on which route you take. The gully between Kings Peak and the so-called Queens Peak are an avalanche danger well into summer. Lovely Kings Peak is marked by an unfortunate radio repeater tower at the top. The route should take about 6 hours to climb.

Victoria and Area Trails

Bear Creek Reservoir (Map 3/B3)
Old (and not so old) logging roads, are the order of the day in the Bear Creek Area.

Bear Hill Regional Park (Map 4/D3)
At 220m (720 ft), Bear Hill is not huge, but it is one of the highest peaks in the South Island lowlands. The trail to the top of this monodock (hill) is short and steep, which is a pretty apt description of most of the trails in the park. Bear Hill is scarred and striated from the glaciers the rubbed it raw nearly 15,000 years ago and each new knoll offers a new angle on the area. Other trails through this 49 ha park hook up with trails in Elk/Beaver Lake Regional Park to the south (see below).

East Sooke Regional Park (Map 3/G7)
A semi-wilderness park with 50 km of easy to moderate trails. The highest point in the park is Mount Maguire, at 272m (892 ft) and a somewhat challenging trail climbs up this peak as well as the scenic Babbington Hill, the second highest point at 239m (784 ft). Other trails lead down to the beach, past old mines, through flowering (in season) meadows, and to the petroglyphs at Aldridge Point. The highlight of the area is the Coast Trail, a challenging, exhilarating 10 km hike along some surprisingly remote bits of coastline.

Elk/Beaver Lake Regional Park Trails (Map 4/D3)
An easy 9 km trail that circles Elk and Beaver Lakes is the big route in this regional park, the most popular of all Capital Region Parks. There are a number of shorter trails that, for the most part, hook up with the main trail.

Francis/King Regional Park Trails (Map 4/C4)
There are 11 km of gentle woodland trails in and around this small park, which is tucked next to the much more popular Thetis Lake Regional Park. Most of the trails are under 1 km long but they can be strung into any number of loops. The trail system is split in half by Munn Road, with the shorter, easier trails east of the road and the longer, more difficult trails to the west. A couple trails, including High Ridge Trail, connect up with trails in Thetis Lake Park.

Gail Wickens Horse Trail (Map 4/D1)
This trail links the many short trails of Centennial Park with John Dean Park, via Haldon Park.

Galloping Goose Trail (Maps 3/F4-4/A5)
Perhaps the most popular multi-use trail on Vancouver Island, the 57 km trail stretches from Victoria to the historic Leechtown. The majority of the easy route follows an old rail grade that once ran from Victoria

---

Trans Canada Trail

Victoria may be the start or the terminus of what will eventually be the world's longest trail stretching some 16,000 km from coast to coast. The Trans Canada Trail is being designed as a multi-use trail that will link communities, parks and greenways.

The Trans Canada Trail route on Vancouver Island starts at the Mile O sign at Beacon Hill in Victoria. Travellers have a variety of ways to make their way north and over the Johnson Street Bridge and to the start of the Galloping Goose Trail. Follow this popular trail west to the Luxton Fairgrounds in Langford. The Trans Canada Trail route then branches north, past Langford Lake to the Trans Canada Highway. Unfortunately, the stretch north to Shawnigan Lake Road currently follows the highway.

Turning west on the Shawnigan Lake Road and then south on the Sooke Lake Road will hook you up with the old railway heading northwest to Lake Cowichan. Outside of a few hiccups (including the closed Kinsol Bridge) the route to Lake Cowichan is in good shape.

From Lake Cowichan west to north Duncan the route will eventually follow the old railbed. For now the Old Cowichan Lake Road makes a fine alternative (especially for bikers). From Duncan the route follows rural roads east and north past the quaint towns of Crofton, Chemainus and Ladysmith.

North of Ladysmith the route is quite tricky and has a major gap (a bridge over the Nanaimo River). Currently, a mix of side roads and the highway can lead you north to the Nanaimo River Road. Head west on this road and then north on White Rapids and Extension Roads. The Abyss Trail, the water pipeline and the Old Comox Railgrade are but a few better options being considered to link Nanaimo with the southern Island communities.

As Extension Road nears the Island Highway, you will meet the Parkway Trail and the beginning of a well established route through Nanaimo. This route links several small parks, quiet city streets and the Nanaimo Waterfront with Departure Bay. From Departure Bay the route sails away towards Horseshoe Bay on the mainland.

By the spring of 2001, Mussio Ventures Ltd. in cooperation with Trails BC, plans to release the **TRANS CANADA TRAIL**, The British Columbia Route guidebook. This book will highlight an uninterrupted 1,750 km route from Victoria to the Alberta Border. The book will offer maps and detailed route descriptions of the entire British Columbia section of this fantastic trail.

---

to the Lake Cowichan Area. To shorten the route, there are many access points along the route. The Trans Canada Trail follows the beginning of the route from the Selkirk Trestle in Victoria to the Luxton Fairgrounds in Langford.

Goldstream Provincial Park (Map 4/A4)
This popular provincial park is dissected by the Trans Canada Highway, as well as a number of fabulous hiking trails. There is even a short trail to Niagara Falls from the northernmost parking lot in the park. No, not that Niagara Falls. This one weighs in at a mere 47.5m (155 ft). You can also reach the falls from the campground along the Arbutus, then Gold Mine Trail, a hike of about 6 km return. Goldstream Park is also home to spawning salmon in fall, pockets of old growth forest and the Mount Finlayson Trail (see below).

Gowlland Tod Provincial Park (Map 4/B3)
An extensive (25 km) network of trails, mostly along old roads, weaves and winds its way around this park on the east side of Finlayson Arm. One of the more scenic trails is the 10 km long Ridge Top Trail, which stretches from Caleb Pike to McKenzie Bight.

Harrison Trail (Map 3/F5)
From Sooke Potholes Provincial Park, a rough, gated old road leads north to the top of the 673m (2,208 ft) Empress Mountain. The mountain makes a fine destination and is a moderate 10 km, return hike. Mountain bikers usually continue past Crabapple Lake and the Sooke Mountain Park to the highway and back to the potholes. This creates a challenging loop trail.

Horth Hill Regional Park (Map 10/C7)
There are a lot of trails packed into this 31 ha North Saanich park, including trails leading up the 136m (446 ft) Horth Hill. The two main trails in the park are the Lookout Trail and the Ridge Trail, both of which lead to viewpoints over the Saanich Peninsula and surrounding islands. Strung end to end, the trails in this park would cover about 5 km but the trails have been bent, twisted, and broken up to fit into the area provided.

Island View Beach (Map 4/E2)
Although there are only a few hundred metres of trails around Island View Park, at low tide you can head out onto the beach for an easy 10 km one-way walk south to Mount Douglas Park. A shorter 1.5 km one-way beach walk north will get you to the tip of Cordova Spit. Check tide tables before you go; least you get stranded on the beach.

John Dean Park (Map 4/D1)
There are eight short (in the 1 to 1.5 km range) easy trails through John Dean Park that can be stitched together into various longer walks.

Lochside Trail (Map 4-10)
The Lochside Trail follows an old rail bed for about 27 km from Swartz Bay to Victoria. Recent development on this route makes it much easier to follow and access but travellers will still find sections that have been paved over and turned into road (including a 4 km section of Lochside Drive). The route hooks up with the Galloping Goose Trail and is an official side trail to the main Trans Canada Trail route.

Lone Tree Hill Regional Park (Map 4/B3)

The signature tree for which this park is named is merely a snag. Still it is worth your while to hike to the top of this 388m (1,273 ft) hill, for the open views from the top. It is a moderate hike, weighing in at slightly over 1 km one-way.

Matheson Lake Park (Map 3/G7, 4/A7)

There are several trails to choose from through this park, including a 4.5 km section of the Galloping Goose (see above). There is swimming and some fishing in Matheson Lake but the big draw for most is the trails, which hook up to Roche Cove Provincial Park to the west, along the Goose running east, and several horse trails to the north. The misnamed Mount Ball (at 151m or 495 ft, this is a mere hill) is a moderate 2 km hike return from the parking lot, while a longer, easier circumnavigation of Matheson Lake is about 3 km.

Mill Hill Park (Map4/C5)

The trail to the top of this 200m (656 ft) hill will take about 20 minutes. For your effort, you will be rewarded with nearly 360 degree views from the site of a former lookout tower. The trail continues down the north side of the hill to hook up with Thetis Lake Park and the Galloping Goose Trail.

Millstream Highlands (Map 4/B4)

A series of mountain bike trails ranging from easy to difficult are found in the Skirt/Miniskirt Mountain area, off Millstream Road. As a general rule, the higher up you are, the easier the riding; the lower down you go, the gnarlier the trails get.

Mount Finlayson Trail (Map 4/B4)

Though it is just over 1 km to the top, the trail that leads to the top of the 419m (1,375 ft) Mount Finlayson is difficult, rugged, and not recommended for anyone who thinks that hiking the Galloping Goose is hard work. This trail is located inside the boundaries of pretty Goldstream Provincial Park.

Mount Douglas Park (Map 4/E4)

Though any lump of land under 305 metres (1,000 feet) is officially considered a hill, the 277m (909 ft) Mount Douglas gets the mount designation because at the time it wasn't considered wise to give the then-Governor a mere hill. Such is the nature of BC politics. Hikers will find a maze of easy to moderate trails throughout the park, including one to the summit of Douglas.

Mount Work Regional Park (Map 4/C3)

11 km of trails connect the 449m (1,473 ft) summit of Mount Work with the McKenzie Bight tidal pools and with a handful of lakes in the park. See also Mount Work Hartland Trails (below).

Mount Work Hartland Trails (Map 4/C3)

Now a part of Mount Work Regional Park, this is the only Capital Regional District sanctioned area for mountain bikers but these are not your typical sanctioned trails. Even hardcore riders will get a kick out of some trails, which range from simple to difficult (no extreme stuff, though, at least, not officially). Bikers can (and quite often do) spend a day exploring the trails in this area.

Princess Margaret Marine Park (Map 10/D6)

The whole of Portland Island is a provincial park—Princess Margaret Provincial Park. The island is circled by a scenic 5 km trail, while two other trails (both about 1.5 km) bisect the island. Ferry service to the island is available from June to September (call 250-727-7700 for the schedule) and camping is possible.

Roche Cove Regional Park (Map 3/G6)

There are several trails to chose from through this 159 ha park, including a 1.5 km section of the Galloping Goose (see above) which connects Roche Cove with Matheson Lake Regional Park, one of a trio of trails that link the two parks. From the parking lot at the northwest corner of the park, you can follow the Goose along the northern shore of Roche Cove, or walk deeper into the heart of the park along the Cedar Grove Trail. This trail heads south and hooks up with Galloping Goose for a 4.5 km loop back to the parking lot.

Sidney Spit (Map 4/F1)

There are no developed trails in Sidney Spit Park but you can wander around the white sand beaches and large tidal flats. The 6 km walk to the tip of Sidney Spit is a certifiable highlight of any trip to the park and is one of the best beach walks in the province. There is a ferry that runs to the island from May to October (call 250-727-7700 for the schedule), or you can get to the island by boat or kayak

Spectacle Lake Park (Map 4/A2)

If you peer very closely at Spectacle Lake, you will note that it looks a bit like a pair of glasses, from whence it gets its name. The park itself is tiny (65 ha), and the trail around it is little less than an hour's stroll. However, a longer trail leads north to, then around, Oliphant Lake, for a 7 km (4 hour), hike. The Oliphant Lake/Johns Creek area also offers about 10 kilometres of multi-use trails along both old roads and connector trails.

Thetis Lake Regional Park (Map 4/B4)

Like many area parks, there is a rat's nest maze of trails around Upper and Lower Thetis Lakes. Trail lead up Seymour Hill and past McKenzie Lake and even hook up (via Panhandle Road just inside the northern park boundary, off Highland Road) with the trails in Francis/King Park (see above). The park is also a popular fishing retreat and offers a find beach for sunbathers.

Witty's Lagoon (Map 4/B6)

There is a short system of trails in this regional park, which is known as a good waterfowl viewing area. A 3km one-way beach walk (at low tide) links up with Devonian Park to the south.

www.backroadmapbooks.com

Winter Recreation

(Cross-country Skiing, Snowmobiling and Other Activities)

Vancouver Island is not blessed with an abundance of snow. Surrounded on all sides by water, much of the climate is too mild for snow. Despite this climate, when the winter rains hit the cities, it will usually be snowing in the mountains.

Snow enthusiasts will find snow in the many alpine and sub-alpine areas that make up the backbone of the Island. Generally speaking, suitable snow conditions last from December through April in the alpine.

Skiers will find a pair of downhill ski hills still in operation—Mount Cain and Mount Washington. Former ski hills were found at such places as Mount Becher, Green Mountain, Mount Arrowsmith and the recently defunct Forbidden Plateau. If you are looking for snow, these are good places to start.

Cross-Country Skiing

Official cross-country ski areas on the Island are limited but as always, there are many places that locals go. If you are not near one of the options listed below, you can set your own track or look for the familiar tracks heading up an old road or trail in your area.

Mt. Cain (Map 33/G1)
This popular regional park really comes alive in the winter. In addition to a downhill ski area, winter recreationists can explore about 15 km of marked, but ungroomed trails in the Mount Cain area. Although most of the cross-country ski routes follow snowed-over logging roads, there are some nice vistas to enjoy.

Mt. Washington Ski Resort (Map 28/E5)
Mount Washington Ski Resort maintains 40km of trails groomed for both classic and skate skiing. The claim to fame for these trails is that they are the most picturesque in the Pacific Northwest. The trails wander into Strathcona Provincial Park, past (or over) several alpine lakes and access a few incredible viewpoints. Backcountry ski touring is a popular alternative in the Forbidden Plateau area. There is a fee to use the trails and rentals are available.

Backcountry Skiing & Snowshoeing

During the winter, most logging roads into the high country are not plowed, turning them into great ski or snowshoe areas. Logging cut blocks can even become mini-bowls for telemarkers and alpine tourists. (Watch out for stumps!) And many of the high alpine hiking trails also provide backcountry skiers or snowshoers with an access to the high country. The difference is, with fragile alpine flowers and other flora safely under a thick blanket of snow, backcountry travellers often have more freedom to roam. With this freedom, locals turn many remote mountains into their own private ski run.

Avalanches are always a danger back there, so go prepared, armed with the proper equipment, the knowledge of how to use it, and the experience to recognize dangers. If you are not confident of your abilities, do not go, or go with someone who knows what to do. If you want to hook up with a local, contact Len Apedaile at the Strathcona Nordic Ski Club, (250) 337-5246.

Below we have described a few of the more popular South Island areas:

Mount Benson Area (Map 16/G4)
There are several trails up to this 1,019 m (3,343 ft) peak, but skiers usually follow a rocky 4wd road from the southeast. This road is found off the Nanaimo Lakes Road and covers about 3.5 km to the top (de-pending on how far down the mountain the snow is). Another option is to trek up the northwest ridge.

Blackjack Ridge (Map 16/E4)
Above the Nanaimo Lakes Road is a nest of logging roads that lead along Blackjack Ridge. If you are new to the area be prepared for plenty of route searching but the peace, solitude make the effort worthwhile.

Labour Day Lake (Map 15/F4)
Also used by snowmobilers, the logging roads and trails around Labour Day Lake are a popular destination for backcountry skiers as well. A veritable maze of logging roads can be followed, or the more adventurous skier can break out into the alpine along McLaughlin Ridge.

Saint Mary's Lakes (Map 15/C1)
Located near Mount Arrowsmith Regional Park, this pair of tiny lakes is a great destination for alpine touring or telemark skiing. To access the area, drive up Pass Main as far as you can get then ski/walk the road through the fringes of Arrowsmith Park and west to the lakes.

McKay Ridge (Map 28/F5)
Located just north of Mount Washington, McKay Lake can be accessed by skiers from either the ski hill or along Branch 62.

Mount Cain Area (Map 33/G1)
From Mount Cain, you can either follow the marked cross-country ski trails or head out into the backcountry. There is an old, weatherworn and almost defeated cabin in the West Bowl area that skiers can stay in (though building a snow cave might prove to be a more reliable shelter). For the serious alpine mountaineer, there is a trio of peaks over 1,500 metres (4,900 ft) to explore in a 5 km radius.

Green Mountain (Map 16/A6)
A former ski hill, Green Mountain is now a critical Wildlife Management Zone for the Vancouver Island Marmot. The marmots hibernate from September to April, so you will not be disturbing them, but if you choose to go, do nothing to upset the habitat for this most endangered of all Canadian animals. Backcountry enthusiasts will find a beautiful alpine area with both old roads and trails to explore.

Mount Becher (Map 28/F7)
From the former cross-country area at the former Forbidden Plateau Ski Area, it is possible to ski to the original ski hill on the island. A winter cabin was built here in 1928 for snowshoers, tobogganers and skiers, who used to hike or ski to the top of Becher, slogging their way uphill from Comox Lake from near the site of the old Bevan Mine. These days, you can drive most of the way to Mount Becher along the Boston Main, and then ski in from the old Forbidden Plateau parking lot. The cabin was torn down in the 1980s, but the spirit of the explorers who opened up this area lives on in the soul of everyone who follows in their footsteps.

Of course, this is just a small sampling of where you can go with skis or snowshoes strapped to your feet. Most anywhere there is snow and a trail, a logging road, or an open alpine area, you can get to on skis. Here are a few other suggestions:

- **Arrowsmith-Moraity Divide** (Map 15/D2-F4)
- **Kwai & Hairtrigger Lakes** (Map 28/D6)
- **Mount Apps Area** (Map 22/D4)
- **Mount Brenton Area** (Map 9/C2)
- **Tangle Mountain Meadows** (Map 15/G5)

Snowmobiling

Many of the snowmobile areas on Vancouver Island access high alpine ridges or mazes of Forest Service roads that can be difficult or dangerous to follow. If you are new to an area, we suggest you contact a local club to get more details or to hook up with a riding partner/guide. Call the BC Snowmobile Federation at (250) 566-4627 for contact information. The riding season starts as early as mid-November and can extend all the way into June at higher elevations.

Bacon Lake (Map 35/G7)
A small area on the west side of Upper Campbell Lake follows the network of logging roads in and around the lake.

Holyoak Lake (Map 9/C2)
Access to the Hollyoak Lake area is along the Copper Canyon Main, a gated road near Chemainus with a manned security post. This area is on private forestland and if you want to ride here, you must have valid BC Snowmobile Federation membership. Contact Blake Erickson of the Mid-Island Sno-Blazers, at (250) 758-0315 or by email at erickson@island.net.

McLaughlin Ridge Area (Map 15/B2-F4)
This large riding area extends along McLaughlin Ridge from Labour Day Lake, over McKinley Peak and on through the Yellow Creek Logging division. Most people access this high alpine ridge off Copper Creek Main or Yellow Creek Main. The Mid-Island Sno-Blazers maintain a survival shelter in the area.

Mount Adrian/Iron River (Map 28/D2- A5)
A sprawling area tucked along the east side of Strathcona Park, this largely undefined area centres around Wowd and Beadnell Lakes. The riding area is accessed from the Island Highway off York Road. Depending on snow conditions and avalanche hazard, you can follow the rat's nest of private logging roads and cross-country trails that offer over 120 km of riding. The variety of terrain will satisfy or challenge novice or experienced snowmobilers. In particular, the difficult climb to the alpine areas around Mount Adrian offering a rewarding vista from the 1,825 m (6,000 ft) level. The North Island Snowmobile Assocation maintains a cabin in the area.

Mount Porter Area (Map 21/G7)
This sprawling alpine area in the high country between Sproat Lake and Great Central Lake is a snowmobilers dream. Though there are some logging roads to follow, much of this area is big, wide, open terrain to play in.

Mount Washington (Map 28/E5)
Just north of the Mt Washington Ski area is a maze of logging roads in the McKay Lake region. Though this area is smaller than some of the other areas on the island, it is still extremely popular, due, no doubt, to its proximity to Courtenay and Comox. Like most snowmobile areas you follow logging roads until you hit snow. Popular access points are either the Piggott Main or Branch 62 off Mount Washington Road.

www.backroadmapbooks.com

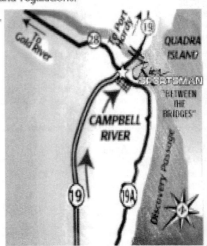

Vancouver Island Mapkey *(Including the Gulf Islands)*

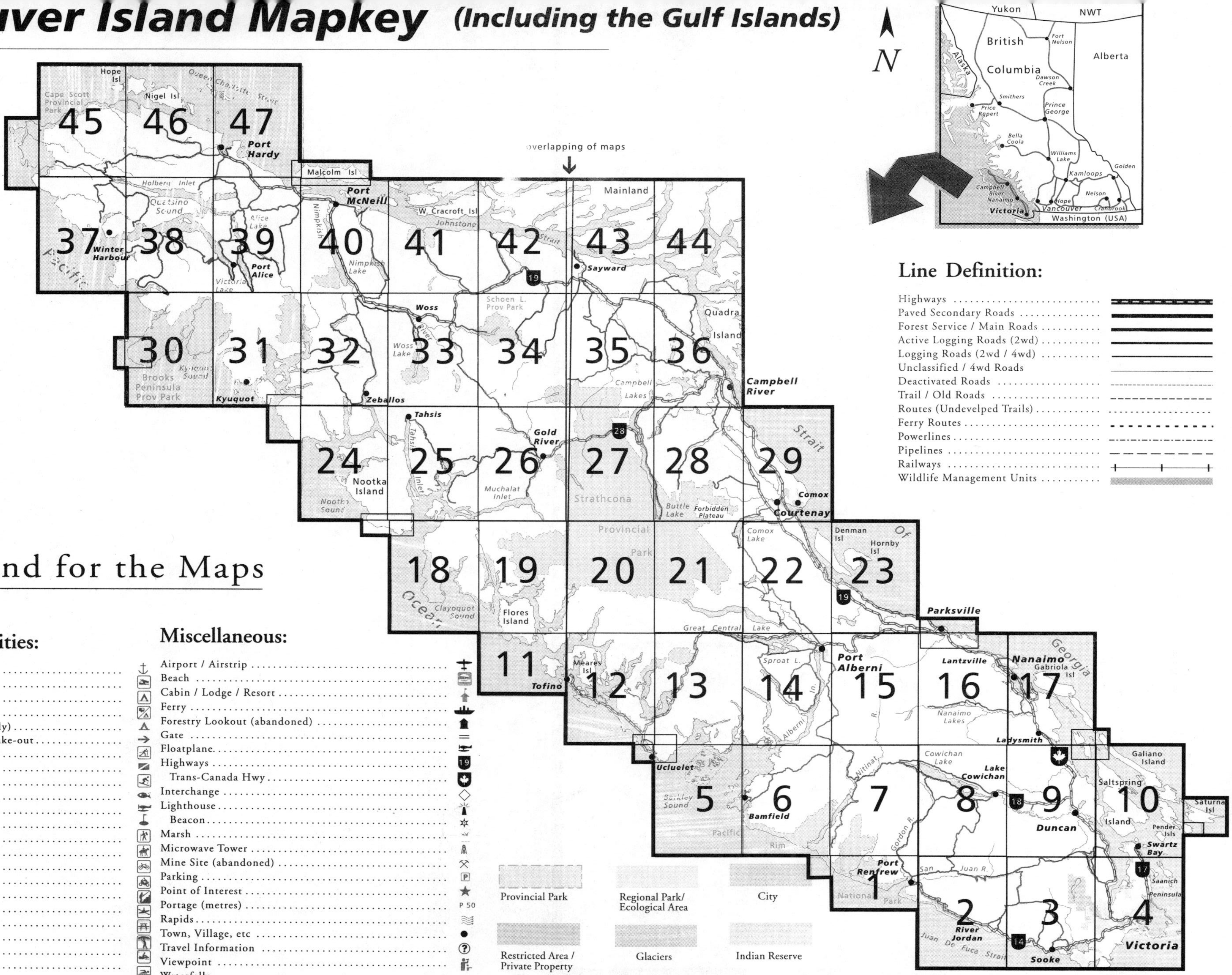

Line Definition:

Highways	
Paved Secondary Roads	
Forest Service / Main Roads	
Active Logging Roads (2wd)	
Logging Roads (2wd / 4wd)	
Unclassified / 4wd Roads	
Deactivated Roads	
Trail / Old Roads	
Routes (Undevelped Trails)	
Ferry Routes	
Powerlines	
Pipelines	
Railways	
Wildlife Management Units	

Legend for the Maps

Recreational Activities:

Anchorage

Boat Launch

Campsite / Limited Facilities

Campsite / Trailer Park

Campsite (trail / water access only)

Canoe / Kayak Access Put-in / Take-out

Cross Country Skiing

Diving

Downhill Skiing

Fishing

Float Plane

Golf Course

Hiking Trail

Horseback Riding

Mountain Biking

Motorbiking / ATV

Mountaineering

Paddling (canoe-kayak)

Picnic Site

Portage

Snowmobiling

Swimming

Miscellaneous:

Airport / Airstrip

Beach

Cabin / Lodge / Resort

Ferry

Forestry Lookout (abandoned)

Floatplane

Gate

Highways

Trans-Canada Hwy

Interchange

Lighthouse

Beacon

Marsh

Microwave Tower

Mine Site (abandoned)

Parking

Point of Interest

Portage (metres)

Rapids

Town, Village, etc

Travel Information

Viewpoint

Waterfalls

Map legend areas:

City

Regional Park / Ecological Area

Provincial Park

Restricted Area / Private Property

Indian Reserve

Glaciers

Index Map Labels:

Yukon
NWT
Alaska
British Columbia
Alberta
Fort Nelson
Dawson Creek
Smithers
Prince George
Golden
Bella Coola
Price Rupert
Williams Lake
Kamloops
Revelstoke
Hope
Nelson
Cranbrook
Vancouver
Campbell River
Nanaimo
Victoria
Washington (USA)

overlapping of maps

N

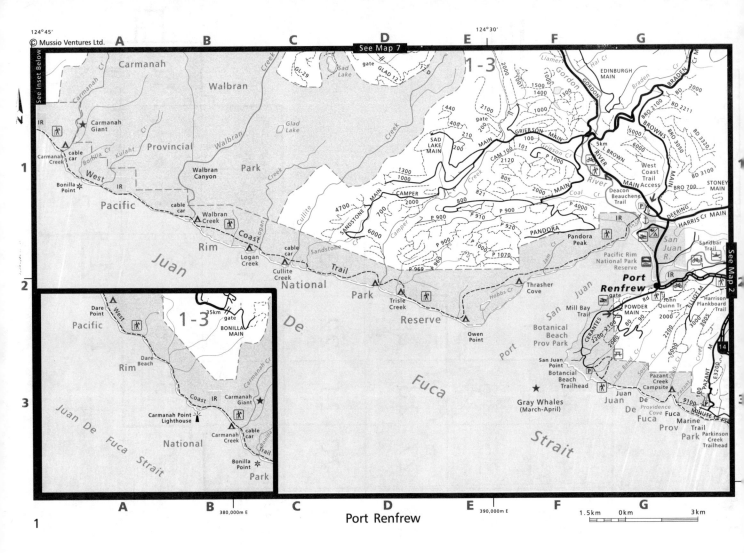

124° 45'

124° 30'

See Map 7

A B C D E F G

1 - 3

Carmanah

Walbran

GL-29

gate
GL-29
GLAD 12

1500
1400

EDINBURGH
MAIN

Liamen Cr

Gordon

Hal Cr

BRADEN

Cr M

BD 2000
BD 2211
BROWNS
BRO 3050
BD 3320

IR

Carmanah
Giant

Provincial

Glad
Lake

1440

2100

2000

1000

1300

BRO 2100

5000

6000

MAIN

BD 3100

Carmanah Cr

cable
car

West

Park

Walbran

400
210

gate
200

GRIERSON
MAIN

100

5km
L BROWN

West
Coast
Trail
Access

BRO 700

STONEY
MAIN

Bonilla
Point

Pacific

IR

Walbran
Canyon

SAD
LAKE
MAIN

200
CAM 100
101

Grierson Cr

1000

P 1000

RIVER

Deacon
Beauchene
Trail

DEERING

HARRIS Cr MAIN

cable
car

Walbran
Creek

Coast

Cullite

1300
1000

2120

805

CAMPER

P 900

P 4000

P
IR

San
Juan
R.

Sandbar
Trail

Rim

Logan
Creek

cable
car

Sandstone

4700

SANDSTONE MAIN

700
6000

2000

821

800
960

P 900

P 910

P 920

P 900

P 1000

PANDORA

Pandora
Peak

IR

Pacific Rim
National Park
Reserve

IR

San

Juan

Port
Renfrew
gate

John
Quinn Tr.

Harrison
Plankboard
Trail

Juan

National

P 969

Inn Cr

P 1070

Thrasher
Cove

Port

Mill Bay
Trail

POWDER
MAIN

80
90

FLUGTIM

2000

14

Cullite
Creek

De

Trisle
Creek

Park

Hobbs Cr

San Juan

2000
80 90

2000

2200

Reserve

Owen
Point

Botanical
Beach
Prov Park

Botanical
Beach
Trailhead

CERANTES

2200 2100
2060

Pazant
Creek
Campsite

Fuca

6000

PAZANT

Fuca

Juan

Juan

De

Providence
Cove

Fuca
Marine
Trail

Parkinson
Creek
Trailhead

Gray Whales
(March-April)

San Juan
Point

P

Tim Banfi

Soup Cr

9100

100
L3200

MINUTE

De

Prov
Park

Strait

Inset (See Inset Below / 1-3)

Dare
Point

Pacific

West

35km
gate

1 - 3

BONILLA
MAIN

Rim

Dare
Beach

Coast

IR

Carmanah Cr

Carmanah
Giant

Carmanah Point
Lighthouse

Coast

Carmanah
Creek

cable
car

Juan De Fuca Strait

National

Bonilla
Point

Trail

Park

A B 380,000m E C D E 390,000m E F G

Port Renfrew

1.5km   0km   3km

1

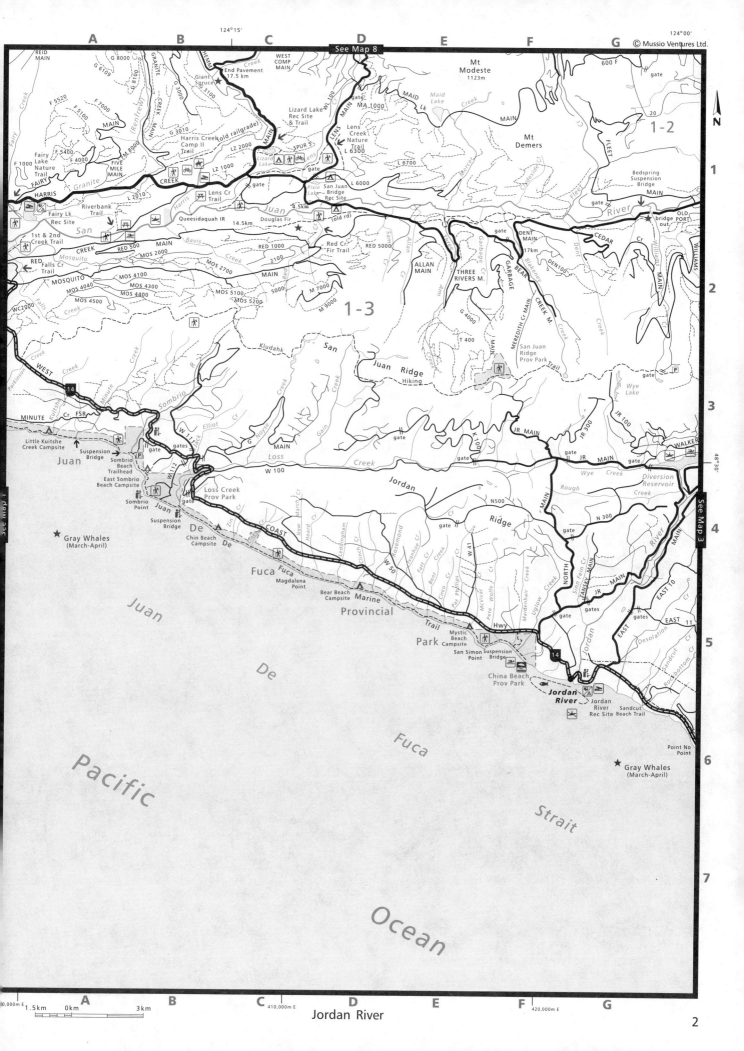

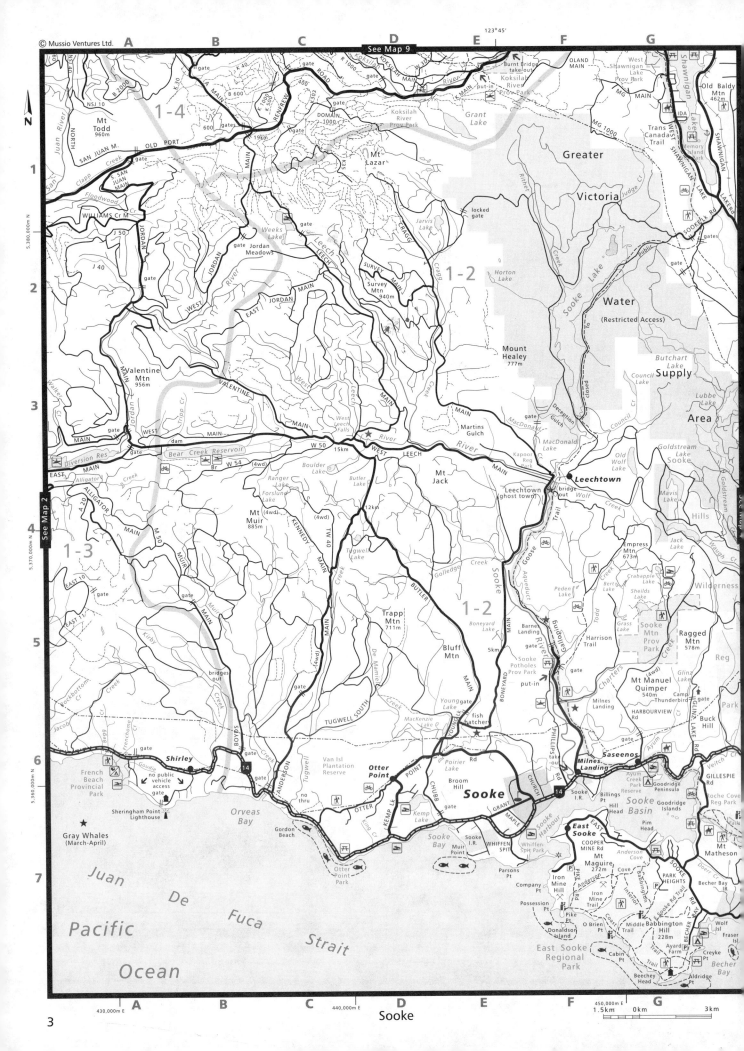

123°45'

N

1-4

Mt Todd 960m

Greater

Victoria

Water

(Restricted Access)

1-2

Supply

Area

1-3

1-2

Leechtown

1-2

Trapp Mtn 711m

Bluff Mtn

Mt Manuel Quimper 540m

Ragged Mtn 578m

Wilderness

Shirley

Otter Point

Sooke

Milnes Landing

Saseenos

East Sooke

COOPER MINE Rd
Mt Maguire 272m

French Beach Provincial Park

Gray Whales (March-April)

Orveas Bay

Sooke Basin

Juan

De

Fuca

Strait

Pacific

Ocean

East Sooke Regional Park

Becher Bay

430,000 m E   440,000 m E   Sooke   450,000 m E

0km   3km

1.5km

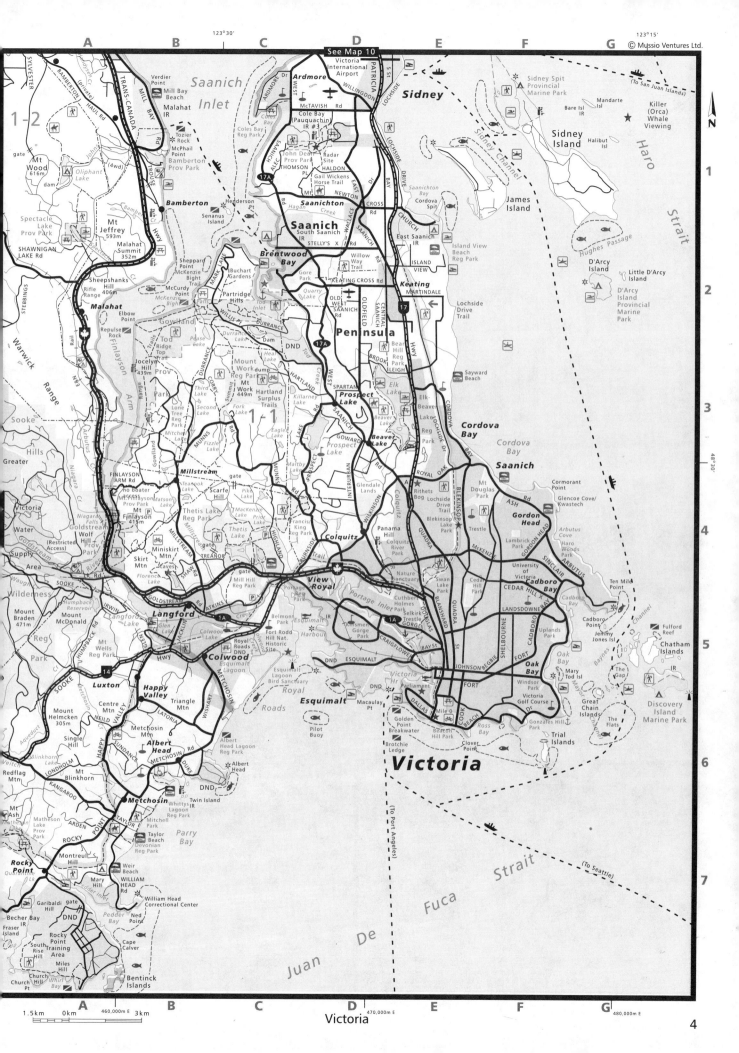

© Mussio Ventures Ltd.

123°30'

123°15'

A **B** **C** **D** **E** **F** **G**

1-2

Saanich Inlet

Ardmore

Victoria International Airport

Sidney

Sidney Spit Provincial Marine Park

Killer (Orca) Whale Viewing

McTAVISH Rd

Mill Bay Beach

Malahat IR

Verdier Point

Mandarte Isl

Bare Isl

Sidney Island

Halibut Isl

(To San Juan Islands)

Mt Wood 616m

gate

Oliphant Lake

(4wd)

dam

Tozier Rock

McPhail Point

Bamberton Prov Park

Cole Bay (Pauquachin) IR #3

John Dean Prov Park

Radar Site

Coles Bay Reg Park

THOMSON PL

HALDON

Gail Wickens Horse Trail

Sidney Channel

James Island

Cordova Spit

Haro Strait

Bamberton

Henderson Pt

NEWTON

Saanichton

CROSS

Saanichton Bay

Cordova Spit

1

Spectacle Lake Prov Park

Mt Jeffrey 593m

Mt Malahat Summit 352m

Senanus Island

Saanich

South Saanich IR

Hagan

East Saanich IR

Island View Beach Reg Park

D'Arcy Island

Little D'Arcy Island

SHAWNIGAN LAKE Rd

Sheepshanks Hill 406m

Sheppard Point McKenzie Bight Trail

Brentwood Bay

STELLY'S X

Willow Way Trail

ISLAND VIEW

D'Arcy Island Provincial Marine Park

Rifle Range

Buchart Gardens

KEATING CROSS Rd

Keating

Hughes Passage

2

Malahat

Elbow Point

Partridge Hills

Gore Park

McCurdy Point

McKenzie Bight

Quarry Lake

OLD WEST SAANICH Rd

MARTINDALE

48°30'

Repulse Rock

Gowlland

Tod Ridge Top Trail

Durrance Lake

dam

Heal Lake

OLDFIELD

CENTRAL

17

Lochside Drive Trail

Jocelyn Hill 439m

Prov

Pease Lake

Mount Work Reg Park

Peninsula

Bear Hill Reg Park

Sayward Beach

3

Sooke

Greater

Hills

Park

Mt Work 449m

Hartland Surplus Trails

Hartland

Killarney Lake

17A

SPARTAN

BROOK

LEIGH

Elk Lake

Elk-Beaver Lake Reg Park

Cordova Bay

Third Lake

Lone Tree Reg Park

Second Lake

Fork Lake

Prospect Lake

Beaver Lake

Cordova Bay

Finlayson Arm

Mt Finlayson 415m

Mitchell Lake

Eagles Lake

Goward

Prospect Lake

Beaver Lake

Saanich

FINLAYSON ARM Rd

no boater access

Yeawok Lake

Fizzle Lake

Maltby Lake

INTERURBAN

Mt Douglas Park

Cormorant Point

4

Victoria

Water Supply Area

Niagara Falls

Goldstream Wolf Hill Prov Park

Millstream

Scarfe Hill

Thetis Lake Reg Park

Prior Lake

MacKenzie Lake

Francis King Reg Park

Glendale Lands

Panama Hill

Rithets Bog

Lochside Drive Trail

Blenkinsop Lake Park

Trestle

Gordon Head

Glencoe Cove/ Kwastech

Haro Woods Park

Lambrick Park

Arbutus Cove

Skirt Mtn

Miniskirt Mtn

Keavesy

Florence Lake

Thetis Lake

HIGHLAND

MUNNS

Colquitz

Colquitz River Park

University of Victoria

Cadboro Bay

Ten Mile Point

5

Wilderness

Mount Braden 471m

Mount McDonald

Reg Park

Mt Wells Reg Park

Glen Lake

Langford Lake

Colwood Lake

Royal Roads Univ

Belmont Park

Fort Rodd Hill Nat. Historic Site

Esquimalt Lagoon

IR

Portage Reg Park

Portage Inlet Park

Kinsmen Gorge Park

Selkirk Trestle

GORGE

Swan Lake Park

Cuthbert Holmes Park

Cedar Hill Park

LANDSDOWNE

Uplands Park

Cadboro Point

Jemmy Jones Isl

Fulford Reef

Chatham Islands

Langford

View Royal

Colwood

Esquimalt Harbour

Esquimalt

CRAIGFLOWER

Victoria Hr

Parliament

Oak Bay

Windsor Park

Mary Tod Isl

The Gap

Discovery Island Marine Park

6

Luxton

Happy Valley

Triangle Mtn

Metchosin

Albert Head Lagoon Reg Park

Esquimalt Lagoon

Royal Roads

DND

Esquimalt

Macaulay Pt

Mile 0

Golden Point Breakwater

Beacon Hill Park

Victoria Golf Course

Gonzales Hill Park

Great Chain Islands

Trial Islands

The Flats

Mount Helmcken 305m

Centre Mtn

Single Hill

Mount Blinkhorn

Albert Head

DND

Albert Head

Twin Island

Pilot Buoy

Royal Roads

Victoria

Ross Bay

Clover Point

Brotchie Ledge

6

Mt Ash

Redflag Mtn

Matheson Lake Prov Park

Mitchell Park

Taylor Beach

Devonian Reg Park

Parry Bay

Whittys IR Lagoon Reg Park

DND

7

Rocky Point

Montreul Hill

Weir Beach

WILLIAM HEAD Rd

Garibaldi Hill

DND

William Head Correctional Center

Ned Point

Becher Bay

Fraser Island

South Rise Hill

Rocky Point Training Area

Cape Calver

Church Hill

Church Pt

Whirl Bay

Miles Hill

Bentinck Islands

Juan De Fuca Strait

(To Port Angeles)

(To Seattle)

N

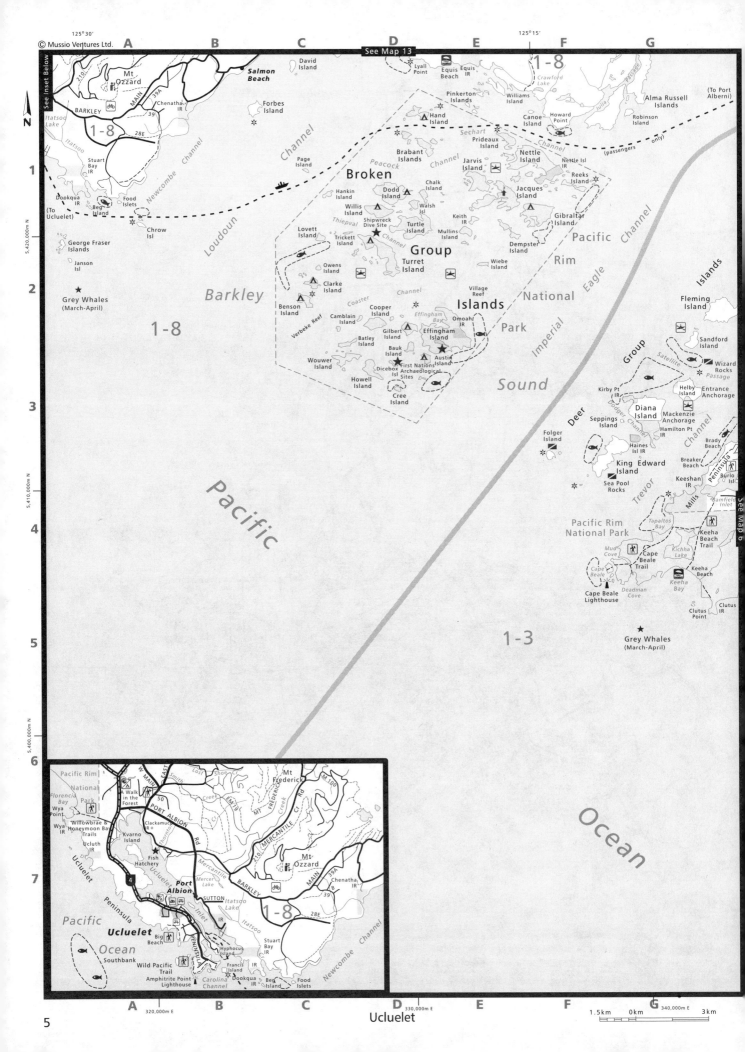

125°30'
125°15'

A **B** **C** **D** **E** **F** **G**

See Map 13

1-8

Mt Ozzard
210
BARKLEY
MAIN
39A
Chenatha IR
39
28E

Salmon Beach

David Island

Forbes Island

1-8

Itatsoo Lake
Itatsoo

Stuart Bay IR

Dookqua IR
(To Ucluelet)
Beg Island
Food Islets

Chrow Isl

Page Island

Loudoun Channel

Newcombe Channel

Lyall Point
Equis Beach
Equis IR

Pinkerton Islands

Williams Island

Canoe Island
Howard Point

Crawford Lake

Julia Passage

Alma Russell Islands

(To Port Alberni)

Robinson Island

(passengers only)

Hand Island

Brabant Islands

Peacock Channel

Sechart Channel

Prideaux Island

Jarvis Island

Nettle Island

Nettle Isl IR

Reeks Island

Broken

Hankin Island

Dodd Isl

Chalk Island

Willis Island

Walsh Island

Shipwreck Dive Site

Turtle Island

Keith IR

Mullins Island

Jacques Island

Gibraltar Island

Group

George Fraser Islands

Janson Isl

★ Grey Whales (March-April)

Barkley

Lovett Island

Trickett Island

Thiepval Channel

Owens Island

Clarke Island

Turret Island

Coaster Channel

Benson Island

Verbeke Reef

Camblain Island

Cooper Island

Effingham Bay

Village Reef

Omoah IR

Islands

Gilbert Island

Batley Island

Bauk Island

Effingham Island

Austin Island

Dempster Island

Wiebe Island

Pacific Rim National Park

Imperial Eagle Channel

Fleming Island

Sandford Island

Wizard Rocks

Satellite Passage

Sound

Group

Deer

Kirby Pt IR

Seppings Island

Dodger Channel

Helby Island

Entrance Anchorage

Diana Island

Mackenzie Anchorage

Hamilton Pt IR

Brady Beach

1-8

5,420,000m N

5,410,000m N

5,400,000m N

1

2

3

4

5

6

7

Wouwer Island

Howell Island

Dicebox Isl

First Nations Archaeological Sites

Cree Island

Folger Island

Haines Isl IR

Sea Pool Rocks

King Edward Island

Trevor

Channel

Keeshan IR

Breaker Beach

Mills

Burlo Isl

Camfield Inlet

Peninsula

Pacific

Pacific Rim National Park

Tapaltos Bay

Mud Cove

Cape Beale Trail

Kichha Lake

Keeha Beach Trail

Cape Beale

Deadman Cove

Keeha Bay

Cape Beale Lighthouse

Clutus Point

Clutus IR

Ocean

1-3

★ Grey Whales (March-April)

See Map 13

See Map 6

Inset: Ucluelet

Pacific Rim National Park

Florencia Bay

Wya Point

Wya IR

A Walk in the Forest

Willowbrae & Honeymoon Bay Trails

Kvarno Island

Ucluth IR

Fish Hatchery

W MAIN
EAST

Smith Cr

Lost Shoe Cr

Mt Frederick

M 100

PORT ALBION

50

Clackamuck Cr

Mercantile Cr Rd

MT FREDERICK

EM79

210

BARKLEY

MAIN

39A

Chenatha IR

39

28E

Mt Ozzard

1-8

Mercantile Rd

Mercer Lake

Port Albion

SUTTON

Itatsoo Lake

Stuart Bay IR

Ucluelet Inlet

Thornton Cr

Peninsula

Pacific

Wild Pacific Trail

Big Beach

Hyphocus Island

Francis Island

Carolina Channel

Ucluelet

PENINSULA

Amphitrite Point Lighthouse

Dookqua IR

Beg Island

Food Islets

Newcombe Channel

Ocean

Southbank

4

A **B** **C** **D** **E** **F** **G**

320,000m E
330,000m E
340,000m E

Ucluelet

1.5km 0km 3km

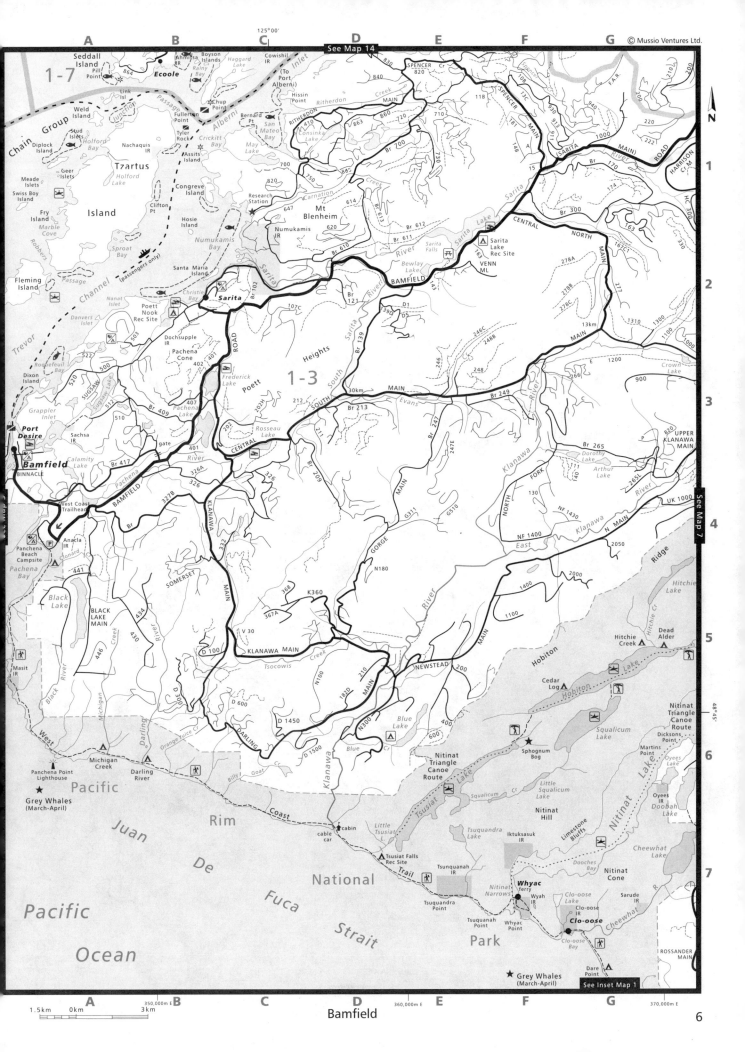

1-7

N

Chain Group

Island

Pacific Ocean

Pacific

Juan

De

Fuca

Strait

National

Park

Bamfield

1-3

Alberni Channel

Trevor Channel

Seddall Island
Pill Point
864
Ecoole
Ahmilsa IR
Boyson Islands
Haggard Lake
Cowishil IR
Rainy Bay
Link Isl
Junction
Weld Island
Fullerton Point
Chup Point
Tyler Rock
Bernard Pt
San Mateo Bay
Hissin Point
Diplock Island
Holford Bay
Nachaquis IR
Crickitt Bay
Assits Island
Congreve Island
May Lake
Meade Islets
Geer Islets
Swiss Boy Island
Fry Island
Marble Cove
Clifton Pt
Hosie Island
Numukamis Bay
Research Station
Numukamis IR
Mt Blenheim
620
647
614
Fleming Island
Robbers Passage
Sproat Bay
Santa Maria Island
Christie Bay
Br 102
Sarita
Poett Nook Rec Site
503
Br 610
Br 611
Br 612
Br 613
Danvers Islet
Nanat Islet
Dochsupple IR
Br 121
Pachena Cone
402
401
107C
Roquefeuil Bay
522
500
520
512
Frederick Lake
Poett Heights
South Sarita River
30km
Dixon Island
SUGSAW
Sugsaw Lake
Br 409
407 Pachena Lake
202H
212
211
Rosseau Lake
Grappler Inlet
510
Port Desire
Sachsa IR
gate
401
326A
326
202
BINNACLE
Bamfield
Calamity Lake
Br 417
BAMFIELD
327B
KLANAWA
West Coast Trailhead
Br
Anacla IR
441
Clonard
Pachena Beach Campsite
Pachena Bay
Somerset
MAIN
434
430
446
BLACK LAKE MAIN
Black Lake
Masit IR
Black River
Michigan River
Darling River
Orange Juice Cr
Michigan Creek
Darling River
Panchena Point Lighthouse
Grey Whales (March-April)
Rim

Spencer Cr
SPENCER 820
830
840
108
11B
13C
781
863
860
720
710
RITHERDON
410
Consinka Lake
Br 700
Carnation Creek
750
730
700
820
865
SARITA MAIN (River)
15
148
A
911
913
917
940
1000
Sarita Lake
Sarita Falls
Bewlay Lake
Sarita Lake Rec Site
CENTRAL NORTH MAIN
143
VENN ML
163
Br 300
174
167C1
278A
278B
278C
271
13km
MAIN
246C
248B
246
248
Evans
BAMFIELD
D1
D5
390
Br 139
Br 213
SOUTH CENTRAL MAIN
Br 249
Br 247
247E
1200
900
Crown Lake
266
E
P
820
UPPER KLANAWA MAIN
Br 265
Dorothy Lake
111
140
Arthur Lake
River
GORGE
G311
G510
130
NF 1430
NF 1400
N180
NORTH FORK
265L
2050
Ridge
Hitchie Lake
UK 1000
N MAIN
Klanawa East River
1400
2000
1100
Hitchie Cr
Hitchie Creek
Dead Alder
368
K360
367A
V 30
D 100
KLANAWA MAIN
Tsocowis Creek
N100
182D
210
MAIN
NEWSTEAD
200
Hobiton
Hobiton Lake
Cedar Log
Squalicum Lake
Nitinat Triangle Canoe Route
Dicksons Point
Martins Point
Oyees Lake
N300
Blue Lake
Blue Cr
400
600
Sphognum Bog
Little Squalicum Lake
Nitinat Hill
Oyees IR
Doobah Lake
D 600
D 1450
DARLING
D 1500
Klanawa River
Billy Goat Cr
Tsunquanah IR
Squalicum Cr
Nitinat Triangle Canoe Route
Iktuksasuk IR
Limestone Bluffs
Cheewhat Lake
Nitinat Lake
Coast
Trail
cable car
cabin
Little Tsusiat
Tsusiat Lake
Tsuquandra Lake
Nitinat Cone
Tsusiat Falls Rec Site
Tsunquanah IR
Tsuquandra Point
Nitinat Narrows
Whyac
ferry
Wyah IR
Wyah Point
Clo-oose Lake
Sarude IR
Cheewhat R
Grey Whales (March-April)
Tsuquanah Point
Whyac Point
Clo-oose
Clo-oose IR
Clo-oose Bay
Dare Point
ROSSANDER MAIN

See Map 7

See Inset Map 1

125°00'

48°45'

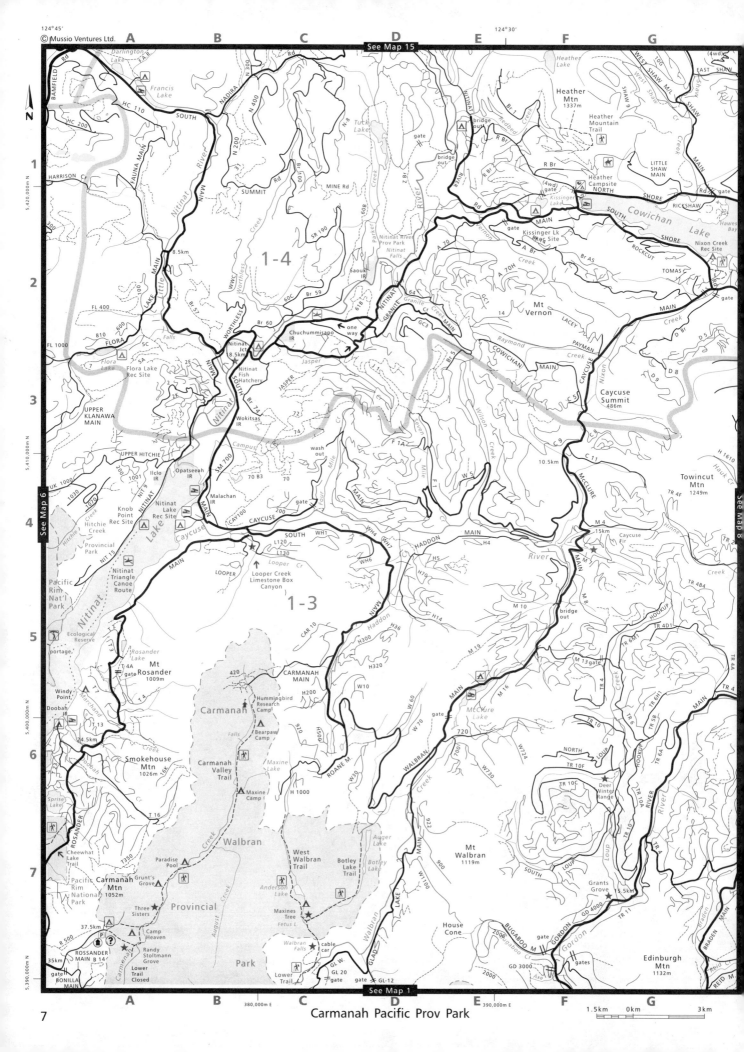

© Mussio Ventures Ltd.

N

1-4

1-3

Carmanah Pacific Prov Park

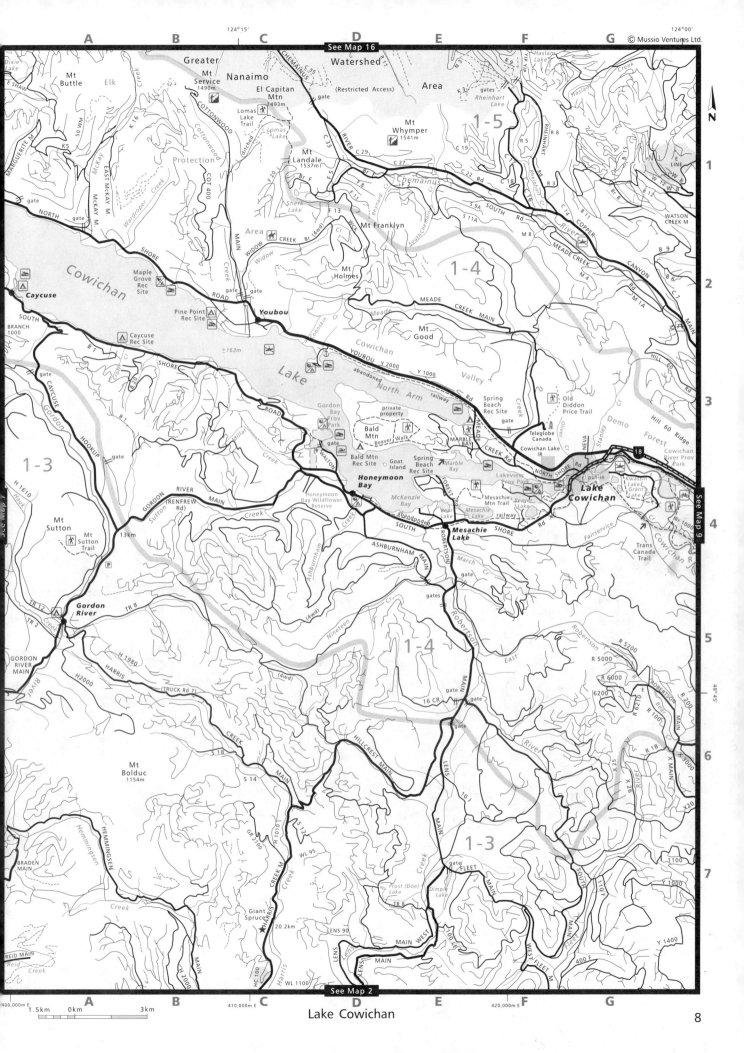

124°15'

124°00'

A   **B**   **C**   **D**   **E**   **F**   **G**

Greater Nanaimo Watershed Area (Restricted Access)

Mt Buttle

Mt Service 1490m

El Capitan Mtn 1493m

Lomas Lake Trail

Mt Landale 1537m

Mt Whymper 1541m

Rheinhart Lake

Protection

Area

Mt Franklyn

Mt Holmes

1-5

1-4

Cowichan

Maple Grove Rec Site

Pine Point Rec Site

Youbou

Caycuse

Caycuse Rec Site

Mt Good

Lake

Cowichan Valley

North Arm

abandoned railway

Spring Beach Rec Site

Old Diddon Price Trail

Teleglobe Canada

Hill 60 Ridge

Demo Forest

1-3

Mt Sutton

Mt Sutton Trail

Gordon Bay Prov Park

Bald Mtn

private property

Beaver Walk

Bald Mtn Rec Site

Goat Island

Spring Beach Rec Site

Marble Bay

Cowichan Lake IR

Lakeview Prov Park

Lake Cowichan

Kwassin Lake

Grant Lake

Cowichan River Prov Park

13km

Honeymoon Bay

Honeymoon Bay Wildflower Reserve

McKenzie Bay

Mesachie Mtn Trail

Mesachie Lake

Bear Lake

railway

Fairservice

Trans Canada Trail

Gordon River

Mesachie Lake

Mt Bolduc 1154m

Ashburnham

1-4

1-3

16 CR

Giant Spruce

20.2km

Prost (Doe) Lake

Dimple Lake

FLEET

1.5km   0km   3km

400,000m E   410,000m E   420,000m E

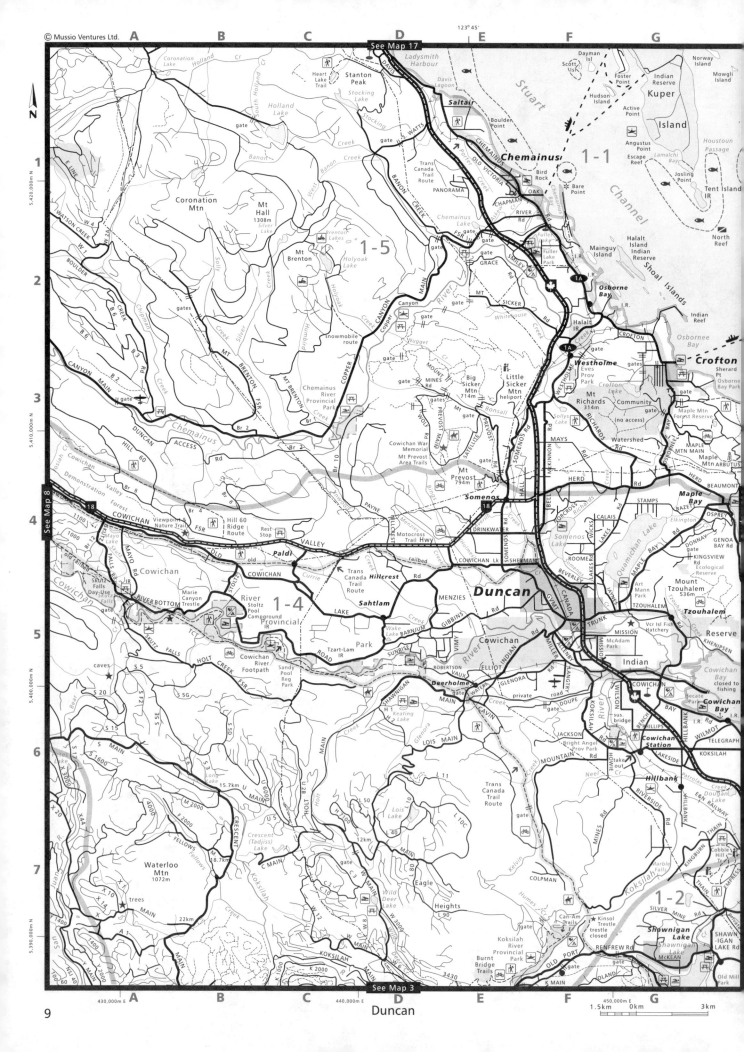

123° 45'

See Map 17

A   B   C   D   E   F   G

1-1

Kuper
Island

1-5

1-4

1-2

See Map 8

See Map 3

A   B   C   D   E   F   G

430,000m E   440,000m E   450,000m E

9   Duncan

1.5km   0km   3km

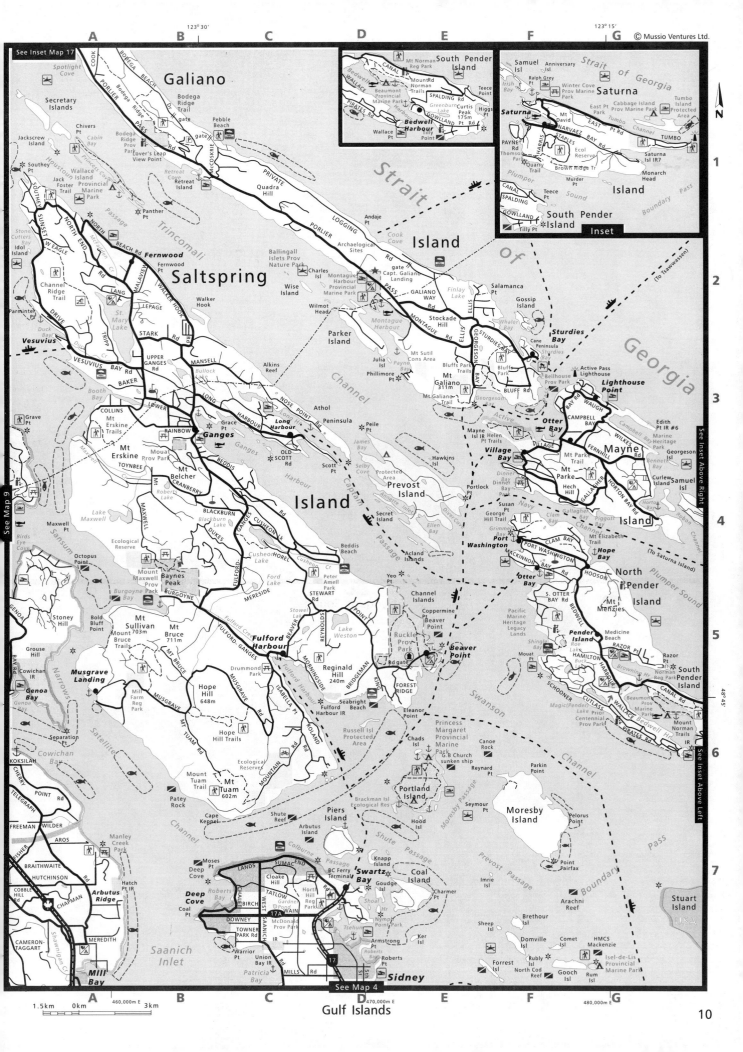

Gulf Islands

10

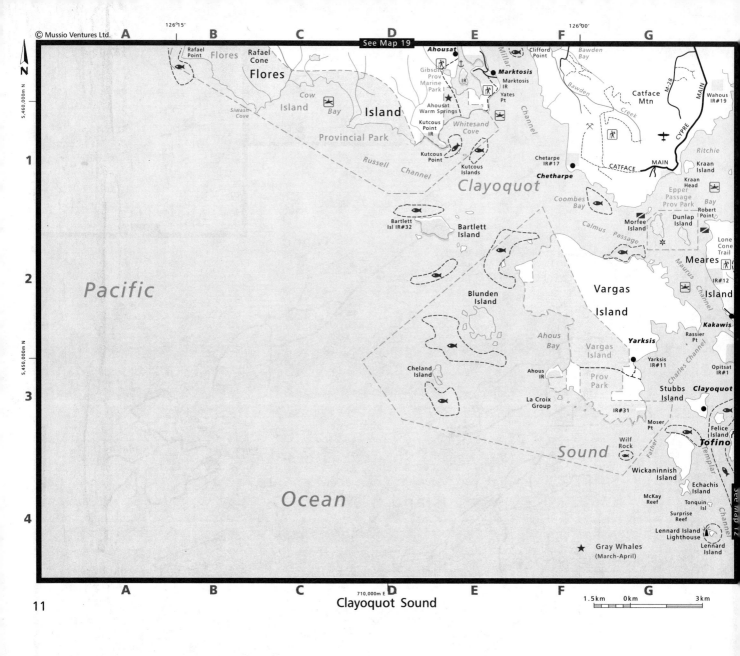

A   126°15'   **B**   **C**   **D**   **E**   **F**   126°00'   **G**

© Mussio Ventures Ltd.

N

5,460,000m N

Rafael Point

Flores

Rafael Cone

Flores

Cow Island

Bay

Island

Siwash Cove

Provincial Park

Russell Channel

Ahousat

Gibsons Prov Marine Park

IR

Ahousat Warm Springs

Kutcous Point IR

Whitesand Cove

Kutcous Point

Kutcous Islands

Clifford Point

Bawden Bay

Marktosis
Marktosis IR

Yates Pt

Millar Channel

Bawden Creek

Catface Mtn

M-28

CATFACE MAIN

Wahous IR#19

Ritchie

CYPRE MAIN

Clayoquot

Chetarpe IR#17

Chetharpe

Coombes Bay

Calmus Passage

Morfee Island

Dunlap Island

Kraan Island

Kraan Head

Epper Passage Prov Park

Robert Point

Lone Cone Trail

1

5,450,000m N

Pacific

Bartlett Isl IR#32

Bartlett Island

Blunden Island

Cheland Island

Ahous Bay

La Croix Group

Ahous IR

Vargas Island

Prov Park

IR#31

Vargas

Island

Maurus Channel

Meares

IR#12

Island

Kakawis

Rassier Pt

Yarksis IR#11

Yarksis

Opitsat IR#1

Charles Channel

Stubbs Island

Clayoquot

2

3

Moser Pt

Wilf Rock

Felice Island

Tofino

Ocean

Wickaninnish Island

McKay Reef

Echachis Island

Tonquin Isl

Surprise Reef

Lennard Island Lighthouse

Lennard Island

Sound

Father

Templar

Channel

See Map 12

★ Gray Whales
(March-April)

4

A   **B**   **C**   710,000m E **D**   **E**   **F**   **G**

11

Clayoquot Sound

1.5km   0km   3km

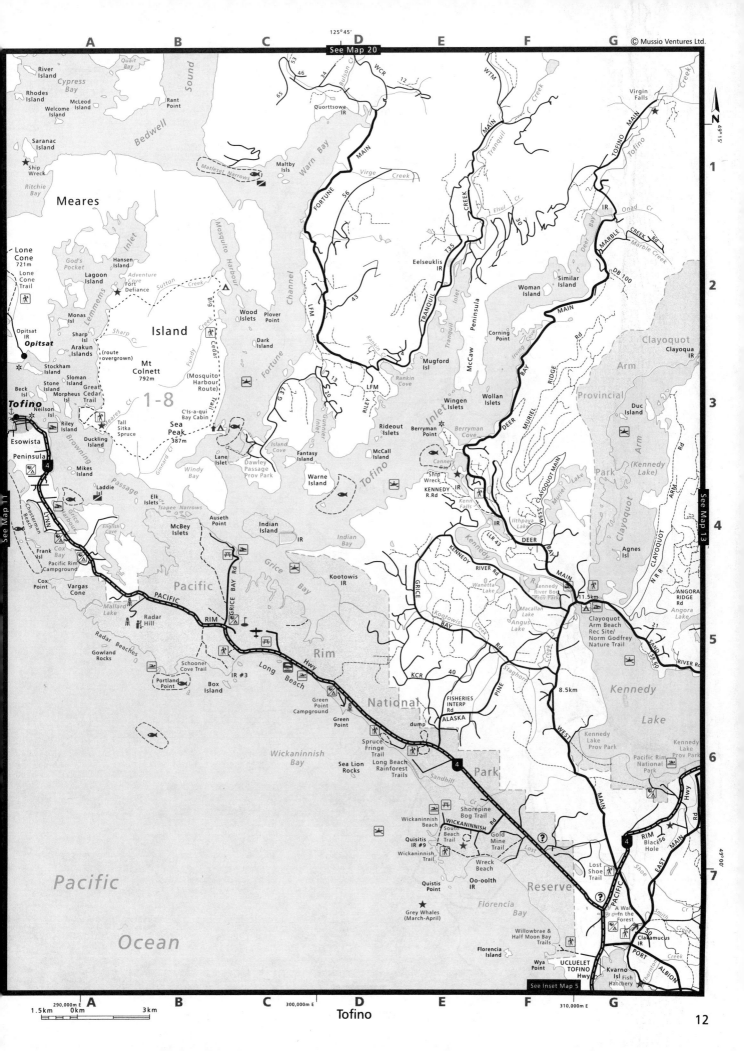

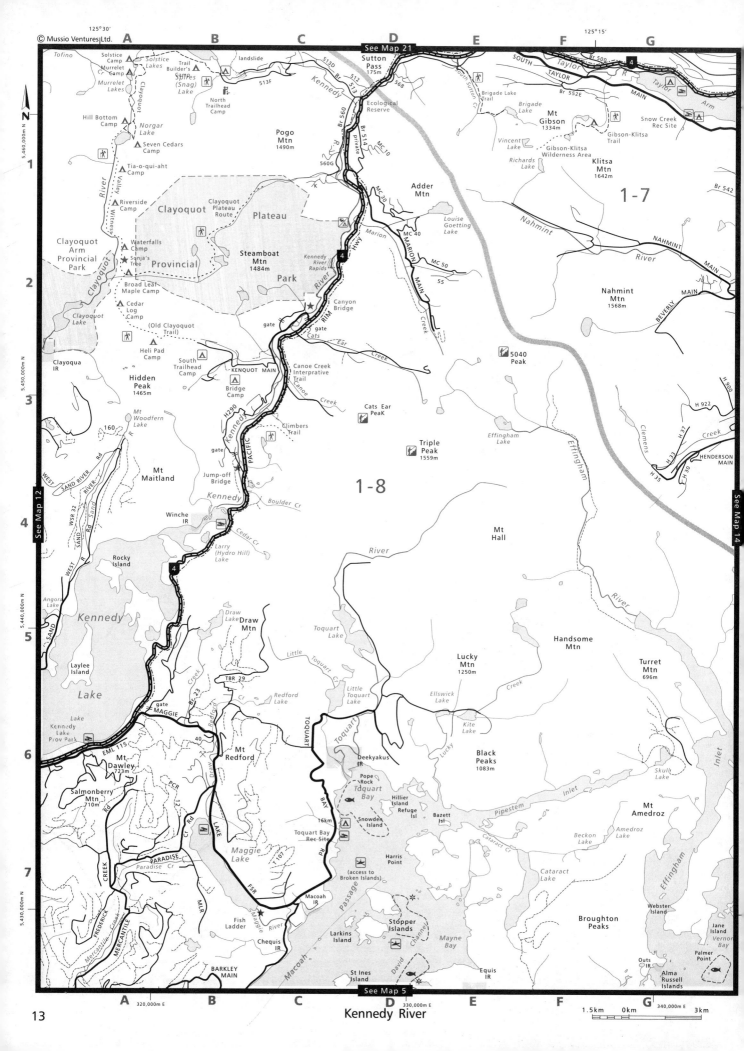

© Mussio Ventures Ltd.

125°30'

125°15'

1-7

1-8

13

Kennedy River

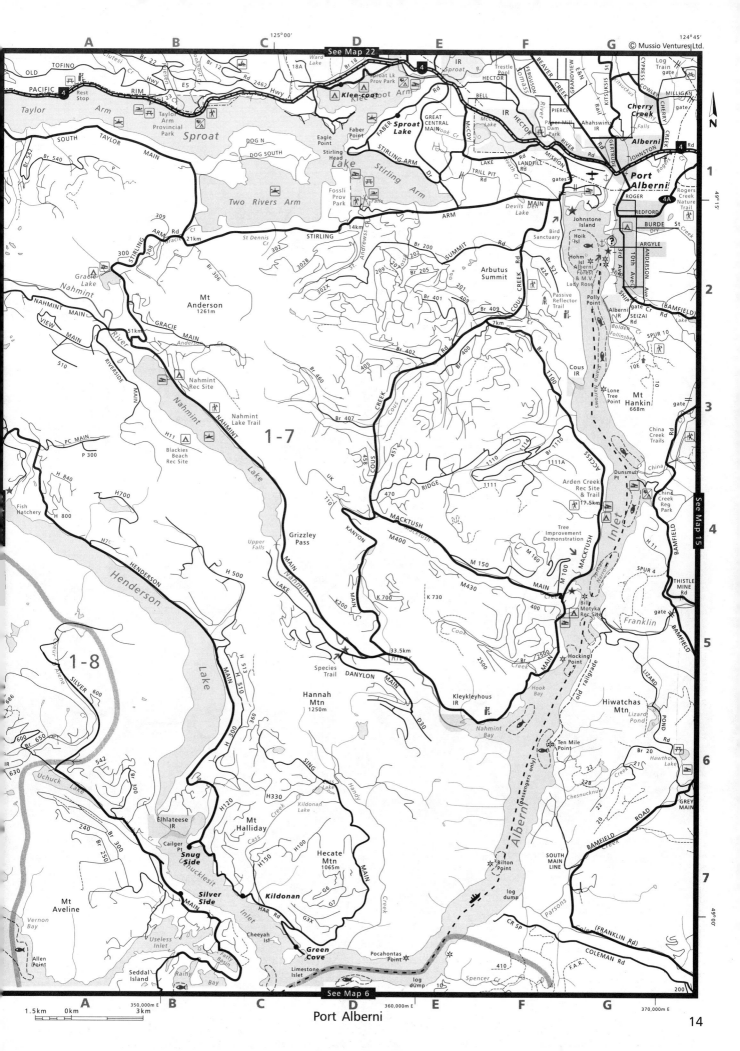

© Mussio Ventures Ltd.

See Map 22

See Map 15

See Map 6

1-7

1-8

1.5km   0km   3km

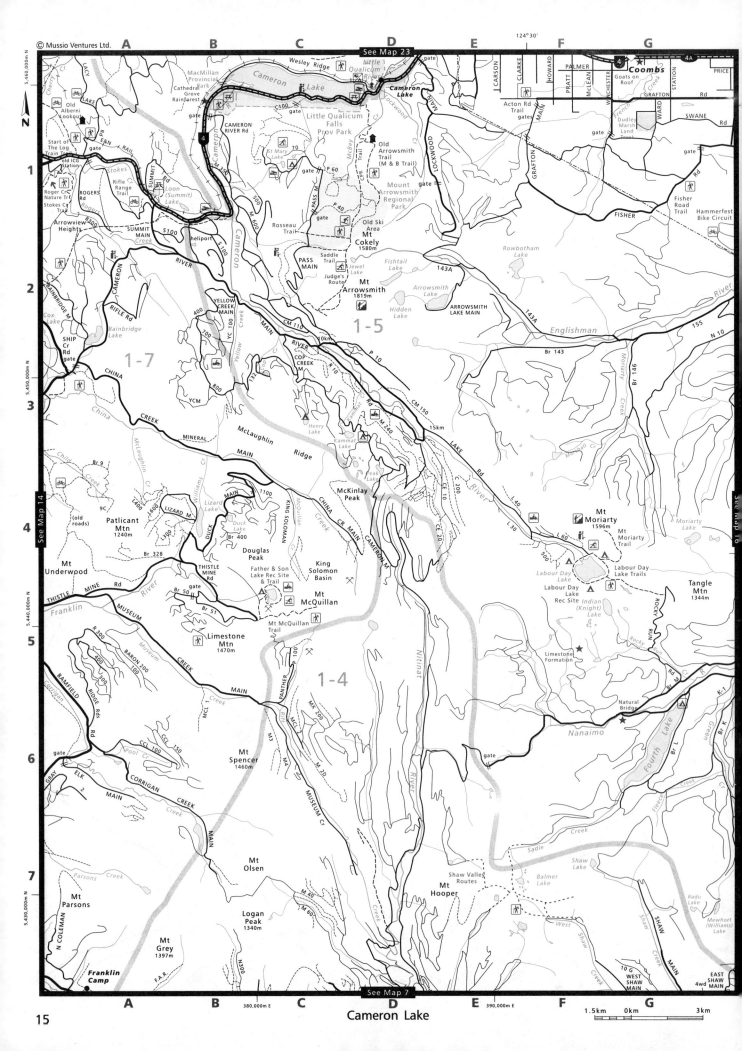

124° 30'

See Map 23

Coombs

Goats on Roof

See Map 14

See Map 16

1-7

1-5

1-4

See Map 7

Cameron Lake

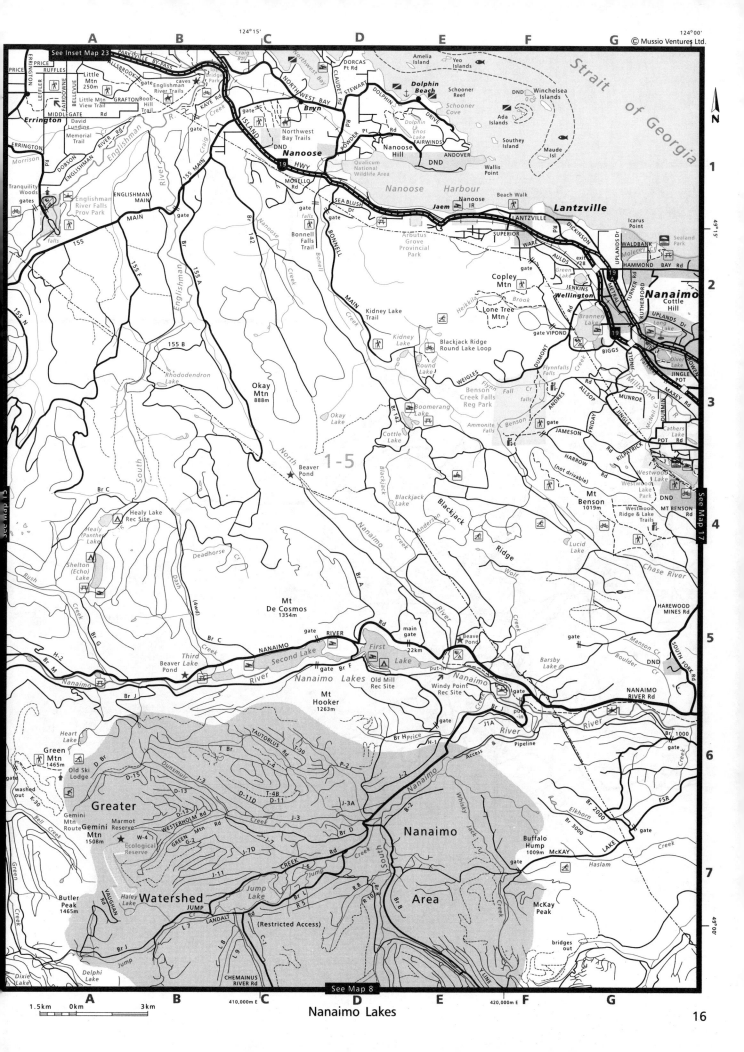

A B C D E F G

Strait of Georgia

1

49°15'

2

3

4

See Map 17

5

6

7

49°00'

1.5km 0km 3km

A B C D E F G

410,000m E 420,000m E

Nanaimo Lakes

16

See Inset Map 23

See Map 23

See Map 8

Price *Errington* *Ruffles*
Lefler *Bellevue* *Fairdowne*

Little Mtn 250m

Errington
David Lundine Memorial Trail

Tranquility Woods

Englishman River Falls Prov Park

falls

155

155 N

155 F

155 A

MAIN

ENGLISHMAN MAIN

155 B

Rhododendron Lake

Okay Mtn 888m

Okay Lake

Beaver Pond

1-5

Br C

Healy Lake Rec Site

Healy Panther Lake

Shelton (Echo) Lake

Br G

Br M

Deadhorse Cr

Mt De Cosmos 1354m

Third Beaver Lake Pond

NANAIMO

Br C

RIVER

Second Lake

Nanaimo Lakes

Mt Hooker 1263m

gate

First Lake

Old Mill Rec Site

Heart Lake

Green Mtn 1465m

Old Ski Lodge

Gemini Mtn Route

Gemini Mtn 1508m

Marmot Reserve

W-4 Ecological Reserve

Greater

Watershed

Butler Peak 1465m

Haley Lake

VAUGHAN Rd

JUMP

Jump

Delphi Lake

Dixie Lake

CHEMAINUS RIVER Rd

Dunsmuir

WESTERHOLM Rd

GREEN Mtn Rd

G-2

TAUTORLUS Rd

T Br

D Br

D-15

D-13

D-12

D-11D

D-11

T-4

T-4B

T-30

J-3

J-7

J-7D

J-11

L 7

LB

L 9

J-3A

J-3

Br D

J-6

CREEK

JUMP

LANDALT Rd

Br L

R S

(Restricted Access)

Jump Lake

P-2

Br H price

H-1

Br A

Nanaimo

Creek

Blackjack Creek

South

Nanaimo

River

Pipeline

Access

Br J

J1A

put-in

Nanaimo

Area

Whisky Jack Cr

B-2

Jack

South

Creek

Nanaimo

River

LAKE

Buffalo Hump 1009m

McKAY

gate

McKay Peak

Haslam

Br 1000

Br 2000

Br 3000

Elkhorn

FSR

Creek

bridges out

Y LINE

Craig Bay

PARKSVILLE BY-PASS

Englishman River Trails

gate

caves

KAYE Rd

Craig Creek

155 MAIN

Br 142

Nanoose Creek

MORELLO Rd

Br

gate

Bonnell Falls Trail

Bonnell Creek

SEA BLUSH Dr

BONNELL

MAIN

Kidney Lake Trail

Kidney Lake

Round Lake

Cottle Lake

Br 142

Boomerang Lake

Blackjack Lake

Andersson Cr

Blackjack Ridge

Wolf

NORTHWEST BAY Rd

NORTHWEST Bay

DOLPHIN DRIVE

CLAUDET Rd

STEWART Rd

POWDER Pt Rd

Bryn

Northwest Bay Trails

DND

Nanoose

19 HWY

Nanoose Hill

Dolphin L

Enos Lake

DORCAS Pt Rd

Dolphin Beach

Schooner Cove

Schooner Reef

Amelia Island

Yeo Islands

DND

Winchelsea Islands

Ada Islands

Southey Island

Maude Isl

Wallis Point

ANDOVER

FAIRWINDS

Qualicum National Wildlife Area

Nanoose Harbour

Jaem

Nanoose IR

Beach Walk

Lantzville

Icarus Point

SUPERIOR

WARE

DICKINSON

AULDS

Green Lake

UPLANDS Dr

WALDBANK

Molecey

HAMMOND BAY Rd

Sealand Park

exit 28

Arbutus Grove Provincial Park

Copley Mtn

Lone Tree Mtn

Heikkila

Brook

JENKINS

Wellington

gate VIPOND

DUMONT

WEIGLES

Flynn

Fall

Cr

falls

Flynnfalls Falls

Benson Creek Falls Reg Park

Ammonite Falls

Benson

ANDRES

JAMESON

FRIDAY

ALLSOP

HARROW

(not drivable)

Mt Benson 1019m

MT BENSON

Westwood Ridge & Lake Trails

Westwood Lake Park

Lucid Lake

Chase River

HAREWOOD MINES Rd

DND

Manson Cr

Boulder

SOUTH FORK Rd

Barsby Lake

NANAIMO RIVER Rd

gate

Nanaimo

Cottle Hill

RUTHERFORD

TURNER Rd

METRAL

BIGGS

JINGLE

MUNROE

KILPATRICK

DURMIN

MAXEY Rd

JINGLE POT

Diver

Millstone

OWEN

Long

Lk

Brannen Lake

19A

19

Cathers Lake Rd

Westwood Lake

put-in

-22km

main gate

Windy Point Rec Site

Beaver Pond

River

Br J

gate

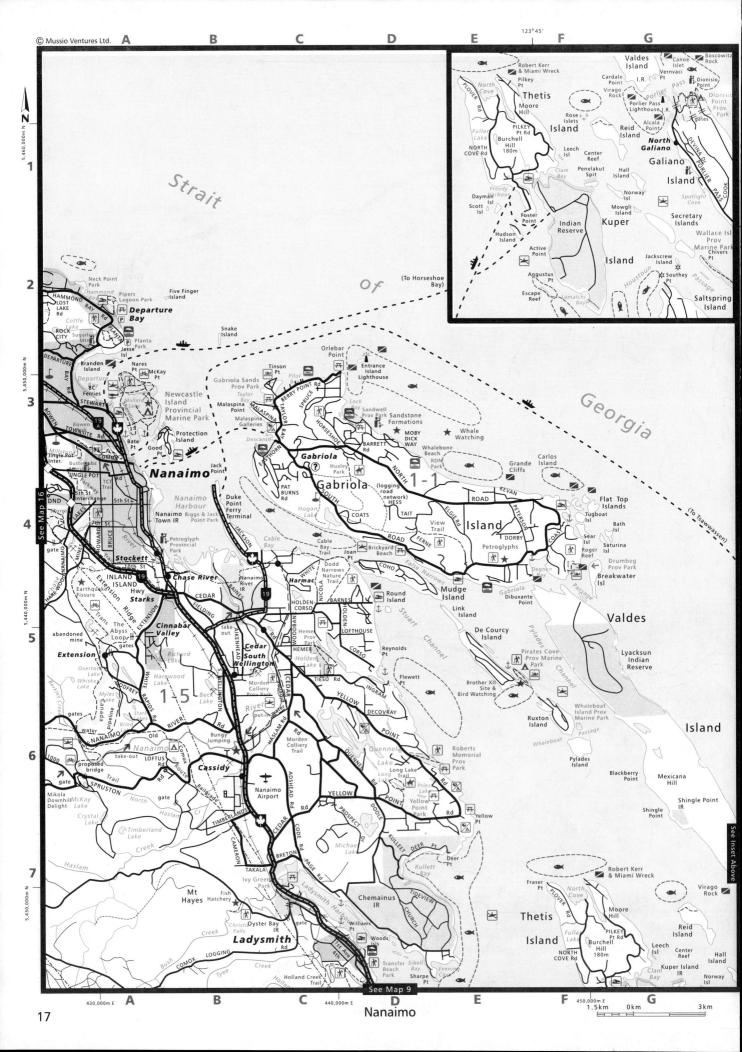

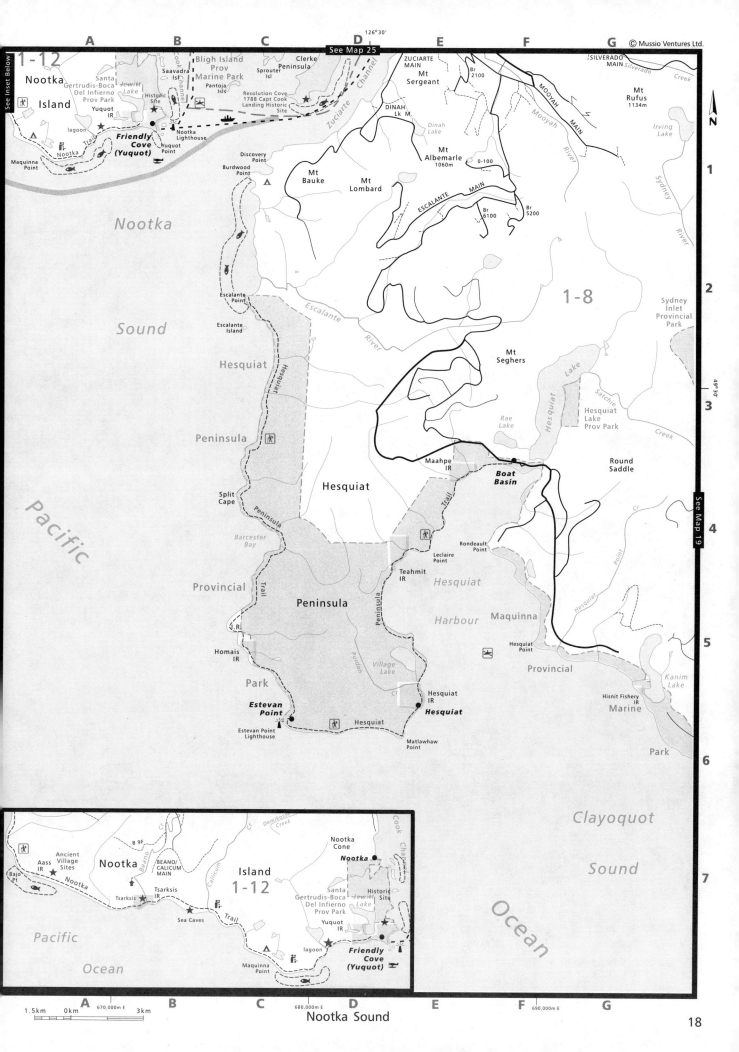

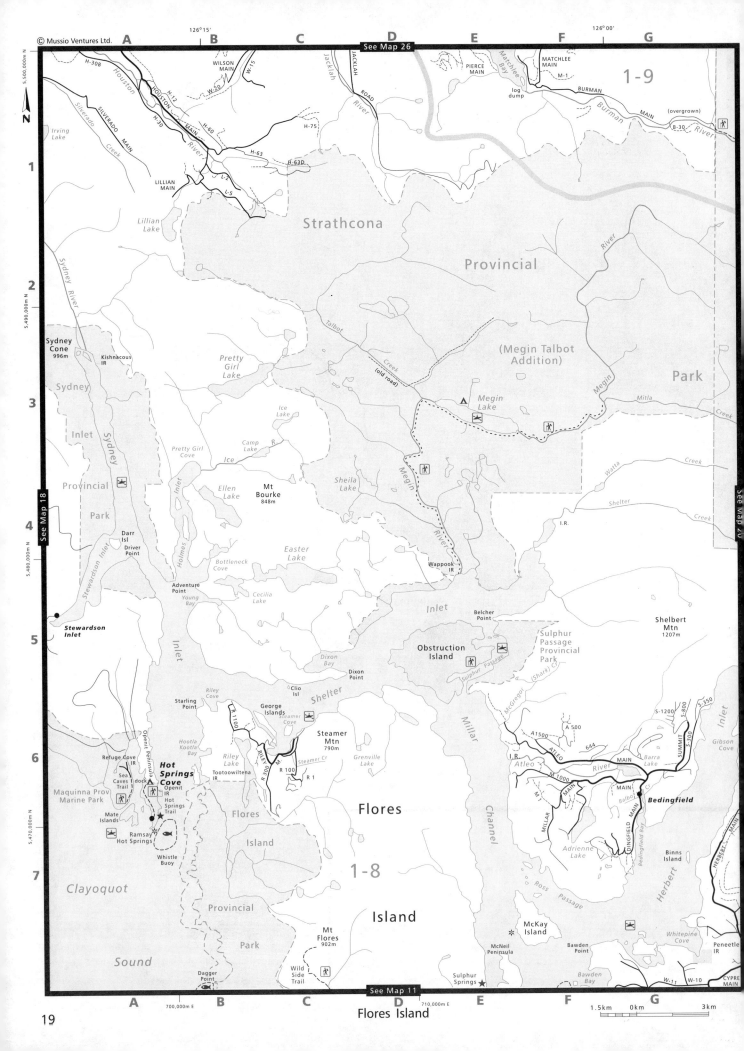

© Mussio Ventures Ltd.

126°15'   126°00'

A   B   C   D   E   F   G

1-9

Houston

H-30B

SILVERADO MAIN

Silverado Creek

Irving Lake

HOUSTON MAIN

H-30

H-12

H-60

WILSON MAIN

W-15

W-20

JACKLAH ROAD

Jacklah River

PIERCE MAIN

MATCHLEE MAIN

M-1

Matchlee Bay

log dump

BURMAN MAIN

B-30

Burman River

(overgrown)

1

LILLIAN MAIN

H-63

H-63D

L-2

L-5

Lillian Lake

Strathcona

Provincial

2

Sydney River

Sydney Cone
996m

Kishnacous IR

Pretty Girl Lake

Talbot Creek

(old road)

(Megin Talbot Addition)

Megin

Park

Mitla

3

Sydney

Inlet

Pretty Girl Cove

Ice Lake

Camp Lake

Ice R

Megin Lake

Megin

4

Provincial

Park

Darr Isl
Driver Point

Holmes Inlet

Ellen Lake

Mt Bourke
848m

Sheila Lake

Bottleneck Cove

Easter Lake

Megin River

Wappook IR

I.R.

Watta Creek

Shelter Creek

5

Stewardson Inlet

Adventure Point

Young Bay

Cecilia Lake

Inlet

Dixon Bay

Dixon Point

Belcher Point

Obstruction Island

Inlet

Sulphur Passage

Sulphur Passage Provincial Park

Shelbert Mtn
1207m

6

Starling Point

Riley Cove

Clio Isl

George Islands

Steamer Cove

Shelter

Steamer Mtn
790m

Grenville Lake

Millar

McGregor Cr

(Shark) Cr

S-1200

S-800

A1500

A 500

ATLEO MAIN

644

S-350

S-300

SUMMIT

Barra Lake

Gibson Cove

Hootla Kootla Bay

Riley Lake

R 1100

RILEY RD

R M.

R 100

Tootoowiltena IR

Steamer Cr

R 1

Channel

I.R.

Atleo River

M 1000

M 1

MILLAR MAIN

Balbot Cr

DINGFIELD MAIN

Bedingfield

HERBERT MAIN

Refuge Cove IR

Openit Peninsula

Hot Springs Cove

Openit IR
Hot Springs IR

Flores

Flores

Island

Adrienne Lake

Bedingfield Bay

Binns Island

Sea Caves Trail

dock

Hot Springs Trail

Maquinna Prov Marine Park

Mate Islands

Ramsay Hot Springs

Whistle Buoy

1-8

Herbert

7

Clayoquot

Provincial

Park

Mt Flores
902m

Wild Side Trail

Ross Passage

McKay Island

McNeil Peninsula

Sulphur Springs

Bawden Point

Bawden Bay

Whitepine Cove

Peneetle IR

W-11

W-10

CYPRE MAIN

Sound

Dagger Point

Flores Island

1.5km   0km   3km

19

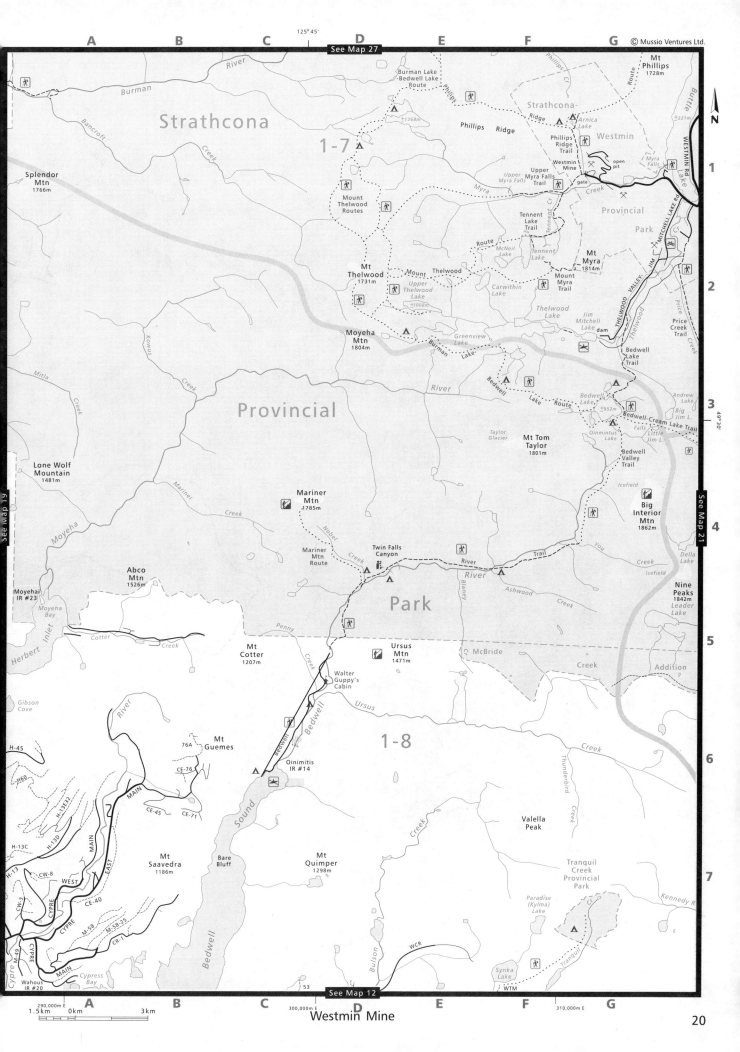

A B C D E F G

N

Burman River

Strathcona

Splendor Mtn 1766m

1-7

Mt Phillips 1728m

Burman Lake-Bedwell Lake Route

+1268m

Phillips Ridge

Strathcona- Westmin

Phillips Cr

+221m

Phillips Ridge Trail

Arnica Lake

Westmin Mine

Mount Thelwood Routes

Upper Myra Falls

Upper Myra Falls Trail

open pit

Myra Falls

WESTMIN Rd

gate

Myra Creek

Provincial Park

Mt Thelwood 1731m

Mount Thelwood

Route

McNeil Lake

Tennent Lake Trail

Tennent Cr

Tennent Lake

Mt Myra 1814m

Upper Thelwood Lake +1008m

Carwithin Lake

Mount Myra Trail

Thelwood Lake

Jim Mitchell Lake

dam

Price Creek Trail

Moyeha Mtn 1804m

Burman Lake

Greenview Lake

Bedwell Lake Trail

Provincial

Kowus Creek

Mitla Creek

Lone Wolf Mountain 1481m

Mariner Creek

Mt Tom Taylor 1801m

Taylor Glacier

Bedwell Lake Route

Bedwell Lake +952m

Bedwell-Cream Lake Trail

Andrew Lake

Big Jim L.

Oinimintus Lake

Little Jim L.

Bedwell Valley Trail

49° 30'

Mariner Mtn 1785m

Nobel Creek

Icefield

Big Interior Mtn 1862m

See Map 21

Moyeha River

Abco Mtn 1526m

Mariner Mtn Route

Twin Falls Canyon

River

Blaney

You Creek

Della Lake

Icefield

Nine Peaks 1842m

Leader Lake

Moyehar IR #23

Moyeha Bay

Cotter Creek

Herbert Inlet

Park

Penny Creek

Mt Cotter 1207m

Ursus Mtn 1471m

McBride Creek

Addition

Gibson Cove

River

Walter Guppy's Cabin

Bedwell

Bedwell

Ursus

1-8

H-45

Mt Guemes

76A

CE-76

Oinimitis IR #14

Thunderbird Creek

H-60

H-13E32

H-13D

H-13C

MAIN

EAST

CE-45

CE-71

Bedwell

Sound

Mt Saavedra 1186m

Bare Bluff

Mt Quimper 1298m

Creek

Valella Peak

Tranquil Creek Provincial Park

H-13

CW-8

WEST

CYPRE

CE-40

Paradise (Kylma) Lake

CW-3

CYPRE

M-58

M-58-25

CR-1

Cypre M-49

CYPRE

MAIN

Wahous IR #20

Cypress Bay

53

Bulson Creek

WCR

Synka Lake

Tranquil Cr

Kennedy R

WTM

See Map 12
290,000m E
1.5km 0km 3km
300,000m E
310,000m E
A B C D E F G
Westmin Mine
20

See Map 19

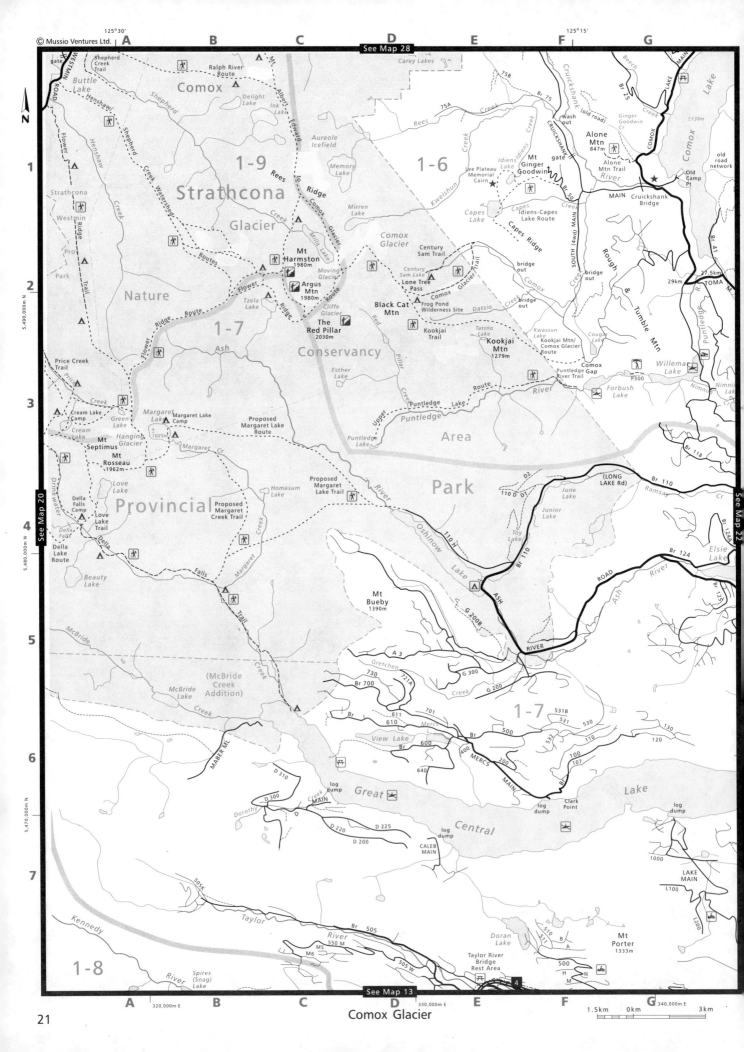

125°30'

125°15'

See Map 28

N

Comox

1-9

Strathcona

Glacier

Nature

Park

1-7

Conservancy

Provincial

1-6

Comox Glacier

Area

Park

1-7

Great Central

Lake

1-8

See Map 13

Comox Glacier

1.5km 0km 3km

320,000m E 330,000m E 340,000m E

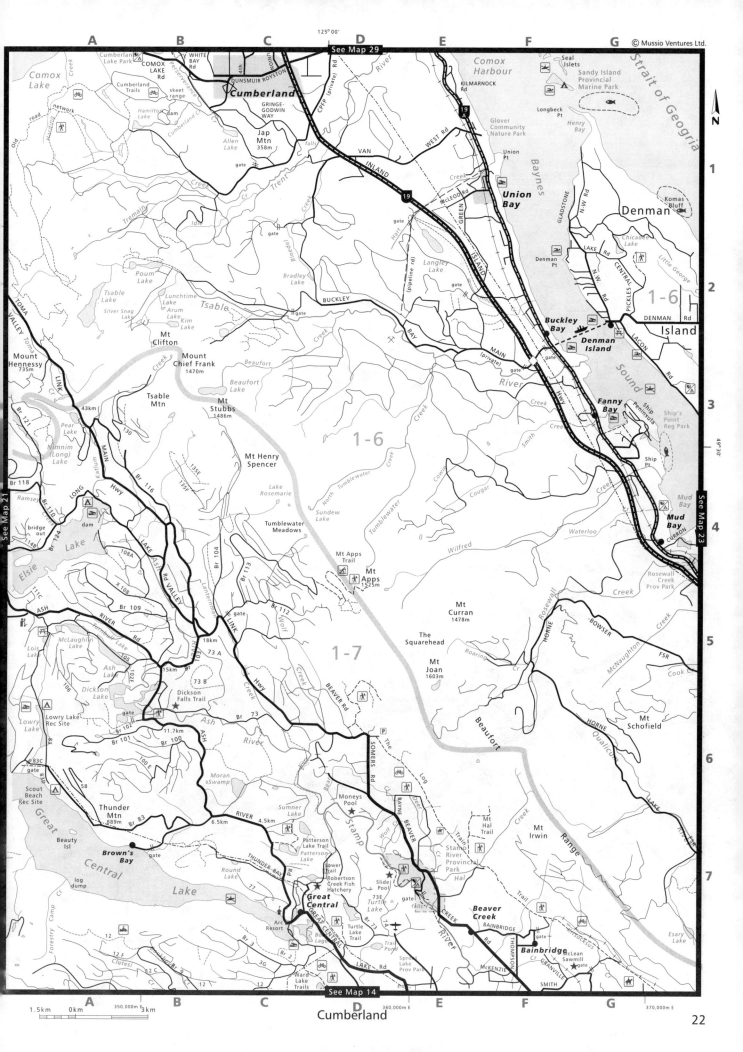

Comox Lake

Cumberland Lake Park
COMOX LAKE Rd
WHITE BAY Rd
4th
Cumberland Trails
skeet range
DUNSMUIR ROYSTON
Cumberland
GRINGE-GODWIN WAY
Allen Lake
Jap Mtn 358m
dam
gate
falls

Comox Harbour
KILMARNOCK Rd
19A
Seal Islets
Sandy Island Provincial Marine Park
Longbeck Pt
Henry Bay

Creek
WEST Rd
Glover Community Nature Park
GLADSTONE
N-W Rd
Komas Bluff

1

Hamilton Lake

UNION
VAN
INLAND
19
McLEOD Rd
GREEN
Union Pt
Union Bay
Baynes
Denman Pt
LAKE Rd
CENTRAL
Denman
Chicadee Lake
Little George Lake

Tremain
Idle
Bloedel
gate
gate
Hart
BUCKLEY
Langley Lake
BAY
gate
MAIN (private)
PICKLES
DENMAN Rd
Island

1-6

2

49° 30'

Poum Lake
Tsable Lake
Silver Snag Lake
Lunchtime Lake
Arum Lake
Kim Lake
Tsable
Mt Clifton
Creek
Bradley Lake
Buckley Bay
Denman Island
gate
LACON Rd
Ship Peninsula
Ship's Point Reg Park

Mount Hennessy 735m
TOMA
LINK
43km
Br 121
Mount Chief Frank 1470m
Tsable Mtn
Mt Stubbs 1486m
Beaufort
Beaufort Lake
Creek
River
Hwy
Fanny Bay
Ship Pt

3

Pear Lake
Nimnim (Long) Lake
Br 118
Ramsey
Br 110
Br 124
bridge out
Br 148
130
MAIN
Br 116
135E
135F
Mt Henry Spencer
Lake Rosemarie
North Tumblewater
Cowie
Smith
Creek
Mud Bay
Mud Bay
CURRON

4

Elsie
111C
ASH
108A
X 108
Br 104
Tumblewater Meadows
Sundew Lake
1-6
Tumblewater
Cougar
Waterloo
Rosewall
Rosewall Creek Prov Park

HWY
Lake
dam
Br 113
Mt Apps Trail
Mt Apps 1525m
Wilfred
Mt Curran 1478m
HORNE
BOWSER
McNaughton
Creek
Mt Schofield

McLaughlin Lake
Torrhill Lake
105
102E
15km
Br 112
Br 109
18km
73 A
LINK
Wolf
1-7
The Squarehead
Mt Joan 1603m
Roaring
Cr
HORNE
Cook
FSR

5

Lois Lake
106
Ash Lake
Dickson Lake
73 B
Dickson Falls Trail
Hwy
Creek
BEAVER Rd
6

Lowry Lake
Lowry Lake Rec Site
Br 102
Br 101
100 E
11.7km
Br 100
ASH
River
RIVER
Moran Swamp
Sumner Lake
SOMERS Rd
P
Log
Beaufort
Mt Hal Trail
Stamp River Provincial Park
Mt Irwin
Range
HORNE
Qualicum
LAKE
Hwy FSR

Scout Beach Rec Site
83C
gate
58
Thunder Mtn 889m
Br 83
6.5km
4.5km
RIVER
Patterson Lake Trail
Patterson Lake
Moneys Pool
BAYNE
Wolf
Deer
Beaver
Trail
Mt Hal
Mt Irwin

Beauty Isl
Brown's Bay
gate
THUNDER BAY Rd
Round Lake
Stamp
Lower Trail
Robertson Creek Fish Hatchery
Slide Pool
gate
falls
73E
Beaver Creek
Trail

Great Central Lake

log dump
12
12 F
Clutesi
Br 3
12 C
3G
12
Ward Lake Trails
Great Central
Arc Resort
Bog Lagoon
Turtle Lake Trail
73E Turtle Lake
Sproat Lake Prov Park
LAKE Rd
Bainbridge
McLean Sawmill
gate
McKenzie
SMITH
Esary Lake
CR GRANVILLE
THOMPSON
BAINBRIDGE Rd

7

1.5km 0km 350,000m E 3km
A   B   C   D   E   F   G   370,000m E
360,000m E

Cumberland

22

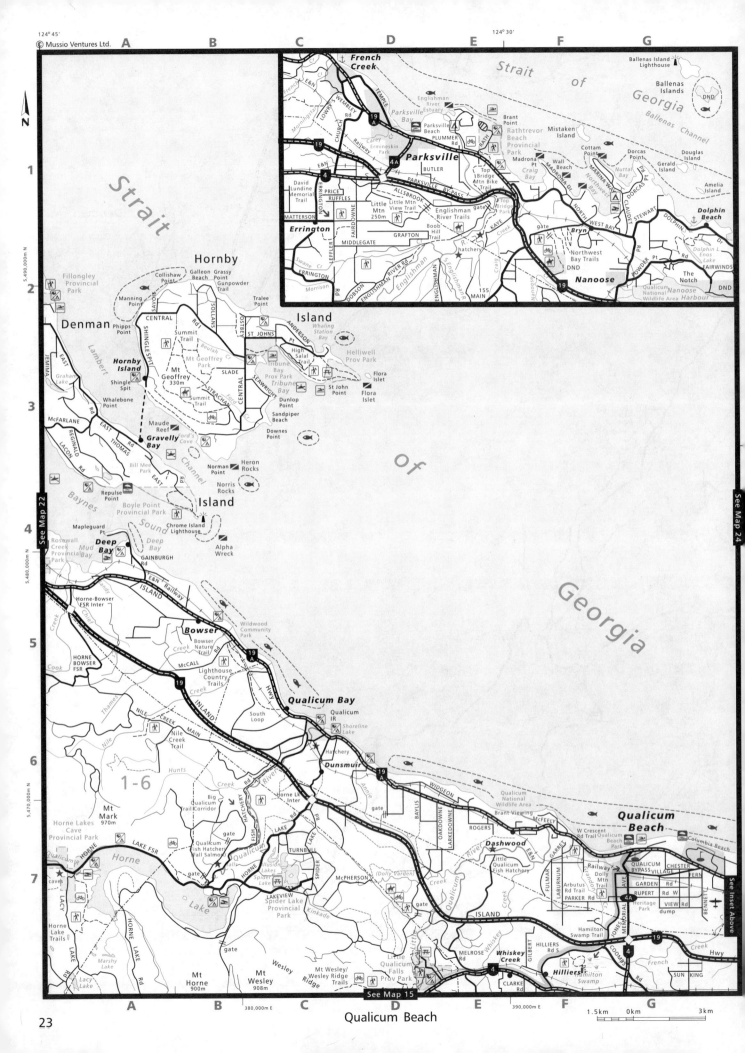

Qualicum Beach

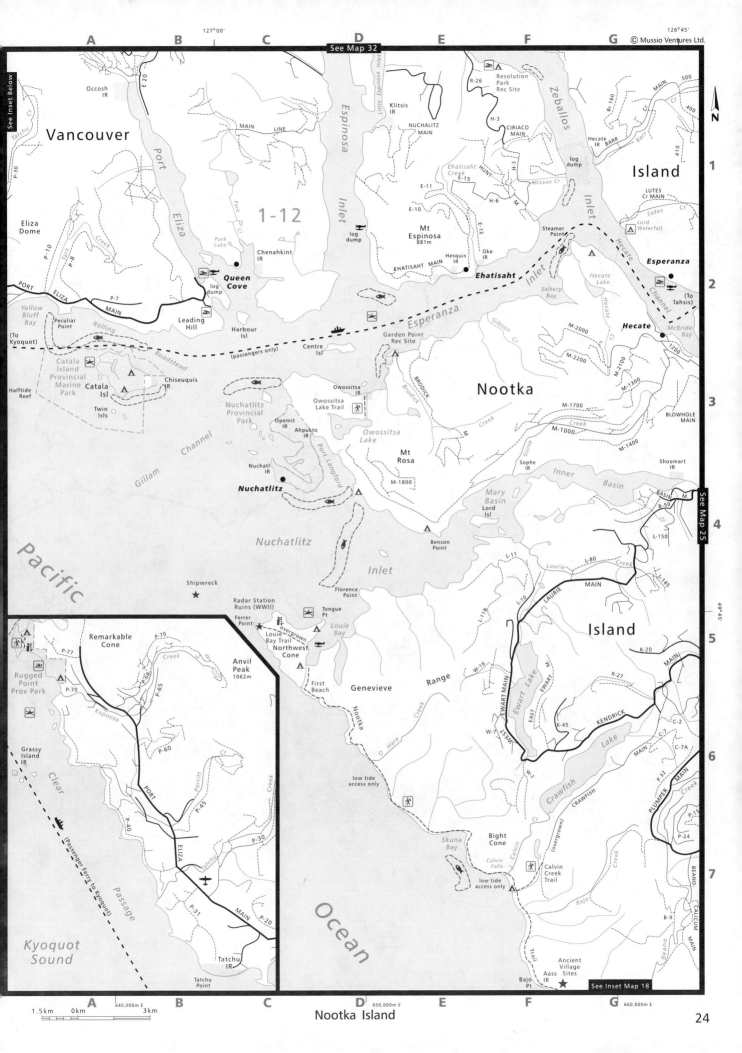

A B C D E F G

127°00'   126°45'
© Mussio Ventures Ltd.

N

1

Vancouver

Island

1-12

Occosh IR

Eliza Dome

Yellow Bluff Bay

Peculiar Point

Halftide Reef

Catala Island Provincial Marine Park

Catala Isl

Twin Isls

Chiseuquis IR

Port Eliza

Park Lake

Chenahkint IR

Queen Cove

Leading Hill

Harbour Isl

Centre Isl

Espinosa Inlet

Little Espinosa Inlet

log dump

Klitsis IR

NUCHALITZ MAIN

Mt Espinosa 881m

Hesquis IR

EHATISAHT MAIN

Oke IR

Ehatisaht

Resolution Park Rec Site

R-26

H-3

CIRIACO MAIN

H-3

H-6

E-15

E-11

E-10

E-12

Steamer Point

Ehatisaht Creek

HUNT

M

McLean Cr

Zeballos

Island

B-160

MAIN

Cr

Cr

Hecate IR

BARR

LUTES Cr MAIN

Lutes Cr

Lord Waterfall

Esperanza

(To Tahsis)

Hecate

McBride Bay

BLOWHOLE MAIN

Shoomart IR

BASIN

2

Pacific

(To Kyoquot)

Rolling Roadstead

(passengers only)

Esperanza Inlet

Garden Point Rec Site

Owossitsa

Owossitsa Lake Trail

Owossitsa Lake

Opemit IR

Ahpukto IR

Nuchatlitz Provincial Park

Nuchatl IR

Nuchatlitz

Gillam Channel

Port Langford

Nuchatlitz

Inlet

Shipwreck ★

Radar Station Ruins (WWII)

Ferrer Point

overgrown

Louie Bay Trail

Northwest Cone

First Beach

Tongue Pt

Louie Bay

Genevieve

Mt Rosa

M-1800

Benson Point

Florence Point

Nootka

Brodick Creek

Gibson Cr

Saltery Bay

Hecate Lake

M-2000

M-2100

M-2200

M-1700

M-1000

M-1400

M-1300

M-1200

Sophe IR

Inner

Basin

Mary Basin

Lord Isl

Range

O Hara Creek

Nootka Creek

Calvin Falls

low tide access only

Skuna Bay

Bight Cone

low tide access only

Calvin Creek Trail

Calvin Cr

Calvin Creek

Laurie Creek

L-11

L-11B

L-10

L-80

L-145

L-150

L-15

LAURIE MAIN

EWART MAIN

WEST

EAST

Ewart Lake

Crawfish Lake

CRAWFISH MAIN

W-16

W-7

W-2

K-20

K-27

K-45

KENDRICK MAIN

C-2

C-7

C-7A

P-32

PLUMPER MAIN

P-24

P-15

BEANO MAIN

CALICUM MAIN

B-9

Island

Ancient Village Sites

Aass IR ★

Bajo Pt

Bajo Cr

3

4

5

6

7

Inset (lower left)

Remarkable Cone

Rugged Point Prov Park

Grassy Island IR

Anvil Peak 1062m

(Passenger Ferry to Kyoquot)

Clear Passage

Kyoquot Sound

Kapoose Creek

Porritt Cr

PORT ELIZA MAIN

Tatchu Cr

Tatchu IR

Tatchu Point

P-77

P-70

P-70

P-76

P-65

P-68

P-60

P-45

P-40

P-30

P-31

P-20

See Inset Below

Tatchu

P-30

E 20

P-10

P-8

P-7

Park Creek

MAIN LINE

PORT ELIZA MAIN

Tlara Creek

Pacific

Ocean

Nootka Island

See Map 25

See Inset Map 18

49°45'

1.5km   0km   3km

640,000m E   650,000m E   660,000m E

24

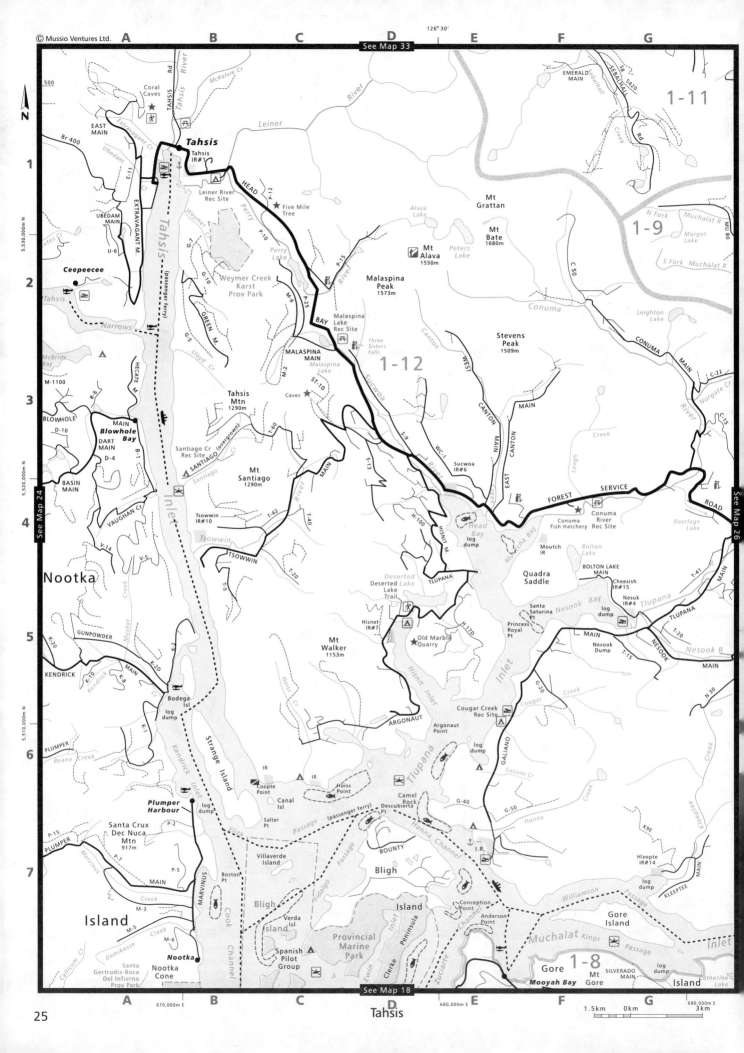

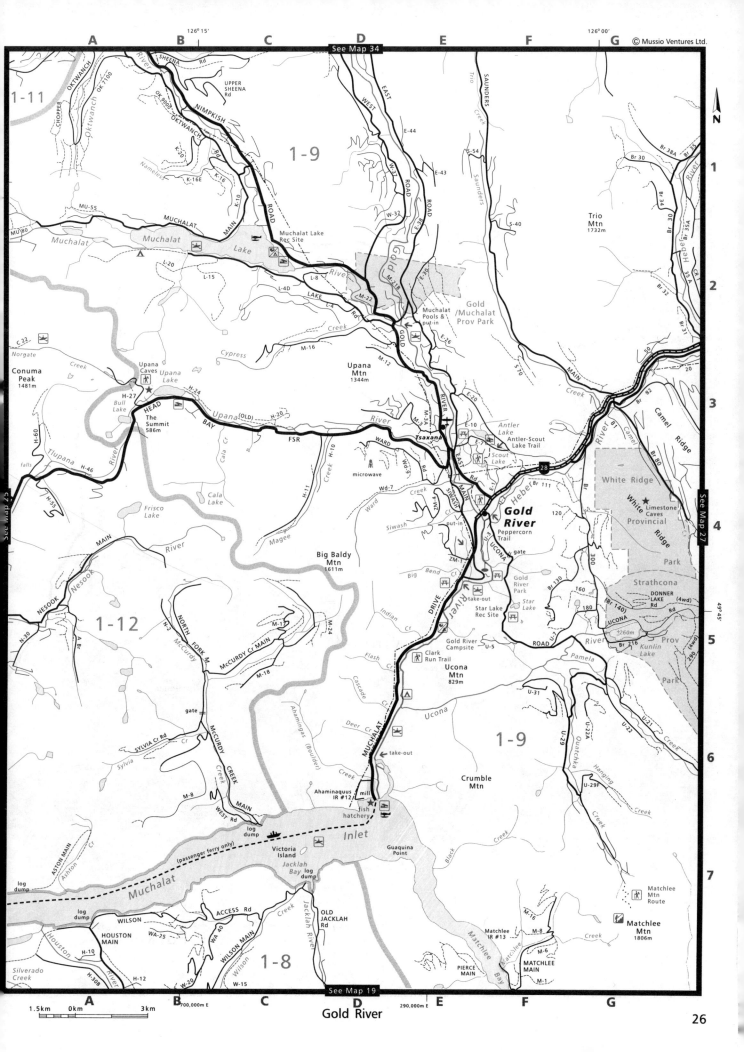

© Mussio Ventures Ltd.

N

126° 15'

126° 00'

A B C D E F G

1-11

1-9

Oktwanch River
CHOPPER
OK-7100
OKTWANCH
OK-9000
OKTWANCH Rd
K-20
K-16E
K-16
K-10
MU-55
MU-80
MUCHALAT MAIN
Muchalat
Muchalat Lake
Muchalat Lake Rec Site
L-20
L-15
L-8
L-4D
L-4
Nameless Cr
SHEENA Rd
UPPER SHEENA Rd
NIMPKISH
ROAD
Muchalat
Lake
LAKE Rd
Creek
M-16
M-12
M-22
Cypress

EAST
WEST
ROAD
E-44
W-31
E-43
W-32
Gold River
M-32B
Saunders Creek
S-54
S-40
E-38
E-30
E-26
Gold/Muchalat Prov Park

Br 38A
Br 35
Br 30
Br 34
Br 30
Trio Mtn
1732m
35A
Br 32
Br 31
Heber River

1

2

3

4

5

6

7

C 22
Norgate Creek
Conuma Peak
1481m
H-60
H-27
H-24
Upana Caves
Upana Lake
Bull Lake
The Summit
586m
HEAD
BAY
Upana (OLD)
H-20
FSR
Upana Mtn
1344m
Upana River
Cala Cr
Cala Lake
H-10
microwave
WARD
Creek
Ward
Creek
H-11
Magee Creek
Siwash
Wd-9
Wd-7
M-3A
E-20
E-10
Antler Lake
Antler-Scout Lake Trail
Scout Lake
Tsaxana
MAIN Rd
28
River
Br 111
Gold River
Peppercorn Trail
put-in
L-3
ZM-1
UCONA
gate
Big Bend
Cr
River

Br 82
Br 81
Camel
River 81
Camel Ridge
White Ridge
White Ridge
Limestone Caves
Provincial
Br 80
Park
300
Br 130
160
180
Strathcona
DONNER LAKE (4wd)
Rd
UCONA
±260m
Br 216
Kunlin Lake
Prov
(4wd)
290
Park
49° 45'

Tlupana River
H-46
H-55
falls
Frisco Lake

1-12

NESOOK
N-30
Nesook Creek
MAIN
A Br
N-2
NORTH FORK M
McCurdy
McCURDY Cr MAIN
M-17
M-24
M-18
gate
SYLVIA Cr Rd
Sylvia Cr
Big Baldy Mtn
1611m
Indian Cr
Flash Cr
Cascade Cr
Deer Cr
Ahamingas (Boulder) Creek
MUCHALAT
DRIVE
take-out
take-out
Clark Run Trail
Gold River Campsite
Ucona Mtn
829m
Ucona River
Gold River Park
Star Lake
Star Lake Rec Site
U-5
U-7
ROAD
Pamela
U-31
U-29
U-29F
U-21
U-22A
U-22
Ouatchka Creek
Hanging Creek

Crumble Mtn

M-8
McCURDY CREEK
WEST Rd
Ahaminaquus IR #12
mill
fish hatchery
log dump
Victoria Island
Jacklah Bay
log dump
Muchalat
(passenger ferry only)
Inlet
Guaquina Point
Black Creek
Matchlee Bay
Matchlee IR #13
Matchlee Mtn Route
Matchlee Mtn
1806m
M-16
M-8
M-6
M-1
PIERCE MAIN
MATCHLEE MAIN

log dump
ASTON MAIN
Ashton Cr
Houston River
HOUSTON MAIN
H-30B
H-10
H-12
WILSON
WA 40
WA-25
WA 40
ACCESS Rd
WILSON MAIN
Wilson
OLD JACKLAH Rd
Jacklah River

Silverado Creek

1-8

Gold River

1.5km 0km 3km

A B C D E F G

700,000 E
290,000 m E

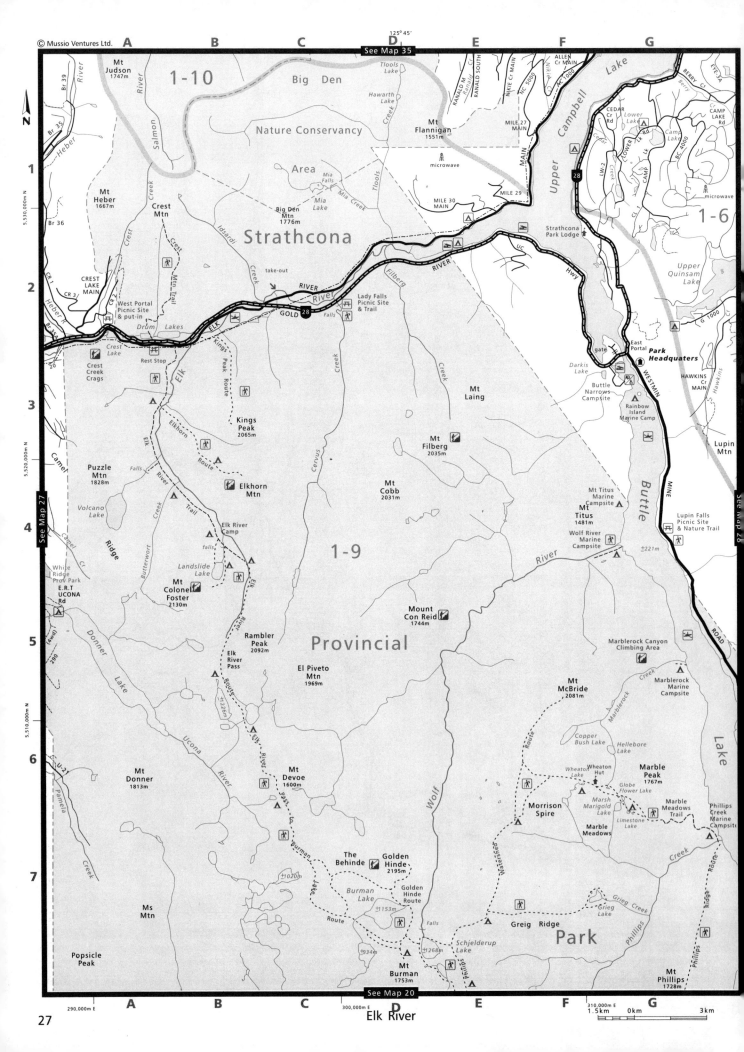

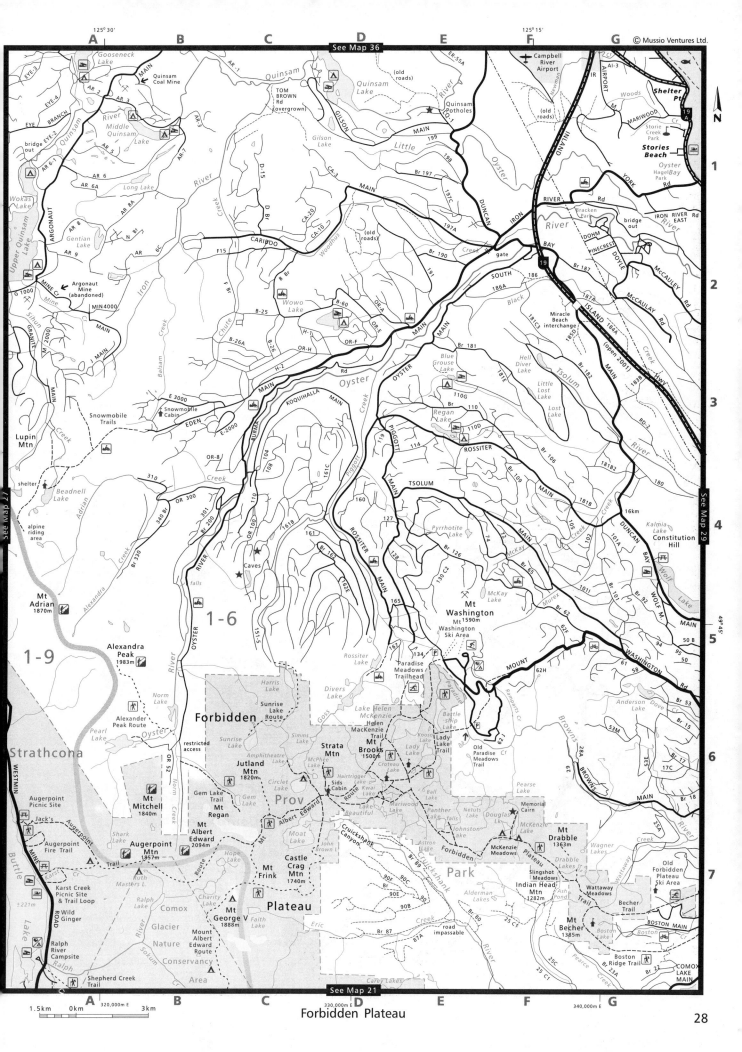

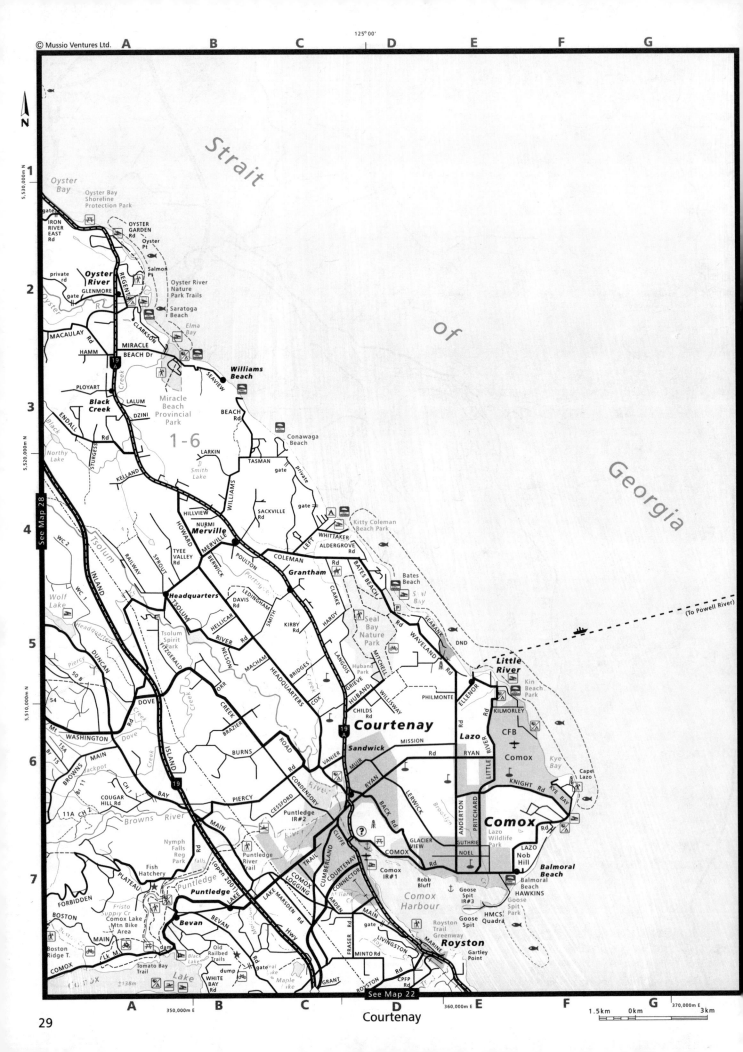

125° 00'

A B C D E F G

Strait

of

Georgia

Oyster Bay

1
Oyster Bay Shoreline Protection Park

gate
IRON RIVER EAST Rd
OYSTER GARDEN Rd
Oyster Pt
Salmon Pt

private rd
Oyster River
GLENMORE
REGENT Rd
CLARKSON
Oyster River Nature Park Trails
Saratoga Beach
Elma Bay

2
gate
Oyster Creek
MACAULAY Rd
HAMM
19A
MIRACLE BEACH Dr
SEAVIEW
Williams Beach

PLOYART
Black Creek
LALUM
DZINI
BEACH Rd

3
ENDALL Rd
Northy Lake
STURGESS
KELLAND
LARKIN
Smith Lake
Miracle Beach Provincial Park
1-6
TASMAN
WILLIAMS
gate
private
Conawaga Beach

See Map 28

Tsolum

WC 2
HILLVIEW
NURMI
Merville
HOWARD
SACKVILLE Rd
COLEMAN
gate
Kitty Coleman Beach Park
WHITTAKER
ALDERGROVE Rd

4
RAILWAY
INLAND
TYEE VALLEY Rd
SPROUT
BERWICK
POULTON
Portly's
Grantham
LEFT
CLARKE
BATES
Bates Beach
Seal Bay

Wolf Lake
WC 1
Headquarters
DAVIS Rd
LEDINGHAM
SMITH
KIRBY Rd
HARDY
Seal Bay Nature Park
Rd
WAVELAND Rd
SEABANK
(To Powell River)

5
Piercy
DUNCAN
FITZGERALD
HELLICAR
NELSON
River Rd
MACHAM
HEADQUARTERS
BRIDGES
LANGOIS
COX
GRIEVE
HUBAND
MITCHELL
WILLISWAY
Huband Park
DND
PHILMONTE
ELLENOR Rd
Little River
Kin Beach Park
KILMORLEY

50 B
54
Mt. WASHINGTON
Br 15A
BROWNS MAIN
Dove Creek Rd
BRAZIER
BURNS
ROAD
CONDENSORY Rd
VANIER
MUIR
CHILDS Rd
19
Courtenay
MISSION
RYAN Rd
Lazo
CFB Comox
Kye Bay
Cape Lazo

6
Br 15
CH 1
COUGAR HILL Rd
BAY
19
PIERCY
CESSFORD Rd
Puntledge IR#2
Sandwick
RYAN Rd
BACK Rd
LERWICK
Brooklyn
ANDERTON Rd
PRITCHARD
LITTLE RIVER Rd
KNIGHT Rd
KYE BAY
Comox

11A CH 2
Jackpot
Browns River
MAIN
Nymph Falls Reg Park
Puntledge River Trail
Comox IR#1
GLACIER VIEW
COMOX Rd
GUTHRIE
NOEL
Lazo Wildlife Park
LAZO Nob Hill
Balmoral Beach

7
PLATEAU
Fish Hatchery
Fristo Supply Cr
Comox Lake Mtn Bike Area
Puntledge
LAKE
Open 2001
COMOX LOGGING
TRAIL
CUMBERLAND
CLIFFE
CONNECTOR
Dillard Cr
Comox IR#1
Robb Bluff
Goose Spit IR#3
Balmoral Beach
HAWKINS
Goose Spit Park
HMCS Quadra

FORBIDDEN
BOSTON
Bevan
BEVAN
Black Lake
Old Railbed Trails
MARSDEN Rd
HWY
FRASER Rd
MAIN Rd
gate
LIVINGSTON Rd
Royston
Royston Trail Greenway
Comox Harbour
Goose Spit
Gartley Point

Boston Ridge T.
MAIN
COMOX
dam
LK M
Tomato Bay Trail
±138m
WHITE BAY Rd
dump
gate
Maple Lake
GRANT
ROYSTON Rd
MINTO Rd
CPFP Rd
MARINE

Comox Lake

See Map 22

A 350,000 E B C **Courtenay** D 360,000 E E F 370,000 E G

1.5km 0km 3km

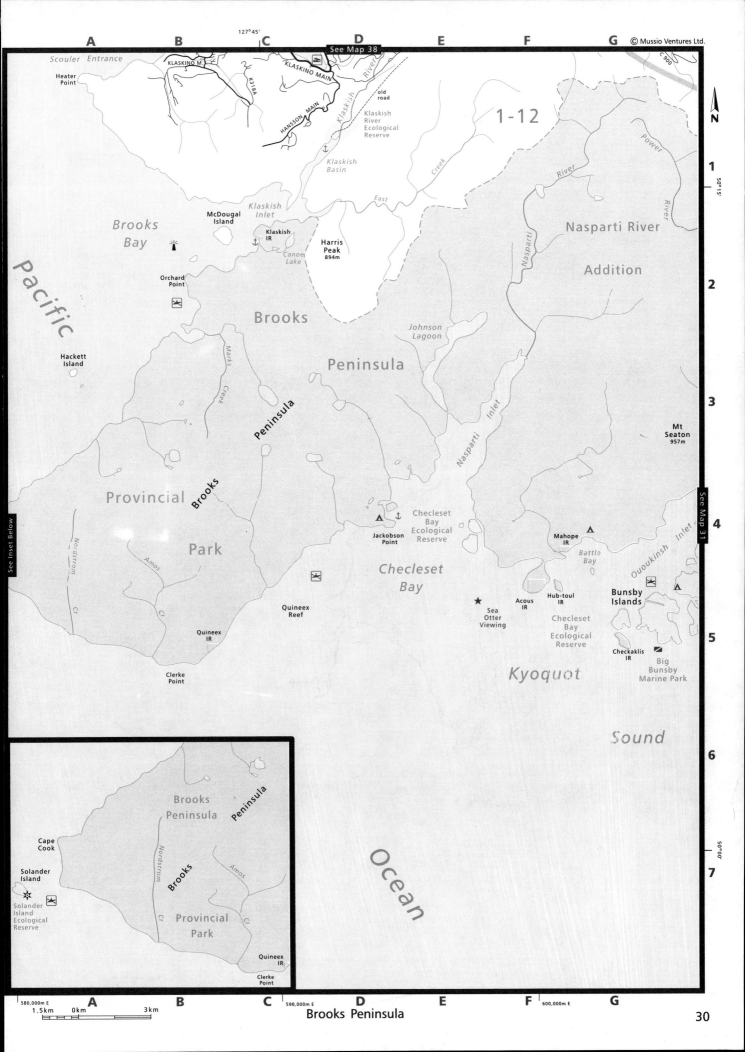

127°45'

See Map 38

A   B   C   D   E   F   G

Scouler Entrance

KLASKINO M.

Heater
Point

K318A

HANSSON MAIN

KLASKINO MAIN

Klaskish River

old
road

1-12

N

50°15'

Klaskish
River
Ecological
Reserve

East   Creek

Klaskish
Basin

Brooks
Bay

McDougal
Island

Klaskish
Inlet

Klaskish
IR

Harris
Peak
894m

1

Pacific

Orchard
Point

Canoe Lake

Brooks

2

50°15'

Hackett
Island

Marks

Creek

Peninsula

Peninsula

Johnson
Lagoon

Naspartar River

Addition

Naspartar

River

Power

River

3

Mt
Seaton
957m

Provincial

Brooks

Park

Nordstrom

Cr

Amos

Cr

Cr

Checleset
Bay
Ecological
Reserve

Jackobson
Point

Naspartar Inlet

Mahope
IR

Battle
Bay

4

See Map 31

Quineex
Reef

Checleset
Bay

Acous
IR

Hub-toul
IR

Ououkinsh Inlet

Bunsby
Islands

Quineex
IR

Sea
Otter
Viewing

Checleset
Bay
Ecological
Reserve

Checkaklis
IR

Big
Bunsby
Marine Park

5

Clerke
Point

Kyoquot

Sound

6

50°00'

7

See Inset Below

Brooks
Peninsula

Peninsula

Cape
Cook

Nordstrom

Brooks

Amos

Solander
Island

Solander
Island
Ecological
Reserve

Cr

Cr

Provincial
Park

Quineex
IR

Clerke
Point

Ocean

580,000m E   A   B   C   590,000m E   D   E   F   600,000m E   G

1.5km   0km   3km

Brooks Peninsula

30

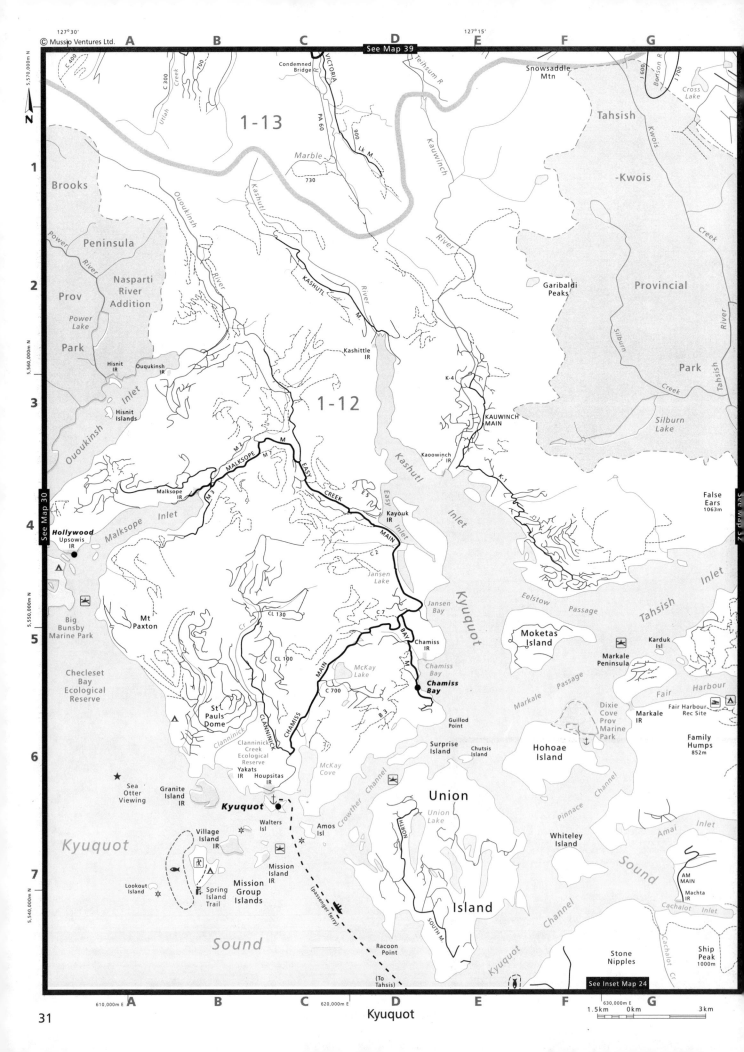

© Mussio Ventures Ltd.

N

C 400
 Utah Creek
C 300
700

1-13

Condemned Bridge CR
VICTORIA R
PA 60
Lk M
900

Marble
730

Snowsaddle Mtn
Berson R
1 600
700
Cross Lake

Tahsish

-Kwois
Kwois

Brooks

Peninsula

Prov

Park

Nasparti River Addition

Power Lake

Power River

KASHUTL
River
M

Kauwinch
River

Kashutl IR

Garibaldi Peaks

Provincial

Park

Silburn
Creek

Silburn Lake

Tahsish River

Ououkinsh
River

Kashutle IR

Hisnit IR
Ouqukinsh IR

Hisnit Islands

1-12

K-4

KAUWINCH MAIN

Kaoowinch IR

Kashutl Inlet

K-1

False Ears
1063m

Ououkinsh Inlet

M3
M
MALKSOPE
M 7
EASY
CREEK
E 5

Malksope IR
M 3

Malksope Inlet

See Map 30

Hollywood
Upsowis IR

Mt Paxton

Big Bunsby Marine Park

CL 130

Cr

CL 100

Checleset Bay Ecological Reserve

St Pauls Dome

Clanninick Creek
Clanninick Creek Ecological Reserve

Sea Otter Viewing

Granite Island IR

Kyuquot

Yakats IR
Houpsitas IR

Kyuquot

Walters Isl

Village Island IR

Mission Island IR

Lookout Island

Spring Island Trail

Mission Group Islands

Sound

Kayouk IR
MAIN
C 2

Jansen Lake

C 7

CHAMISS
MAIN
BAY
M

Chamiss IR

Chamiss Bay

McKay Lake

C 700

B 3

Amos Isl

McKay Cove

Guillod Point

Surprise Island

Chutsis Island

Jansen Bay

Jansen Bay

Kyuquot Inlet

Eelstow Passage

Moketas Island

Markale Peninsula

Chamiss Bay

Hohoae Island

Union

Union Lake

Island

SOUTH M

MAIN
H

Whiteley Island

Dixie Cove Prov Marine Park

Markale IR

Markale Passage

Karduk Isl

Fair Harbour

Fair Harbour Rec Site

Family Humps
852m

Pinnace Channel

Amai Inlet

Racoon Point

(passeger ferry)

Crowther Channel

Kyuquot Channel

AM MAIN

Machta IR

Cachalot Inlet

Stone Nipples

Ship Peak
1000m

(To Tahsis)

See Inset Map 24

See Map 32

5,570,000m N
5,560,000m N
5,550,000m N
5,540,000m N

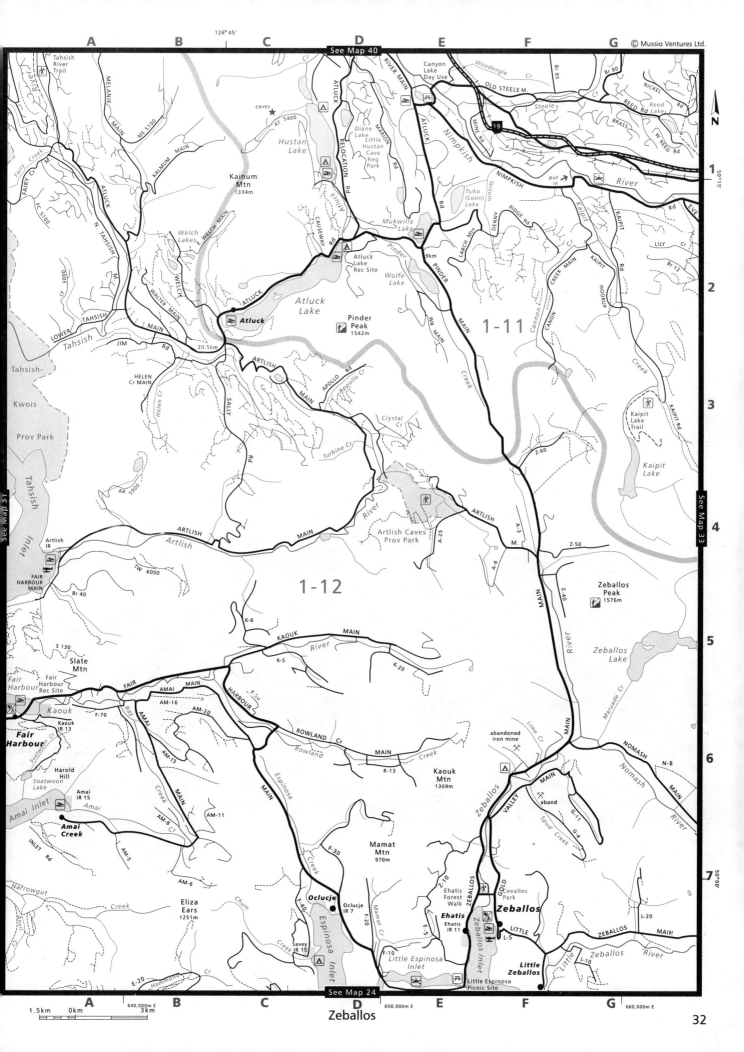

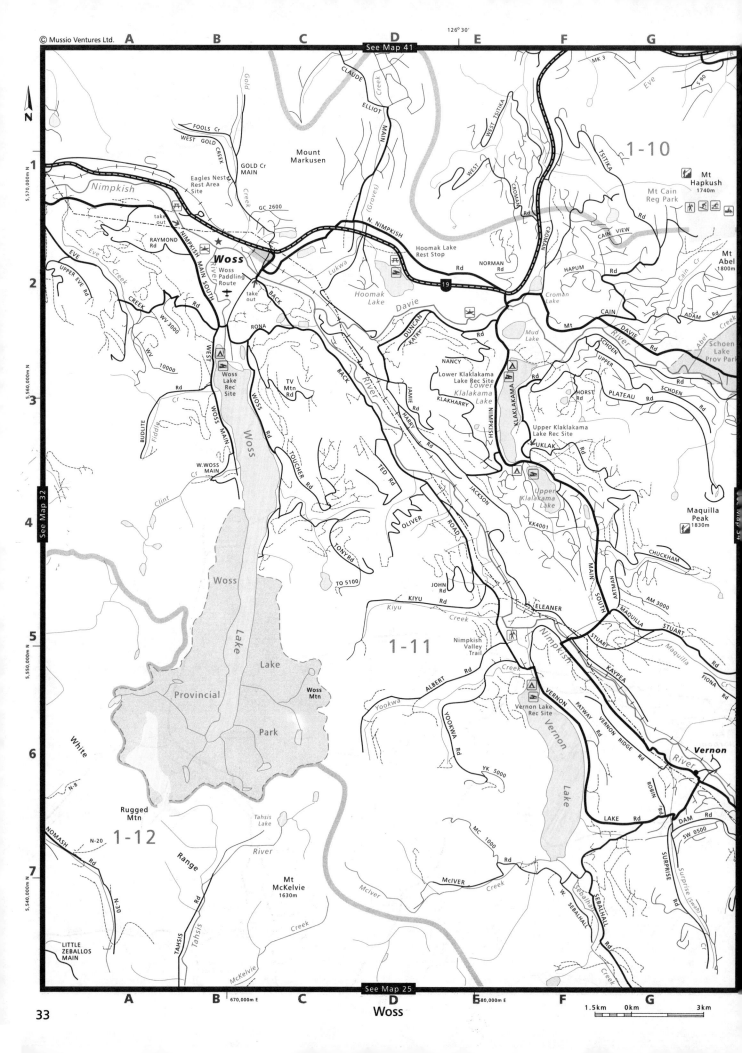

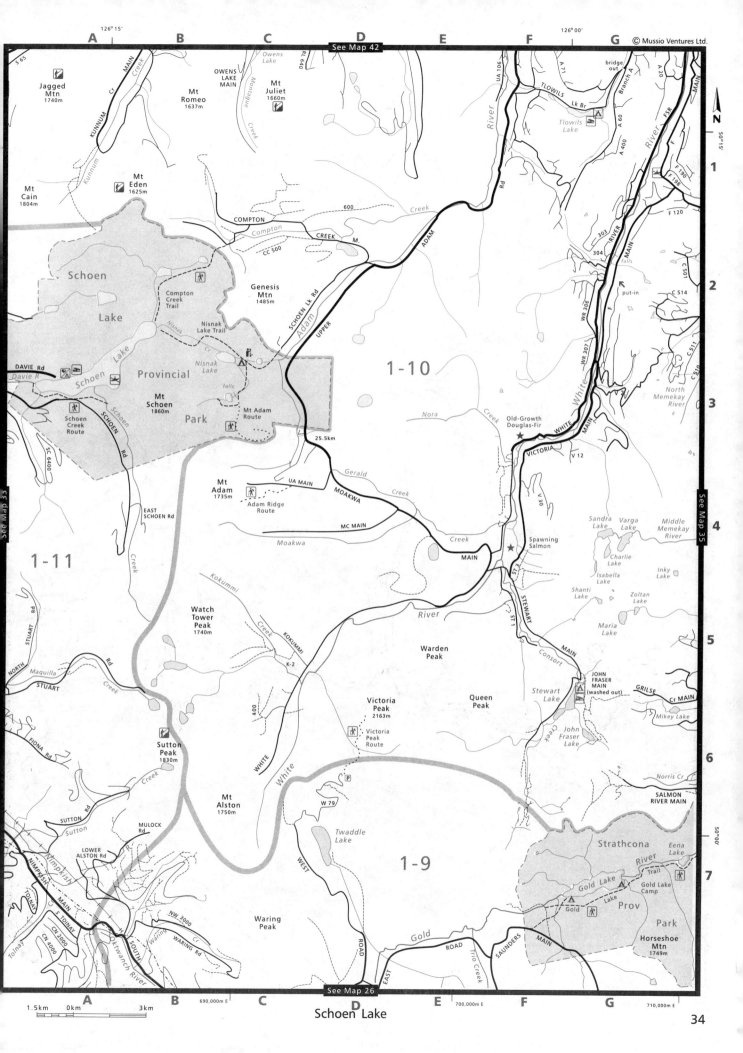

Jagged
Mtn
1740m

OWENS
LAKE
MAIN

Owens
Lake

Mt
Juliet
1660m

bridge
out

TLOWILS

Lk Br

Tlowils
Lake

Mt Cain
1804m

Mt
Romeo
1637m

Mt
Eden
1625m

KUNNUM Cr

Kunnum Cr

MAIN

Montague Creek

Compton Creek

COMPTON

Creek

600

CC 500

M.

CREEK

ADAM

UA 106

A 71

A 60   Branch A

A 20

F 198

F 190

F 120

303

304

RIVER MAIN

River

Schoen

Lake

Provincial

Park

Compton
Creek Trail

Genesis
Mtn
1485m

SCHOEN Lk Rd

UPPER   Adam

Nisnak Lake Trail

Nisnak
Cr

Nisnak
Lake

falls

1-10

Nora   Creek

Old-Growth
Douglas-Fir

WR 306

WR 307

White

C 501

C 514

C 511

C 510

North
Memekay
River

DAVIE Rd

Davie R

SCHOEN Rd

Schoen

Mt
Schoen
1860m

Mt Adam
Route

25.5km

VICTORIA   V 12

WHITE MAIN

Schoen Creek
Route

SC 6400

Schoen

Creek

EAST
SCHOEN Rd

Mt Adam
1735m

Adam Ridge
Route

UA MAIN

MOAKWA

Gerald

Creek

MC MAIN

Moakwa

Creek

MAIN

Spawning
Salmon

ST 3

V 30

Sandra
Lake

Varga
Lake

Middle
Memekay
River

Charlie
Lake

Isabella
Lake

Inky
Lake

Zoltan
Lake

1-11

STUART Rd

NORTH STUART

Maquilla

Creek

Watch
Tower
Peak
1740m

Kokummi

Creek

KOKUMMI

K-2

River

Warden
Peak

MAIN

Consort

STEWART

ST 1

Shanti
Lake

Maria
Lake

JOHN
FRASER
MAIN
(washed out)

GRILSE
Cr MAIN

Mikey Lake

Sutton
Peak
1830m

FIONA Rd

Sutton   Rd

Creek

400

WHITE

White

Victoria
Peak
2163m

Victoria
Peak
Route

P

Queen
Peak

Stewart
Lake

John
Fraser
Creek

John
Fraser
Lake

Norris Cr

SALMON
RIVER MAIN

SUTTON Rd

Sutton

LOWER
ALSTON Rd

MULOCK
Rd

Mt Alston
1750m

W 79

Twaddle
Lake

1-9

Strathcona

Eena
Lake

Nimpkish

S TOINAY

CN 2000

CN 4000

Tolnay

MAIN

SOUTH

Aktwanch River

NW 3000

Waring Cr

WARING Rd

Waring
Peak

WEST

ROAD

EAST   ROAD

Gold

ROAD

Trio Creek

SAUNDERS   MAIN

River   Gold Lake

Gold

Gold Lake
Camp

Prov   Park

Horseshoe
Mtn
1749m

50°15'

N

1

2

3

See Map 35

4

5

6

50°00'

7

See Map 33

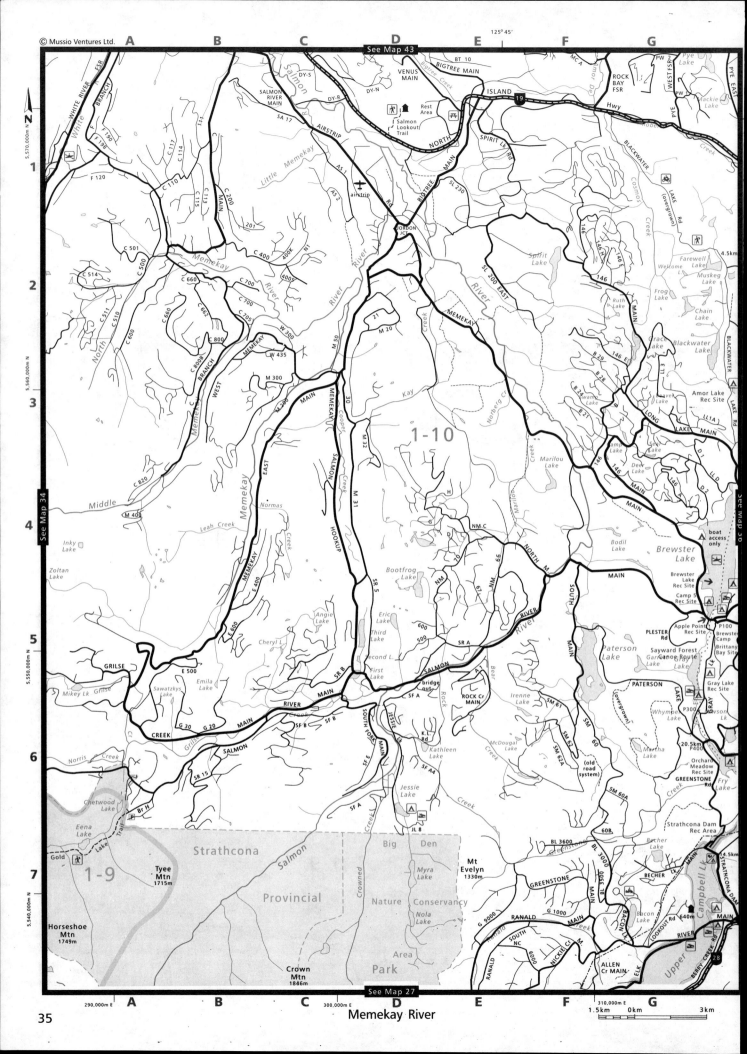

See Map 34

See Map 30

35

Memekay River

1-10

1-9

Strathcona

Provincial

Nature Conservancy

Area

Park

Big Den

Myra Lake

Nola Lake

Mt Evelyn 1330m

Tyee Mtn 1715m

Horseshoe Mtn 1749m

Crown Mtn 1846m

125° 45'

19 Hwy

ISLAND

Brewster Lake

Paterson Lake

Campbell Lk

Upper Campbell Lk

290,000m E

5,570,000m N

5,560,000m N

5,550,000m N

5,540,000m N

300,000m E

310,000m E

1.5km   0km   3km

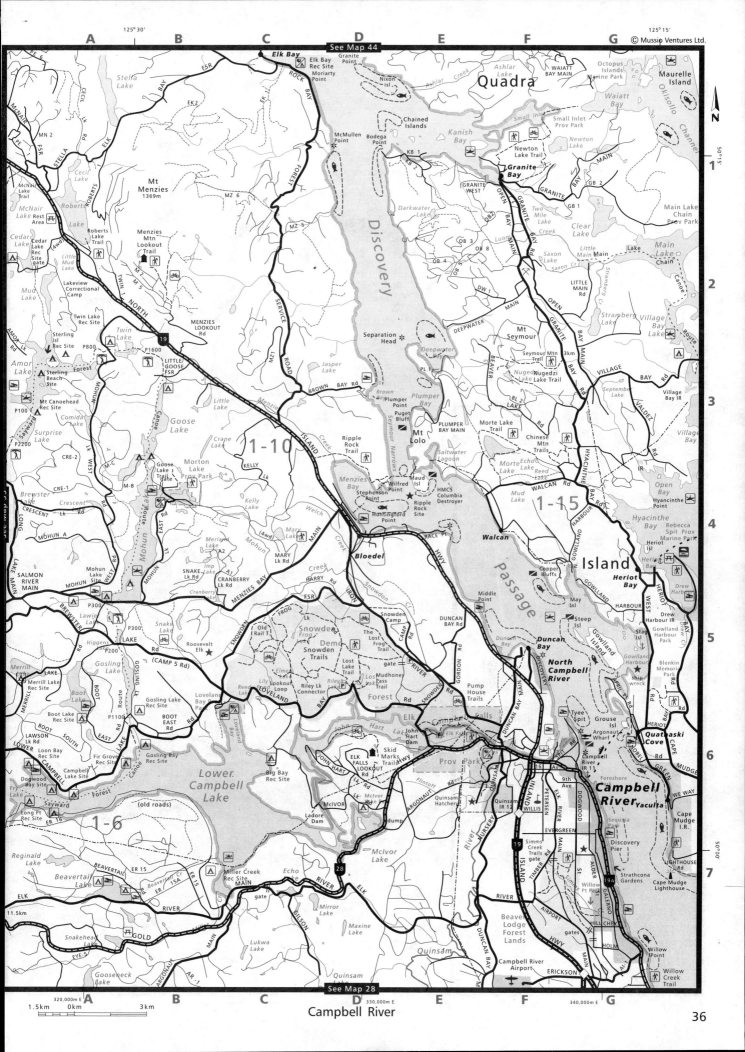

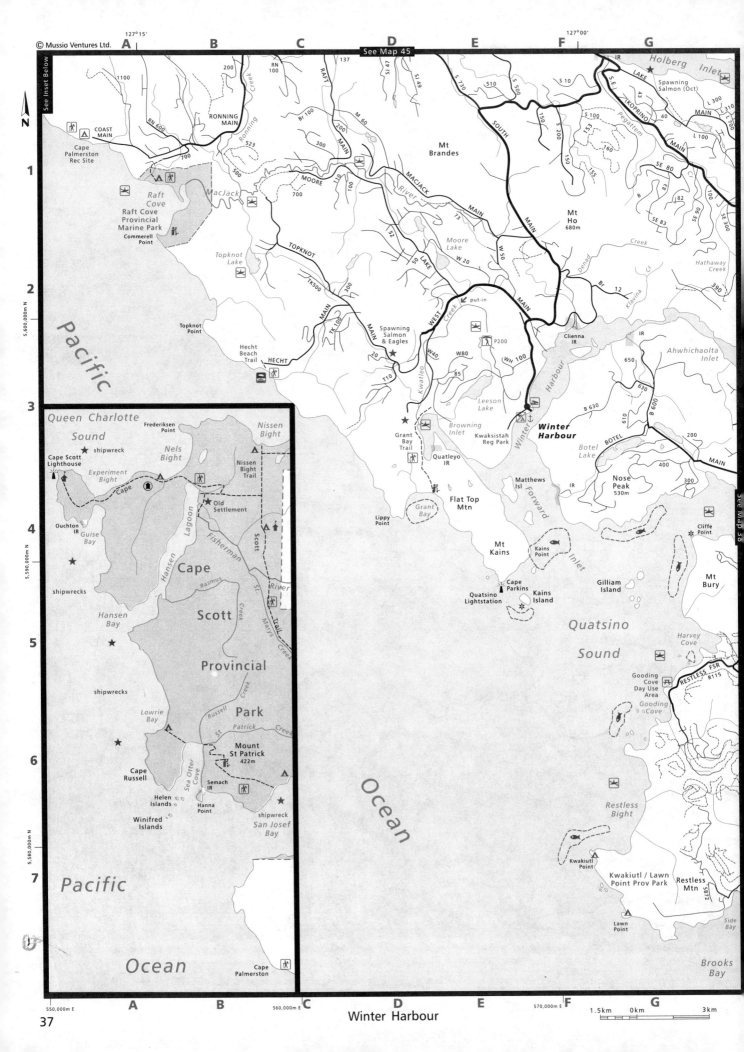

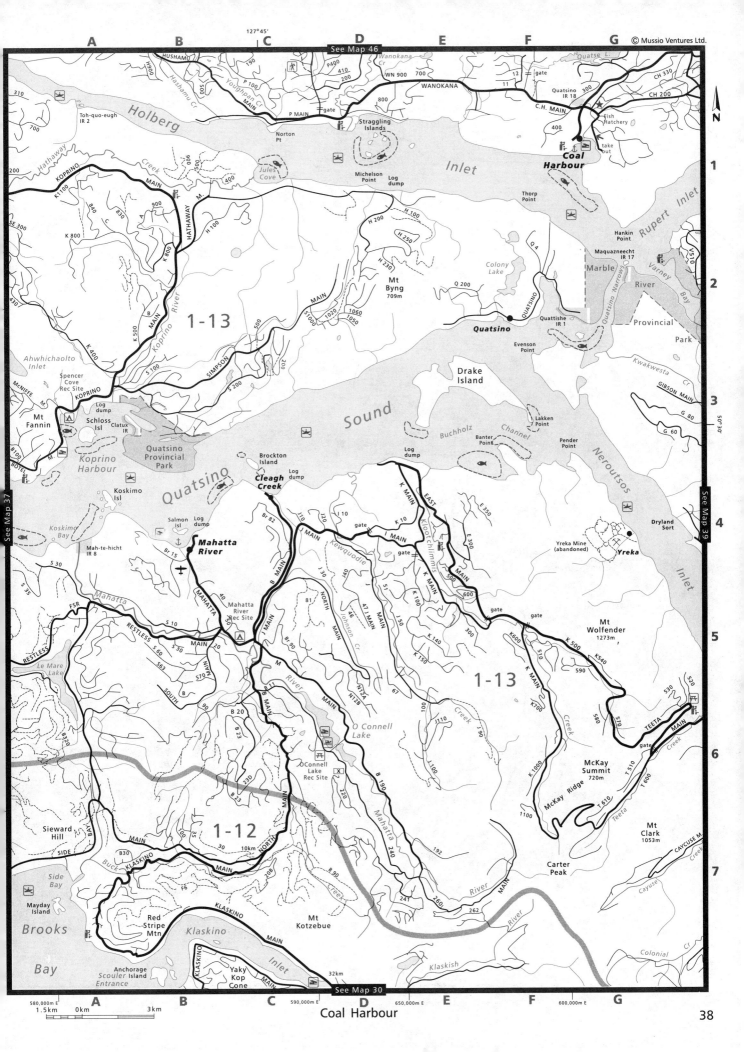

© Mussio Ventures Ltd.

127°45'

N

Holberg   **Inlet**

Toh-quo-eugh IR 2

Wanokana Cr

WANOKANA

gate

Quatsino IR 18

C.H. MAIN

CH 330

CH 200

Fish Hatchery

take out

Coal Harbour

Hathaway Creek

Straggling Islands

Norton Pt

HUSHAMU

Youghpan Cr

P MAIN

gate

Jules Cove

Michelson Point

Log dump

Thorp Point

Hankin Point

Maquazneecht IR 17

Rupert Inlet

KOPRINO MAIN

HATHAWAY M

H 100

H 250

H 230

H 200

H 100

1-13

Mt Byng 709m

Colony Lake

Q 4

Q 200

Marble River

Varney Bay

Quatsino Narrows

Provincial

Koprino River

SIMPSON

MAIN

S 1000

1020

1060

1050

1100

200

S 100

S 200

Quatsino

QUATSINO

Quattishe IR 1

Evenson Point

Kwakwesta Cr

GIBSON MAIN

G 80

G 60

50°30'

Ahwhichaolto Inlet

McNIFFE M

Mt Fannin

Spencer Cove Rec Site

KOPRINO

B 100 BOTEL

Log dump

Schloss Isl

Clatux IR

Quatsino Provincial Park

Koprino Harbour

Koskimo Isl

Quatsino   **Sound**

Drake Island

Buchholz Channel

Lakken Point

Banter Point

Pender Point

Neroutsos

1-13

Dryland Sort

Koskimo Bay

Mah-te-hicht IR 8

Salmon Isl

Log dump

Br 15

Mahatta River

Brockton Island

Log dump

Cleagh Creek

Log dump

Br 82

J 10

J 10

K MAIN

K 10

EAST

E 350

E 300

Kloot-chlimms

Yreka Mine (abandoned)

Yreka

Inlet

See Map 39

Le Mare Lake

FSR

RESTLESS

Mahatta

MAHATTA

S 10

MAIN

S 30

Mahatta River Rec Site

J MAIN

Kewquodie

gate

gate

MAIN

E 300

500

600

MAIN

gate

gate

Mt Wolfender 1273m

K 600

K 500

K 540

K 700

530

520

590

RESTLESS

S 35

S 30

S 60

S 63

570

MAIN

J MAIN

81

NORTH MAIN

Johnson Cr

J 6

47 J MAIN

J 50

K 100

K 140

K 150

300

K MAIN

K 510

580

570

TEETA

MAIN

Side Bay

Mayday Island

S 30

B 320

B

90

B 20

B 23

M

B MAIN

NORTH MAIN

23D

10km

B 30

B 23

O Connell Lake

O Connell Lake Rec Site

X

N12B

67

B 190

J 110

J 100

K 1000

McKay Ridge

1100

T 610

Teeta

McKay Summit 720m

T 510

T 600

gate

Creek

Mt Clark 1053m

CAYUSE

1-12

Sieward Hill

SIDE BAY

KLASKINO

MAIN

100

35

30

B 208

B 90

Buck Creek

Klaskino

Red Stripe Mtn

KLASKINO MAIN

Mt Kotzebue

192

241

260

262

Carter Peak

Cayuse Cr

Brooks

Bay

Klaskino

Anchorage Scouler Island Entrance

Yaky Kop Cone

F6

KLASKINO MAIN

32km

Klaskish Inlet

Klaskish River

Mahatta River

MAIN

Colonial Cr

See Map 30

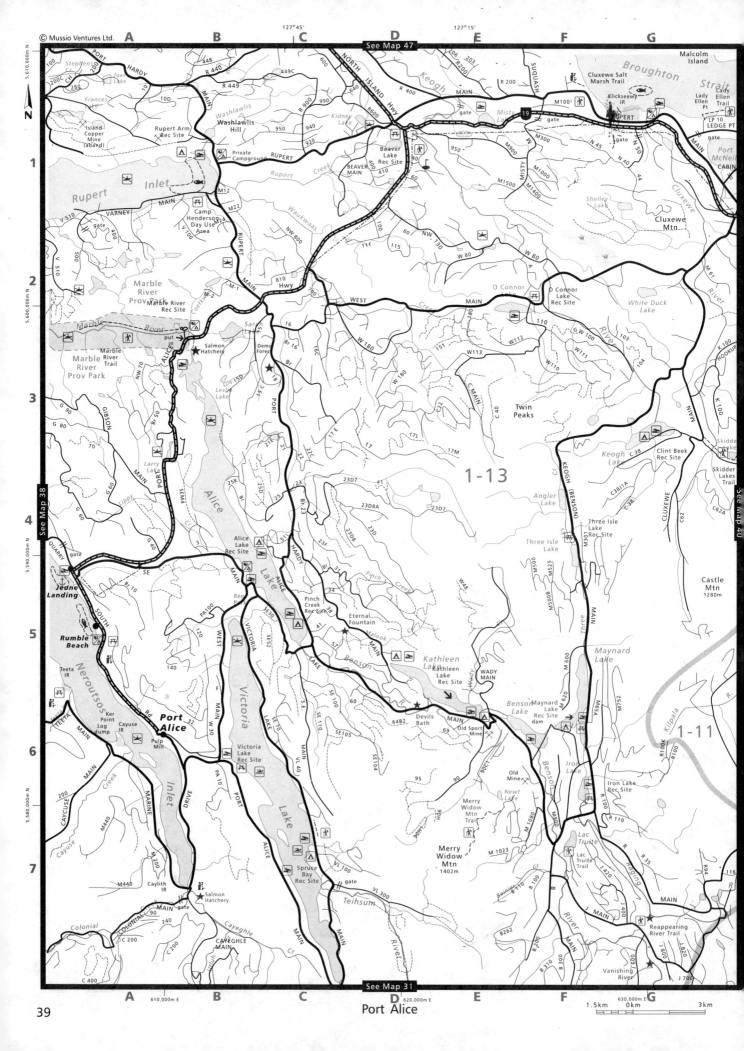

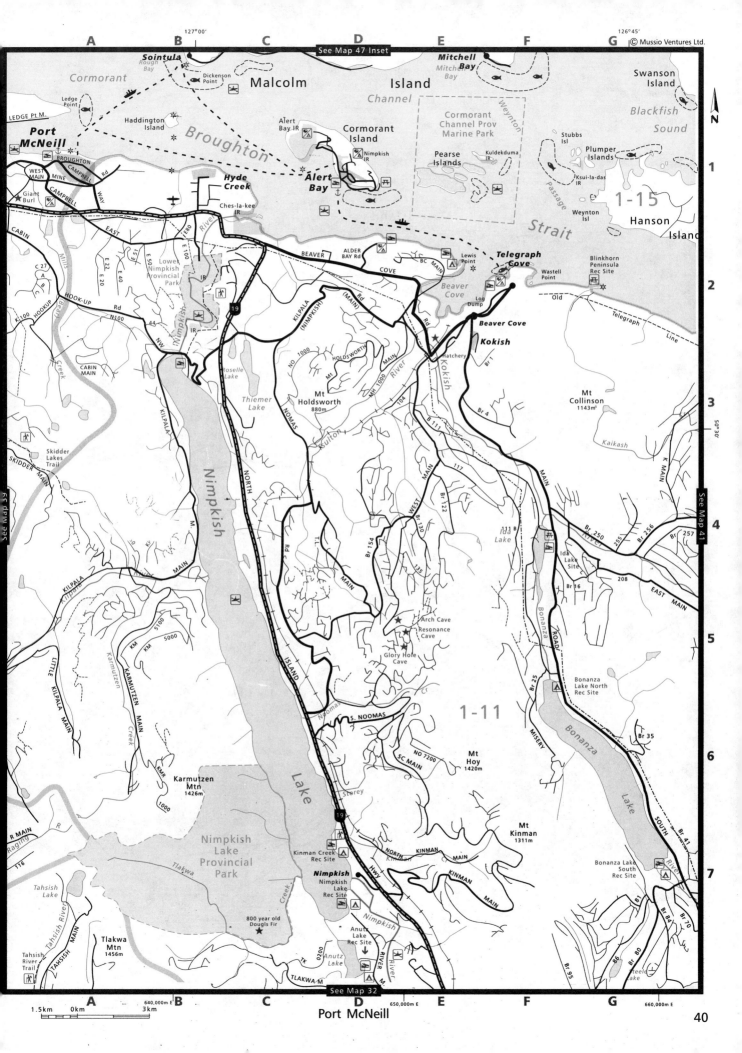

Cormorant
Sointula
Rough Bay
Dickenson Point
Malcolm   Island
Mitchell Bay
Mitchell Bay
Swanson Island
Ledge Point
Haddington Island
Broughton
Cormorant Island
Channel
Cormorant Channel Prov Marine Park
Blackfish Sound
N
LEDGE Pt M.
Port McNeill
BROUGHTON
WEST MAIN
MINE
CAMPBELL   Rd
Hyde Creek
Alert Bay IR
Nimpkish IR
Alert Bay
Pearse Islands
Kuldekduma IR
Stubbs Isl
Plumper Islands
Iksui-la-das IR
1
Giant Burl
CAMPBELL WAY
EAST
E 80
Ches-la-kee IR
Weynton Isl
1-15
Hanson Island
CABIN
HOOK-UP   Rd
E 51
E 50
E 22
E 40
E 20
E 100
N100
Lower Nimpkish Provincial Park
IR
19
BEAVER
ALDER BAY Rd
COVE
BC MAIN
Lewis Point
Telegraph Cove
Wastell Point
Blinkhorn Peninsula Rec Site
2
C 27
A B C
HAISLA
Mills   Creek
NW
44
IR
KILPALA (NIMPKISH)   MAIN
Rd
Beaver Cove
Log Dump
Beaver Cove
Kokish
Old
Telegraph   Line
Strait
SKIDDER MAIN
Roselle Lake
NO 1000
Mt Holdsworth 880m
HOLDSWORTH
MH 1000
River
104
Kokish
Hatchery
Br 1
Br 4
Mt Collinson 1143m
Kaikash
K MAIN
See Map 41
3
50°30'
Skidder Lakes Trail
Thiemer Lake
Sulton
WEST   MAIN
117
Br 122
Br 250
Br 256
Br 257
50°30'
4
See Map 39
KILPALA   MAIN
KILPALA
KM 5100
KM 5000
Karmutzen   Creek
NOMAS
NORTH   ISLAND   M.
TL MAIN
Br 130
Br 154
135
MAIN
Ida Lake
208
EAST MAIN
Br 16
Br 35
5
LITTLE KILPALA MAIN
KMR
1000
Karmutzen Mtn 1426m
Rd
Noomas
Arch Cave
Resonance Cave
Glory Hole Cave
1-11
Cr
S. NOOMAS
MISERY
ROAD
Bonanza   Lake
Bonanza Lake North Rec Site
Br 25
6
R MAIN
Raging   R
116
Nimpkish Lake Provincial Park
Tlakwa
Lake
Storey
NO 7200
SC MAIN
Mt Hoy 1420m
Mt Kinman 1311m
SOUTH
Br 41
7
Tahsish Lake
Tahsish River Trail
Tahsish River
TAHSISH MAIN
Tlakwa Mtn 1456m
800 year old Dougls Fir
Tlakwa   Creek
Kinman Creek Rec Site
Nimpkish
Nimpkish Lake Rec Site
19
Hwy
Anutz Lake Rec Site
TK
0200
Anutz Lake
TLAKWA M
NORTH   KINMAN
KINMAN   MAIN
Nimpkish   River
RIVER   M
Bonanza Lake South Rec Site
Br 70
Br 84
Br 95
Br 80
Br 81
86
Steele Lake

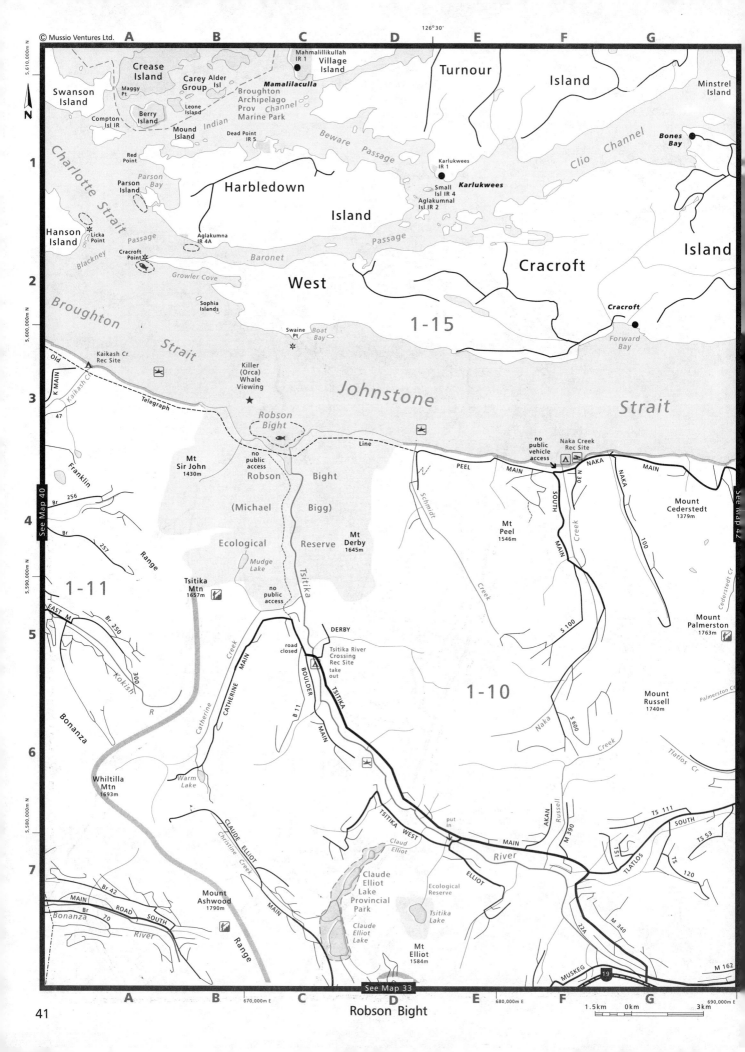

© Mussio Ventures Ltd.

A **B** **C** **D** 126°30' **E** **F** **G**

N

5,610,000 m N

Swanson
Island

Crease
Island

Carey
Group

Alder
Isl

Mahmalillikullah
IR 1

Village
Island

Turnour

Island

Minstrel
Island

Maggy
Pt

Compton
Isl IR

Berry
Island

Leone
Island

Mound
Island

Mamalilaculla

Broughton
Archipelago
Prov
Marine Park

Indian

Channel

Beware

Passage

Karlukwees
IR 1

Karlukwees

Bones
Bay

Red Point

1

Parson
Island

Parson
Bay

Dead Point
IR 5

Harbledown

Island

Small
Isl IR 4

Aglakumnal
Isl IR 2

Clio

Channel

Island

Hanson
Island

Licka
Point

Aglakumna
IR 4A

Passage

Cracroft

Blackney

Cracroft
Point

Baronet

Passage

West

2

Broughton

Strait

Growler Cove

Sophia
Islands

Cracroft

Forward
Bay

5,600,000 m N

Swaine
Pt

Boat
Bay

1-15

Johnstone

Old

K MAIN

Kaikash Cr
Rec Site

Killer
(Orca)
Whale
Viewing

Strait

3

47

Telegraph

*Robson
Bight*

Line

no public
vehicle
access

Naka Creek
Rec Site

Franklin

Mt
Sir John
1430m

no public
access

Robson

Bight

PEEL

MAIN

SOUTH MAIN

GEN

NAKA

NAKA

MAIN

See Map 40

Br 256

(Michael

Bigg)

Mt
Derby
1645m

Mt Peel
1546m

Mount
Cederstedt
1379m

See Map 42

4

5,590,000 m N

Br

257

Range

Ecological

Reserve

Mudge
Lake

Tsitika

Creek

Cederstedt Cr

Tsitika
Mtn
1657m

no public
access

1-11

EAST M

Br 250

DERBY

Tsitika River
Crossing
Rec Site
take
out

1-10

Mount
Palmerston
1763m

5

300

Catherine

Creek

CATHERINE MAIN

road
closed

B 11

BOULDER MAIN

TSITIKA

S 100

Naka

Russell

S 600

Creek

Mount
Russell
1740m

Kokish

R

Bonanza

Tlatlos Cr

6

5,580,000 m N

Whiltilla
Mtn
1693m

Warm
Lake

TSITIKA WEST

put
in

MAIN

River

AKAN

M 390

TS 111

TS 53

SOUTH

TS 151

TS 120

Br 42

CLAUDE ELLIOT

Christine Creek

Claude
Elliot

ELLIOT

Ecological
Reserve

TLATLOS

7

MAIN

ROAD

SOUTH

Mount
Ashwood
1790m

Claude
Elliot
Lake
Provincial
Park

Tsitika Lake

22A

M 340

Bonanza

Br
70

River

MAIN

Range

Claude
Elliot
Lake

Mt
Elliot
1584m

MUSKEG

19

M 162

A **B** 670,000m E **C** See Map 33 **D** **E** 680,000m E **F** **G** 690,000m E

1.5km 0km 3km

Robson Bight

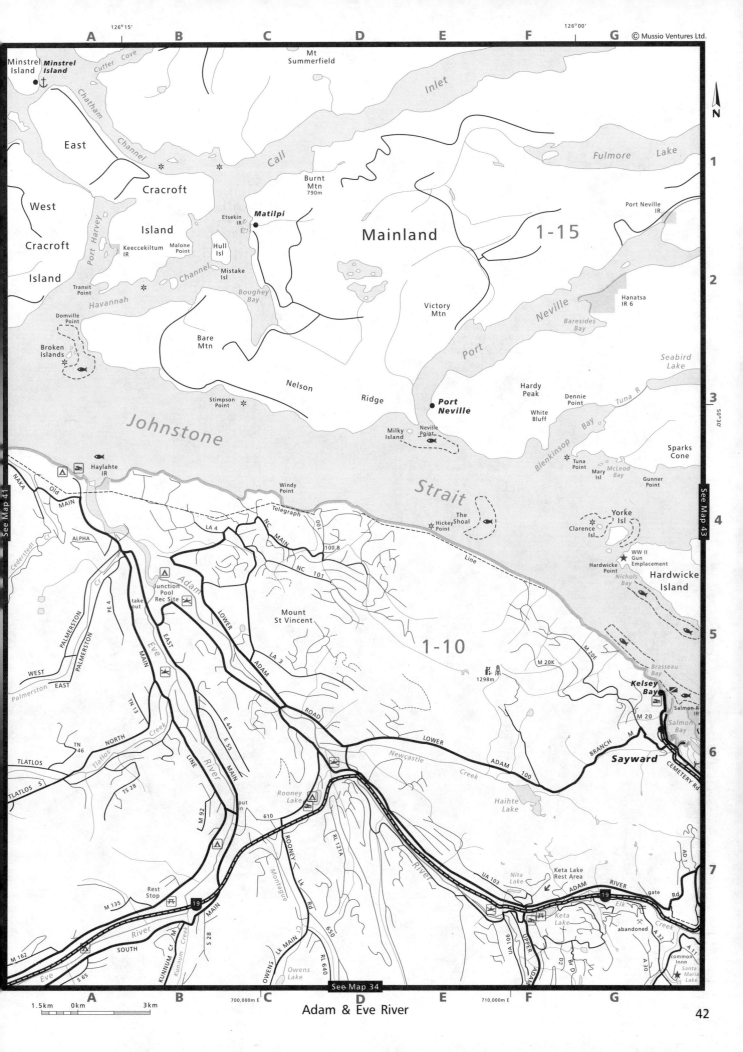

© Mussio Ventures Ltd.

A · B · C · D · E · F · G

126°15' 126°00'

Minstrel
Island   *Minstrel
Island*

Cutter Cove

Mt
Summerfield

Call

Inlet

Fulmore Lake

East

Chatham

Channel

Cracroft

Burnt
Mtn
790m

Port Neville
IR

Island

Etsekin
IR   *Matilpi*

Mainland

1-15

West

Port Harvey

Keeccekiltum
IR   Malone
Point   Hull
Isl

Mistake
Isl

Cracroft

Transit
Point

Havannah

Channel

Boughey
Bay

Victory
Mtn

Port

Neville

Hanatsa
IR 6

Baresides
Bay

Island

Domville
Point

Bare
Mtn

Broken
Islands

Nelson

Seabird
Lake

Stimpson
Point

Ridge

Hardy
Peak

Dennie
Point

Tuna R

Johnstone

*Port
Neville*

White
Bluff

Milky
Island   Neville
Point

Blenkinsop Bay

Tuna
Point   Mary
Isl   McLeod
Bay

Sparks
Cone

Gunner
Point

See Map 41

Haylahte
IR

Windy
Point

Telegraph

Strait

The
Hickey Shoal
Point

Line

Clarence
Isl   **Yorke
Isl**

WW II
Gun
Emplacement

Hardwicke
Point

Nichols
Bay

See Map 43

50°30'

Hardwicke
Island

NAKA

Old

MAIN

ALPHA

LA 4

NC   MAIN

100

100 B

NC 101

Brasseau
Bay

Cedarstedt Cr

Adam

Junction
Pool
Rec Site

LOWER

Mount
St Vincent

LA 3

1-10

1298m

M 20K

M 20E

**Kelsey
Bay**

Salmon R
IR

PE 4

take
out

EAST

ADAM

Salmon
Bay

WEST

Palmerston

Palmerston

Eve

ROAD

M 20

PALMERSTON

East

E 44

E 55

LOWER

Newcastle

ADAM   100

M

BRANCH

Sayward

CEMETERY Rd

Tlatlos

TN
46   NORTH

Creek

Creek

TN 13

LINE

River

MAIN

put in

Rooney
Lake

Haihte
Lake

AD 1

TLATLOS

TS 28

M 92

610

RL 121A

River

UA 103

Nita
Lake

Keta Lake
Rest Area

ADAM   RIVER

Elk

gate
Rd

Rest Stop

19

M 135

SOUTH

KUNNUM Cr M

Kunnum Creek

S 28

Montague

Rd

RL 640

Owens Lk Main

Owens
Lake

650

UPPER   ADAM

UA 106

19

Keta
Lake

abandoned

A 32

M 162

S 65

Eve   River

See Map 34

UPPER   ADAM   D2   Br D   A 11

Common Inon

Santa
Maria
Lake

A 30

1.5km   0km   3km

Adam & Eve River

42

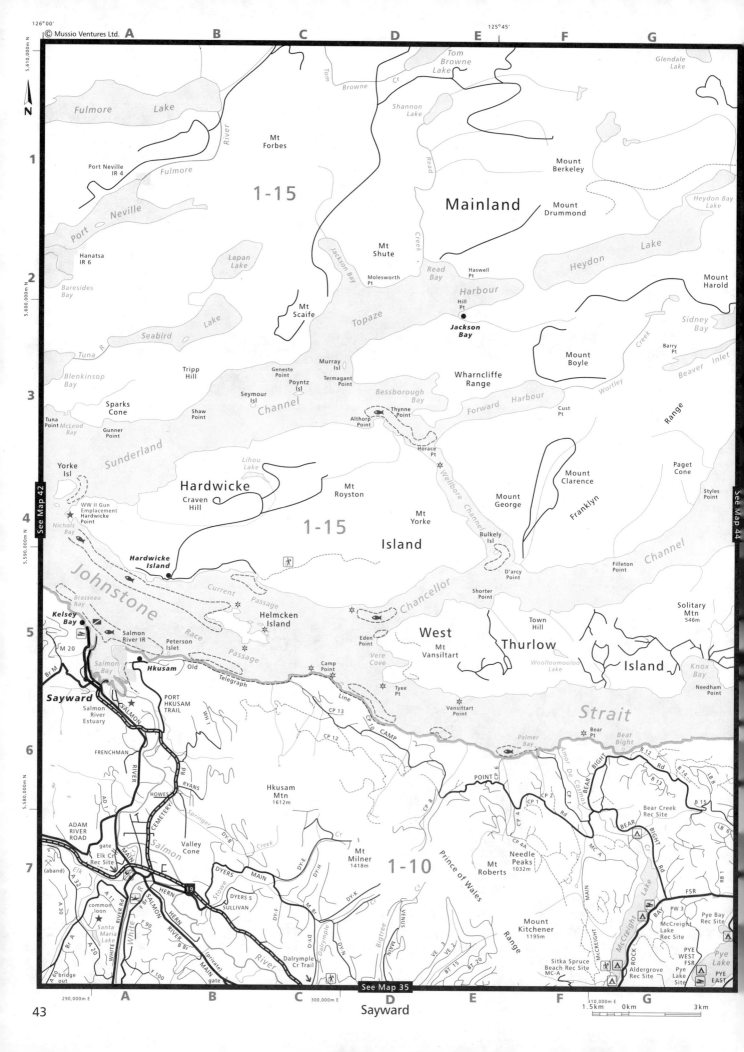

126°00'

125°45'

5,610,000m N

A **B** **C** **D** **E** **F** **G**

Fulmore *Lake*

Mt Forbes

1-15

Tom Browne Lake

Browne Cr

Shannon Lake

Glendale Lake

Mount Berkeley

Mainland

Mount Drummond

Heydon Bay Lake

Port Neville IR 4

Fulmore River

Port Neville

Hanatsa IR 6

Lapan Lake

Mt Shute

Read Creek

Read Bay

Molesworth Pt

Haswell Pt

Heydon Lake

Mount Harold

1

5,600,000m N

Baresides Bay

Tuna R.

Seabird Lake

Mt Scaife

Jackson Bay

Harbour

Hill Pt

Topaze

Jackson Bay

Sidney Bay

Barry Pt

Beaver Inlet

2

Blenkinsop Bay

Sparks Cone

Tripp Hill

Geneste Point

Poyntz Isl

Murray Isl

Termagant Point

Channel

Bessborough Bay

Wharncliffe Range

Mount Boyle

Wortley Creek

Range

3

Tuna Point

McLeod Bay

Gunner Point

Seymour Isl

Shaw Point

Althorp Point

Thynne Point

Horace Pt

Forward Harbour

Cust Pt

See Map 42

Yorke Isl

WW II Gun Emplacement Hardwicke Point

Nichols Bay

Hardwicke

Craven Hill

Lihou Lake

Mt Royston

1-15

Mt Yorke

Island

Wellbore Channel

Mount George

Mount Clarence

Franklyn

Paget Cone

Styles Point

See Map 44

4

5,590,000m N

Johnstone

Brasseau Bay

Hardwicke Island

Current Passage

Bulkely Isl

D'arcy Point

Filleton Point

Channel

5

Kelsey Bay

M 20

Bt M

Salmon River IR

Peterson Islet

Race Passage

Helmcken Island

Eden Point

Vere Cove

Chancellor

Shorter Point

West

Mt Vansiltart

Town Hill

Thurlow

Woolloomooloo Lake

Island

Solitary Mtn 546m

Knox Bay

Needham Point

Hkusam

Old Telegraph

Camp Point

Tyee Pt

Vansittart Point

Strait

Bear Pt

Bear Bight

6

5,580,000m N

Sayward

Salmon River Estuary

PORT HKUSAM TRAIL

SALMON

FRENCHMAN

RIVER

HOWES

RYANS Rd

WH 1

Line

CP 13

CP 12

CP 10

CAMP

POINT

Amor De Cosmos

Palmer Bay

BEAR

BIGHT

B 12

B 13

B 14

LB 8

Rd

Rd

7

5,570,000m N

ADAM RIVER ROAD

Elk Cr Rec Site

(aband)

common loon

Santa Maria Lake

A 11

A 30

A 20

60 Bt A

bridge out

F 60

CEMETERY

MAIN

Salmon

Valley Cone

DY-B

Springer

Creek

Cr

Mt Milner 1418m

1-10

Hkusam Mtn 1612m

Prince of Wales

Mt Roberts

Needle Peaks 1032m

CP 1

CP 2

CP 4

CP 8

CP 44

MC-A

Bear Creek Rec Site

BEAR BIGHT Rd

LB 6

B 15

LB 8

ELK

WHITE RIVER Rd

SALMON RIVER Rd

HERN

HERN

19

DYERS MAIN

DYERS S

SULLIVAN

Stowe

DY-E

DY-H

DY-F

M Br

DY-K

DY-O

DY-N

Bigtree MAIN

VENUS

VE 3

VE 2

BT 15

BT 20

Mount Kitchener 1195m

Range

MAIN

MCCREIGHT

ROCK BAY Rd

McCreight Lake

PW 3

FSR

RB 1

Pye Bay Rec Site

Sitka Spruce Beach Rec Site MC-A

Aldergrove Rec Site

McCreight Lake Rec Site

Pye Lake Site

PYE WEST FSR

Pye Lake

PYE EAST

White R

Dalrymple Cr Trail

See Map 35

A **B** **C** **D** **E** **F** **G**

290,000m E

300,000m E

310,000m E

1.5km   0km   3km

Sayward

43

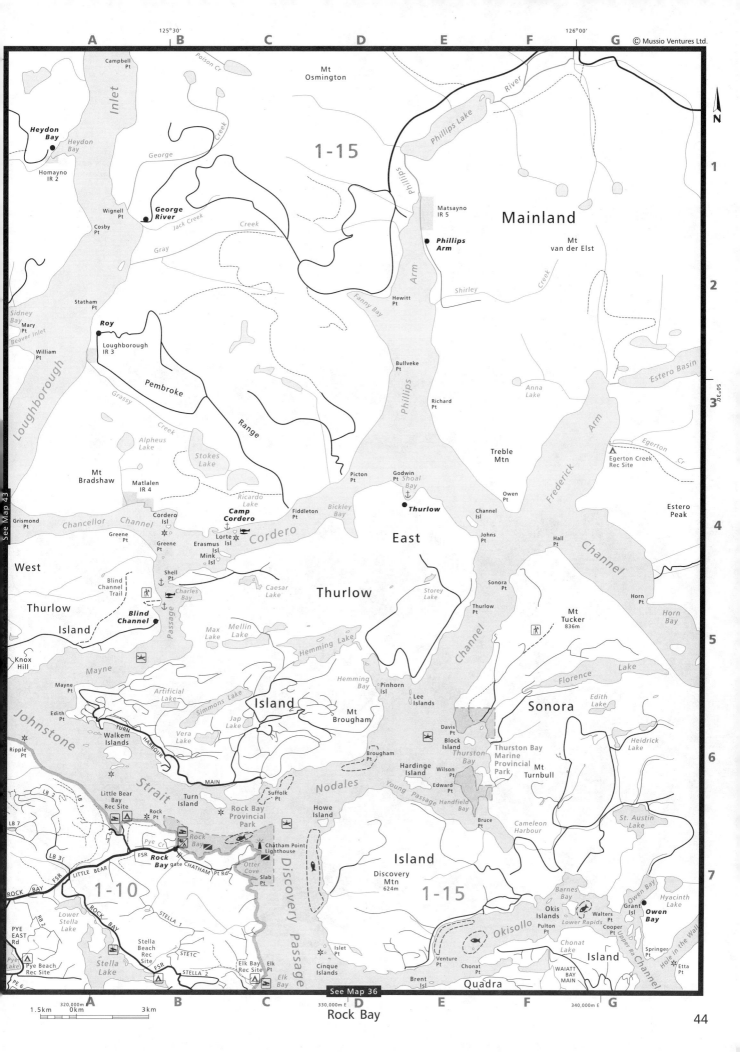

A   B   125°30'   C   D   E   F   126°00'   G

1-15

Mt Osmington

Campbell Pt

Poison Cr

George Creek

Jack Creek

Gray

Creek

Phillips Lake

River

Mainland

Matsayno IR 5

Mt van der Elst

Inlet

Heydon Bay

Homayno IR 2

Wignell Pt

Cosby Pt

Statham Pt

George River

Phillips Arm

Phillips Arm

Hewitt Pt

Fanny Bay

Shirley

Creek

Sidney Bay

Mary Pt

Beaver Inlet

William Pt

Roy

Loughborough IR 3

Pembroke

Range

Grassy Creek

Alpheus Lake

Stokes Lake

Bullveke Pt

Richard Pt

Phillips

Anna Lake

Estero Basin

50°30'

Loughborough

Mt Bradshaw

Matlalen IR 4

Ricardo Lake

Picton Pt

Bickley Bay

Godwin Pt   Shoal Bay

Thurlow

Treble Mtn

Owen Pt

Channel Isl

Frederick

Arm

Egerton Cr

Egerton Creek Rec Site

Estero Peak

4

Grismond Pt

Chancellor   Channel

Greene Pt

Cordero Isl

Camp Cordero

Lorte Isl

Erasmus Isl   Mink Isl

Greene Pt

Fiddleton Pt

Cordero

East

Johns Pt

Hall Pt

Channel

West

Thurlow

Island

Blind Channel Trail

Shell Pt

Charles Bay

Blind Channel

Passage

Caesar Lake

Max Lake

Mellin Lake

Thurlow

Storey Lake

Sonora Pt

Thurlow Pt

Mt Tucker 836m

Horn Pt

Horn Bay

5

Knox Hill

Mayne Pt

Mayne

Artificial Lake

Simmons Lake

Jap Lake

Hemming Lake

Hemming Bay

Pinhorn Isl

Lee Islands

Florence Lake

Edith Lake

Ripple Pt

Edith Pt

Walkem Islands

Vera Lake

Island

Mt Brougham

Brougham Pt

Davis Pt   Block Island

Thurston Bay

Sonora

Thurston Bay Marine Provincial Park

Mt Turnbull

Heidrick Lake

St. Austin Lake

6

Johnstone

Strait

TURN HARBOUR

MAIN

Little Bear Bay Rec Site

Rock Pt

Turn Island

Suffolk Pt

Rock Bay Provincial Park

Howe Island

Nodales

Young Passage

Hardinge Island

Wilson Pt

Edward Pt

Handfield Bay

Bruce Pt

Cameleon Harbour

Island

Barnes Bay

Okis Islands

Lower Rapids

Walters Pt

Cooper Pt

Grant Isl

Owen Bay

Hyacinth Lake

7

LB 2

LB 1

LB 7

LB 3

ROCK BAY

ROCK   BAY FSR

LITTLE BEAR   FSR

Pye Cr

Rock Bay

gate   CHATHAM Pt Rd

Otter Cove

Slab Pt

Chatham Point Lighthouse

Discovery

Passage

1-10

Lower Stella Lake

Stella Beach Rec Site

STELLA 1

STE1C

STELLA 2

Elk Bay Rec Site

Elk Bay

Islet Pt

Cinque Islands

Discovery Mtn 624m

1-15

Venture Pt

Chonat Pt

Brent Isl

Okisollo

Chonat Lake

WAIATT BAY MAIN

Quadra

Pulton Pt

Island

Upper Ra Channel

Hole In the Wall

Springer Pt

Etta Pt

PYE EAST Rd

Pye Lake

PE 6

Pye Beach Rec Site

Stella Lake

See Map 43

See Map 36

Rock Bay

1.5km   320,000m E   0km   3km   330,000m E   340,000m E

A   B   C   D   E   F   G

44

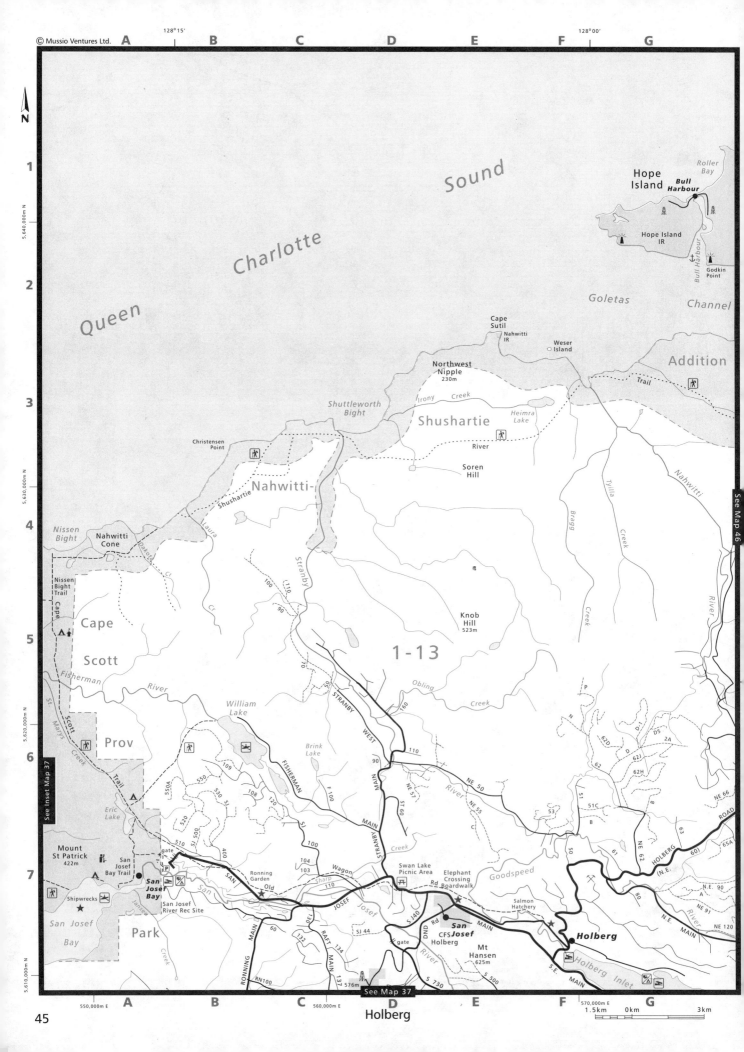

© Mussio Ventures Ltd.

128°15'   128°00'

A   B   C   D   E   F   G

Queen   Charlotte   Sound

Hope
Island   *Bull
Harbour*

*Roller
Bay*

Hope Island
IR

Godkin
Point

Goletas   *Channel*

Addition

Cape
Sutil

Nahwitti
IR

Weser
Island

Northwest
Nipple
230m

Irony   *Creek*

Shushartie

*Heimra
Lake*

Trail

Shuttleworth
Bight

River

Tyilla

Nahwitti

Christensen
Point

Soren
Hill

Nahwitti-

Shushartie

Laura

Bragg

Creek

River

*Nissen
Bight*

Nahwitti
Cone

Dakota

100

110

Creek

90

Knob
Hill
523m

Nissen
Bight
Trail

1-13

Cape

Cape

Scott

Fisherman

River

William
Lake

70

Obling   *Creek*

St. Marys Creek

Scott

Prov

Brink
Lake

109

108

550A

550

SJ

120

F 100

FISHERMAN

550

500

510

400

520

SJ

100

STRANBY MAIN

WEST

90

110

160

River

NE 50

NE 57

ST 60

NE 55

110

P

N

62D

D-1

D5

2A

D

62J

62

62H

51

51C

B

C-1

53

50

61

NE 62

HOLBERG

ROAD

60)

65A

N.E.
90

N.E.
91

NE 66

NE 120

Eric
Lake

Mount
St Patrick
422m

San
Josef
Bay Trail

gate

San Josef
River Rec Site

**San
Josef
Bay**

Shipwrecks

*San Josef
Bay*

Ronning
Garden

Old

San

SAN

RONNING

RN100

60

132

RAFT MAIN

134

137

104

103

Sharp

SJ 44

110

Wagon

Josef

Josef

SJ 140

River

gate

Swan Lake
Picnic Area

Elephant
Crossing
Boardwalk

Salmon
Hatchery

Goodspeed

80

S.E.

MAIN

N.E.

Holberg Inlet

Holberg

**San
Josef**
CFS
Holberg

Mt
Hansen
625m

S 140

DND   *Rd*

S 730

S 500

576m

Park

See Map 37

See Map 46

See Inset Map 37

45

550,000m E   **A**   560,000m E   **C**   **D**   570,000m E   **F**   **G**

5,640,000m N

5,630,000m N

5,620,000m N

5,610,000m N

Holberg

1.5km   0km   3km

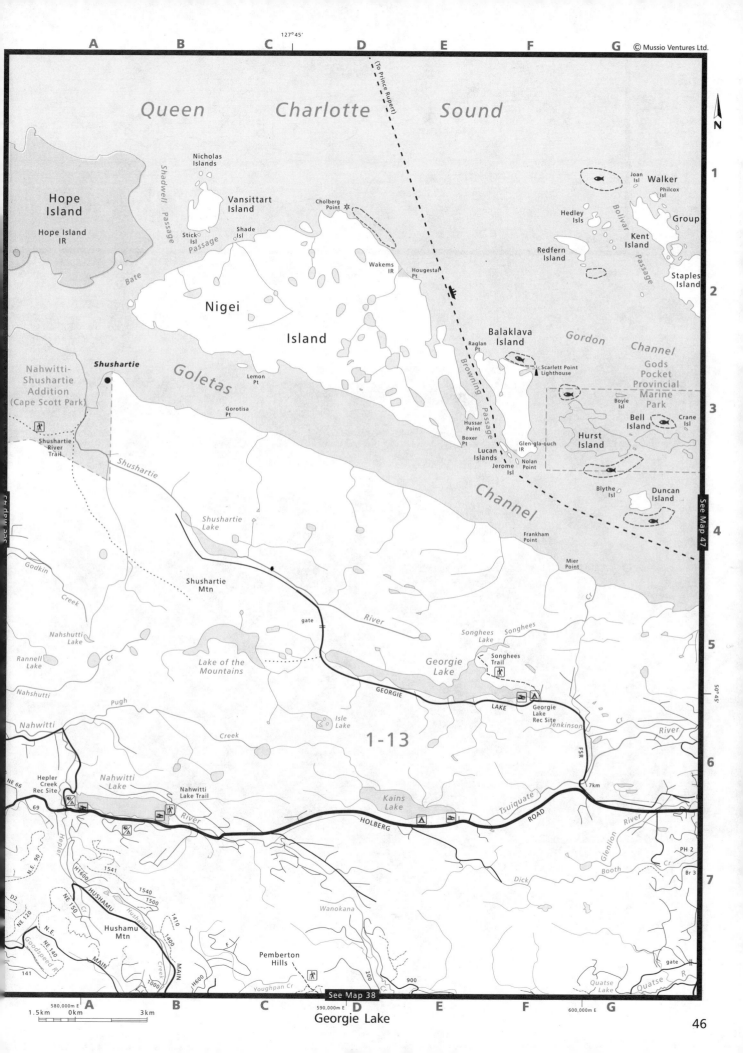

127°45'

© Mussio Ventures Ltd.

N

Queen   Charlotte   Sound

(To Prince Rupert)

1

Nicholas
Islands

Hope
Island

Vansittart
Island

Cholberg
Point

Joan
Isl   Walker

Philcox
Isl

Hedley
Isls

Group

Hope Island
IR

Stick
Isl

Shade
Isl

Shadwell
passage

Wakems
IR

Redfern
Island

Kent
Island

Bolivar

passage

Staples
Island

2

Nigei

Hougesta
Pt

Balaklava
Island

Gordon   Channel

Island

Raglan
Pt

Scarlett Point
Lighthouse

Gods
Pocket
Provincial
Marine
Park

Nahwitti-
Shushartie
Addition
(Cape Scott Park)

Shushartie

Goletas

Lemon
Pt

Hussar
Point

Browning Passage

Boyle
Isl

Bell
Island

Crane
Isl

3

Shushartie
River
Trail

Gorotisa
Pt

Boxer
Pt

Lucan
Islands

Glen-gla-ouch
IR

Hurst
Island

Shushartie

Jerome
Isl

Nolan
Point

Blythe
Isl

Duncan
Island

Channel

See Map 47

Godkin

Shushartie
Lake

Frankham
Point

4

Creek

Shushartie
Mtn

Mier
Point

50°45'

Nahshutti
Lake

Lake of the
Mountains

gate

River

Songhees
Lake

Songhees

Georgie
Lake

Songhees
Trail

5

Rannell
Lake

Nahshutti

Pugh

GEORGIE

Isle
Lake

1-13

Georgie Lake
Rec Site

LAKE

Jenkinson

River

Nahwitti

Creek

FSR

6

Hepler
Creek
Rec Site

Nahwitti
Lake

Nahwitti
Lake Trail

Kains
Lake

Tsuiquate

7km

NE 66

69

River

HOLBERG

ROAD

Glenlion River

Booth

PH 2

Br 3

1541

1540

1500

Dick

Quatse

7

D2

NE 120

NE 150

N.E.
140

HUSHAMU

1600

Hushamu
Mtn

1410

1400

Wanokana

Cr

gate

141

Goodspeed R.

MAIN

H600

Creek

Pemberton
Hills

Youghpan Cr

200

900

Quatse Lake

Quatse R

See Map 38

580,000m E
1.5km   0km   3km

590,000m E

600,000m E

Georgie Lake

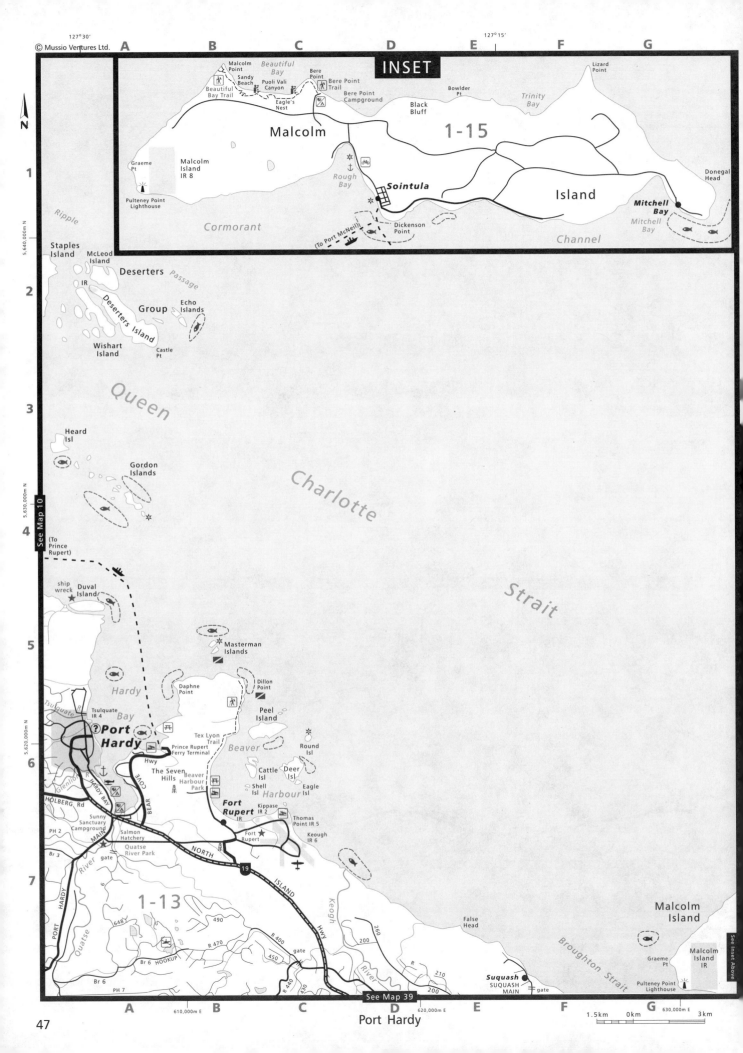

INDEX

This comprehensive index is intended to help guide you to the map or reference page you are interested in. If the specific item is not labelled try picking the most prominent land feature in the area. This will guide you to the right map and reference page.

#

1st and 2nd Creek Trail .... Map 2/A2
2nd Lake .... Map 4/B3
3rd Lake .... Map 4/B3

A

Ada Islands .... Map 16/F1
Adam River .... Map 34/E2, 42/B5; .... Ref 25,27
Adrienne Lake .... Map 19/F6
Agnes Island .... Map 12/G4
Ahousat Warm Springs .. Map 11/E1; Ref 6
Al Stopper Island .... Map 13/D7
Alava Lake .... Map 25/E2
Alberni Inlet .... Map 14/F6
Alberni Trails .... Map 15/A1; Ref 55
Albert Head .... Map 4/B6
Albert Head Lagoon Regional Park .... Map 4/C6; Ref 33
Aldergrove Rec Site ... Map 43/G7; Ref 39
Alert Bay .... Map 40/D1; Ref 29
Alice Lake .... Map 39/B24; Ref 20
Alice Lake Rec Site .... Map 39/B4
Allen Lake .... Map 22/B1
Alligator Creek .... Map 3/A4
Alma Russell Island .... Map 5/G1, 13/G7
Alone Mountain Trail .... Map 21/G1; Ref 47
Alpheus Lake .... Map 44/A3
Alto Lake .... Map 19/C7
Amai Creek .... Map 32/A7
Amai Inlet .... Map 31/G7
Amedroz Lake .... Map 13/G7
Amelia Island .... Map 16/E1
Ammone Falls .... Map 16/F4
Amor De Cosmos Creek .... Map 43/F6
Amor Lake .... Map 36/A3; Ref 20
Amos Creek .... Map 30/Inset
Amos River .... Map 30/A4
Anderson Creek .... Map 16/D4
Anderson Lake .... Map 7/C7; Ref 11
Andrew Lake .... Map 20/G3
Angie Lake .... Map 35/C5
Angora Lake .... Map 12/G5 13/A5
Angus Lake .... Map 12/F5
Antler Lake .... Map 26/E3; Ref 11, 20, 52
Anutz Lake Rec Site .... Map 40/D7; Ref 42
Anutz River .... Map 40/C7; Ref 20
Apple Point Rec Site ... Map 35/G5; Ref 39
Arakun Island .... Map 12/A2
Arbutus Creek .... Map 4/A3
Arbutus Grove Prov Park .... Map 16/E2; .... Ref 35
Arden Creek Rec Site .... Map 14/G4; .... Ref 43
Ardmore .... Map 4/D1
Armor Lake Rec Site ... Map 35/G3; Ref 39
Arnica Lake .... Map 20/G1
Arrowsmith Lake .... Map 15/D2; Ref 11
Artificial Lake .... Map 44/B5
Artlish Caves Prov Park .... Map 32/D3
Artlish River .... Map 32/B4; Ref 25
Artlish Caves Prov Park .... Map 32/E4; Ref 35
Art Mann Park .... Map 9/64
Arum Lake .... Map 22/B2
Ash Lake .... Map 22/A5; Ref 11
Ash River ...... Map 21/C3, 22/A4; Ref 24
Ashew Creek .... Map 9/E2
Ashlar Creek .... Map 36/E1
Ashwood Creek .... Map 20/F5
Atleo River .... Map 19/F6
Atluck Lake .... Map 32/C2; Ref 20, 42
Aureole Icefield .... Map 21/C1
Aurthur Lake .... Map 6/G4
Austin Island .... Map 5/D2
Averill Creek .... Map 9/E4
Award Lake .... Map 14/D1
Axe Creek .... Map 7/F7
Ayum Creek Park Reserve .... Map 3/G4; Ref 33

B

Bacon Lake .... Map 35/G7; Ref 62
Backwater Lake .... Map 35/F2
Bainbridge Lake .... Map 15/A2; Ref 11
Bainbridge .... Map 22/F7
Bajo Creek .... Map 24/G7
Balaklava Island .... Map 46/E3
Balbo Creek .... Map 19/G6
Bald Mountain Rec Site .. Map 8/D3; Ref 43
Bald Mountain Trails ...... Map 8/D3; Ref 47
Baldy Mountain .... Map 16/F2; Ref 50
Ballenas Islands .... Map 23/Inset/G1
Ballingall Islets Provincial Nature Park .... Map 10/C2; Ref 31
Balmer Lake .... Map 15/F7
Bamber Creek .... Map 4/A1
Bamberton Prov Park ...... Map 4/B1; Ref 33
Bamfield .... Map 6/A3
Bancroft Creek .... Map 20/B1
Banifield Inlet .... Map 5/G4
Banon Creek .... Map 9/C1
Bare Island .... Map 4/G1
Baresides Bay .... Map 42/G2, 43/A2
Barington Lake .... Map 7/A1
Baronet Passage .... Map 41/B2
Barra Lake .... Map 19/F6
Barsby Lake .... Map 16/F5
Bartlett Island .... Map 11/D2
Battleship Lake .... Map 28/E6; Ref 11
Bavis Creek .... Map 2/B2
Bawden Bay .... Map 19/F7
Bawden Creek .... Map 11/F1
Bayle Point Provincial Park .... Map 23/A4
Baynes Sound .... Map 22/F2, 23/A4
Bazan Bay .... Map 4/D1
Bazett Island .... Map 13/E7
Beano Creek .... Map 18/Inset, 24/G7
Bear Creek Reservoir Map 3/B3; Ref 11, 60
Bear Creek .... Map 9/A6, 40/A2
Bear Creek Rec Site .... Map 43/G7; Ref 39
Bear Creek Resevoir ...... Map3/B3; Ref 11
Bear Hill Regional Park .... Map 4/D3; Ref 33, 59
Bear Lake .... Map 8/E4; Ref 11
Beaufort Creek .... Map 22/B3
Beaumont Marine Park .... Map 10/G5/Inset; Ref 31
Beauty Lake .... Map 21/A4
Beaver Cove .... Map 40/B2
Beaver Creek .... Map 22/E7
Beaver Harbour .... Map 47/B6
Beaver Inlet .... Map 43/G2
Beaver Lake .... Map 4/D3, 9/A6; Ref 11
Beaver Lake Rec Site .... Map 39/D1; Ref 20, 41
Beaver Lodge Forest Lands Trail .... Map 36/67; Ref 46
Beaver Point .... Map 10/E5
Beaver Point Provincial Park .... Map 10/D5
Beavertail Lake .... Map 36/A7; Ref 20
Becher Bay .... Map 3/G7
Becher Lake .... Map 35/G7
Beck Island .... Map 12/A3
Beckon Lake .... Map 13/F7
Bedingfield Bay .... Map 19/G7
Bedwell Harbour .... Map 10/Inset
Bedwell Lake .... Map 20/G3
Bedwell River .... Map 20/E4; Ref 24, 53
Bedwell Sound .... Map 12/B1 20/B7
Bedwell Valley Trail .... Map 20/G4
Bedwell-Cream Lake Trail .... Map 20/G3
Beech Creek .... Map 21/G1
Beg Island .... Map 5/A1/Inset
Belkinson Lake .... Map 4/E4
Bell Creek .... Map 16/A7
Bell Island .... Map 46/G3
Bellhouse Provincial Park .... Map 10/F3; Ref 31
Belmont Park .... Map 4/C5
Bench Trail .... Map 23/B3
Bennett Bay .... Map 10/G3; Ref 31
Benson Creek .... Map 16/F3
Benson Lake .... Map 39/E5; Ref 20
Benson River .... Map 39/E7; Ref 25
Bessborough Bay .... Map 43/D3
Beware Passage .... Map 41/C1
Big Bay Rec Site .... Map 36/C6; Ref 39
Big Bunsby Prov Marine Park .... Map 30/G4; Ref 35
Big Interior Mountain .... Map 20/G4
Big Qualicum River .... Map 22/G6, 23/B7; Ref 24, 55
Big Jim Lake .... Map 20/G3
Bigtree Creek .... Map 35/D1
Bigtree Lake .... Map 43/D7
Billy Goat Creek .... Map 6/C6
Bings Creek .... Map 9/D4
Binns Island .... Map 19/G7
Black Island .... Map 44/E6
Black Lake .... Map 6/A5; Ref 11
Black River .... Map 6/A6
Blackburn Lake .... Map 10/B4
Blackfish Sound .... Map 40/G1
Blackies Beach Rec Site .... Map 14/B4; Ref 43
Blackjack Creek .... Map 16/D4
Blackjack Lake .... Map 16/D4; Ref 11
Blackjack Ridge ..... Map 16/E3; Ref 50, 61
Blackwater Lake .... Map 35/G3
Blakeney Creek .... Map 2/F2
Blaney Creek .... Map 20/E4
Blenkinshop Bay .... Map 43/A2
Bligh Island .... Map 25/D7; Ref 29
Bligh Island Prov Marine Park .... Map 18/C1, 25/C7; Ref 35
Blind Channel .... Map 44/A4
Blind Lake .... Map 17/A6; Ref 12
Blinkhorn Lake .... Map 4/A6
Blinkhorn Peninsula Rec Site .... Map 40/G2; Ref 42
Bloedel Creek .... Map 22/C2
Blowhole Bay .... Map 25/A3
Blue Creek .... Map 6/D6
Blue Grouse Lake .... Map 28/E3; Ref 12
Blue Lake .... Map 6/D6
Bluffs Park .... Map 10/E3
Blunden Island .... Map 11/E2
Blythe Island .... Map 46/G4
Boat Basin .... Map 18/F4
Bodil Lake .... Map 35/F4
Boerlage Lake .... Map 25/G4
Bonanza River .... Map 40/G6; Ref 20, 42
Bonell Creek .... Map 16/D2
Bones Bay .... Map 41/G1
Boneyard Lake .... Map 3/E5; Ref 12
Bonsall Creek .... Map 9/E3
Boomerang Lake .... Map 16/D3; Ref 12
Boot Lake Rec Site .... Map 36/A5; Ref 20, 39
Bootfrog Lake .... Map 35/D4
Booth Bay .... Map 10/A3
Boston Main .... Maps 28/G7, 29/A7; Ref 47
Botanical Beach Provincial Park .... Map 1/F3; Ref 57
Botley Lake .... Map 7/D7; Ref 12, 53
Bottleneck Cove .... Map 19/B4
Boulder Creek .... Map 13/C4 16/G5
Boulder Lake .... Map 3/C4; Ref 12
Boundary Pass .... Map 10/G7
Boyle Point Park .... Map 23/A4; Ref 31
Boyston Islands .... Map 6/B1
Bracie Creek .... Map 14/B2
Barkey Park .... Map 28/F1
Braden Creek .... Map 1/G1 7/G7
Bradley Lake .... Map 22/C2
Bragg Creek .... Map 45/F4
Brannen Lake .... Map 16/G2; Ref 12
Brasseau Bay .... Map 42/G5 43/A4
Breakwater Island .... Map 17/F4
Brenton Lakes .... Map 9/C2
Brentwood Bay .... Map 4/C2
Brethour Island .... Map 10/F7
Brewster Camp .... Map 35/G4; Ref 39
Brewster Lake .... Map 35/G4; Ref 20, 39
Brigade Lake .... Map 13/E1; Ref 55
Bright Angel Prov Park .... Map 9/G6; Ref 33, 48
Brink Lake .... Map 45/B6
Brittany Bay Rec Site .... Map 35/G5; Ref 39
Broken Group Islands .... Map 5/D2; Ref 29, 37
Brooks Bay .... Map 38/A7
Brooks Peninsula Provincial Park .... Map 30/G5, 31, 32/A6; Ref 35
Brooks Point Regional Park .... Map 23/A4; Ref 31
Broughton Archipelago Marine Park .... Map 41/B1
Broughton Strait .... Map 39/G1
Brown's Bay .... Map 22/B7
Browning Inlet .... Map 37/D3
Browning Passage .... Map 12/A4
Buck Creek .... Map 38/B7
Buckley Bay .... Map 22/F2
Bugaboo Creek .... Map 7/F7
Bull Harbour .... Map 45/G1
Bulson Creek .... Map 12/D1
Bunsby Island .... Map 30/G5
Burman Lake-Bedwell Lake Route .... Map 20/E1
Burman River .... Map 19/G1, 20/B1; Ref 25
Burnt Bridge Trails .... Map 9/E7; Ref 48
Bush Creek .... Map 17/A7
Butchart Lake .... Map 3/G3
Butte Creek .... Map 21/A1
Buttertub Slough .... Map 17/A3
Buttertub Marsh Sanctuary .... Map 17/A3; Ref 51
Buttle Lake .... Map 20/G1, 27, 28/A7; Ref 12, 58

C

C'ls-a-qui Bay Cabin .... Map 12/C3
C'onard Creek .... Map 6/A4
Cabbage Island Marine Park .... Map 10/Inset; Ref 31
Cachalot Creek .... Map 24/Inset
Cadboro Bay .... Map 4/F5
Caesar Lake .... Map 44/B4
Calamity Lake .... Map 6/A4
Call Inlet .... Map 42/C1
Callicum Creek .... Map 18/Inset
Calmuus Passage .... Map 11/F1
Camel Rock .... Map 25/D6
Cameron Lake .... Map 15/C1; Ref 12
Cameron River .... Map 15/D3
Camp 5 .... Map 35/G4; Ref 39
Camp Henderson ...... Map 39/B1; Ref 42
Camp Lake .... Map 19/B3
Camp Lake .... Map 35/G3
Campbell Lake Rec Site .... Map 36/B6; Ref 39
Campbell River   Map 36/G6; Ref 24, 27
Camper Creek .... Map 1/D2
Campus Creek .... Map 7/B3
Can-Am Trails .... Map 9/F7
Cannery Bay .... Map 12/E3
Canoe Creek .... Map 13/C3
Canon .... Map 32/G2
Canyon Lake .... Map 32/E1; Ref 42
Canyon View Trail ...... Map 36/E6; Ref 46
Cape Beale Trail .... Map 5/B4
Cape Cook .... Map 30/Inset
Cape Mudge .... Map 36/G7
Cape Scott Trail .... Map 37/Inset/A4
Cape Scott Prov Park .... Map 37/Inset, 45/A5; Ref 35, 52
Cape Lazo .... Map 29/F6; Ref 47

Capes Creek .... Map 21/E1
Capes Lake .... Map 21/E1
Captain Passage .... Map 10/D4
Cape Palmerston Rec Site .... Map 37/A1; Ref 42
Cardero Point .... Map 17/F4
Carey Lake .... Map 21/D1
Carlos Island .... Map 17/E4
Carmanah Creek .... Map 1/A1/Insert, Map 7/B7
Carmanah Valley Trail ... Map 7/B6; Ref 53
Carmanah Walbran Provincial Park .... Map 1/B1, 7/B7; Ref 33
Carnation Creek .... Map 6/D1
Carolina Channel .... Map 5/Inset
Carter Peak .... Map 38/F7
Carwithen Lake .... Map 20/F2
Case Creek .... Map 14/C7
Case Lake .... Map 14/D6
Cassidy .... Map 17/B6
Catala Island .... Map 24/A3; Ref 35
Cataract Creek & Lake .... Map 13/E7
Catherine Lake .... Map 25/G7
Cats Ear Creek .... Map 13/C2
Caycuse Rec Site .... Map 8/B2; Ref 43
Caycuse Creek .... Map 7/E5
Caycuse River .... Map 7/D4; Ref 24
Cayeghie Creek .... Map 39/B7
Cayuse Creek .... Map 38/G7, 39/A6
Cecilia Lake .... Map 19/B5
Cedar .... Map 17/C5
Cedar Lake .... Map 35/G4; Ref 20
Cedar Lake Rec Site ... Map 36/A2; Ref 20
Cedarstedt Creek .... Map 41/G4, 42/A4
Ceepeecee .... Map 25/A2
Centre Island .... Map 24/D2
Century Sam Lake .... Map 21/D2
Century Sam Trail ..... Map 21/D2; Ref 47
Chamiss Bay .... Map 31/D6
Chancellor Channel .. Map 43/D4, 44/A4
Channel Island .... Map 44/E4
Charles Channel .... Map 11/G2
Charles Island .... Map 10/C2
Charlie Lake .... Map 34/G4
Charlotte Strait .... Map 40/A2
Charters River .... Map 3/F5
Chase River .... Map 16/G4, 17/B5
Chatham Islands .... Map 4/G5; Ref 29
Checleset Bay .... Map 30/E5
Cheewhat Lake .... Map 6/G7
Cheewhat Lake Trail .... Map 7/A7
Cheewhat River .... Map 6/G7
Cheeyah Island .... Map 14/C7
Chemainus Bay .... Map 9/F2
Chemainus Lake .... Map 9/E2; Ref 12
Chemainus River .... Map 8/F2, 9/D3; Ref 24
Chemainus River Prov Park .... Map 9/C3; Ref 33
Cherry Creek .... Map 14/G1, 15/A1
Chesnucknuw Creek .... Map 14/G6
Chetharpe .... Map 11/F1
Chetwood Lake .... Map 35/A6
China Beach Provincial Park .... Map 2/F5
China Creek .... Map 15/A3
China Creek Regional Park .... Map 14/G4; Ref 43, 55
Chickadee Lake .... Map 22/G2
Child Creek .... Map 15/A3
Chipman Creek .... Map 9/A2
Chonat Lake .... Map 44/F7
Christie Falls Trail .... Map 17/B7; Ref 51
Cinnabar Valley .... Map 17/A5
Cinque Islands .... Map 44/C7
Circlet Lake .... Map 28/C6; Ref 12
Clapp Creek .... Map 3/A1
Clarke Island .... Map 5/D2
Claude Elliot Park Map 41/D7; Ref 20, 35
Clay Bank .... Map 16/B1; Ref 55
Clayoquot .... Map 11/G3
Clayoquot Arm .... Map 12/G4
Clayquot Arm Beach Rec Site .... Map 12/G5; Ref 43
Clayoquot Arm Provincial Park .... Map 12/G3, 13/A2; Ref 35
Clayoquot Lake .... Map 13/A2
Clayoquot Plateau Provincial Park .... Map 13/B2; Ref 35
Clayoquot Plateau Route .... Map 13/A1; Ref 54
Clayoquot River .... Map 13/A1
Clayquot Sound .... Map 11/G4
Clayoquot Witness Trail .... Map 13/A1; Ref 54
Clear Lake .... Map 36/G1
Clear Passage .... Map 24/Inset
Clemens Creek .... Map 13/G3
Clesklagh Creek .... Map 38/A1
Cliffe Glacier .... Map 21/C2
Climbers Trail .... Map 13/C3; Ref 55
Clint Beek Rec Site .... Map 39/G3; Ref 42
Clio Channel .... Map 40/F1
Cloagh Creek .... Map 38/C4
Clo-oose .... Map 6/G7
Cluxewe River .... Map 39/G1; Ref 25
Clydside Creek .... Map 2/F1
Coal Harbour .... Map 38/F1
Cobble Hill Trails and Rec Site .... Map 9/G7; Ref 43, 48
Cochrane Road/Nile Creek Main .... Map 23/B6; Ref 55
Coeur D'Alene Creek .... Map 14/A6
Colburne Passage .... Map 10/D7
Coleman Creek .... Map 14/G7
Coles Bay Regional Park .... Map 4/C1; Ref 33
Colliery Dam Park ..... Map 17/A4; Ref 51
Colonial Creek .... Map 39/A7
Colquitz River .... Map 4/D4
Colwood Lake .... Map 4/B5
Colwood .... Map 4/B4
Comida Lake .... Map 36/A3
Comorant Channel Plateau Prov Park .... Map 40/E1; Ref 35
Comorant Island .... Map 40/D1
Comox Creek .... Map 21/F2
Comox Creek Nature .... Map 21/D2
Comox Glacier Trail .... Map 21/D2; Ref 47
Comox Harbour .... Map 22/E1
Comox Lake .. Map 21/G1, 29/A7; Ref 12
Comox Lake Mountain Bike Area .... Map 29/A7; Ref 47
Compton Creek .... Map 34/C1
Compton Island .... Map 41/A1
Congreve Island .... Map 6/B1
Consinka Lake .... Map 6/D1
Consort Creek .... Map 34/E5
Conuma Fish Hatchery .... Map 25/F4
Conuma River Rec Site .... Map 25/F3; Ref 39
Cook Channel .... Map 18/Inset
Cook Creek .... Map 14/F5
Coombes Bay .... Map 11/F1
Cooper Creek .... Map 35/D3
Cordero Channel .... Map 44/C4
Cordova Bay .... Map 4/E3
Cornation Lake .... Map 9/A1
Corning Point .... Map 12/F2
Corrigan Creek .... Map 15/A6
Cotter Creek .... Map 20/A5
Cottle Lake .... Map 16/D3
Cougar Creek Rec Site .... Map 25/E6; Ref 39
Cougar Lake .... Map 21/F3
Courtenay .... Map 29/C7
Council Lake .... Map 3/G3
Cous Creek .... Map 14/E3; Ref 24
Cow Bay .... Map 11/C1
Cowichan Bay .... Map 9/G5, 10/A6
Cowichan Lake . Map 7/G1, 8/C3; Ref 12
Cowichan River .... Map 8/G4, 9/A5; Ref 24, 27
Cowichan River Prov Park .... Map 8, 9/B5; Ref 48
Cowichan Station .... Map 9/G6
Cox Bay .... Map 12/A4
Cox Lake .... Map 15/A2
Crabapple Lake .... Map 3/G4; Ref 12
Cragg Creek .... Map 3/D2
Crane Lake .... Map 36/B3
Crawfish Lake .... Map 24/F6
Crawford Lake .... Map 5/F1
Cream Lake .... Map 21/A3
Crease Island .... Map 41/A1
Crescent Lake .... Map 36/A4
Cresent (Tadjiss) Lake .... Map 9/C7
Crickett Bay .... Map 6/C1
Crofton .... Map 9/G3
Crofton Lake .... Map 9/G3
Croman Lake .... Map 33/F2
Cross Lake .... Map 31/G1; Ref 20
Croteau Lake .... Map 28/E6; Ref 12
Crown Lake .... Map 6/G3; Ref 12
Crowned Creek .... Map 35/D7
Cruickshank River .... Map 21/F1
Crystal Lake .... Map 17/A6; Ref 12
Culltite Creek .... Map 1/C2
Cumberland .... Map 22/C1
Cumberland Lake Park .... Map 22/A1
Current Passage .... Map 43/B4
Currie Creek .... Map 9/C4
Cusheon Creek .... Map 10/C4
Cusheon Lake .... Map 10/B4; Ref 12
Cypre River ... Map 12/G1, 20/A7; Ref 24
Cypress Bay .... Map 12/A1 20/A7
Cypress River .... Map 20/A7

D

D'Arcy Island Provincial Marine Park .... Map 4/G2; Ref 30, 31
Dakota Creek .... Map 45/A4
Dalrymple Creek .... Map 43/C7
Daphne Point .... Map 47/A5
Dark Island .... Map 12/C3
Darkis Lake .... Map 31/G1; Ref 20
Darlington Lake .... Map 7/A1; Ref 12
Darling River .... Map 6/B6
Dash Creek .... Map 16/B5
Datsio Creek .... Map 21/E2
David Channel .... Map 13/D7
David Island .... Map 13/C7 5/C1
Davie River .... Map 33/D2, 34/A3; Ref 25,27
Davis Lagoon .... Map 9/D1
Dawley Passage Prov Park .... Map 12/C4; Ref 36
Dayman Island .... Map 9/F1
De Courcy Island .... Map 17/E5; Ref 30
De Mamiel Creek .... Map 3/D5
Deacon Beauchene Trail .... Map 1/G1; Ref 57
Deadhorse Creek .... Map 16/B4
Deep Bay .... Map 23/A4
Deep Cove .... Map 10/B7
Deepwater Bay .... Map 36/D2
Deer Bay .... Map 12/G2
Deer Group Islands .... Map 5/G3, 6; Ref 30
Deer Island .... Map 47/C6
Delphi Lake .... May 16/A7; Ref 13
Demikosse Creek .... Map 18/Inset
Delight Lake .... Map 21/B1
Della Falls Camp .... Map 21/A4
Della Lake .... Map 20/G4; Ref 56
Delphi Lake .... Map 16/A7; Ref 13
Denman Islands .... Map 22/G2, 23/A3; Ref 30, 49
Dent Creek .... Map 2/G2
Departure Bay .... Map 17/A2
Delta Falls Trail .... Map 21/A4
Deserted Lake .... Map 25/D5; Ref 52
Deserters Island .... Map 47/A2
Devil's Bath .... Map 39/D6; Ref 6
Devils Den Lake .... Map 14/F1
Devonian Regional Park .... Map 4/B7
Diana Island .... Map 5/G3
Diane Lake .... Map 32/D1; Ref 20
Dick Booth Creek .... Map 46/G7
Dickson Lake .... Map 22/A6; Ref 13
Diddon Price Trail .... Map 8/F3; Ref 48
Dillon Point .... Map 47/B5
Dinah Lake .... Map 18/E1
Dionisio Point Prov Park .... Map 17/Inset; Ref 31
Diplock Island .... Map 6/A1
Discovery Isl Marine Park .... Map 4/G6; Ref 31
Discovery Passage .... Map 36/D7
Diver Lake .... Map 16/G3; Ref 13
Diversion Reservoir .... Map 2/G4, 3/A3; Ref 13
Dixi Cove Provincial Park .... Map 31/F6; Ref 36
Dixie Lake ...... Map 8/A1, 16/A7; Ref 13
Dixie Lake .... Map 15/G7
Dodger Channel .... Map 5/G3
Dogwood Bay .... Map 36/A6; Ref 40
Domville Island .... Map 10/F7
Donegal Head .... Map 47/Inset/G1
Donner Lake .... Map 27/A5; Ref 13
Doobah Cree .... Map 7/A6
Doobah Lake .... Map 6/G6
Doran Lake .... Map 21/E7; Ref 13
Dorothy Creek .... Map 21/C7
Dorothy Lake .... Map 6/G4
Dougan Lake .... Map 9/G7; Ref 13
Douglas Lake .... Map 28/E7; Ref 13
Drake Island .... Map 38/E3
Draw Creek .... Map 13/B6
Draw Lake .... Map 13/B5
Drinkwater Creek .... Map 21/A4
Drum Lake .... Map 27/A2; Ref 13, 58
Drumbeg Provincial Park .... Map 17/F4; Ref 31
Drummond Park .... Map 10/C5
Duc Island .... Map 12/G3
Duck Bay .... Map 10/A2
Duck Creek .... Map 10/A2
Duck Lake .... Map 15/B4
Duckling Island .... Map 12/A3
Dudley Marsh .... Map 15/G1
Duke Point .... Map 17/B4
Duncan .... Map 9/F2
Duncan Island .... Map 46/G4
Duncan Lake .... Map 35/F5
Dunlap Island .... Map 11/G1
Dunsmuir Creek .... Map 16/B6
Dunsmuir Point .... Map 14/G4
Durrance Lake .... Map 4/C2; Ref 13
Duval Island .... Map 47/A5

E

East Cracroft Island .... Map 42/B1
East Klanawa River .... Map 6/G4
East Sooke .... Map 3/F7
East Sooke Regional Park .... Map 3/G7; Ref 59
Easter Lake .... Map 19/C4
Echachis Island .... Map 11/G3
Echo Lake .... Map 36/C7; Ref 20
Ecoole .... Map 6/B1
Edith Lake .... Map 44/F5
Eena Lake .... Map 34/G7
Eena Lake .... Map 35/A7
Effingham Inlet .... Map 13/G6
Effingham Island .... Map 5/D2
Effingham Lake .... Map 13/E3
Effingham River .... Map 13/F4
Egerton Creek .... Map 44/G3
Ehatisaht .... Map 24/E2
El Capitan Mountain ... Map 8/C1; Ref 48
Elephant Crossing Boardwalk .... Map 45/E7
Eliza Creek .... Map 24/Inset
Elk Bay Rec Site .... Map 36/C1, 44/C7; Ref 40
Elk Creek Rec Site .... Map 43/A; Ref 40
Elk Falls Park .... Map 36/E6; Ref 36
Elk Falls Trail .... Map 36/E6; Ref 46
Elk Islets .... Map 12/B4
Elk Lake .... Map 4/D3; Ref 13, 59
Elk River .... Map 27/C2; Ref 25, 58
Elkhorn Creek .... Map 16/G6
Elkington Creek .... Map 9/G4
Ellen Lake .... Map 19/B4
Ellswick Lake .... Map 13/E6
Elsie Lake .... Map 21/G4, 22/A4; Ref 13
Emila Lake .... Map 35/B5
Englishman River Falls Provincial Park .... Map 16/A1; Ref 33
Englishman River .... Map 15/G2, 16/A1; Ref 24
Englishman River South .... Map 16/B1; Ref 55
Englishman River Trails .. Map 23/Inset/D1
Enos Lake .... Map 16/E1
Entrance Island .... Map 17/D3
Epper Passage Prov Park .... Map 11/G1; Ref 36
Epinosa Inlet .... Map 24/D1
Equis Beach .... Map 5/E1
Eric Lake .... Map 35/D5
Eric Lake .... Map 45/A6

Errington .... Map 16/A1
Esary Lake .... Map 22/G7; Ref 13
Escalante River .... Map 18/D2
Escape Reef .... Map 9/G1
Esperanza Inlet .... Map 24/E2
Esperanza .... Map 24/G2
Espinosa Creek .... Map 32/C7
Espinosa Inlet .... Map 32/D7
Esquimalt Harbour .... Map 4/C5
Esquimalt Lagoon Bird Sanctuary ....
.... Map 4/C5
Estevan Point .... Map 18/C6
Esther Lake .... Map 21/C3
Estowista Island .... Map 11/G3
Evans Creek .... Map 6/E3
Eve Creek .... Map 33/A2
Eve River ....
.... Map 33/G1, 42/B5; Ref 25,27
Eves Provincial Park .... Map 9/F3
Ewart Lake .... Map 24/F5
Extension .... Map 17/A5; Ref 51

F

Fair Harbour ....
.... Map 31/G5, 32/A1, 36/A6; Ref 42
Fair Harbour River Rec Site ....
.... Map 31/G6, 32/A1; Ref 40
Fairy Creek .... Map 2/A1; Ref 57
Fairy Lake Rec Site ....
.... Map 2/A1; Ref 13, 43
Falls Creek .... Map 2/A2
Family Humps .... Map 31/G6
Fanny Bay .... Map 22/G3
Fanny Bay .... Map 44/D2
Fantasy Island .... Map 12/C4
Farewell Lake .... Map 35/G2; Ref 20
Father & Son Lake ....
.... Map 15/C1; Ref 13, 43, 56
Father Templar Channel .... Map 11/G3
Fatty Basin .... Map 14/C7
Felice Island .... Map 11/G3
Fellows Creek .... Map 9/B7
Fernwood .... Map 10/A2
Fetus Lake .... Map 7/C7; Ref 13
Fillongley Provincial Park ....
.... Map 23/A2; Ref 31
Finlayson Arm .... Map 4/A3
Fir Grove Rec Site ....
.... Map 36/A6; Ref 40
First Lake .... Map 16/C5
First Lake .... Map 35/D5
First/Second Creek Trail ....
.... Map 2/A2; Ref 57
Fisher Road Trail .... Map 15/G1; Ref 55
Fisherman Creek ....
.... Map 37/Inset/A4; Ref 25
Fisherman River .... Map 45/A5
Fishtail Lake .... Map 15/D2; Ref 13
Flat Top Islands .... Map 17/F4
Fleece Creek .... Map 15/G6
Fleet Creek .... Map 2/F1
Fleming Island .... Map 5/G, 26/A2
Floodwood Creek .... Map 3/A1
Flora Island .... Map 23/C3
Flora Lake Rec Site ....
.... Map 7/A3; Ref 13, 43
Florence Lake .... Map 4/B4; Ref 14
Florence Lake .... Map 44/F5
Florencia Bay .... Map 12/F7
Flores Island ....
.... Map 11/D1, 19/D7; Ref 36
Flower Ridge Trail .... Map 21/A1
Flynn Fall Creek .... Map 16/F3
Folger Island .... Map 5/F3
Forbes Island .... Map 5/B1
Forbush Lake .... Map 21/F3; Ref 14
Forbidden Plateau ....
.... Map 28/D-G7; Ref 47, 57
Ford Lake .... Map 10/B4
Fork Lake .... Map 4/B3
Forrest Island .... Map 10/F7
Forslund Lake .... Map 3/C4
Fort Rupert .... Map 47/B6
Forward Bay .... Map 41/G2
Forward Harbour .... Map 43/E3
Fossil Prov Park ... Map 14/E2; Ref 36, 56
Foster Point .... Map 9/F1
Four Mile Creek .... Map 7/C4
Fourth Lake .... Map 15/G6
Frances Lake .... Map 38/A1
Francis King Regional Park ....
.... Map 4/C4; Ref 59
Francis Lake .... Map 7/A1; Ref 14
Frank Island .... Map 12/A4
Franklin Camp .... Map 15/A7
Franklin River ....
.... Map 14/G5, 15/A5; Ref 24
Fraser Island .... Map 4/A7
Fredrick Lake .... Map 6/B3; Ref 14
French Beach Prov Park ....
.... Map 3/A6; Ref 33
French Creek .... Map 3/C1, 15/G1
Friendly Cove .... Map 18/B1/Inset
Friesen Creek .... Map 14/A1
Frog Pond Wilderness Site .... Map 21/D2
Fry Gravel Pit Rec Site ....
.... Map 36/A6; Ref 40
Fry Island .... Map 6/A2
Fry Lake .... Map 35/G6
Fry Trestle Rec Site ..... Map 36/A6; Ref 40
Fulford Harbour .... Map 10/C5
Fuller Lake .... Map 9/F2; Ref 14
Fuller Lake Park .... Map 17/F7/Inset
Fulmore Lake .... Map 42/F1 43/A1

G

Gabriola Island ... Map 17/D4; Ref 30, 49
Gabriola Sands Prov Park ....
.... Map 17/B3; Ref 31
Gain Creek .... Map 2/D3
Galiano Island ....
.... Map 10/C2, 17/Inset; Ref 30, 49
Galloping Goose Regional park ....
.... Map 3/F5, 4/A6; Ref 33, 59
Ganges .... Map 10/B3
Ganges Harbour .... Map 10/B3
Garbage Creek .... Map 2/E2
Garden Point Rec Site ....
.... Map 24/D3; Ref 40
Gardner Pond Map10/C7
Garibaldi Peaks .... Map 31/F2
Garrett Lake .... Map 35/G5
Geer Islets .... Map 6/A1
Gem Lake Trail .... Map 28/C6; Ref 57
Gemini Mountain Route ....
.... Map 16/A6; Ref 51
Genoa Bay .... Map 7/F1
George Creek .... Map 44/B1
George Islands .... Map 19/C6
George River .... Map 44/B1
Georgie Lake Rec Site ....
.... Map 46/F5; Ref 20, 42
Gerald Creek .... Map 34/D3
Gibralter Island .... Map 5/D2
Gibson Cove .... Map 20/A6
Gibson-Klitsa Trail ..... Map 13/F1; Ref 56
Gibson-Klitsa Wilderness Area ....
.... Map 13/F1
Gibson Prov Marine Park ....
.... Map 11/E1; Ref 36
Gilbert Island .... Map 5/D2
Gillam Channel .... Map 24/B3
Gillian Island .... Map 37/G4
Glad Lake .... Map 1/C1
Glaver Comm Nature Park .... Map 22/E1
Glen Lake .... Map 4/B5; Ref 14
Glendale Lake .... Map 43/G1
Glenlion River .... Map 46/ G7, 47/A6
Glenora Creek .... Map 9/D6/E5
Glinz Lake .... Map 3/G5
God's Pocket Prov Park ....
.... Map 12/A2; Ref 36
Godkin Creek .... Map 46/A4
Gold Creek .... Map 33/B1
Gold Lake Camp .... Map 34/G7
Gold Lake .... Map 34/F7
Gold Lake Trail .... Map 34/G7; Ref 52
Gold Prov park .... Map 26/E2; Ref 25
Gold Mine Trail .... Map 12/E7
Gold Muchalat Provincial Park ....
.... Map 26/D2; Ref 36
Gold River ....
.... Map 34/D7 36/A7 26/E2-6; Ref 28
Goldstream Lake .... Map 3/G3
Goldstream River ... Map 4/A4; Ref 33, 59
Golledge Creek .... Map 3/E4
Gooche Island .... Map 10/F7
Gooding Cove Rec Site ....
.... Map 37/G6; Ref 42
Goodspeed River .... Map 45/G6
Goose Lake Trail .... Map 36/B4; Ref 46
Gooseneck Lake .... Map 36/A7
Gordon Bay Prov Park ....
.... Map 8/C4; Ref 33
Gordon Island .... Map 47/A4
Gordon River ....
.... Map 1/F1 7/G7. 8/A4; Ref 24
Gore Island .... Map 25/G7
Gosling Bay Rec Site ... Map 36/B6; Ref 40
Gosling Lake Rec Site ....
.... Map 36/A5; Ref 20, 40
Gossip Island .... Map 10/F3
Gowland Harbour .... Map 36/G5
Gowland Island .... Map 36/F5
Gowland Tod Provincial Park ....
.... Map 4/B3; Ref 33, 59
Grace Lake .... Map 35/G3; Ref 21
Gracie Lake .... Map 14/A2; Ref 14
Graham Lake .... Map 23/A3
Grande Cliffs .... Map 17/E4
Granite Creek .... Map 2/A1, 7/D2
Grant Lake .... Map 3/E1
Grant Bay Trail .... Map 37/D4; Ref 52
Granville Lake .... Map 19/D6
Grappler Inlet .... Map 6/A3
Grass Lake .... Map 3/G5; Ref 14
Grassy Creek .... Map 44/A3
Gravelly Bay .... Map 23/A3
Gray Creek .... Map 44/B1
Gray Lake Rec Site .... Map 35/G5; Ref 40
Great Central Lake ....
.... Map 21/E6, 22; Ref 14
Great Chain Islands .... Map 4/F5
Green Cove .... Map 14/C7
Green Creek .... Map 16/A7
Green Lake .... Map 16/G2; Ref 14
Green Lake .... Map 21/A3
Green Mountain . Map 16/A6; Ref 51, 61
Green Point Campground ..... Map 12/D6
Greenstone Creek .... Map 35/F6
Greenview Lake .... Map 20/E2
Gretchen Creek .... Map 21/D5
Grice Bay .... Map 12/C5
Grice Harbour .... Map 12/A4
Grilse Creek .... Map 35/B6
Guise Bay .... Map 37/Inset/A4
Gunnier Inlet .... Map 12/D3

H

Habiton Lake .... Map 6/G5
Hadden Creek .... Map 7/C5
Haggard Island .... Map 6/C1
Hahwitti Lake Trail .... Map 46/B6
Hahwitti-Shushartie Addition ... Map 46/A3
Haihte Lake .... Map 42/E6
Haines Island .... Map 5/G3
Halalt Island Indian Reserve ..... Map 9/G2
Haley Lake .... Map 16/A7
Hall Island .... Map 17/G7/Inset
Hamilton Lake .... Map 22/A1
Hamilton Swamp .... Map 23/F7
Hammerfest Bike Circuit ....
.... Map 15/G1, 16/A2; Ref 55
Handy Creek .... Map 14/D7
Hanging Glacier .... Map 21/A3
Hanna Channel .... Map 25/E7
Hanna Creek .... Map 25/F6
Hansen Bay .... Map 37/Inset/A5
Hansen Island .... Map 12/A2
Hanson Island .... Map 41/A2
Hanson Lagoon .... Map 37/Inset/A4
Happy Valley .... Map 4/B5
Harbour Island .... Map 24/B2
Harding Creek .... Map 22/A1
Hardinge Island .... Map 44/D5
Hardwicke Island .... Map 42, 43/A4
Hardy Bay .... Map 47/A5
Hardy Peak .... Map 42 F3
Harewood Lake .... Map 17/A5; Ref 14
Harmac .... Map 17/C5
Harris Creek ....
.... Map 2/C1, 8/C7; Ref 24, 57
Harris Peaks .... Map 30/C1
Harrisons Plankboard Trail ....
.... Map 1/G2; Ref 57
Harvey Cove .... Map 37/G5
Haslam Creek ....
.... Map 8/G1, 16/G7, 17/A7
Hathaway Creek .... Map 38/A1
Hause Bay .... Map 7/G1
Havannah Channel .... Map 42/A2
Hawkins Island .... Map 10/D4
Hawthorn Lake .... Map 14/G6; Ref 14
Head Bay .... Map 25/E4
Heal Lake .... Map 4/C3
Healy Lake .... Map 16/A4; Ref 14
Heard Island .... Map 47/A3
Heart Lake .... Map 16/A6; Ref 14
Heart Lake Trail .... Map 9/D1; Ref 48
Heath Creek .... Map 14/F1
Heather Lake .... Map 7/F1; Ref 14, 43
Heather Lake Trail .... Map 9/C1; Ref 48
Heber River ... Map 26/F3, 27/A1; Ref 26
Hecate Park .... Map 9/G5
Hectate .... Map 24/G2
Hectate Channel .... Map 24/G2
Hectate Lake .... Map 24/G2
Heidrick Lake .... Map 44/G6
Heimra Lake .... Map 45/E3
Helby Island .... Map 5/G3
Helliwell Prov Park .... Map 23/C3; Ref 31
Helmcken Island .... Map 43/B5
Helper Creek Rec Site ....
.... Map 46/A7; Ref 42
Hemer Prov Park ....
.... Map 17/C5; Ref 33, 51
Hemming Lake .... Map 44/C5
Henderson Lake .... Map 14/B5
Henry Lake .... Map 15/C3; Ref 14
Henshaw Creek .... Map 21/A1
Henshaw/Shepherd Creek Routes ....
.... Map 21/A1
Herbert Inlet .... Map 19/G7, 20/A5
Heriot Bay .... Map 36/F4
Hesquiate .... Map 18/E6
Hesquiat Harbour .... Map 18/E5
Hesquiat Lake .... Map 18/F3
Hesquiat Lake Provincial Park ....
Map 18/F3; Ref 36
Hesquiate Peninsula Provincial Park ....
.... Map 18/C3; Ref 36, 52
Hesquiat Point Creek .... Map 18/G4
Heydon Bay Lake .... Map 43/G1
Heydon Lake .... Map 43/F2
Hidden Lake .... Map 15/D2; Ref 14
Hill 60 Ridge Route ..... Map 9/B4; Ref 48
Hillier Island .... Map 13/D6
Hinne Creek .... Map 7/G4
Hisnit Inlet .... Map 25/D5
Hitchie Creek .... Map 7/A4
Hitchie Creek Prov Park ....
.... Map 7/A4; Ref 33
Hitchie Lake .... Map 6/G4
Hkusam .... Map 43/F3, 43/A5
Hobbs Creek .... Map 1/E2
Hoggan Lake .... Map 17/C4
Hohoae Island .... Map 31/F6
Hois Creek .... Map 25/C6
Holberg Inlet .... Map 37/G1, 38/A1
Holberg .... Map 45/F7
Holden Lake .... Map 17/C5; Ref 14
Holford Lake .... Map 6/A1
Holland Creek .... Map 9/B1
Holland Lake .... Map 9/C1; Ref 14
Hollywood .... Map 31/A5
Holmes Creek .... Map 9/E4
Holmes Inlet .... Map 19/B4
Holt Creek .... Map 9/C6
Holyoak Creek .... Map 9/C2
Holyoak Lake .... Map 9/C2; Ref 62
Homasum Lake .... Map 21/B4
Hoomak Lake .... Map 33/D2; Ref 21
Hook Bay .... Map 14/F5
Hook Creek .... Map 14/E1
Hoomak Lake .... Map 33/D2; Ref 52
Hope Bay .... Map 10/G5
Hope Island .... Map 45/G1, 46/A1
Hornby Island .... Map 23/B2; Ref 30, 49
Horne Lake .... Map 23/B7; Ref 14, 56
Horne Lake Caves Park ....
.... Map 23/A7; Ref 6, 36

Horton Lake .... Map 3/E2
Horth Hill Regional Park .... Map 10/C7; Ref 34, 59
Hosie Island .... Map 6/B2
Hot Springs Cove .... Map 19/A6; Ref 6
Houston River .... Map 19/A1
Houstoun Passage .... Map 9/G1
Howard Point .... Map 5/F1
Howe Island .... Map 44/C6
Hudson Island .... Map 9/F1
Humbird Creek .... Map 9/C3
Humes Creek .... Map 9/E7
Humpback Bay .... Map 43/F6
Humpback Reservoir .... Map 4/A5
Hurst Island .... Map 46/F3
Hushamu Creek .... Map 46/B7
Hustan Lake .... Map 32/C1; Ref 21
Hyacinth Lake .... Map 44/G7
Hyde Creek .... Map 40/B1

I

Ice Lake .... Map 19/C3
Ice River .... Map 19/B3
Ida Lake Rec Site .... Map 40/F4; Ref 42
Idiens Creek .... Map 21/E1
Idiens Lake .... Map 21/E1
Idiens-Capes Lake Route .... Map 21/F1; Ref 47
Idle Creek .... Map 22/B2
Idol Island .... Map 10/A2
Illusion Lake .... Map 23/C7
Imperial Eagle Channel .... Map 5/F2
Indian Island .... Map 12/C4
Indian Lake .... Map 15/F5; Ref 14
Ink Lake .... Map 21/B1
Inner Basin .... Map 24/F4
Invy Green Park .... Map 17/B7
Inwood Creek .... Map 9/C4
Iron Lake Rec Site .... Map 39/F6; Ref 42
Irony Creek .... Map 45/D3
Irving Cove .... Map 12/F2
Irving Lake .... Map 18/G1, 19/A1
Isel-de-Lis Provincial Marine Park .... Map 10/E5; Ref 31
Island View Beach Regional Park .... Map 4/E2; Ref 34, 59
Isle Lake .... Map 46/C5
Itatsoo Creek .... Map 5/A1/Inset
Itatsoo Lake .... Map 5/A1/Inset
Ithpaya Lake .... Map 12/F4

J

Jack Creek .... Map 44/B1
Jack Elliot Creek .... Map 2/B3
Jack Foster Trial .... Map 10/A1
Jack Lake .... Map 3/G4
Jacklah River .... Map 19/D1, 26/D7; Ref 26
Jackscrew Island .... Map 10/A1
Jackson Bay .... Map 43/D2
Jackson River .... Map 19/C1
Jacob Creek .... Map 3/A6
James Island .... Map 4/E1; Ref 30
Jansen Bay .... Map 31/D5
Jansen Creek .... Map 31/D4
Jansen Lake .... Map 45/A7
Jap Lake .... Map 44/B6
Jarvis Lake .... Map 3/D2; Ref 14
Jasper Creek .... Map 7/C3
Jasper Lake .... Map 36/C3
Jessie Lake .... Map 35/D6
Jeune Landing .... Map 39/A4
Jim Mitchell Lake .... Map 20/G2
John Dean Prov Park .... Map 4/D1; Ref 34, 59
John Fraser Lake .... Map 34/F5
John Hart Lake .... Map 36/D6
John Quinn Trail .... Map 1/G2; Ref 57
Johns Creek .... Map 4/A1
Johnson Lagoon .... Map 30/E2
Johnston Lake .... Map 28/E7; Ref 15
Johnstone Island .... Map 14/G1
Johnstone Strait .... Map 41/A2, 44/A6
Jordan River .... Map 2/G5, 3/B2; Ref 24, 45
Juan de Fuca Marine Trail .... Map 1/G3, 2/B4; Ref 57
Juan de Fuca Prov Park .... Map 2/B4; Ref 34
Judge Creek .... Map 3/G1
Judge's Route .... Map 15/D2
Jules Cove .... Map 38/C1
Julia Passage .... Map 5/G1
Jump Creek .... Map 16/B7
Jump Lake .... Map 16/C7
June Lake .... Map 21/F4; Ref 15
Junction Pool Rec Site .... Map 42/B5; Ref 40

K

Kaikash Creek Rec Site .... Map 41/A3; Ref 42
Kains Island .... Map 37/F5
Kains Lake .... Map 46/D6; Ref 21
Kaipit Creek .... Map 32/G2
Kaipit Lake .... Map 32/G3; Ref 52
Kakawis .... Map 11/G2, 12/A2
Kammat Lake .... Map 15/C3; Ref 15
Kanim Lake .... Map 18/G5
Kanish Bay .... Map 36/E1
Kaouk River .... Map 32/A1
Kapoor Regional Park .. Map 3/E4; Ref 34
Kapoose Creek .... Map 24/Inset
Karlukwees .... Map 41/A3
Karmutzen Creek .... Map 40/A6
Kashuti Inlet .... Map 31/C4
Kashuti River .... Map 31/B1
Kathleen Lake .... Map 35/D6
Kathleen Lake .... Map 39/D5; Ref 21, 42
Katlum Creek .... Map 22/A3
Kauwinch River .... Map 31/D1
Kay Creek .... Map 35/D3
Keating Lake .... Map 9/D6
Keeha Bay .... Map 5/B4
Keeha Bay Trail .... Map 5/B4
Kelsey Bay .... Map 42/G6, 43/A4
Kelvin Creek .... Map 9/E6
Kemp Lake .... Map 3/D6; Ref 15
Kendrick Creek .... Map 25/A5
Kendrick Inlet .... Map 25/A6
Kennedy Lake Bog Provincial Park .... Map 12/F5; Ref 36
Kennedy Lake .... Map 12/G6, 13/A5; Ref 15
Kennedy Lake Provincial Park .... Map 12/G6, 13/A6; Ref 36
Kennedy River .... Map 12, 13, 20, 21; Ref 28
Kennedy River Rapids .... Map 13/C2
Kent Island .... Map 46/G1
Keogh Lake .... Map 39/G3; Ref 21
Keogh River .. Map 39/D1, 47/D7; Ref 26
Kewquodie Creek .... Map 38/C6
Kichha Lake .... Map 5/G4
Kidney Lake .... Map 16/E3
Kidney Lake .... Map 39/C1; Ref 55
Kilarney Lake .... Map 4/C3
Kildonan Lake .... Map 14/C7/D6
Kilpala River .... Map 40/A5
Kim Lake .... Map 22/B2
King Edward Island .... Map 5/F3
Kinman Creek .... Map 40/D7
Kinman Creek Rec Site .... Map 40/D7; Ref 42
Kinsol Trestle .... Map 9/F7
Kirby Creek .... Map 3/B6
Kissinger Lake .... Map 7/F1
Kissinger Rec Site .... Map 7/F1; Ref 45
Kite Lake .... Map 13/E6
Kitsucksus Creek .... Map 22/G7
Klaklakama Lakes .... Map 33/E3; Ref 20
Klaklakama Lake, Lower .... Map 33/F3; Ref 42
Klaklakama Lake, Upper .... Map 33/F4; Ref 42
Klanawa River .... Map 6/D6
Klasin River .... Map 38/D1; Ref 24
Klaskino Inlet .... Map 38/B7
Klee Arm .... Map 14/D1
Kleecoot .... Map 14/D1
Kleeptee Creek .... Map 25/G7
Klokish River .... Map 38/D7
Klootclimmis Creek .... Map 38/E4
Kludahk Hiking Trail .... Map 2/C2
Knob Point Rec Site .... Map 7/A4; Ref 45
Knox Bay .... Map 43/G5
Kokish .... Map 40/B2
Kokis River ... Map 40/F4, 41/A5; Ref 26
Koksilah River .. Map 3/D1, 9/D7; Ref 28
Koksilah River Provincial Park .... Map 3/D1, 9/E7; Ref 34
Kokummi Creek .... Map 34/B4
Komas Bluff .... Map 22/G2
Kookjai Trail .... Map 21/D2; Ref 47
Kootowis Creek .... Map 12/E5
Koprino Harbour .... Map 38/A3
Koprino River .... Map 38/B3
Koskimo Bay .... Map 38/A4
Kowus Creek .... Map 20/B3
Kraan Island .... Map 11/G1
Kuitshe Creek .... Map 2/A3
Kulaht Creek .... Map 1/A1
Kullett Bay .... Map 17/D7
Kunlin Lake .... Map 26/G5; Ref 15
Kunnum Creek .... Map 34/B1 42/B7
Kuper Island .... Map 9/G1, 17/Inset; Ref 30
Kvarno Island .... Map 12/G7, 5/Inset
Kwakiuti Lawn Point Provinvial Park .... Map 37/G7; Ref 36
Kwartleo Creek .... Map 37/D2
Kwassun Lake .... Map 21/E3
Kweishun Creek .... Map 21/D1
Kwois .... Map 31/F1
Kwois Creek .... Map 31/G2
Kyoquot .... Map 31/B7
Kyoquot Sound .... Map 24/Inset, 31
Kyuquot Channel .... Map 24/Inset

L

La Mare Lake .... Map 38/A5
Labour Day Lake ... Map 15/F4; Ref 15, 45
Labour Day Lake Trails .... Map 15/F4; Ref 56, 61
Lac Truite .... Map 39/F7; Ref 52
Lacy Lake .... Map 23/A7; Ref 15
Lady Lake .... Map 28/E6; Ref 15
Ladysmith .... Map 17/C7
Ladysmith Harbour ...... Map 17/C7, 9/D1
Lagoon Island .... Map 12/A2
Lake Beautiful .... Map 28/D7; Ref 15
Lake Helen McKenzie .... Map 28/E6; Ref 15
Lake Maxwell .... Map 10/A4
Lake of the Mountains .... Map 46/B4
Lake Rosemarie .... Map 22/C4
Lake Weston .... Map 10/D5; Ref 15
Lambert Channel .... Map 23/A3
Landslide Lake .... Map 27/B4; Ref 15
Lane Islet .... Map 12/C4
Langford Lake .... Map 4/B5; Ref 15
Langley Lake .... Map 22/E2
Lantzville .... Map 16/F1
Lapan Lake .... Map 43/B2
Larkins Island .... Map 13/D7
Larry Lake .... Map 13/B4; Ref 15
Larry Lake .... Map 39/B3
Laura Creek .... Map 45/A4
Laurie Creek .... Map 24/F4
Lawier Lake .... Map 36/A4
Laylee Island .... Map 13/A5
Leader Lake .... Map 20/G5
Lee Islands .... Map 44/E5
Lee Plateau Memorial Cabin ... Map 21/E1
Leech Island .... Map 17/G7/Inset
Leeson Lake .... Map 37/D3
Leetch River .... Map 3/C2
Legion Trail .... Map 3/G1; Ref 48
Leighton Lake .... Map 25/G2
Leiner River Rec Site .... Map 25/C1; Ref 26, 40
Lemmens Inlet .... Map 12/A2
Lennard Island .... Map 11/G4
Lens Creek .... Map 2/D1
Lens Creek Trail .... Map 2/B1
Leslie Lake .... Map 39/B3
Lighthouse Point .... Map 10/G3
Lighthouse Country Trail .... Map 23/B6; Ref 55
Lihou Lake .... Map 43/A
Lillian Lake .... Map 19/A2
Limestone Inlet .... Map 14/C7
Limestone Mountain .... Map 15/B5; Ref 56
Link Island .... Map 17/D5
Little Bear Bay Rec Site .... Map 44/A6; Ref 41
Little Espinosa Picnic Site .... Map 32/E7; Ref 41
Little Hustan Cave Park .... Map 32/D1; Ref 6
Little Jim Lake .... Map 20/G3
Little Lake .... Map 36/B3
Little Mountain View Trail .... Map 23/Inset/D1; Ref 55
Little Nitinat River .... Map 7/B1
Little Qualicum Falls Park .... Map 15/C1, 23/D7; Ref 36
Little Qualicum River .... Map 15/D1,23/E7; Ref 24
Little Squalicum Lake .... Map 6/F6
Little Toquart Creek .... Map 13/C5
Little Toquart Lake .... Map 13/C6
Little Zebellos .... Map 32/F7
Little Zebellos River .... Map 32/G7
Lizard Lake ..... Map 2/C1; Ref 15, 45, 57
Lizard Lake .... Map 15/B4
Lizard Pond .... Map 14/G6; Ref 15
Lochside Trail .... Map 4-10; Ref 59
Lockwood Creek .... Map 15/D1
Logan Creek .... Map 1/C2
Log Train Trail .... Map 14, 15/A1, 22; Ref 56
Lois Lake .... Map 9/D7; Ref 15
Lois Lake .... Map 22/A5
Lomas Lake .... Map 8/C1; Ref 48
Lone Cone Trail ... Map 11/G2, 12; Ref 54
Lone Tree Prov Park .... Map 4/B3; Ref 34, 60
Long Beach .... Map 12/E6; Ref 37
Long Lake .... Map 16/G, 29/B6; Ref 15
Long Lake Trail .... Map 17/D6
Long Point Rec Site .... Map 36/A6
Loon Bay Rec Site .... Map 36/A6; Ref 41
Loon Lake .... Map 15/A1; Ref 16
Loon Lake .... Map 28/F3
Looper Creek .... Map 7/B5
Lord Island .... Map 24/E4
Loss Creek .... Map 2/C3
Loss Creek Provincial Park .... Map 2/B4
Lost Lake .... Map 28/F3; Ref 196
Lost Shoe Creek .... Map 12/G7, 5/Inset
Lost Shoe Trail .... Map 12/G7
Loudoun Channel .... Map 5/B2
Loughborough Inlet .... Map 44/A3
Louie Bay Trail .... Map 24/D5; Ref 52
Louise Goettwg Lake .... Map 13/D1
Loup Creek .... Map 7/G6
Lourie Bay .... Map 37/Inset/A5
Love Lake .... Map 21/A4; Ref 56
Loveland Bay Prov Park .... Map 36/B6; Ref 36
Lower Campbell Lake .... Map 36/B6
Lower Memekay River .... Map 34/G4
Lower Nimpkish Prov Park .... Map 40/B2; Ref 36
Lower Stella Lake .... Map 44/A7
Lowry Lake .... Map 22/A6; Ref 16
Lowry Lake Rec Site .... Map 22/A6; Ref 45
Lubbe Lake .... Map 3/G3
Lucid Lake .... Map 16/F4; Ref 16
Lucky Creek .... Map 13/E6
Lukwa Creek .... Map 33/D1
Lukwa Lake .... Map 36/C7
Lunchtime Lake .... Map 22/B2
Luxton .... Map 4/B5

M

Macallan Lake .... Map 12/F5
MacDonald Lake .... Map 3/E3; Ref 16
Mackenzie Lake .... Map 3/D6, 4/C4
Mackie Lake .... Map 35/G2
Mactush Rec Site .... Map 14/F5; Ref 45
MacMillan Prov Park .. Map 15/B1; Ref 36
Macoah Passage .... Map 13/C7
Maggie Lake .... Map 16/B7; Ref 16
Maggie River .... Map 13/C7
Mahatta River ...... Map 38/B5; Ref 26, 42
Maid Lake .... Map 2/E1

Main Lake Chain . Map 36/G2; Ref 27, 32
Malahat .... Map 4/B1
Malaspina Lake Rec Site .... Map 25/C3; Ref 41
Malby Lake .... Map 4/C4
Malcolm Island .... Map 40/C1, 47/G7/Inset; Ref 52
Malcolm Point .... Map 47/Inset/B1
Malinguy Island .... Map 9/F2
Mallard Lake .... Map 17/A3
Malook Creek .... Map 39/D5
Manley Creek Park ... Map 10/A7; Ref 34
Manso Creek .... Map 16/G5
Maple Bay .... Map 9/G4
Maple Grove Rec Site ... Map 8/B2; Ref 45
Maple Lake .... Map 29/C7; Ref 16
Maple Mountain Centennial Park .... Map 10/A3; Ref 48
Maple Mountain Memorial Park .... Map 9/G3; Ref 48
Maple Mountain Trail .. Map 9/G3, 10/A3
Maquila Creek .... Map 34/A5
Maquinna Prov Marine Park .... Map 18/F5, 19/A6; Ref 36
Marble Creek .... Map 12/G2
Marble Falls .... Map 9/G7
Marble River .... Map 38, 39/A2; Ref 26, 28, 36, 52
Marble River Rec Site .... Map 39/A2; Ref 42
Margaret Creek .... Map 21/B4
Margaret Lake .... Map 21/A3
Margot Lake .... Map 25/G2
Marie Canyon Site .... Map 9/B5
Mariner Creek .... Map 20/B4
Mariner Mtn Route .... Map 20/D4
Mariwood Lake .... Map 28/D6; Ref 16
Marshall Creek .... Map 15/F3
Marshy Lake .... Map 23/A7; Ref 16
Martha Lake .... Map35/G6; Ref 21
Marvinus Creek .... Map 25/A7
Mary Basin .... Map 24/E4
Mary Lake .... Map 36/C4; Ref 21
Masterman Islands .... Map 47/B5
Matchee Mountain .... Map 26/G7; Ref 53
Mate Islands Warm Spring .... Map 19/A7; Ref 6
Matheson Lake Park .... Map 3/G6, 4/A7; Ref 16, 34, 60
Matilpi .... Map 42/C1
Matson Lake .... Map 4/B4
Matthews Point Regional Park .... Map 10/E3; Ref 34
Maude Island .... Map 16/F1
Mavis Lake .... Map 3/G4
Max Lake .... Map 44/B5
Maxwell Creek .... Map 10/A3
May Lake .... Map 6/C1
Maynard Lake .... Map 39/ F5; Ref 21
Maynard Lake Rec Site .... Map 39/F5; Ref 43
Mayne Bay .... Map 13/E7
Mayne Island ...... Map 10/G3; Ref 30, 50
Mayo Lake .... Map 9/A4; Ref 16
McBey Islets .... Map 12/B4
McBride Bay .... Map 25/A3
McBride Creek Addition .... Map 20/G5, 21/A5
McBride Creek .... Map 21/A5
McBride Lake .... Map 21/A6; Ref 16
McCall Island .... Map 12/D3
McClure Lake .... Map 7/E5; Ref 16
McCoy Lake .... Map 14/E1
McCreight Lake .... Map 42/F7; Ref 21
McCreight Lake Rec Site .... Map 43/G7; Ref 41
McDonald Prov Park .... Map 10/C7; Ref 34
McFadden Creek .... Map 10/A2
McGregor Creek .... Map 19/F6
McIvor Lake .... Map 36/D7; Ref 21
McKay Island .... Map 19/F7
McKay Lake .... Map 17/A6; Ref 16
McKay Reef .... Map 11/G4
McKay Ridge .... Map 28/F5
McKenzie Lake .... Map 28/F7; Ref 17
McKenzie Lake .... Map 3/C4; Ref 17
McLaughlin Creek .... Map 15/A3
McLaughlin Lake .... Map 22/A5; Ref 17
McLaughlin Ridge .. Map 15/B2-F4; Ref 62
McNair Lake Trail .... Map 36/B4; Ref 46
McNeil Lake .... Map 20/F2
McQuillan Creek .... Map 15/C4
Meade Islets .... Map 6/A1
Meares Island .... Map 11/G2, 12/B2
Megin Lake .... Map 19/D3
Megin River .... Map 19/E4/F3; Ref 24
Megin Talbot Addition .... Map 19/E4
Mellin Lake .... Map 44/B5
Memory Lake .... Map 21/C1; Ref 34
Menzies Creek .... Map 36/C3
Menzies Creek .... Map 9/D4
Menzies Mountain Lookout Trail .... Map 36/B2; Ref 46
Mercantile Creek ...... Map 13/A7, 5/Inset
Mercer Creek .... Map 2/E1
Mercer Lake .... Map 5/Inset
Merchand Creek .... Map 7/A6
Mercs Lake .... Map 21/D6
Merrill Lake Rec Site .. Map 36/A5; Ref 41
Merry Widow Mtn .... Map 39/E7
Mesachie Lake .... Map 8/E4; Ref 17
Mesachie Mountian Trail .... Map 8/E4; Ref 48
Metchosin .... Map 4/A6
Metchosin Creek .... Map 4/A6
Mewhort (Williams) Lake .... Map 15/G7
Menzies Mountain Trail .... Map 36/B2; Ref 46
Michael Lake .... Map 17/D6; Ref 17
Michigan Creek .... Map 6/A6
Mikes Island .... Map 12/A3
Mikey Lake .... Map 34/G5
Mikola Downhill Delight .... Map 17/A6; Ref 51
Mill Bay .... Map 10/A7
Mill Hill Regional Park .... Map 4/C5; Ref 34, 60
Milla Lake .... Map 21/C2
Millar Channel .... Map 11/E1, 19/E6
Miller Creek Rec Site Map 36/C7; Ref 41
Mills Creek .... Map 40/A2
Mills Peninsula .... Map 5/G4
Millstone River .... Map 16/G2, 17/A3; Ref 25
Millstream .... Map 4/B4
Millstream Creek .... Map 4/B4; Ref 57
Milnes Landing .... Map 3/F6
Mimnim Creek .... Map 21/G3
Minstral Island .... Map 41/G1, 42/A1
Miracle Beach Prov Park .... Map 29/B3; Ref 37
Minute Creek .... Map 2/A3
Mirren Lake .... Map 21/C2
Mirror Lake .... Map 36/D7; Ref 21
Mission Group Island .... Map 31/B7
Mitchell Bay ...... Map 40/E1, 47/Inset/G1
Mitchell Lake .... Map 4/B3; Ref 17
Mitla Creek .... Map 19/G3, 20/A3
Mr Canoehead Rec Site .... Map 36/A3; Ref 41
Moakwa Creek .... Map 34/C4
Moat Lake Rec Site .... Map 4/B3; Ref 17
Mohun Creek ...... Map 36/B4; Ref 21, 41
Montague Creek Island .... Map 42/C7
Montague Harbour Prov Park .... Map 10/D2; Ref 32
Mooyah Bay .... Map 25/E7
Mooyah River .... Map 18/F1
Morden Colliery Historic Park .... Map 17/B5; Ref 34, 51
Moresby Island .... Map 10/F7; Ref 30
Morfee Island .... Map 11/G1
Moriarty Creek .... Map 14/G3
Moriarty Lake .... Map 15/G4; Ref 17
Morrison Creek .... Map 16/A1; Ref 55
Morpheus Island .... Map 12/A3
Morris Creek .... Map 34/G6
Morton Lake .... Map 36/B4; Ref 21, 37
Mosquito Creek .... Map 2/A2
Mosquito Harbour .... Map 12/B2
Mouat Prov Park .... Map 10/B3; Ref 32
Mount Adrian ...... Map 28/D2-A5; Ref 62
Mount Arrowsmith Regional Park .... Map 15/C1; Ref 56
Mount Ashwood .... Map 41/B7
Mount Apps Trail .... Map22/D5; Ref 56
Mount Arrowsmith ..... Map 15/D2; Ref 56
Mount Becher .... Map 28/F7; Ref 61
Mount Benson ...... Map 16/F4; Ref 51, 61
Mount Cain Park .... Map 33/G1; Ref 53, 61
Mount Douglas Park ..... Map 4/E4; Ref 60
Mount Finlayson Trail .... Map 4/B4; Ref 60
Mount Hankin .... Map 14/G3; Ref 56
Mount Horne .. Map 15/B1, 23/B7; Ref 56
Mount Maxwell Prov Park .... Map 10/A5; Ref 32
Mount McQuillan ...... Map 15/C5; Ref 57
Mount Moriarty .... Map 15/F4; Ref 57
Mount Porter Area ..... Map 21/G7; Ref 62
Mount Prevost Park ...... Map 9/D4; Ref 48
Mount Richards .... Map 9/F3; Ref 48
Mount Sutton .... Map 8/A4; Ref 48
Mount Thelwood Routes .... Map 20/E2/D1
Mount Tzouhalem .... Map 9/G5; Ref 48
Mount Washington .... Map 28/ E5; Ref 47, 62
Mount Work Hartland Dump Trails .... Map 4/C3; Ref 60
Mount Work Regional Park ...... Map 4/C2
Moving Glacier .... Map 21/C2
Mowgli Island .... Map 17/Inset
Moyeha River .... Map 16/G2, 17/A3, 20/C3; Ref 25
Mt Cain .... Map 33/G1; Ref 61
Mt Douglas Park .... Map 4/E4
Mt McQuinllan Trail .... Map 15/C5
Mt Woodfern Lake .... Map 13/A3
Mt Alava .... Map 25/D2
Mt Apps Trail .... Map 22/D4
Mt Hat Trail .... Map 22/E6
Mt Washington Ski Resort .... Map 28/ E5; Ref 61
Mt Wesley Ridge Trails .... Map 23/D7
Muchalat Lake .... Map 36/C2; Ref 21, 41
Mud Bay .... Map 22/G4
Mud Lake .... Map 36/A2; Ref 21
Mudge Island .... Map 17/D5
Mugford Island .... Map 12/E3
Muir Creek .... Map 3/B6
Mukwilla Lake .... Map 32/A2; Ref 21
Muriel Lake .... Map 12/F4; Ref 17
Museum Creek .... Map 15/B5
Musket Creek .... Map 25/A5
Myles Lake .... Map 17/A5
Myra Creek .... Map 20/F1

N

Nahmint Bay .... Map 14/F6
Nahmint Lake Rec Site .... Map 14/B3; Ref 17
Nahmint River .... Map 13/F3, 14/A2/D5; Ref 25
Nahshuttie Lake .... Map 46/A5
Nahwitti Lake .... Map 46/A6; Ref 21
Nahwitti River .... Map 45/G4, 46/B6; Ref 26
Nahyshutti Creek .... Map 46/A5
Naka Creek Rec Site .. Map 41/F6; Ref 41
Nanaimo Lakes .... Map 15/G6, 16/D5; Ref 17
Nanaimo .... Map 17/A3
Nanaimo Parkway Trail .... Map 16/G3; Ref 51
Nanaimo River ..... Map 8/F1, 16/F6, 17/A6; Ref 25, 28
Nanoose Creek .... Map 16/C2
Nanoose Harbour .... Map 16/E1
Naparti Inlet .... Map 30/E2
Narrowgut Creek .... Map 24/Inset, 32/A7
Nasparti River .... Map 30/F2 31/A2
Neel Creek .... Map 9/F6
Neilson Island .... Map 12/A3
Neroutsos Inlet .... Map 38/F5, 39/A5
Nesook Bay .... Map 25/F5
Nesook River .... Map 25/G5
Newcastle Creek .... Map 42/E6; Ref 52
Newcastle Isl Prov Park .... Map 17/A3; Ref 32
Newton Lake .... Map 36/F1
Niagara Creek .... Map 4/A4
Nicholas Bay .... Map 43/A4
Nigei Island .... Map 46/C2
Nile Creek .... Map 23/A6
Nimnim (Long) Lake ... Map 22/A3; Ref 17
Nimpkish .... Map 40/C7; Ref 22
Nimpkish River .... Map 32/F1, 33/Al; Ref 26, 29
Nimpkish Lake Prov Park .... Map 36/B4; Ref 37
Nimpkish Lake Rec Site .... Map 40/D7; Ref 43
Nisnak Lake .... Map 34/B2
Nissen Bight Trail .... Map 45/A4
Nita Lake .... Map 42/E7; Ref 22
Nitinat Lake Rec Site .... Map 6/G6, 7/A4; Ref 45
Nitinat River .... Map 7/B3, 15/D5; Ref 25, 34
Nitinat Triangle .... Map 6/F6, 7; Ref 27
Nixon Creek Rec Site .... Map 7/G2; Ref 45, 48
Nobel Creek .... Map 20/D4
Nodales Channel .... Map 44/D6
Nola Lake .... Map 35/D7
Nomash River .... Map 32/G7
Noomas Creek .... Map 40/D6
Nootka Island .... Map 18/A1/Inset, 24/F3; Ref 53
Nootka .... Map 18/Inset, 25/B7
Nootka Sound .... Map 18/B2
Nora Creek .... Map 34/E3
Nordstrom .... Map 30/A4
Nordstrom Creek .... Map 30/Inset
Norgar Lake .... Map 13/A1
Norgate River .... Map 25/G3
Norris Rocks .... Map 23/B4
North Galiano Island .... Map 17/Inset
North Memekay River .... Map 34/G3
North Nanaimo River .... Map 16/D4
North Pender Island .... Map 10/G5
Northwest Bay Trails .... Map 16/C1, 23/Inset/F2; Ref 55
Norway Island .... Map 9/G1, 17/G7/Inset
Nose Peak .... Map 37/F4
Noyse Creek .... Map 2/C3
Nuchatlitz .... Map 24/C3
Nuchatlitz Inlet .... Map 24/C4
Nuchatlitz Provincial Park .... Map 32/D3; Ref 37
Nugedzi Lake .... Map 36/F3
Nugget Creek .... Map 9/D3
Numukamis Bay .... Map 6/B2
Nymph Falls .... Map 38/B3; Ref 47

O

O'Connell Lake .... Map 38/D6, 39/E2; Ref 22, 43
Oak Bay .... Map 4/F5
Obling Creek .... Map 45/D5
Obstruction Island .... Map 19/E5
Octopus Islands Marine Park .... Map 36/G1; Ref 32
Okay Lake .... Map 16/D3
Okis Islands .... Map 44/F7
Old Marble Quarry .... Map 25/D5
Old Baldy Mountain Trail .... Map 3/G1; Ref 48
Old Mill Rec Site .... Map 16/D5; Ref 45
Old Rail Grade Rec Site .... Map 35/G5; Ref 46
Old Schoen Lake Fire Trail ..... Map 34/A3
Old Wolf Lake .... Map 3/G3
Oliphant Lake .... Map 4/A1
Onad Creek .... Map 12/G2
Open Bay .... Map 36/G4
Opitsat .... Map 12/A2
Orchard Meadow Rec Site .... Map 35/G6; Ref 41
Orange Juice Creek .... Map 6/B6
Orveas Bay .... Map 3/B6
Osborn Bay .... Map 9/F2/G3
Osbourne Bay Park .... Map 9/G3
Oshinow Lake .... Map 21/D4; Ref 17
Otter Bay .... Map 10/F5/G3
Otter Point .... Map 3/D6
Otter Point Park .... Map 3/C7
Ououkinish Inlet .... Map 30/G4, 31/A3
Ououkinsh River .... Map 30/A1
Overton Lake .... Map 17/A5
Owen Point .... Map 1/E2
Owens Lake .... Map 34/C1, 42/C7
Owossitsa Lake .... Map 24/D3

Owossitsa Lake Trail ... Map 24/D3; Ref 53
Oyees Lake ... Map 6/G6
Oyster River Park Trails ... Map 28, 29/A2; Ref 46

P

Pacific Rim National Park ... Map 1/C2, 5-7, 12/D5; Ref 37, 54
Palmerston Creek ... Map 41/G5, 42/A5
Panchena Bay ... Map 6/B4; Ref 25
Panchena Lake ... Map 6/B3; Ref 17
Panchena Point ... Map 6/A6
Pandora Peak ... Map 1/F2
Pantoja Islands ... Map 18/C1
Panther Lake ... Map 28/E7; Ref 17
Paper Mill Dam Park ... Map 14/F1
Paradise Creek ... Map 13/A7
Paradise Lake ... Map 20/F7
Paradise Meadows (Forbidden Plateau) ... Map 28/E6; Ref 58
Park Lake ... Map 24/B2
Parker Creek ... Map 7/D2
Parker Island ... Map 10/D3
Parkinson Creek ... Map 2/A3
Parksville ... Map 23/Inset/D1
Parry Bay ... Map 4/B7
Parson Bay ... Map 41/A1
Parsons Creek ... Map 14/F7, 15/A7
Part Alice ... Map 39/A6
Passive Reflector Trail ... Map 14/F2; Ref 56
Paterson Park ... Map 35/G5
Patrolas Creek ... Map 9/G6
Patterson Lake ... Map 22/C7; Ref 17
Patterson Lake Trail ... Map 22/C7
Peak (Henry) Lake ... Map 15/D4
Pear Lake ... Map 22/A3; Ref 17
Pearl Lake ... Map 28/A6; Ref 17
Pearse Islands ... Map 40/E1
Pease Lake ... Map 4/B3
Pedder Bay ... Map 4/A7
Peder Lake ... Map 3/F5
Peel Island ... Map 47/B6
Pegattem Creek ... Map 37/G1
Pender Island ... Map 10/G5, 10/Inset; Ref 30, 50
Penny Creek ... Map 20/C5
Perry Lake ... Map 25/C2; Ref 22
Perry River ... Map 25/C2; Ref 26
Perserverance Creek ... Map 22/B1
Peters Lake ... Map 25/E2
Petes Lake ... Map 9/A6
Petroglyph Prov Park .. Map 17/B4; Ref 34
Phillips Lake ... Map 44/E1
Phillips Arm ... Map 44/D3/E1
Phillip Ridge Trail ... Map 20/G1; Ref 58
Piers Island Sidney ... Map 10/D7
Pike Lake ... Map 4/C4
Pinch Creek Rec Site ... Map 39/D6; Ref 43
Pinder Creek ... Map 32/E3
Pinder Peak ... Map 32/D2
Pine Point Rec Site ... Map 8/B2; Ref 45
Pinhorn Island ... Map 44/D5
Pinkerton Islands ... Map 5/E1
Pipers Lagoon Park ... Map 17/A2
Pirates Cove Marine Park ... Map 17/E5; Ref 32
Pixie Lake ... Map 2/D1; Ref 17
Pizzle Lake ... Map 4/B3
Plumber Sound ... Map 10/G5
Plumper Bay ... Map 36/E3
Plumper Harbour ... Map 25/A6
Plumper Island ... Map 40/G1
Poett Nook Recreational Site ... Map 6/B2
Point No Point ... Map 2/G6
Poirer Lake ... Map 3/D6
Poison Creek ... Map 44/B1
Pool Creek ... Map 15/A6
Porritt Creek ... Map 24/Inset
Port Alberni ... Map 14/G1
Port Alice ... Maps 37/G4, 38/D1, 39/B2; Ref 30
Port Desire ... Map 6/A3
Port Eliza ... Map 24/B1
Port Hardy ... Map 47/A6
Port Hkusam Trail ... Map 43/A5
Port McNeill ... Map 40/A1
Port Neville ... Map 43/A1
Port Renfrew ... Map 1/G2
Port Washington ... Map 10/F5
Portage Inlet ... Map 4/D4
Porte Neville ... Map 42/E3
Porter Creek ... Map 9/E1
Portland Island ... Map 10/D7; Ref 30
Poum Lake ... Map 22/A2
Power River ... Map 30/G2
Pretty Girl Cove ... Map 19/B4
Pretty Girl Lake ... Map 19/B3
Prevost Island ... Map 10/D4; Ref 32
Prevost Passage ... Map 10/F7
Price Creek Trail ... Map 20/G2
Priest Lake ... Map 17/D6; Ref 17
Princess Margaret Marine Park ... Map 10/E6; Ref 32, 60
Prior Lake ... Map 4/C4
Prior Centennial prov Park ... Map 10/F5
Proposed Margaret Creek Trail ... Map 21/B4
Proposed Margaret Lake Route ... Map 21/B3
Prospect Lake ... Map 4/C3; Ref 17
Protection Island ... Map 17/A3
Providence Cove ... Map 1/G3
Pugh Creek ... Map 46/A5
Pulteney Point ... Map 47/Inset/A1
Puntledge Lake ... Map 29/B7; Ref 25
Puntledge River ... Map 21/G2, 29/A7; Ref 29
Puntledge River Trail ... Map 21/F3; Ref 47
Purdon Creek ... Map 18/E5
Pye Bay ... Map 44/A7
Pye Bay Rec Site ... Map 43/G7; Ref 41
Pye Beach Rec Site ... Map44/A7; Ref 41
Pye Creek ... Map 44/B7
Pye Lake ... Map 35/G1, 43/G7, 44/A7; Ref 22
Pye Lake Rec Site ... Map 43/G7; Ref 41
Pylades Island ... Map 17/F6

Q

Quadra Island ... Map 36/F3, 44/F7; Ref 30, 50
Quait Bay ... Map 12/A1
Qualicum ... Map 23/C6
Qualicum Beach ... Map 23/G7
Qualicum Fish Hatchery ... Map 23/B7
Qualicum National Wildlife Area ... Map 16/D1, 23/E7/Inset/G2
Qualicum River ... Map 22/G6, 23/B7
Quamichan Lake ... Map 9/G4; Ref 18
Quarantine Lake ... Map 4/A7
Quarry Regional Wilderness Park ... Map 9/G7; Ref 34
Quathaski Cove ... Map 36/G6
Quatse Lake ... Map 38/G1, 46/G7; Ref 22
Quatsie Prov Park ... Map 38/B3
Quatsie River ... Map 46/G7, 47/A7; Ref 26
Quatsino Park ... Map 38/B3; Ref 37
Quatsino Sound ... Map 37/F4, 38/B4; Ref 30
Queen Charlotte Sound ... Map 37/Inset/A3
Queen Cove ... Map 24/B2
Quennell Lake ... Map 17/D6; Ref 18
Quinsam Lakes ... Map 27/G2, 28/A-D1; Ref 22
Quinsam River ... Map 28/D1, 36/E7; Ref 26
Quinsam Nature Trails ... Map 36/E6; Ref 46

R

Radar Station Ruins ... Map 24/C5
Radu Lake ... Map 15/G7
Rae Lake ... Map 18/F3
Raft Cove ... Map 37/A1; Ref 37, 53
Raging River ... Map 39/G7, 40/A7
Rainier Creek ... Map 39/D7
Ralph River Route ... Map 21/B1
Ramsey Creek ... Map 21/G4, 22/A4
Ramsey Hot Springs ... Map 19/A6
Ranald Creek ... Map 35/F7
Ranger Lake ... Map 3/C4; Ref 18
Rankin Cove ... Map 12/D3
Rannell Lake ... Map 46/A5
Rasmus Creek ... Map 37/Inset/A5
Rathtrevor Beach Provincial Park ... Map 23/Inset/E1; Ref 37
Ray Creek ... Map 32/B6
Raymond Creek ... Map 7/F2
Read Creek ... Map 43/D1
Reagan Lake ... Map 28/E3; Ref 18
Rebecca Spit Marine Park ... Map 36/G4; Ref 32
Red Creek ... Map 2/C2; Ref 57
Red Creek Fir Trail ... Map 2/D2
Red Pillar Creek ... Map 21/D3
Redbed Creek ... Map 7/E1
Redford Creek ... Map 13/B6
Redford Lake ... Map 13/B6
Reed Lake ... Map 32/G1
Rees Creek ... Map 21/D1
Refuge Island ... Map 13/D6
Reginald Lake ... Map 36/A7; Ref 22
Reid Creek ... Map 7/G7
Reid Island ... Map 17/G7/Inset
Resolution Cove Historic Site ... Map 18/C1
Resolution Park Rec Site ... Map 24/E1; Ref 41
Resonance Cave ... Map 40/E5
Restless Bight ... Map 37/G6
Reufern Island ... Map 46/F1
Reynard Creek ... Map 8/D1
Rheinhart Lake ... Map 8/F1; Ref 18
Rheinhart Creek ... Map 8/F1
Rhodes Island ... Map 11/G1, 12/A1
Rhododendron Lake ... Map 16/B3
Richard Lake ... Map 17/A5
Richardo Lake ... Map 44/B3
Richards Creek ... Map 9/F4
Rideout Islets ... Map 12/D3
Rifle Range Trail ... Map 15/A1
Rift Creek ... Map 15/C6
Riley Island ... Map 12/A3
Riley Lake ... Map 19/B6
Ripple Rock Trail ... Map 36/D4; Ref 46
Ritch Creek ... Map 3/E1
Ritchie Bay ... Map 11/G1, 12/A1
Ritherdon Creek ... Map 6/D1
River Island ... Map 12/A1
Riverbank Trail ... Map 2/A2
Robert Kerr & Mami Wreck ... Map 17/G7/Inset
Roberts Lake ... Map 10/B4
Roberts Lake ... Map 36/A1; Ref 22
Roberts Memorial Park ... Map 17/E6; Ref 34
Robertson Creek Fish Hatchery ... Map 22/C7; Ref 56
Robinson Island ... Map 5/G1
Robson Bight Park ... Map 41/C4; Ref 37
Roche Cove Regional Park ... Map 3/G6; Ref 34, 60
Rock Bay Prov Park ... Map 44/B6; Ref 37
Rocky Island ... Map 13/A4
Rocky Point ... Map 4/A7
Rockyrun Creek ... Map 15/G5
Roger Creek Nature Trail ... Map 15/A1
Rogers Creek ... Map 15/A1; Ref 57
Rolling Roadstead ... Map 24/A2
Ronning Creek ... Map 37/B1
Rooney Lake ... Map 42/C6; Ref 22
Rosander Lake ... Map 7/A5
Roselle Lake ... Map 40/B3; Ref 22
Rosewall Creek ... Map 22/G5
Rosewall Creek Provincial Park ... Map 22/G4, 23/A4; Ref 38
Ross Bay ... Map 4/E6
Ross Passage ... Map 19/F7
Rosseau Lake ... Map 6/C3; Ref 18
Rosseau Trail ... Map 15/B2
Rossiter Lake ... Map 28/D5
Rough Bay ... Map 47/Inset/C1
Rough Creek ... Map 2/G4
Round Lake ... Map 16/E3, 22/C7; Ref 18
Rowboat Island ... Map 17/F4
Rowbotham Lake ... Map 15/E2; Ref 18
Rowland Creek ... Map 32/D6
Royal Roads ... Map 4/C5
Ruckle Prov Park ... Map 10/D5; Ref 32
Rugged Point Provincial Park ... Map 24/Inset; Ref 38
Rumble Beach ... Map 39/A5
Rupert Arm Rec Site ... Map 39/B1; Ref 43
Rupert Creek ... Map 39/C1
Rupert Inlet ... Map 38/G1, 39/A1
Rush Creek ... Map 16/A5
Russell Creek ... Map 37/Inset/A6, 41/E7
Russell Island Protected Area ... Map 10/D6; Ref 32
Ruxton Island ... Map 17/F6

S

Saanichton Bay ... Map 4/D1
Saavadra Island ... Map 18/B1/Inset
Sad Lake ... Map 1/C1
Sadje Creek ... Map 15/F7
Sahtlam ... Map 9/D5
Saint Mary's Lakes ... Map 15/C1; Ref 61
Sally Creek ... Map 9/B2
Salmon Bay ... Map 42/G
Salmon Lookout Trail ... Map 35/D1; Ref 47
Salmon River ... Map 27/A1, 35/D1, 42/A7, 43/A5
Salmon River Estuary ... Map 43/A5
Saltair ... Map 9/E1
Saltwater Lagoon ... Map 36/E3
Saltspring Island ... Map 10/B4; Ref 30, 50
Samuel Island ... Map 10/Inset
San Josef Bay ... Map 37/Inset/A6, 45/A7
San Josef Campsite ... Map 45/A7
San Josef River Rec Site ... Map 45/C7; Ref 43
San Juan Bridge ... Map 2/D1; Ref 45
San Juan Ridge/Kludahk Trail ... Map 2/C-G3; Ref 57
San Juan River ... Map 1, 2/B1, 3/A1; Ref 25, 29
San Mateo Bay ... Map 6/C1
San Simon Point ... Map 2/E5
Sand River ... Map 13/A4
Sandbar Trail ... Map 1/G2
Sandra Lake ... Map 34/G4
Sanduct Creek ... Map 2/G5
Sandwell Park ... Map 17/D3; Ref 32
Sandy Island Prov Park ... Map 22/F1; Ref 32
Sanford Island ... Map 5/G2
Sannich Inlet ... Map 4/B1, 10/A7
Sansum Narrows ... Map 10/A5
Santa Gertrudis-Boca Del Infierno Park ... 18/Inset; Ref 38
Santa Maria Island ... Map 6/B2
Santa Maria Lake ... Map 42/G7, 43/A7; Ref 22
Santiago Creek Rec Site ... Map 25/B4; Ref 41
Sara Lake ... Map 39/B3
Saranac Island ... Map 11/G1, 12/A1
Sarita ... Map 6/B2
Sarita Falls ... Map 6/E2
Sarita Lake ... Map 6/E1; Ref 18
Sarita Lake Rec Site ... Map 6/E2; Ref 45
Sarita River ... Map 6/G1
Saseenos ... Map 3/G6
Satchie Creek ... Map 18/G3
Satellite Channel ... Map 10/B6, 5/G3
Saturna Island ... Map 10/Inset; Ref 30
Sawatzky Lake ... Map 35/B5
Sayward Forest ... Map 42/G6, 43/A5
Sayward Canoe Route ... Map 35/G5, 36/A5; Ref 27
Sayward Salmon Bay ... Map 43/A5
Schmidt Creek ... Map 41/D4
Schoen Lake ... Map 33/G3, 34/A2; Ref 22, 38
Schoen Lake Park Trail ... Map 34/B2; Ref 53
Schooner Beach Trail ... Map 12/C5
Schooner Cove ... Map 16/E1
Scott Island ... Map 9/F1
Scout Beach Rec Site .. Map 22/A6; Ref 45
Sea Caves Trail ... Map 19/A6
Seabird Lake ... Map 42/G3, 43/B2
Seal Islets ... Map 22/F1
Seal Lake ... Map 35/G3
Sear Island ... Map 17/F4
Sebalhall Creek ... Map 25/G1, 33/F7
Seal Bay Regional Park ... Map 29/D5; Ref 47

Reference 68

Sechart Channel .... Map 5/E1
Second Lake .... Map 16/C5
Second Lake .... Map 35/D5; Ref22
Secretary Islands ..... Map 10/A1, 17/Inset
Sepping Island .... Map 5/G3
Seven Mile Creek .... Map 7/D4
Shannon Lake .... Map 43/D1
Sharp Creek .... Map 45/C6
Sharp Island .... Map 12/A2
Shaw Creek .... Map 15/G7, 7/G1
Shaw Lake .... Map 15/F7
Shaw Valley Routes ...... Map 15/E7; Ref 48
Shawnigan Lake .... Map 3/G1, 9/G7
Sheila Lake .... Map 19/D4
Sheilds Lake .... Map 3/G5
Shelly Lake .... Map 39/F1
Shelter Creek .... Map 19/G4
Shelter Inlet .... Map 19/D5
Shelton (Echo) Lake .... Map 16/A4
Shepherd Creek .... Map 21/A1
Shepherd Creek Trail .... Map 21/A1
Sherk Lake .... Map 8/C1
Shields Lake .... Map 3/G5,Ref 43
Ship Creek .... Map 31/G7
Ships Point Reg Park .... Map 22/G3
Shoal Islands .... Map 9/G2
Shorepine Bog Trail .... Map 12/E7
Shushartie .... Map 46/A3
Shushartie Lake .... Map 46/B4
Shushartie River .... Map 46/B3
Shute Passage .... Map 10/D7
Sidney .... Map 4/D1
Sidney Bay .... Map 43/G2, 44/A2
Sidney Island .... Map 4/G1; Ref 30
Sidney Spit Prov Marine Park ....
.... Map 4/F1; Ref 32; Ref 60
Silborn Creek .... Map 31/G3
Silburn Lake .... Map 31/G3
Silver Creek .... Map 9/B2
Silver Lake .... Map 9/C2; Ref 18
Silver Snag Lake .... Map 22/A2
Silverado Creek ...... Map 18/G1, 19/A1
Similar Island .... Map 12/F2
Simmons Lake .... Map 44/B5
Sitka Spruce Beach Rec Site ....
.... Map 43/F7; Ref 41
Skidder Lakes Trail .... Map 39/G3; Ref 53
Skidmarks .... Map 36/D6; Ref 47
Skutz Falls Campsite .... Map 9/A5
Slide Bay .... Map 38/A7
Slide Pool .... Map 22/D7
Sloman Island .... Map 12/A3
Small Inlet Prov Park .... Map 36/G1
Smith Creek .... Map 5/Inset
Snake Lake .... Map 36/B5
Snakehead Lake .... Map 36/A7; Ref22
Snow Creek Rec Site ....
.... Map 13/G1; Ref 45
Snowden Island .... Map 13/D6
Snowden Trails .... Map 36/C5; Ref 47
Sointula .... Map 40/B1, 47/Inset/D1
Solander Island .... Map 30/Inset
Somass River ... Map 14/F1, 22/E7; Ref 25
Someone Lake .... Map9/C2; Ref 18
Sombrio Beach Trailhead ....
.... Map 2/B3; Ref 57
Sombrio Point .... Map 2/B4
Sombrio River .... Map 2/B3
Somenos Lake .... Map 9/F4
Somner Lake .... Map 22/C7
Songhees Creek .... Map 46/F5
Songhees Lake .... Map 46/F5
Songhees Trail .... Map 46/F5; Ref 53
Sonora Island .... Map 44/F5
Sooke Basin .... Map 3/G6
Sooke Bay .... Map 3/D7
Sooke Harbour .... Map 3/E7
Sooke Hills Wilderness Regional Park ....
.... Map 3/G7; Ref 34
Sooke Lake .... Map 3/F2
Sooke Mountain Prov Park ....
.... Map 3/G5; Ref 35
Sooke Potholes Prov Park .... Map 3/F5
Sooke River .... Map 3/F6; Ref 25, 29
South Beach Trail .... Map 12/E7
South Chemainus Creek .... Map 8/E2
South Holland Creek .... Map 9/B1
South Nanaimo River .... Map 16/E7
South Otter Bay Protected Area ....
.... Map 10/F5; Ref 32
South Pender Island ..... Map 10/G6/Inset
South Sarita River .... Map 6/D2
South Sutton Creek .... Map 13/E1
South Wellington .... Map 17/B5
Southey Island .... Map 16/F1
Spanish Pilot Group .... Map 25/C7
Spectacle Creek .... Map 4/A2; Ref 35
Spectacle Lake ....
.... Map 4/A2; Ref 18, 49, 60
Spencer Creek .... Map 6/F1
Spencer Cove Rec Site ....
.... Map 38/A3; Ref 43
Spider Lake .... Map 23/C7; Ref 18
Spider Lake Provincial Park ....
.... Map 23/C7; Ref 38
Spire Lake .... Map 13/B1, 21/B7
Spirit Lake .... Map 35/F2; Ref22
Spit Trail .... Map 23/B3
Spring Beach Rec Site .... Map 8/E4; Ref45
Spring Island .... Map 31/B7; Ref 53
Springer Creek .... Map 43/A6
Sprish Lake .... Map 7/A6
Sproat Lake ....
.... Map 13/G1, 14/A-D1; Ref 38
Sproat Lake Park .... Map 22/D7
Sproat Narrows .... Map 14/G4
Sproat River .... Map 14/E1
Sprouter Island .... Map 18/C1
Spruce Bay Rec Site ... Map 39/C7; Ref 43
Spruce Fringe Trail .... Map 12/D6
Squalicum Lake .... Map 6/G6
St. Andrews Creek .... Map 14/D2
St. Austin Lake .... Map 44/G6
St. Ines Island .... Map 13/C7
St. Mary Lake .... Map 10/A2; Ref 19
St. Mary Lake .... Map 15/C1; Ref 19
St. Marys Creek ....
.... Map 45/A5, 37/Inset/B5
St. Patrick Creek .... Map 37/Inset/A6
Staghorn Creek .... Map 12/F5
Stamp Falls Park .... Map 22/E7
Stamp Narrows .... Map 14/G3
Stamp River .... Map 22/D6, 22/E7; Ref 38
Staples Island .... Map 47/A2, 46/G2
Star Lake Rec Site .... Map 26/F5; Ref 41
Stark Lakes .... Map 17/A6
Steamer Creek .... Map 19/C6
Steele Creek .... Map 32/F1
Steele Lake .... Map 40/G7
Stella Beach Rec Site ....
.... Map 44/A7; Ref 41
Stella Lake ...... Map 36/A1, 44/A7; Ref22
Stephens Creek .... Map 38/G1, 39/A1
Sterling Beach Rec Site ....
.... Map 36/A3; Ref 41
Sterling Island Rec Site ....
.... Map 36/A3; Ref 41
Stewardson Inlet .... Map 18/G5, 19/A5
Stewart Lake .... Map 34/F5; Ref 22
Stirling Arm .... Map 14/D1
Stockett .... Map 17/A4
Stockham Island .... Map 12/A3
Stocking Lake .... Map 9/C1; Ref 19
Stokes Lake .... Map 44/B3
Stone Island .... Map 12/A3
Stone Nipples .... Map 31/G7
Stocking Lake .... Map 9/C1; Ref 19
Storey Creek .... Map 40/C6
Story Lake .... Map 44/D4
Stowe Creek .... Map 43/B7
Stowell Lake .... Map 10/C5
Stramberg Lake .... Map 36/G2
Stranby River .... Map 45/C4; Ref 26
Strange Island .... Map 25/B6
Strathcona Dam Rec Site ....
.... Map 35/G7; Ref 41
Strathcona Provincial Park ....
.... Map 19/E2, 20/B3, 33/B7; Ref 38, 57
Strathcona Westmin Provincial Park ....
.... Map 20/G1, 21/A2; Ref 38
Stuart Channel .... Map 17/D5, 9/F1
Stuart Island .... Map 10/G7
Stubbs Island .... Map 11/G3
Stud Islets .... Map 6/A1
Sturdies Bay .... Map 10/F3
Sucwoa River .... Map 25/D3
Sugar Loaf Mnt Park Map17/A2
Sugsaw Lake .... Map 6/A3
Sulphur Passage .... Map 19/E5; Ref 38
Summit Trail .... Map 23/B3
Sunderland Channel .... Map 43/A3
Sundew Lake .... Map 22/C4
Sunrise Lake Route ..... Map 28/C6; Ref 57
Sunrise Reef .... Map 11/G4
Suquash .... Map 47/E7
Surprise Creek .... Map 33/G7
Surprise Lake .... Map 36/A3
Sutton Creek .... Map 34/A6
Swamp Lake .... Map 35/F3
Swan Lake Pinic Area .... Map 45/E5;
Swan Lake Rec Site .... Map 45/D7
Swanson Channel .... Map 10/F6
Swanson Island .... Map 40/G1, 41/A1
Swartz Bay .... Map 10/D7
Swiss Bay Island .... Map 6/A1
Sydney Inlet .... Map 19/A3
Sydney Inlet Prov Park ....
.... Map 18, 19/A3; Ref 38
Sydney River .... Map 18/G1, 19/A2
Synka Lake .... Map 20/D7

T

Tahsis .... Map 25/B1
Tahsis Inlet .... Map 25/A2
Tahsis Lake .... Map 33/C7; Ref22
Tahsis River ..... Map 25/B1, 33/B7; Ref 26
Tahsish .... Map 31/F1
Tahsish Inlet .... Map 31/G5, 32/A4
Tahsish Lake .... Map 40/A7; Ref 54
Tahsish River ....
. Map 31/G2, 32/A1, 33/A7; Ref 26, 53
Tahsish-Kwois Park .... Map 32/A3; Ref 38
Talbot Creek .... Map 19/D3
Tapaltos Bay .... Map 5/G4
Tara Creek .... Map 24/A2/Inset
Tatchu Creek .... Map 24/Inset
Tatsno Lake .... Map 21/E3
Taylor Arm .... Map 13/G1, 14/A1
Taylor Arm Provincial Park ....
.... Map 14/B1; Ref 38
Taylor River Bridge Rest Area ... Map 21/E7
Taylor River .... Map 13/F1, 21/C7; Ref 25
Teeta Creek .... Map 38/G6
Teihsum River .... Map 31/D1, 39/C7
Telegraph Cove .... Map 40/F2
Tennent Lake .... Map 20/F2
Tennent Lake Trail .... Map 20/F2
Tent Island .... Map 9/G1; Ref 30
Tex Lyon Trail .... Map 47/B6; Ref 53
Thames Creek .... Map 23/A5
The Abyss Loop .... Map 17/A5
The Pumphouse .... Map 36/F6; Ref 46
Thelwood Creek .... Map 20/G2
Thelwood Lake .... Map 20/F2
Thetis Isalnd ....
.... Map 9/G1, 17/F7/Inset; Ref 30
Thetis Lakes .... Map 4/C5; Ref 19, 35, 60
Thetis Lake Regional Park ....
.... Map 4/B4; Ref 60
Thiemer Lake .... Map 40/C2
Third Lake .... Map 16/A5
Third Lake .... Map 35/D5
Three Arm Creek .... Map 2/E2
Three Ilse Lakes .... Map 39/F4; Ref 22
Three Ilse Lake Rec Site ....
.... Map 39/C7; Ref 43
Thunderbird Creek .... Map 20/F6
Thurlow .... Map 43/E5, 44/A4
Thurlow Island .... Map 44/A4
Thurston Bay .... Map 44/E6
Thurston Bay Marine Provincial Park ....
.... Map 44/E6; Ref 38
Tiakwa Creek .... Map 40/B7
Timberland Lake .... Map 17/A7; Ref 19
Tiupana Inlet .... Map 25/E5
Tlatlos Creek .... Map 41, 42/A6
Tlowils Lake .... Map 34/F1; Ref22
Tlupana River .... Map 25/G5
Todd Creek .... Map 3/F5
Todd Inlet .... Map 4/C2
Tofino .... Map 12/A3
Tofino Creek .... Map 13/A1
Tofino Inlet .... Map 12/C4
Tolnay Creek .... Map 34/A7
Tom Brownie Creek .... Map 43/C1
Tom Brownie Lake .... Map 43/D1
Toma Creek .... Map 22/A3
Tonqui Island .... Map 11/G4
Top Bridge Mountain Park ....
.... Map 16/B1, 23/Inset/E1; Ref 55
Topaze Harbour .... Map 43/D2
Topknot Lake Map37/B2
Toquart Bay .... Map 13/D6
Toquart Bay Rec Site .. Map 13/C6; Ref 45
Toquart Lake .... Map 13/C6
Toquart River .... Map 13/C5; Ref 25
Toy Lake .... Map 21/E4; Ref 19
Trail Islands .... Map 4/F6
Trail Pond .... Map 22/D7; Ref 19
Tranquil Creek .... Map 12/F1, 20/D7
Tranquil Creek Provincial Park ....
....
Map 20/F7; Ref 38
Tranquil Elsue .... Map 12/E2
Tranquil Inlet .... Map 12/E3
Tranquility Woods Campsite .... Map 16/A1
Transfer Beach Park .... Map 17/D7
Trasher Cove .... Map 1/E2
Tremain Creek .... Map 22/A2
Trent River ..... Map 22/C1, 29/E7; Ref 25
Trevor Channel .... Map 5/G3, 6/A2
Tribune Bay Prov Park ....
.... Map 23/B2; Ref 32
Trincomali Channel .... Map 10/C3
Trinity Bay .... Map 47/Inset/F1
Trio Creek .... Map 34/E7
Trisle Creek .... Map 1/D2
Tsable Lake .... Map 22/A2
Tsable River .... Map 22/D3; Ref 25
Tsiko Lake .... Map 32/E1; Ref22
Tsitika Crossing Rec Site ....
.... Map 41/C4; Ref 41
Tsitika Lake .... Map 41/D7
Tsitika River .... Map 41/C4; Ref 29
Tsocowis Creek .... Map 6/C5
Tsowwin River .... Map 25/C4
Tsuiquate River .... Map 46/F6
Tsulton River .... Map 40/D3
Tsuquandre Lake .... Map 6/E7
Tsusiat Lake .... Map 6/E7
Tsolum Spirit Park .... Map 29/B5
Tuck Lake .... Map 7/D1; Ref 19
Tugboat Island .... Map 17/F4
Tugwell Creek .... Map 3/C6
Tugwell Lake .... Map 3/D4
Tumblewater Creek .... Map 22/D4
Tumbo Island .... Map 10/Inset; Ref 33
Turbull Lake .... Map 22/A5; Ref 19
Turn Island .... Map 44/B6
Turnbull Lake .... Map 22/A5; Ref 19
Turnour Island .... Map 41/E1
Turtle Lake .... Map 22/D7; Ref 19
Twaddle Lake .... Map 34/D6
Twin Islets .... Map 24/A3
Twin Lake .... Map 36/A2; Ref22
Twin Peaks .... Map 39/F3
Two Rivers Arm .... Map 14/C1
Tyilla Creek .... Map 45/F4
Tzartus Island .... Map 6/A1
Tzeia Lake .... Map 21/B2
Tzuhalem .... Map 9/G5
Tzuhalem Creek .... Map 9/G5

U

Uchuck Creek .... Map 14/A6
Uchuck Lake .... Map 14/A6
Uchuklesit Inlet .... Map 14/B7
Ucluelet .... Map 5/Inset
Uglow Creek .... Map 2/F5
Union Bay .... Map 22/E1
Union Island .... Map 31/D7
Upana Caves .... Map 26/B3; Ref 6
Upana Lake .... Map 26/B3; Ref 19, 22
Upper Campbell Lake ....
.... Map 27/F1, 35/G7; Ref 23
Upper Kla-anch River .... Map 34/A7
Upper Myra Falls Trail .... Map 20/F1
Upper Passage Provincial Park ....
.... Map 11/G1
Upper Thelwood Lake .... Map 20/E2
Ursus Creek .... Map 20/E6
Useless Inlet .... Map 14/B7

V

Valdes Island .... Map 17/G6/Inset
Vanishing River .... Map 39/G7; Ref 6
Vansittart Island .... Map 46/B1
Varga Lake .... Map 34/G4
Vargus Island .... Map 11/F2
Vargus Island Provincial Park ... Map 11/F2
Varney Bay .... Map 38/G2

Veitch Creek .... Map 3/G6
Vera Lake .... Map 44/B6
Verda Island .... Map 25/C7
Vernon .... Map 33/G7
Vernon Bay .... Map 13/G7, 14/A7
Vernon Creek .... Map 7/E2
Vernon Lake .... Map 33/F6; Ref 23, 40
Vesuvius .... Map 10/A2
Victoria .... Map 4/E5
Victoria Harbour .... Map 4/D5
Victoria International Airport .... Map 4/D1
Victoria Lake .... Map 39/B6; Ref 23, 40
View Lake .... Map 21/D6; Ref 19
View Trail .... Map 17/D4
Village Bay Lake .... Map 36/G2
Village Bay .... Map 10/G3
Village Island .... Map 40/C1
Village Lake .... Map 18/E5
Village Reef .... Map 5/D2
Villaverde Island .... Map 25/C7
Virago Rock .... Map 17/G7/Inset
Virge Creek .... Map 12/D1

W

Wady Creek .... Map 39/E6
Wake Lake .... Map 9/D5
Walatt Bay .... Map 36/G1
Walbran Creek ....
.... Map 1/B1, 7/D7; Ref 25
Walcan .... Map 36/E4
Walken Island .... Map 44/A5
Walker Creek .... Map 3/A3
Wallace Island .... Map 10/A1; Ref 50
Wallace Island Provincial Marine Park ......
.... Map 10/A1; Ref 33
Walter Guppies Cabin .... Map 20/D4
Wanetta Lake .... Map 12/E5
Wanokana Creek ..... Map 38/D1, 46/D7

Ward Lake Trails .... Map 22/C7; Ref 57
Waring Creek .... Map 34/B7
Warm Lake .... Map 41/B6
Warn Bay .... Map 12/C1
Warne Island .... Map 12/D4
Warta Creek .... Map 19/G4
Washiawlis Creek .... Map 39/B1
Waugh Creek .... Map 3/G4
Waukwaas Creek .... Map 39/B1
Webster Island .... Map 13/G7
Weeks Lake .... Map 3/C1; Ref 19
Welch Lake .... Map 32/B2
Welcome Island .... Map 12/A1
Weld Island .... Map 6/A1
Wellington .... Map 16/G2
Wesley Ridge Trail ....
.... Map 15/C1, 23/D7; Ref 57
West Banon Creek .... Map 9/C1
West Coast Trail Access .... Map 1/G1
West Coast Trail ....
.... Map 1/A1, 6/A5; Ref 37, 54
West Cracroft Island .. Map 41/D2, 42/A2
West Croman .... Map 33/E2
West Leetch River .... Map 3/C3
West Shaw Creek .... Map 7/G1, 15/F7
West Shawnigan Lake Provincial Park ....
.... Map 3/G1, 9/G7; Ref 35
West Thurlow Island .... Map 43/D5
Westwood Lake ...Map 16/G4; Ref 19, 52
Westmin Mine .... Map 28; Ref 58
Westwood Ridge & Lake Trails ....
.... Map 16/G4
West Walbran Trail ..... Map 7/C7; Ref 54
Weymer Creek Prov Park ....
.... Map 25/B2; Ref 38
Whaleboat Passage .... Map 17/F6
Whalebone Island Prov Park ....
.... Map 17/F6; Ref 33
Whirl Bay .... Map 4/A7
Whiskey Jack Creek .... Map 16/F7
Whiskey Lake .... Map 17/A5
White Creek .... Map 43/A7
White Duck Lake .... Map 38/F2
White Ridge .... Map 34; Ref 38
White River ....
.. Map 34/F4, 35/A1, 43/A7; Ref 26, 29,
Whitehouse Creek .... Map 9/E2
Whitepine Cove .... Map 19/G7
Whittys Lagoon Provincial Park . Map 4/B6
Whyac .... Map 6/F7

Wichannish Island .... Map 11/G3
Wickaninnish Bay .... Map 12/C6
Wickaninnish Trail .... Map 12/E7
Wild Deer Creek .... Map 9/D7
Wild Deer Lake .... Map 9/D7; Ref 19
Wilfred Creek .... Map 22/F4
Willemar Lake .... Map 21/G3; Ref 19
William Head .... Map 4/B7
William Lake .... Map 45/B6
Williams Creek .... Map 2/G2, 15/B4
Williams Island .... Map 5/E1
Williamson Passage .... Map 25/G7
Willis Island .... Map 5/D2
Willow Creek Trail ..... Map 36/G7; Ref 47
Willow Point .... Map 36/G7
Willowbrae & Honeymoon Bay Trails ....
.... Map 5/Inset, 12/F7
Wilson Creek .... Map 7/E3
Winchelsea Islands .... Map 16/F1
Windy Bay Rec Site ...... Map 16/E5; Ref 45
Wingen Islets .... Map 12/E3
Winter Cove Marine Park ....
.... Map 10/Inset/F1; Ref 33
Winter Harbour .... Map 37/E3
Wise Island .... Map 10/C2
Witty's Lagoon Regional Park ....
.... Map 4/B6; Ref 35, 60
Wizard Rocks .... Map 5/G2
Wolf Creek .... Map 3/F4, 16/F5
Wolf Lake ...... Map28/G5, 29/A5; Ref 19
Wolfe Lake .... Map 32/E2; Ref23
Wollan Islets .... Map 12/E3
Woman Island .... Map 12/F2
Woss .... Map 33/B2
Woss Lake .... Map 33/B3; Ref 40
Wye Creek .... Map 2/G4
Wye Lake .... Map 2/G3

Y

Yarksis .... Map 11/G2
Yellow Bluff Bay .... Map 24/Inset
Yookwa Creek .... Map 33/E6
Yorke Island .... Map 42/G4, 43/A3
You Creek .... Map 20/G4
Youghpan Creek .... Map 38/C1
Young Bay .... Map 19/B5
Young Lake .... Map 3/D6; Ref 19

Z

Zeballos .... Map 32/F6
Zeballos Inlet .... Map 24/F1, 32/F7
Zeballos Lake .... Map 32/G5
Zeballos Rec Site .... Map 32/F7; Ref 45
Zeballos River .... Map 32/F6; Ref 26
Zoltan Lake .... Map 34/G4
Zuclarte Channel .... Map 18/D1